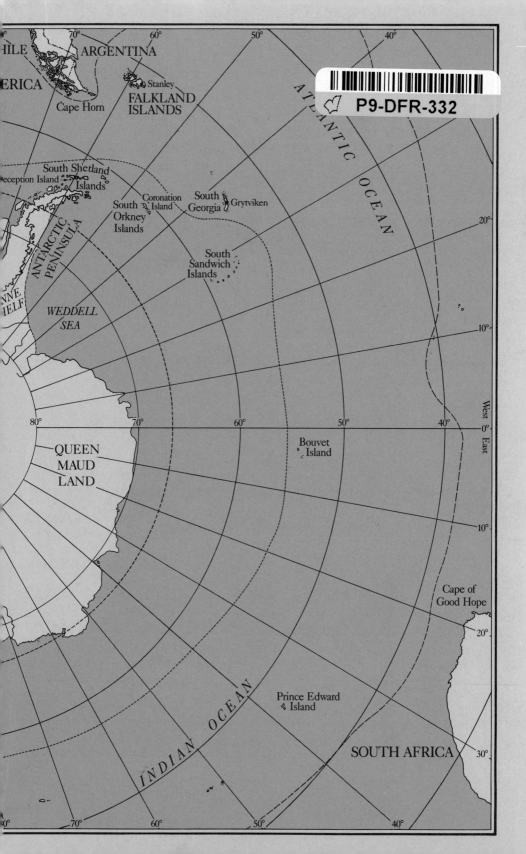

P9-DFR-332

RODGERS, EUGENE   08/15/90
BEYOND THE BARRIER
(2) 1990 919.8904RODG
9201 04 105973 01 1   (IC=1)

B920104105973011B

919.8904 Rodg

Rodgers, Eugene.

Beyond the barrier :

SEP 2 6 1990			
OCT 2 1 1990			
NOV 2 0 1990			
FEB 0 4 1991			
MAR 1 9 1991			
FEB 1 6 1995			
FEB 1 9 1997			
MAR 2 2 2004			

AUG 1 4 1990

VESTAL PUBLIC LIBRARY

0 00 10 0100827 3

VESTAL PUBLIC LIBRARY
VESTAL, NEW YORK 13850
1-607-754-4243

BEYOND THE BARRIER

EUGENE RODGERS

 BEYOND

NAVAL INSTITUTE PRESS

Annapolis, Maryland

THE BARRIER

The Story of Byrd's
First Expedition to Antarctica

Copyright © 1990
by the United States Naval Institute
Annapolis, Maryland

All rights reserved. No part of this book may be reproduced
without written permission from the publisher.

LIBRARY OF CONGRESS CATALOGING-IN-PUBLICATION DATA
Rodgers, Eugene.
Beyond the barrier : the story of Byrd's first expedition to
Antarctica / Eugene Rodgers.
p.   cm.
Includes bibliographical references.
ISBN 0-87021-022-X (alk. paper) :
1. Byrd Antarctic Expedition.   2. Byrd, Richard Evelyn,
1888–1957.   I. Title.
G850.1928.B95R63   1990
919..8904--dc20   89-28450
                                                                      CIP

Printed in the United States of America on acid-free paper ∞

3   5   7   9   8   6   4   2
First printing

LOVINGLY DEDICATED TO MY MOTHER,
CATHERINE SLATTERY RODGERS,
AND MY WIFE,
CAROL HUBER RODGERS

Contents

Preface

THIS book began in 1963 when I became Public Information Officer for the U.S. Antarctic Research Program, the civilian scientific effort supported logistically by the U.S. Navy's Operation Deep Freeze. In boning up for my assignment, I looked for books about America's antarctic hero, Admiral Byrd, and his expeditions; but I could find no histories or biographies specifically about Byrd. The only books available then were the original works by Byrd and his men, which were dated. They assumed an awareness of the society and technology of the 1920s and 1930s and a general knowledge about the well-publicized expedition and Byrd himself, who was famous before he ever went to Antarctica. These books were technically detailed but revealed little about the inner workings of the expeditions, the interplays of the personalities involved, or the conflicts, mistakes, canceled plans, unachieved goals, and other negative occurrences. Curiously, American social histories of the 1920s and 1930s and even general histories of antarctic exploration gave scant attention to Byrd's expeditions. I learned, however, that Byrd's explorations had indeed been historically important, so I decided to write a book myself and give the late admiral his due when I got the opportunity.

During my assignment I got a clue about why Byrd had been neglected. A public television crew arrived in Antarctica to film a series about current American activities in antarctic science and exploration. The director disclosed to me that he wanted to interweave films, photographs, and other material about Byrd's expeditions throughout the programs, but Byrd's eccentric son would not cooperate. The director ended up using material from England's Scott expeditions.

When I began researching this book in the mid-1960s, I was astonished at the rebuffs I received to my interview requests. As a writer, I have usually found people cooperative about telling their stories, especially when, like members of Byrd's expeditions, they have something to be proud of. One former Byrd man with whom I had become friendly on my assignment refused to meet with me. I had worked closely with another of Byrd's veterans who would reply only in writing to written questions and would not talk to me about Byrd. He did not answer some questions at all and answered many perfunctorily. Two other of Byrd's alumni did not reply at all to my letters asking for information. Another agreed to an interview on a certain day when he would be in Washington, D.C. I traveled from Pittsburgh to meet him but, when I arrived, he told me he no longer had the time and could not talk to me, giving the impression he had thought better of it.

Another of Byrd's associates (not a member of the first expedition) invited me to his house in response to my request for an interview. When he answered the door, he just stared at my offered hand. He pointed to the tape recorder in my other hand and said, sneering, "Only writers with weak minds use tape recorders." He let me in and asked if I'd have a drink. I declined. Smirking, he said, "Good for you—I'd have kicked you out if you'd accepted." The interview went downhill from there, and he responded to virtually nothing I asked. Trembling with rage, he warned me to interview only men of "character" and not Byrd's "detractors." His only purpose in granting the interview seems to have been to intimidate me. Bernt Balchen, a member of Byrd's first expedition who had written a biography containing revelations about and charges against Byrd, as revealed in the epilogue to this book, identified this man as a key figure in the group of Byrd's partisans who had threatened legal actions and forced Balchen and his publisher to censor portions of his book.[1]

An official of a society whose members have been to Antarctica or are otherwise interested in antarctic affairs saw a letter I had written to an expedition member in which I summarized Byrd's strengths, accomplishments, and faults. Objecting to the critical part, the official, a Ph.D. scientist, wrote me in 1986 on society letterhead, "If this is one of your conclusions, I doubt if I will want to buy your book, or even give it a good review in our Society's newsletters. . . . [I] hope you don't come out with an exposé." Calling criticism of Byrd hogwash, he wrote further "I don't think the world is out there waiting to hear it from you or anyone else." He sent a carbon copy to the man who had tried to intimidate me.

I surmised that at least part of the problem was that the regular navy and scientists opposed to Byrd had taken over the government-sponsored expeditions and relegated Byrd to a back seat, and that the takeover had resulted in some bitter pro-Byrd and anti-Byrd factionalism that lingered long after his death. Probably neither side liked the possibility that a book would stoke the conflict.

I thought another factor might be the kind of reticence revealed by an incident I had observed in Antarctica. Sir Charles Wright, an aged man who had been on Scott's last expedition, had returned to Antarctica as a guest of the United States. During the taping of a radio interview, he mentioned how bad the meals in the hut had been back in 1911, then stopped himself and said, "I shouldn't have said that. It will embarrass the cook and the expedition." As far as I was concerned, Scott's expedition was dusty history, but to old Sir Charles it was a contemporary event. Byrd's veterans likewise might have been bristling at the thought that their expeditions were being treated as history, regarding the unpublished details as nobody's business but their own.

I still think both guesses are valid as far as they go. But neither explains the degree of evasion and animosity I encountered. I felt as if Byrd's intimates were sitting on some unspeakable secret.

I believe I came to understand the situation during my research. As this book reveals, Byrd was not the superhero or plaster saint of the legend that he and some of his associates created; in fact, reality sometimes strayed far from the image. In particular, Byrd's main defense to charges about his honesty was that he was of such sterling character that he would never lie. The record shows, however, that he often misstated the facts to suit his purposes. To maintain his reputation, the explorer had a cadre of relatives and supporters whose own reputations were threatened by those they called Byrd's detractors, who presumably included not only his enemies but neutral writers who might question the image.

For almost thirty years after Byrd's death, his son refused researchers access to any of the admiral's papers. Working behind the scenes, moreover, as his father had often done, the late Richard E. Byrd, Jr., orchestrated the attacks on Balchen's book and, incredibly, on a book revering Byrd by the late Dr. Paul Siple, the disciple of the admiral whom Siple loved as a second father. The younger Byrd objected to statements such as "the admiral was happy as a boy," "he dressed meticulously," and "his hair was turning white," considering the words to be subtle assaults on his father's image. In both attacks, the son procured the cooperation of many prominent persons, some bearing names well known in the worlds of journalism and publishing; fortunately, Siple and his publisher, Putnam, successfully resisted the attempt to censor their book.[2]

An unbiased writer on Byrd, Lisle Rose, whose work *Assault on Eternity: Richard E. Byrd and the Exploration of Antarctica 1946–47* was angrily condemned by Byrd's partisans, said recently in a private communication that ". . . there seems to be no end of individuals prepared even at this late . . . date to go into paroxysms of defense at any mention of a possible blemish on the Admiral's perfect character. . . . I have to caution you that *any* description of Byrd as less than perfect or saintly will stimulate the wrath of the older antarctic community. It happened to me."

Byrd's idolators seem so opposed to complete, frank treatments of Byrd and his expeditions that they would rather he be forgotten than that the legend he and they created be compromised. Partly because they stifled research and writing on him, Byrd is little remembered. His name was recently dropped from the "Richard E. Byrd" airport in his home state of Virginia, but there was no outcry. No one seemed to care.

Those who felt strongly against Byrd, on the other hand, would not relish helping an author whose findings might be favorable to the admiral. Those critical of Byrd but whose reputations were nevertheless linked to his would not want to risk damage from any fallout. Besides, most of the critics clearly felt it was unseemly to air their iconoclastic attitudes in public. Many of Byrd's men, remembering how intensely he could hate an associate whose loose tongue threatened to undermine his image, have probably kept silence out of respect for his wishes.

Not all Byrd's associates were hostile or unwilling to help. Dr. Siple graciously gave me a long interview shortly before his death and while he was suffering from the effects of a stroke. Although he spoke guardedly and never criticized Byrd, he obviously tried to be as frank as he felt he could. Henry Harrison, while in his eighties and at a time when he was not feeling well, was also guarded but generously completed many sections of a long questionnaire I sent him. The late Dean Smith, when in his mid-eighties, blind, and suffering from congestive heart failure, listened to his wife, Beth, read an identical questionnaire to him and dictated to her all the answers he had. Several members of Byrd's second expedition, now all deceased, also spoke with me: Admiral Richard Black, George Grimminger, Dr. Thomas Poulter, and Captain Finn Ronne.

I gleaned original information from several other sources, primarily the papers of Admiral Byrd and his family at Ohio State University; diaries, correspondence, and other records of the members and associates of Byrd's expeditions in the U.S. National Archives; and Bernt Balchen's papers at the Air Force History Center. I wish to express my appreciation to Mrs. Ruth Siple for allowing me access to the restricted Siple papers in the National Archives.

I have revealed all the pertinent facts concerning Byrd's first antarctic expedition as I learned or deduced them, pro and con, and I have tried not to judge Byrd himself as good or bad or to take sides on issues that remain controversial. I have accepted at face value what Byrd said and what others said about him and the expedition, especially regarding his life and career before 1927, except when those statements do not make sense or when there is evidence to the contrary. This book is not a biography of Byrd, of course, but the story of a key part of his career. I hope that readers will find it as interesting and enlightening to be taken beyond the barriers of illusion that Byrd erected as to go beyond the barriers to geographical discovery that he encountered. I believe the fundamental questions of ethics and leadership raised by the actions of this fascinating, complex man are worthy of a debate that has so far been discouraged.

Dean Smith, who was a pilot on the expedition, said that the major reward the experience gave him was a measure of maturity. I would like my readers to share in that personal growth while participating vicariously in the excitement that once captivated millions of armchair adventurers. The true story of Byrd's first expedition to Antarctica, with the elements of human drama revealed by newly available records of the expedition, rivals fictional tales of voyages to other planets.

I am grateful to librarians in the Library of Congress and the city libraries of Washington, D.C., Hartford, and Richmond for their help; to Roxy Montana for acquiring for me many of the books about Byrd and the expedition; to Jane Hemmin, for moral support and encouragement at the beginning; to Lissa Karp, for typing help before word processors; and to my in-laws, Harvey and Betty Huber, for their hospitality and kindnesses in connection with my research trips.

The late Dr. Kenneth Bertrand, Professor of Geography at Catholic University, provided insights from his research on Byrd's expeditions. I wish to recognize the aid and advice of Dr. Franklin Burch and the late Herman Friis, and especially the exceptionally generous assistance and helpfulness of Ms. Alison Wilson, all of the National Archives.

Ohio State University's officials considerately allowed me access to Byrd's papers the school had recently acquired from Byrd's estate (except a few papers OSU had not yet made public under the terms of the acquisition), even though processing and preservation of the voluminous collection has not been completed. I particularly want to thank Dr. Raimund E. Goerler, University Archivist; Dr. Robert A. Tibbetts, Curator of Rare Books & Manuscripts; and Mr. Robert Keller, assistant to Dr. Tibbetts, for going out of their way to help.

BEYOND THE BARRIER

.1.

Dick Byrd

TWENTY airplanes buzzed a salute over the tops of Broadway's sky-scrapers. Hundreds of people leaned out windows and dumped waste-baskets of ticker tape on the crowd of cheering thousands lining the street. Thirty-seven-year-old Lieutenant Commander Dick Byrd, tipping his white navy hat in acknowledgment, marched at the head of a parade of dignitaries. At that moment, he occupied center stage of America's Roaring Twenties.

It was Tuesday, 22 June 1926. Six weeks before, headlines had screamed that Byrd and the man walking beside him, navy enlisted man Floyd Bennett, had become the first men to fly over the North Pole. They had made the flight on their own after taking leave from the service, with Byrd navigating and Bennett piloting.

People were fledglings then, and they exulted at every "first" flight made with their flimsy plywood and canvas wings. As an adolescent world power, America rejoiced at every accomplishment that proved the superiority of Americans.

Many people pressing the barriers at the curbs as Byrd passed by were surprised that the young officer was not more physically imposing. He was slightly built and only average in height. But he was appropriately handsome—blue-eyed and cleft-chinned, with thick, wavy brown hair flecked with gray.

New York City had declared a school holiday for the historic welcoming home. The daring aviators had sailed into the harbor that morning after the long return voyage from their arctic island base. The whistles and horns of nearly every vessel in port greeted the men with a cacaphony of screams and belches. A delegation of political, military, business, and scientific personages received Byrd and Bennett at the pier. They all paraded to city hall for the ceremonies.

There Jimmy Walker, the playboy mayor, presented Byrd the keys to the city, which he accepted in an address carried over two radio stations, his accent proclaiming his Virginian origin. Then an old admiral called for three cheers for the heroes, which were followed by a congressman's leading the crowd in singing "Carry Me Back to Old Virginny." The police officer in charge was crying, too choked with emotion to sing.

Afterward Byrd lunched with a thousand members of the Advertising Club, many of whom were his friends from the world of business, then took a train for Washington, D.C.

That night at the Washington auditorium, Byrd stood before a crowd of six thousand that included most of the government's leading figures and many of his political friends. President Coolidge bestowed on the hero the National Geographic Society's Hubbard Medal for outstanding achievement in polar exploration. In his remarks, Coolidge praised Byrd and his pioneering use of the new technologies of aviation and radio:

> Word that the north pole had been reached by airplane for the first time was flashed around the globe on May 9. . . . An American naval officer . . . had attained in a flight of 15 hours and 30 minutes what Admiral Peary . . . achieved, seventeen years before, only after weary months of travel over frozen arctic wastes.
>
> In no way could we have a more striking illustration of the scientific and mechanical progress since the year 1909. Then Peary's trip to the pole on dog sleds took about two-thirds of a year. He reached his goal on April 6. It was September 6 before news of the achievement reached the outside world.
>
> The naval officer of 1926, using an American invention, the airplane, winged his way from his base and back again in less than two-thirds of a day, and a few hours later the radio had announced the triumph to the four quarters of the earth. Scientific instruments perfected by the navigator . . . were in no small way responsible for success. . . . His

deed will be but the beginning of scientific exploration considered difficult of achievement before he proved the possibilities of the airplane.

Lieutenant Commander Richard Evelyn Byrd . . . you have brought things to pass. . . .[1]

In his acceptance address, Byrd modestly reviewed his arctic achievements. Then he declared, "America will not rest until the . . . unexplored regions in the . . . antarctic have been taken by aircraft from the column of the unknown, and in so doing much valuable scientific data will be given to the world. And the United States must plant its flag at the south pole. It has never been there or anywhere near it."[2]

Byrd's honors made headlines in the next morning's papers. In line with the sentiments of the 1920s, many featured a picture of Byrd and his mother gazing fondly into each other's eyes after they had embraced at the pier. Byrd's high, sloping forehead over heavy-lidded eyes, set wide and deep, and his small, delicate mouth were the most distinctive features in his photographs.

Byrd's story shared the front pages with the kidnapping account of the evangelist Aimee Semple McPherson and the latest report on the futility of trying to enforce prohibition. The newspapers of 1926 were all heavily influenced by tabloid journalism, then in its heyday, presenting life in America as a melodrama. Their audiences hissed at mobster Al Capone, wept at the death of movie star Rudolf Valentino, gasped at the death of murderess Ruth Snider, rooted for fighters Dempsey or Tunney, clucked at lovers Peaches and Daddy Browning, and cheered for hero Dick Byrd. They idolized Lieutenant Commander Byrd because he combined four starring parts—aviator, scientist, explorer, and businessman—into one, and because his sterling character epitomized the true-blue all-American man. He achieved success in each role, and Americans worshipped success.

The New York *Sun* captured Byrd's persona in an interview after the north polar flight. Published in *Literary Digest*, which reprinted noteworthy news stories, the interview reflected not only Byrd's philosophical bent but also the culture of his times. It began:

"What were you thinking about when you crossed the pole in the air?"

For one transitory second the eaglet folded up his wings and dropped his fine dark eyes in humility.

"Do you really want to know?" he answered, lifting his glance and recovering his calm. "I have not been asked that."

"Do you mind?"

"No!"

And then the real Byrd cast off his armor of reserve and addressed the earthbound.

"I thought of the infinitesimal proportions of mortal man, of the frailty of the atoms that occupy the spaces, of the limitations of those who have taken over the conduct of civilization. . . ."[3]

Richard Evelyn Byrd was born 25 October 1888 to a distinguished, Episcopalian, but not moneyed family of Winchester, Virginia, one of the renowned "first families of Virginia," with roots deep in history. He traced his paternal ancestry to a founder of Richmond and, further back, to William the Conquerer. Dick's father had been Speaker of the House in the Virginia state assembly, and brother Harry was governor of Virginia. (Harry Byrd would go on to national prominence as a senator.) Dick's mother was descended from Lord Delaware.

Dick's self-assurance propelled him into the limelight at an early age. When he was only twelve, his parents sent him on his own to visit a family friend in the Philippines. The *New York Times* ran the story of the boy voyager and his Philippine adventures, calling him the youngest globe-trotter of his time.

At the age of fifteen, Byrd enrolled at the Virginia Military Institute, where he decided his career would be with the navy and its far-ranging ships. Unable to get into Annapolis immediately, he went to the University of Virginia to await an appointment, which came in 1908.

Always active in sports, Byrd made the prestigious midshipman football team as second-string quarterback. In his second year, in the game against Princeton, he was caught under a big pile-up. The other men hauled themselves up, but Byrd stayed on the ground, writhing in pain. The doctors found he had broken his right foot in three places. The foot never healed properly, and Byrd could not rejoin the team; but he was able to participate in gymnastics. In a practice session during his last year, however, Byrd tried a trick on the flying rings and missed. He crashed to the ground, dislocating his weak right ankle and fracturing the foot again, this time in two places. On cruise after graduation (Byrd was better at athletics and social events than studies and finished in the middle of his class) he fell down a hatch, once again landing on the right foot and shattering the bones. Surgeons nailed them together, and he spent three months in the hospital.

Having no use on its ships for officers so physically vulnerable, the uncompromising navy declared him unsuitable for promotion. His years of career preparation undone and his ambitions dashed, Byrd had to retire as a lowly ensign. "Career ended. Not enough income to live on; no chance of coming back; trained for a seafaring profession; temperamentally disinclined to business. A fizzle," the depressed Byrd wrote about his forced retirement.[4]

He did not let bitterness destroy him. With the World War raging, he managed to win his way back to active duty in a few days and even wangled a promotion to lieutenant (junior grade), retroactive to the day before retirement—although he was still on the retired list. In a limbolike status, he could resign from active duty whenever he wanted but could not be promoted except under extraordinary circumstances. He was named commander of Rhode Island's naval militia.

Byrd still had to salvage his career for the long term. Aviators were emerging as the new knights of warfare, and Byrd figured that the objections to having a lame officer on a ship would not bar a man from flying a plane. "My one chance of escape from a life of inaction was to learn to fly," he wrote.[5] The navy acceded to his petition to train as a pilot at Pensacola.

After he had learned to fly, Byrd suggested to the navy that the service assign aviators such as he to attempt the first transatlantic crossing by air. He proposed winging instead of shipping the world's largest flying boat to the war in Europe. The navy bought the idea and ordered Byrd to set up a facility in Nova Scotia that would serve double duty as a base for the mission and as a submarine patrol station.

The war ended before preparations for the flight were completed, but the navy kept the project going. The navy did not assign Byrd to the flight, though, because it was reserved for those who had been unable to get foreign duty during the war, duty much sought after by career officers. Furious at what he considered an inane bureaucratic ruling, Byrd complained to his superiors. Although they would not let him fly, they assigned him to work out a navigation system for the flight.

Navigation methods and instruments had been designed for ships. Airplanes changed positions much more quickly, were less steady, and could not stop for sightings. Byrd modified several navigational instruments for aviation and developed the artificial-horizon bubble-sextant that became known as the Byrd sextant. He also helped to devise the drift indicator to compensate for winds. Officially, the first aircraft to navigate out of sight of land used developments he made or supervised for the flying boat's transatlantic attempt.[6]

Byrd's efforts paid off, but the glory for the first transatlantic flight went to the pilot, Lieutenant Commander A. C. Read, who made the milestone crossing in May 1919 from Nova Scotia to the Azores.

Aviation had no clear future, however. The Wright brothers had made their epochal flight less than sixteen years before. Commercial air service in the United States was negligible, and even military aviation was thought to have limited use. Byrd, at the age of thirty, decided to remain on active duty while he pondered what to do with his life.

The navy transferred him to Washington, D.C., to serve as a liaison with Congress. Ironically, Byrd helped to lead what became infamous as the crucifixion of Billy Mitchell, the aviation pioneer. General William Mitchell, believing that military aviation would not reach its full potential until it had been separated from the two traditional services, had launched his campaign to merge the army and navy air units into a powerful, independent air force. Getting nowhere with his superiors, he had gone over their heads to Congress, which was receptive to his ideas. Naval leaders realized that Mitchell's concept would not only cost them their air arm but would also reduce their turf and budget. Byrd volunteered to help stop him. As part of the strategy, Byrd pushed through bills that created the navy's Bureau of Aeronautics and the Naval Air Reserve. Byrd himself organized the first two reserve units. (Mitchell was defeated for the moment, court-martialed for insubordination, and forced out of the army, although his efforts contributed to the establishment of the U.S. Air Force in 1947.) As Admiral Chester Nimitz said much later, Byrd would have been one of the greatest figures in American naval history simply for his contributions to the aeronautics program.[7] Those efforts earned him valuable IOUs from admirals in the top ranks of the service.

He cashed some in to get a promotion. The navy agreed that his services for aeronautics had been extraordinarily meritorious and persuaded Congress to pass a special bill advancing him to lieutenant commander. "It was simply a recognition of the fact that I had plugged strenuously for the service I am so devoted to," Byrd wrote.[8]

Byrd realized that to advance as a forcibly retired officer he would have to continue to perform out-of-the-ordinary jobs. He still believed fervently in aviation and concluded that it remained his most promising route to success. He also felt that aviation had to be promoted, as did hundreds of other aviators trained during the war, who were zealously trying to create a market for their skills. Piloting demanded courage, skill, and muscle, but the fliers hoped to prove that aircraft could be made safe and reliable and that aviation could even revolutionize civilization if given the chance. Aviators were trying mightily to whip up enthusiasm among both the war-sickened public who thought of airplanes as abhorrent military weapons and the hard-nosed businessmen who dismissed aviation as too big a gamble for investment. Byrd devoutly believed that aviation was an instrument of international good will and lasting peace. Those he talked with on the subject said he could go on for hours about it. He said aviation "would do more to promote human welfare than any other human agency."[9]

Byrd proposed risking a solo transatlantic flight in a navy plane. He was turned down. He pleaded for assignment to a transatlantic dirigible flight. The request was granted, but the huge aircraft crashed during a test flight, ending the project. Twice he applied for positions on projects to explore the vast expanses of the Arctic with aircraft. The first time he was turned down, and the second time the project was scrubbed.

Byrd's frustration apparently became unbearable when his ambition to fly the Arctic was thwarted. The saga of attempts to reach the North and South Poles by land had taken place during his lifetime. People of his generation could remember the tales of hardship, suffering, and death that accompanied long, unsuccessful journeys until Peary announced discovery of the North Pole sixteen years before and the Norwegian Roald Amundsen achieved the South Pole thirteen years before. The aviator who faced the same challenges and conquered them in a flight of less than a day was guaranteed to become a hero.

It seemed that the only way Byrd could get his career moving was to strike out on his own. Presumably after much soul-searching he determined to take the risk—and to undertake a private air expedition to the north polar region the summer of 1925.

He cadged offers of philanthropic aid from Ford and Rockefeller, but he needed the help of the navy too. The service, however, had already promised to assist the seasoned arctic explorer Commander Donald B. MacMillan in a similar expedition. The navy arranged a compromise by making Byrd's group an official navy air unit attached to the MacMillan expedition. Byrd's orders called for him to search for land between Greenland and the North Pole and allowed him to try to fly over the pole if success seemed possible. There was little doubt he would seize any chance to make the attempt.[10]

Byrd found himself in a race. Amundsen, in partnership with the American explorer Lincoln Ellsworth, had gotten up an air expedition to reach the pole that summer. Amundsen and Ellsworth took off for the pole, but their planes were forced down and they barely survived. Bad weather unfortunately prevented Byrd from doing any serious flying at all during the few weeks his expedition was in the field, and all he gained was experience.

The following year, the Australian explorer Hubert Wilkins offered Byrd the position of second in command of an arctic expedition,[11] but the American wanted to mount his own effort. He dedicated it to the sole purpose of reaching the North Pole—just as Amundsen had devoted all his resources to singular efforts to reach the poles, unencumbered by any sophisticated exploratory or scientific responsibilities. Byrd was joined by his best friend, Floyd Bennett, a chief machinist's mate. Bennett had gotten to know Byrd during his Pensacola days and had been with him on the first arctic trip.

Bennett would fly while Byrd navigated—Byrd never was a good pilot. The leader tried to get his venture recognized again as an official expedition, but the navy demurred.[12] Byrd procured a small ship and recruited fifty members for his expedition, primarily by writing to nearly all the men in the naval reserves who had more than fifteen years of service. He also included some navy men who took leave from active duty and several civilians from among thousands who volunteered when they read about the project. The expedition would sail to the takeoff point on Spitsbergen, a Norwegian island 750 miles from the pole.

Byrd again was in a race. Wilkins had journeyed to Alaska, intending to fly across the pole to Spitsbergen. But Wilkins's two planes crashed in March before he could make the attempt. The other competitors were Amundsen and Ellsworth again, with their new partner, the Italian Umberto Nobile, who was providing a dirigible for the attempt. They were also basing at Spitsbergen. Neither Byrd nor the others spoke of competition, however, because each of them sought recognition for being the first to fly over the North Pole, not fame for beating other contestants in a polar derby.

Byrd got the jump on the other group, which was still waiting for Nobile to show up when Byrd's ship pulled into the island's harbor on 29 April. Early on the morning of 9 May 1926, he and Bennett took off in the Fokker that Byrd had named the *Josephine Ford*, after the daughter of his major benefactor. They returned late that afternoon and announced they had flown over the pole. Reporters who had traveled to Spitsbergen for the flights flashed word of the accomplishment around the globe.

On the voyage back to the United States Byrd's party stopped in London, where the members were disappointed to learn that people in Norway and Italy were disputing Byrd's claim to have reached the pole, saying the flight time was impossibly short. These people asserted that their countrymen Amundsen and Nobile and the American Ellsworth shared honors for the first flight over the pole when their dirigible cruised over three days later.

Several members of Byrd's expedition were together when they read a report from Italy about the challenge. All but Bennett laughed it off as more of Mussolini's posturing. He studied the account carefully, then crumpled up the newspaper and hurled it to the floor.[13]

There were no doubts among the patriotic Americans who acclaimed Byrd nationwide. New York's greeting was one of the wildest the city had ever given a celebrity. The military presented him with the Distinguished Service Cross and the Distinguished Flying Cross. An enthusiastic Congress awarded him the Congressional Medal of Honor and tried to promote him immediately to admiral, but he declined, saying the advancement was not justified by his exploits. He also doused a movement to appoint him to the new position of assistant secretary of the navy for aviation, preferring to remain on his own.[14] He did accept elevation to commander. There was resentment among regular officers, but an act of Congress was the only way someone retired on disability could win promotion.

Byrd maintained the momentum of his fame by immediately taking aim at another of aviation's major challenges: the first nonstop flight from the United States to Europe. He persuaded Rodman Wanamaker, the department store magnate, to sponsor the effort. Wanamaker assigned the business details of the project to the suave Grover Whalen, the general manager of the store in New York City and a celebrity himself as head of the city's busy welcoming committee (and later a colorful New York City police commissioner).

Byrd chose a three-engine Fokker like the one he had used for the north polar flight. Multiengine planes were still in the pioneering stage, but they were still safer than single-engine planes: the multiengine aircraft could still fly if one engine failed. On the other hand, there were more things that could go wrong to abort a project that stretched a plane to its limits. Byrd stated publicly many times that his flight was to be nothing less than a scientific experiment. He claimed the risks he faced were the same as those encountered by a laboratory researcher, like a chemist testing explosives. He explained that his spectacular flights were designed solely to show where and how future aviators and passengers could fly, to pave the way for the airliners of the future. He intended to equip the plane with every safety and survival device known to aviation; nothing was to be left to chance. Echoing Amundsen, Byrd said that on dangerous projects "the adventure involved varies directly as preparation. . . . The more the amateur, the greater the adventure."[15]

Byrd planned his ocean crossing for the next period when generally good flying weather would prevail over the North Atlantic, beginning in April 1927. The Byrd-Wanamaker organization painstakingly worked out a special weather forecasting service for his route with ships that routinely plied the same lane, with the Radio Corporation of America, and with the U.S. Weather Bureau. The project leased, and spent $30,000 to recondition, a runway for the heavily loaded Fokker at Roosevelt Field on Long Island.

Fokker built the plane at its New Jersey plant. Tony Fokker himself was the pilot for the first test flight on 20 April. In a lapse from Byrd's usual cautious approach, he and the rest of the transatlantic crew—Bennett and radioman George Noville—went along on the maiden flight. The aircraft climbed into the air without incident; but when the pilot tried to level off to land, he discovered the plane was nose heavy. Hitting the ground nose first, the plane somersaulted onto its back. Bennett smashed several ribs, punctured a lung, and severely injured his back. Byrd broke his wrist, and Noville sustained internal injuries; Fokker was only bruised. People who rushed to help found Byrd and Fokker screaming at each other.[16]

The plane was badly damaged but repairable. Byrd minimized the severity of the accident to the press because, he later explained, bad publicity would defeat a major purpose of the flight, which was to improve aviation's reputation.[17] The delay was particularly exasperating because others had decided to try the nonstop flight. Byrd once again found himself in an unwanted race. In Virginia, Commander Noel Davis took off in another three-engine plane. In Paris, two Frenchmen named Nungesser and Coli took off for New York in a single-engine plane. Davis's aircraft crashed, killing him. Nungesser and Coli never arrived in New York, presumably having come down and perished somewhere in the vast ocean.

Two other planes, both single-engine craft, appeared at Roosevelt Field, the best takeoff point for the New York–Paris flight. One was piloted by Clarence Chamberlain but owned by businessman Charles Levine, who planned to go along. The other was flown by a little-known stunt flier and airmail pilot—Charles Lindbergh. The Lone Eagle, as the newspapers began calling him, planned to fly the two days and a night alone, tricky business when piloting was almost an athletic feat and navigating was a delicate art.

Byrd was helpful and courteous to the others. He generously offered them his runway and weather service and proferred them expert advice on navigation. The public's sentimental favorite was "Lindy," but the smart money was on Byrd because of his superior background and resources and his early start. The bettors could not know that the "mishap" suffered by Byrd's plane would cause a long delay.

At the christening of the aircraft, the *America*, on 21 May, Byrd was rising to speak when a messenger dashed up with a note. Byrd looked at it, stuffed his speech notes into his pocket, and announced that Lindbergh had landed in Paris. Byrd called for a celebration in honor of the new hero.

Lindbergh's success deprived Byrd's mission of some of its purpose and denied Byrd much of the glory that might have been his, but he had to continue his "experiment." He tried, though, to get Wanamaker to change the destination from Paris to Rome; but Wanamaker was sponsoring the flight chiefly because of his love for France and so refused. Byrd, therefore, postponed departure until the Lindbergh hysteria passed its peak, to avoid the appearance of horning in on the Lone Eagle and, probably, to increase his own publicity.[18] Chamberlain and Levine meanwhile switched their destination to Germany and made a successful flight.

At last, on 29 June 1927, the *America* took off with navigator Byrd, radioman Noville, and pilots Bert Acosta—replacing Bennett, who was still hospitalized from his serious test-flight injuries—and Bernt

Balchen—a young Norwegian whom Byrd added to the crew because of his uncommon ability to fly on instruments.[19] Byrd had been sworn in as an airmail officer, and his plane was carrying the first transatlantic airmail.

Although the crossing for the most part went smoothly, the landing was unexpectedly dangerous. When the crew arrived over France the day after their takeoff, they were crushed to find the country around Paris socked in by heavy clouds and rain, without a chance of landing. Byrd elected to fly to the coast and ditch in the shallow water. Miraculously, Balchen brought the plane down without mishap in the ocean near the Normandy coast, and the men rowed ashore in their emergency raft.

On his return to New York, Byrd became the first celebrity ever to have a second ticker-tape parade. He made appearances in person and on the radio and was seen all over the country in newsreels. Articles about him or by him were published in the leading magazines, and he wrote papers on navigation and aviation for technical publications. Universities proudly bestowed honorary degrees on him.

The successful transatlantic flights—Lindbergh's in particular—triggered what fliers and flying enthusiasts had been seeking for aviation since the war: the public's respect and enthusiasm and, most of all, financial support. Aviation exploded into a red-hot business, and from then on the job of aviation's promoters would be to keep enthusiasm high.

Byrd still thirsted for achievement in the air. His attempts while in the navy had been discouraging. His first arctic expedition had been disappointing. Few people, surely, would remember in years to come that his plane was the third to cross from the United States to Europe. Even the north polar flight had been unfulfilling: it had been a spectacular stunt that boosted aviation but directly contributed nothing lasting to mankind, and it had been tainted by challenges to the claim. Floyd Bennett, too, apparently found the north polar flight unsatisfying. When he learned that he and Byrd were to receive the Congressional Medal of Honor, the enlisted man's reaction was surprisingly unenthusiastic. He told his friend Balchen, "I don't want to go down to Washington and get another medal for that north polar thing."[20]

Byrd planned to claim his place in history by combining aviation and exploration. He announced he would devote his career to discovery by air. Exploration was then a profession that entrepreneurs could aspire to, and its practitioners were astounding the public. Roy Chapman Andrews had recently found a million-year-old dinosaur egg in the Mongolian desert; William Beebe was finding nightmarish fish in tropical seas; another explorer, Douglas Burden, found the dragonlike "Grand Lizard of Komodo"; and archaeologist Howard Carter uncovered the splendid, long-lost tomb of King Tut. "At this rate," wrote a thrilled observer, "there is no telling what wild freak might turn up in the prodigious spaces yet left to the daring traveler."[21]

Exploration of the vast white spaces in the hostile polar regions was especially romantic and had made contemporary heroes of Ellsworth, MacMillan, Amundsen, and Wilkins as well as Byrd. The legendary British antarctic explorer Sir Ernest Shackleton had died on an expedition only five years before. Even before Byrd returned from Paris after the transatlantic flight, he had officially announced his initial plans: he would fly to the South Pole and explore the millions of square miles of unknown territory in Antarctica—the coldest, windiest, snowiest, driest, most desolate, and most mysterious part of the earth. The unseen area was known to be greater than the total of all other unexplored areas on earth. "Somebody has to explore [the antarctic], and it is the job I have picked out for myself," he said.[22] "The expedition will be in many respects one of the most novel expeditions which ever moved its way into the regions of ice."[23]

.2.

Mobilizing

Byrd's intrepid flight to the remote South Pole would be the center-piece of a unique expedition designed to dramatize what airplanes and other modern technologies could do for antarctic exploration. Aircraft, so frail then, had never flown in Antarctica. Pointing out that the south polar flight would be much more perilous than the one over the North Pole, the *New York Times* asserted that Byrd's achievement would be the "greatest feat in the history of exploration and aviation."

Byrd would fly several hours longer than on his arctic flight while battling fiercer winds, weaving through treacherous mountain passes, and nursing straining engines through thin air over the high, expansive south polar plateau. Scanning the horizon as he soared on high, Byrd would observe in this one flight more than prior explorers hugging the ground on their dog sledges surveyed in a whole season. He would look down on a realm covered by a vast sheet of snow-topped ice reported to average almost half a mile deep. In places he would peer down the black maws of crevasses cavernous enough to swallow a surface traveler, dog team and all, without a trace. Except for mountains he might discover, probably the only bare earth he would spot would be the peaks that poked up through the thick ice in a known range that snaked across his route. Barring unlikely observations, he

14

would glimpse no people, no animals, no trees or other plants—absolutely nothing to eat or give shelter. In the unheated plane he would feel the bite of polar cold said to drop well down into the minus range even during summer flying weather. At any time, but particularly on takeoff and landing, gales reported to blow all the time in some sections might fling his fragile craft to the ground. If he were forced down, by no means improbable, he would be plunged into an alien land not meant for human survival. No daredevil, Byrd did not look forward to the ordeal, but he would put up with the travail to win acclaim at the finish.

Byrd proposed flying from a base on the rim of Antarctica, a continent as large as the United States and western Europe combined. He would land at the pole, roughly in the middle of the continent, to plant the flag and, he said, to make scientific observations—he was no scientist but liked to be thought of as one.[1] He accepted the risk of a crash upon landing or subsequent takeoff due to the unknown and potentially hazardous surface conditions, the strong winds, and the weakness of engines gasping for air at the nine-thousand-foot altitude of the pole. He hoped to keep going all the way across Antarctica to another base or recovery operation on the opposite side, winging over sprawling territory that men had never penetrated.[2]

Byrd had ordered two Fokkers: a big three-engine, four-passenger aircraft for the demanding polar flight, and a smaller one-engine plane for nearby reconnaissance. After the transatlantic flight, before leaving Europe, Balchen had visited Tony Fokker in Holland; they worked up preliminary designs that used Balchen's expertise in ski-flying.[3] The determining factor in Byrd's carefully considered choice was that Fokkers were long-proven. He had flown them on both the north polar and transatlantic projects. Thirty persons died in the summer of 1927 in transatlantic attempts, and Byrd did not want to risk his life or chances of success any more than necessary by using newer types of planes, even one made by an American company.

Byrd fixed on the shore point closest to the pole for his base. He planned to set up advance headquarters in the country nearest his camp, New Zealand. Chile offered the services of her navy to recover him after his long transcontinental flight. Balchen introduced Byrd to a Norwegian relative who owned a huge whaling factory ship. The owner volunteered to piggyback Byrd's assemblage on his ship's annual voyage to antarctic waters, sailing from California on 20 October.[4]

Byrd's troops would stay in Antarctica during December, January, and February (the southern hemisphere's summer and the only time that ships could get through the icy antarctic seas) and would be evacuated by the whaler before the ocean froze them in for the winter.

The burden of mounting a first-class expedition proved much bigger than Byrd had expected. The mission had to be self-sufficient for a year or so, the time it would take if he could not escape from Antarctica before the world's wintriest of winters sealed him in. He had to make sure he thought of all the right things in the right quantities, from toilet paper and playing cards to geophysical instruments and spare parts for the planes. Then he had to beg or buy everything and ship it halfway around the world. Byrd was swamped in a sea of details.

Fortunately, pressure to get underway lessened when Byrd realized that no one else was going to fly in Antarctica in 1927 and beat him to the pole. On 4 August 1927, he announced that he was postponing his departure for a year to make "the most careful preparations" and to allow Floyd Bennett, second in command, more time to recuperate from *America*'s test-flight crash. Byrd explained that thorough planning was necessary to bring everyone back alive and do good scientific work.[5]

The *New York Times* felt it was necessary to defend his position in an editorial because the postponement revived talk, stemming from the long delay in *America*'s takeoff, that Byrd was too much of a perfectionist, or at worst a procrastinator.[6] As one of his financial angels, the *Times* had a stake in his reputation.

Byrd had come to realize that even one more year would be hardly enough time to get ready in light of his ambitions: to explore large, unseen regions of the globe; to seek out data from places scientists had never reached; and to test the emerging technologies of aviation and radio. Appreciating anew the value of wisdom gained through experience, he solicited intelligence from antarctic veterans. He sent Balchen back to Norway to confer with the wise old polar hand Roald Amundsen.[7] In Spitsbergen after the north polar flight, Amundsen had graciously given Byrd tips about antarctic exploration and offered to assist him. Helped by Amundsen's recommendations, Balchen assembled polar materials and recruited other Norwegians skilled in ice and snow. Byrd also corresponded steadily with the experienced Amundsen, who gave the American invaluable advice on exploration and extensive help in procuring manpower, equipment, and supplies.

Whether by choice or not, Byrd apparently had little contact with veterans of the Scott or Shackleton expeditions. Most probably, Byrd felt he had more to learn from the consummately skillful, businesslike Amundsen. Nevertheless, Byrd did ask an associate going to England to talk with former Scott expedition members about ice conditions and alternate sites for bases.[8] One of the British explorers, E. M. Joyce, expressed an interest in joining the American, but nothing came of his feeler.

(Amundsen and England's Captain Robert F. Scott had raced to the South Pole. In 1911, their rival expeditions established seaside bases 580 miles apart in Antarctica. On 19 October, Amundsen's party set out for the pole, about 790 straight-line miles away. On 1 November, Scott's party took off on a trek of about 850 straight-line miles. Without radio, neither party knew when the other left. On 14 December, Amundsen and his four companions reached the South Pole after a thoroughly planned and professionally executed journey. The men encountered relatively few difficulties and returned safely. Scott's party, on the other hand, experienced extreme hardships, primarily because its mission had been poorly planned and amateurishly executed. Scott and his four teammates reached the pole, marked by the Norwegian flag, on 16 January 1912. On the way back, the men were trapped in a blizzard without enough food or fuel. All died.)

Byrd felt that he might turn up something amazing in the little-known south frigid zone. He liked to talk about the possibility, backed up by at least one scientist, that in searching antarctic lowlands he might discover a snow-free netherworld of weird plants and animals, perhaps even inhabited by natives like Eskimos. Byrd let his imagination roam for the readers of *Popular Mechanics*: "Does it seem reasonable that lands which for months of the year are swept by sunshine twenty-four hours a day should not somewhere support life? . . . Somewhere in these tremendous areas there must be lowlands where temperatures rise sufficiently to permit vegetable and animal life—the latter very possibly as different from any we know as the penguin is different from birds of climes with which we are familiar. In some antarctic valley, perhaps, shut in by towering mountains, a thrilling discovery may await us. We may find forms of life completely new to us. Who knows what link with prehistoric times might be there? If the elemental and sturdy penguin can live through the extremes of winter, in warmer lowlands there should be animals able to do the same."[9]

Most scientists would have been delighted simply to glean basic facts about the strange land and its minerals, the great ice sheet that covered them, the ghostly aurora that shimmered overhead, the hardy plants and animals that clung to life near the shore, the surrounding ocean and sea floor, and the unseen geophysical forces about the south magnetic pole that deflected compass needles and caused static and blackouts in radios. Byrd pointed out that whatever his expedition learned about the ocean and its denizens could help the whaling, sealing, and fishing industries. In organizing his scientific program, he drew on his experiences as coordinator of scientific projects for the planned 1924 arctic flight of the dirigible *Shenandoah*, a flight that was canceled, and as supervisor of aerial photography, meteorology, and geomagnetic recording for the MacMillan-Byrd expedition. Leading professionals and scientific organizations helped him to plan the scientific program and select personnel and equipment.[10]

Byrd aimed to pioneer the use of radio for antarctic exploration. Commercial broadcasting had begun less than seven years earlier. Home radio sets were altering evening hours for American families, who now gathered eagerly around to hear the likes of the Happiness Boys and the A & P Gypsies. The first networks, NBC and CBS, had been formed only months earlier. Plans were being laid for a new section of Manhattan, to be called Radio City. The pervasive, invisible radio waves predictably were being blamed by fearmongers for natural disasters, from various crop failures to the floods that devastated New England that year; but radio's potential help to exploration was enormous. People familiar with the frustrations of coordinating expeditionary, military, or other logistic movements were excited by the prospect that field parties, planes, ships, bases, and the United States would all be able to communicate instantly. Using Morse code (more complex voice technology was unreliable), expedition members could discuss problems, opportunities, and changes in plans and efficiently coordinate activities. Previous expeditions had unavoidably suffered wasted efforts and even tragedy because the isolated segments did not know what was happening with the others, for months and sometimes years at a time. Like a central nervous system, radio links would enable the disparate parts of Byrd's expedition to function smoothly together.

Although Byrd expected radio to make a big difference in field operations, he had doubts about the effectiveness of the link with the United States on the other side of the globe. Regular communications had never been sustained over such a long distance. Shortwave radio had been around only three years and was still in its infancy. The *New York Times*, which was sending a reporter on the trip and hoped he might transmit stories directly to the newspaper's radio room, took charge of arranging the link to the United States. The paper approached RCA for help, but the company claimed direct transmission was impossible. Relaying messages through a chain of radio operators might not be timely, however, and the charges would be too expensive. The *Times*, therefore, developed its own methods. Its engineers set up a special transmitter and receiver on Long Island, away from all the static and radio noise of New York City, and connected the station to Times Square by leased telephone lines. Byrd did not expect to get through often or to be understood well when he did, especially since he would be able to take a transmitter of only limited power. The navy built two radio sets for the expedition and offered to relay ship transmissions and other messages when necessary through the worldwide communications system that the service was forming.[11]

In keeping with the spirit of the Twenties, Byrd wanted everything about his venture to be as up-to-date as airplanes and radio and as thoroughly American as possible. He had experts design new types of polar clothing, huts, tents, and trail gear. Nutritionists devised a powdered fruit extract to prevent the curse of scurvy, the disease that caused bleeding and weakness in polar explorers, sailors, and others who did not eat fresh foods; scientists suspected a vitamin prevented the sickness but had not identified the nutrient. Characteristically thoroughgoing, Byrd wished his expedition to be the best prepared ever.[12]

In sharp contrast to his overall sophistication, however, Byrd chose primitive technology for his ground transportation: dog teams. Primarily, they would haul cargo from the ship to the site several miles inland where quarters were to be constructed, would pull scientists through areas chosen for inspection, and would set out emergency food and fuel caches along the route of the south polar flight. Byrd contemplated taking twenty-five dogs, sufficient for two teams and a squad of subs. Reliability was the key: dog sledges were the time-tested method of polar travel. Motorized vehicles specifically adapted to a terrain of ice and snow riven by crevasses had not been fully developed, although Byrd expected to try a Model "A" Ford equipped with caterpillar treads, and possibly tractors and propeller-driven sledges.

Byrd placed special emphasis on choosing the right people to accompany him. In the early, naive stage of planning, he had invited eight Greenland Eskimos, including two squaws, whom he had met on the MacMillan-Byrd expedition. He even entertained the notion that they might start a colony in Antarctica. He went so far as to ask permission of Greenland's government for the Eskimos to leave; but, for unreported reasons, nothing came of the idea. Byrd anticipated taking fifty men, from roustabouts and cooks to pilots and scientists (women, at least non-Eskimo women, were unthinkable as explorers then). He tried to pick his key people early so they could join him in forming the expedition, and he was lucky to have a strong core of a dozen or so men who had served with him before and wanted to go with him again. Other candidates were recommended by his advisors. As word of the expedition spread, applications from adventure seekers arrived in Byrd's daily mail by the dozens and then hundreds from homes and offices, mansions and hovels all over the world. The unsolicited applications were screened for minimum requirements. Applicants had to have needed skills. Related experience, such as naval service or cold-weather work, helped. All his team members had to pass a physical exam by Byrd's medical consultants, and most had to be athletic enough to go up in airplanes if necessary.[13] Most also had to be willing to work without pay; Byrd eliminated a major cash drain by doing away with salaries whenever possible.

Byrd himself interviewed the most promising candidates. He believed that hardship such as they all would face brought out both the best and the worst in people, so he tried hard to fathom these extremes in his interviewees. He looked for those who could keep their heads while in protracted danger, get along well with others under trying circumstances, and be neither excessively annoyed by others nor annoying to them under conditions of close confinement and lack of privacy. The men had to display a sense of loyalty and a willingness to be a team player. Byrd believed that a single man could spread dissatisfaction to infect an entire expedition. "Of the thousand or more men who lost their lives in the attempt to conquer the arctic, many of the deaths were caused by disloyalty or mutiny," Byrd wrote. Accordingly, Byrd, a member of the Masonic fraternal order, greatly favored fellow Masons presumably because of the loyalty they show their brethren. A British antarctic explorer cautioned the commander to handcuff the first man who showed any disloyalty and keep him so until returning to civilization. Byrd added a pair of handcuffs to his supplies. In the event they had to spend the winter in Antarctica, the men had to be able to withstand the mental strain of being cooped up in small huts with little to do during several months of perpetual darkness and bitter cold, when cabin fever was a threat. At least one explorer had gone stir crazy there. Byrd prudently accepted a donation of straitjackets.[14]

He found the personnel decisions tough to make.[15] Since exceedingly few applicants had past experience on polar expeditions, he admitted he was at a loss for firm criteria to judge their suitability. In the end, he relied on gut feelings.

Influential persons, particularly those Byrd relied on for support, put him in a quandary when they lobbied to place unqualified candidates on his roster. He complained that this pressure was one of his biggest headaches, and he continually had to exert his diplomatic skills to maintain high manpower standards.[16]

Byrd had trouble mobilizing people in only one field—science. He often proclaimed that science was the main purpose for the venture, and the *New York Times* reported that he would have "the finest staff of scientifically trained men mustered for polar study . . . since Scott perished." One problem, of course, was the small number of professionally qualified men who were willing and able to endure the hardships. Probably, too, not many young scientists wanted to risk two years of their careers for uncertain rewards. In the ice desert where Byrd planned to base there was little life for biologists to study, and known land of interest to geologists was far away. Other scientists, especially meteorologists and geophysicists who needed winter records—on the aurora, for example—may have been deterred by Byrd's desire to spend just a few months and not stay the winter. He pressed on with his search, questioning his contacts and sifting through his mail to find the right specialists.[17]

Among Byrd's many problems, one towered far above the others:

the need to raise money and donations. He first estimated that he would require, besides contributed goods and services, half a million dollars in cash—a fortune at that time. A four-bedroom house in New York City's fashionable close-in suburbs cost less than $20,000; a subway ride, a nickel. In large part because of modern equipment and new technology, Byrd's expedition would be one of the most expensive ever.

He could count on little help from Washington, D.C. Government was relatively small then (the national budget for 1927 was only about $4 billion) and left as much activity as possible to private enterprise, including projects like Byrd's. Taxes took only a pittance from the rich, who owned much of the country's wealth. Although Byrd hated to plead for money, he had to beg most of his funds from the plutocrats and the giant business firms they controlled.

Without the incentive of charitable tax deductions, the wealthy had no direct reason to give away money. Sometimes Byrd could argue broad business reasons, such as promoting aviation so that Ford could boost sales of the planes it made then. In other cases the commander looked for personal motives. He appealed to a sense of philanthropic duty. He appealed to vanity by promising to name newly discovered places after patrons or by dedicating parts of the expedition, such as buildings at his base, to supporters. After he secured his initial pledges, mainly from those who had bankrolled his north polar project, he spread the word about the support he was getting from business leaders to nudge others onto the bandwagon.[18]

Byrd had a stronger inducement to offer when necessary: advertising endorsements in return for donations of products. In newspapers and magazines and over the air, the companies that made Maxwell House coffee, Oakite cleanser, Beechnut peanut butter, and a host of other products boasted about the projected use of their brands on the expedition. The sponsors held him closely to his bargain. When his steward noted in a wire-service interview that the expedition was taking "one ton of lard," without naming the brand, Byrd caught hell from the Crisco people.[19]

Byrd took nothing for himself from donations, but, assuming donations would cover all of the expedition's expenses, he planned to keep every cent he could make by exploiting his expedition's adventurous aspects, hawking his story for lucrative sums to the media. A feature syndicate affiliated with the *New York Times* picked up both domestic and foreign newspaper syndication rights to stories and photographs for $60,000. The paper assigned reporter Russell Owen, who had covered the north polar flight race, to write stories almost daily about Byrd's preparations and to accompany him to Antarctica. *National Geographic* bought the magazine story. Putnam signed a book contract that gave Byrd a hefty royalty of twenty percent. A lecture bureau offered him a minimum of $50,000. Paramount purchased exclusive permission to film Byrd's activities for newsreels and a documentary, assigning two cameramen to participate in the expedition. Byrd earned his living as a show business property. The contracts usually called for full payment only if he accomplished his most spectacular objectives. Ruminating about his lecture deals, Byrd said that "if there be no story to tell or no film to portray the story, a tour may well shrink to a half a dozen friendly engagements with little or no profit." Byrd regarded this split between expedition financing and personal income as his own business and did not reveal it to the public or the men he recruited. He could even be misleading about his finances, as when he explained to his men that he retained the exclusive right to sell pictures because ". . . the selling of the photographs of the expedition was one of the methods of financing it."[20]

Although most antarctic explorers were forced to commercialize their enterprises to some extent, none, Byrd included, liked to. He went much further than others, however, even though the commercialism created a circus atmosphere that tended to obscure his serious purposes. By diversifying his sources of support he avoided having to answer to a small controlling group or a single patron like Wanamaker who could overrule Byrd's decisions.[21] Besides, promotion was simply the American way in the Twenties. Americans considered public relations and advertising to be just as progressive as aviation and radio. The country had canonized businessmen as the saints of the era of Coolidge prosperity. Tellingly, the best-selling nonfiction book of 1926 had been *The Man Nobody Knows*, which depicted Christ as the foremost businessman and Peter as the top advertiser and salesman.

The reigning Babbitry demanded that explorers build and carefully maintain images based on middle-class ideals. Another famous explorer of the time, Roy Chapman Andrews, remarked that "unless you have the personality and ability to sell yourself as well as your plan, you are just out of luck."[22] Byrd tenaciously guarded his reputation as a heroic and responsible public figure. "Success depends on more than hard work—fame will help you to success," he advised a colleague. Occasionally calling on professional public relations counsel, Byrd became adept at exploiting the era's tabloid journalism while avoiding the pitfalls that any kind of scandal or even unfavorable gossip could open.[23] No celebrity was safe from the dangers. To an associate who doubted that Lindbergh could be knocked off his pedestal, Byrd commented, "Hell, he can be knocked off. Lindbergh isn't the angel everyone thinks he is. He's been out with women and smoked and drank when he felt like it. . . . But he isn't to blame. The press put him in that position."[24] Byrd was well aware he was in the same position in regard to public support, and his job drew heavily on his political skills and instincts. Like his politician brother Harry, the commander was well-connected and used contacts, pulled strings, and maneuvered pragmatically behind the scenes while cultivating his statesmanlike public front.

People sometimes misunderstood Byrd because they did not know he had two faces—his real one and his hero mask—or did not know which one he was wearing; the difference sometimes seemed fuzzy to Byrd himself. To keep him in focus, one had to remember that he was in the business of generating and selling adventurous stories and a heroic image—Byrd called it the "hero business"—and that in America during the Twenties there was no place for major exploration except as part of such a business.[25]

American business methods were among Byrd's distinctive contributions to polar exploration. While stationed in Rhode Island, he had commuted up the coast to courses at Harvard Business School. He had once labored nights at the office of a friend's small company, in which he had invested, to save it from failure. Over the years he had seriously considered offers to join several companies.[26] He ran his expedition like a bottom-line organization, not only making it efficient but winning the confidence of executives whom he approached for support. Byrd lived the life of an executive, although he said he did not like its tedium or the obligation to attend numerous benefits and join various business and civic clubs.

Byrd worked out of temporary offices in New York City, the business, shipping, and mass communications capital of the United States, in the early months of his planning. In the winter of 1927–28, the owner of the Biltmore Hotel lent Byrd and his key aides living accommodations and a third-floor suite of rooms for offices that became his permanent headquarters until embarkation.[27]

Byrd incorporated his expedition and, in businesslike fashion, established operating units devoted to segments such as aviation, sledging, and science. He stocked his Biltmore rooms with all the appropriate office paraphernalia, including "Byrd Antarctic Expedition" letterhead. He hired a business manager, thirty-six-year-old Richard G. Brophy, to administer day-to-day details while Byrd tackled fundraising and other major problems. Little is known about Brophy except that he had been a newspaperman, had established chambers of commerce in various towns, and had been a sales promotion manager just before joining Byrd. Brophy became the highest paid man on the expedition by far, at a salary of $1,000 a month.

As preparations got into gear, the expedition competed for the attention of Americans with the other big stories that were breaking about that same time: trials of political and business leaders on charges stemming from the Teapot Dome Scandal; the execution of anarchists and convicted murderers Sacco and Vanzetti; Jack Dempsey's defeat by Gene Tunney in the controversial "long count" heavyweight-championship fight; the *New York Daily News*'s grisly front-page photograph of Ruth Snyder frying in the electric chair; and the opening of the Holland tunnel, an engineering marvel, between Manhattan and New Jersey.

The undertaking burgeoned and grew more complex. Plans changed frequently. Byrd soon added another plane and tripled the number of sledge dogs to seventy-five, for example. The owner of the whaling ship that would carry the expedition had to change his plans also, and he notified Byrd that the ship could take him only as far as New Zealand. The American would have to get from there to his bivouac and back on his own, so he had to buy a ship of his own for the last leg of the journey. Byrd heeded the advice of Amundsen, who had authoritatively recommended a Norwegian sailing vessel he had served on in his youth. It was a wooden ship with exceptional strength for ice fields and appropriately named the *Samson*. Amundsen considered it the best polar ship in Europe. Byrd bought the vessel and ordered it to sail to New York. Because of the assault by a multitude of problems, Byrd claimed that this preliminary phase was the hardest part, and his co-workers began calling it the "Battle of New York City."[28]

Since aviation was so important, it commanded much of Byrd's attention; and the excitement it generated caught the fancy of the public, few of whom had ever seen an airplane. In mid-March of 1928, Bennett, Balchen, and a couple of mechanics flew to Canada in a new aircraft Byrd had bought, a Bellanca monoplane, for cold weather and snow tests. On the way the crew stopped at St. Alban's, Vermont, on Lake Champlain. Their arrival was a momentous event in town history. The fire alarm signaled the plane's approach, and the schools let out so the children could watch the landing. More than two thousand people witnessed the touchdown on the bay, and afterward the crew was feted at a public reception in the town hall. Byrd did not keep the Bellanca for long, as it turned out, selling it and replacing it with a donated Fairchild having extra-large windows and viewing ports for aerial photography.[29]

Other episodes pointed out the danger of flying in the prototypical aircraft of the day. Oscar Omdahl, a veteran of Amundsen's air expeditions who had joined Byrd, took leave to be the pilot for Mrs. Frances Grayson, a feminist who wanted to be the first woman to fly the Atlantic. They took off for Newfoundland, where the flight would officially begin, and were never seen again. A second Byrd pilot, Harry J. Brooks, was killed in a crash apparently unrelated to the expedition.[30] Every few days the newspapers reported that someone else had died in an airplane accident. The news was not comforting to those contemplating flying into the perils of Antarctica.

Coming to grips with logistic and political imperatives, Byrd overhauled his polar flight plans. He gave up the idea of a singularly difficult and chancy transantarctic attempt, substituting a round trip to the pole from his base. He also switched from a Fokker of demonstrated reliability to a recently developed all-metal Ford trimotor. Whatever the technical merits of the Ford, politics were undoubtedly involved. Edsel Ford had been one of Byrd's chief financial backers, while Byrd's relations with Tony Fokker had been frigid ever since *America*'s test-flight crash.[31] Although Ford donated the plane, he had not yet contributed cash for the antarctic effort, perhaps wanting to be sure that Byrd used a Ford plane for the polar flight.

Bennett and Balchen flew the Ford to Canada in March 1928 for snow trials. On returning, they told newsmen one of the white lies Byrd felt was necessary to protect himself from criticism by his benefactors or the general public. The crew announced that the Ford had performed faultlessly. Actually they had found that it was underpowered, and Byrd had to install a new, larger center engine.[32]

Byrd's enterprise continued to grow larger as his perception of antarctic realities sharpened. He added twenty more dogs, for instance, bringing the total to ninety-five. He came to appreciate that the chance of making his way to Antarctica, setting up a base, laying down emergency caches, flying to the pole, and doing some exploring and scientific studies all in one brief summer as he had hoped was impossibly small. He did not absolutely commit himself to what sailors termed "wintering over"; but instead of figuring on staying three months for sure and a year if he had to, he judiciously began preparing for one definite year and a contingent second year.[33]

For his advance headquarters, Byrd chose Dunedin in southern New Zealand, the jump-off point for many antarctic-bound groups. Acquiring last-minute provisions to be loaded there and coordinating staging operations in a place so distant further complicated management of the expedition. Moreover, he had to contend with diplomatic sensitivities. Great Britain claimed the section of Antarctica due south of New Zealand where Byrd planned to camp, and New Zealand administered that claim. The U.S. government did not recognize any antarctic claims, asserting that only the establishment of a settlement made them valid. However, as a private citizen, Byrd asked for and received British permission to base there and bring back penguins and other specimens.[34]

Byrd helped to launch a promotion in March to stoke public interest and support. The Boy Scouts of America began a nationwide competition, similar to what had been run for other expeditions, to choose one of its members to go with Byrd. Also serving to promote Byrd's interests that spring was publication of his first book, *Skyward*, an autobiography ghostwritten by explorer and author Commander Fitzhugh Green. It was worded in the Horatio Alger vein popular then. The saintly view of himself that Byrd acquiesced in projecting was exemplified by the caption for a photograph showing him visiting crippled French veterans after his transatlantic flight: "After Byrd's greeting, one man, a cripple since the war, rose and walked."[35] Shortly after publication, Green wrote a version for boys under his own name.

The executive editor of the *New York World* talked Byrd into another promotion. Two Germans and an Irishman had made the first successful east-to-west Atlantic flight, but their plane, the *Bremen*, had been forced down on an island off Labrador. They found comfortable quarters but had no easy way to get home. The editor wanted to support a "rescue" by Byrd, to benefit both the newspaper and Byrd's expedition. Byrd did not want to marry himself or his enterprise officially to the scheme, probably because of his contract with the *Times*, but he "allowed" Bennett and Balchen to take the Fort trimotor on their own to retrieve the downed crew. Bennett and Balchen were both ill with the flu but wanted to go, so they flew north along with the *World*'s star reporter Charles J. V. Murphy. Bennett, still not fully recovered from his test-flight crash a year before, continued to get sicker. He went to bed at their first stop in Canada, while Balchen and Murphy flew on and completed the mission. Bennett developed double lobar pneumonia and slipped downhill until his condition became critical. Lindbergh flew serum up to Canada. Bennett's wife, Cora, and Byrd went up to be with the sick man.[36]

On 26 April, Bennett died. Byrd was devastated. Bennett had been the commander's closest friend and right-hand man in mounting the expedition. Bennett's death, moreover, was occasioned by two of Byrd's projects, the rescue and *America*'s crash, and Byrd always felt a keen responsibility for the welfare of those who worked with him. For a while Byrd lost interest in everything. He soberly announced that he would name his south polar plane and newly discovered antarctic land after Bennett.[37]

Balchen thought there may have been another element in the impact of Bennett's death on Byrd. As Balchen later related, he tried to console Cora when he saw her at the Biltmore after Bennett's death: "I said . . . 'I'm going to miss Floyd terribly. . . . I know he will be a great loss to the commander.' She turned on me with eyes blazing. 'Bernt, how can you say anything like that?' she cried. 'This is the luckiest thing that ever happened to Byrd.' She didn't say any more. And I didn't know what to say. So I didn't say anything."[38] At the time, the quiet Norwegian did not tell anyone what was on his mind.

.3.

The Battle of
New York City

BYRD had to break out of mourning to cope with deepening fiscal difficulties. On 19 May 1928, with only about five more months until he would have to leave, the *New York Times* ran an editorial pointing up that he did not have enough money; in particular, he was short of funds to finance a top scientific staff. The paper called for an effort to arouse public support.[1]

Well-known businessmen and other public figures responded by forming a committee, similar to one that had helped Admiral Peary, to solicit donations and take care of some of the expedition's business. Known as the Byrd Aviation Associates, the committee held its first meeting on 30 May. Its letterhead bore many imposing names: Ford, Rockefeller, Astor, Vanderbilt, Guggenheim, Pulitzer, Charles Evans Hughes, Bernard Baruch. Astor served as chairman. At the same time, leading government and military aeronautics officials formed an advisory group. *The Nation* magazine, sounding the theme of patriotism and reminding readers of the story of Columbus and Isabella, suggested that even higher government officials, including the president, should become directly involved.[2]

Byrd and his supporters stepped up promotional activities. One of his foremost allies, Charles V. Bob, a friend to many celebrities, was reaping millions from the sale of mining stock and grandly promised $100,000 to erect a seventy-five-foot lighted cross on top of Broadway Temple to guide aviators. The cross would be christened the "Richard E. Byrd" beacon. In a ceremony at the Bankers Club, Mayor Walker gratefully accepted the gift for the city, and Byrd proudly accepted for aviation. Other promotions included the exhibit of a bronze bust of Byrd in Washington, D.C. Byrd also helped to inaugurate an exhibit of antarctic maps at the American Museum of Natural History that would be displayed throughout the expedition so the citizenry could follow his progress.[3]

The first of June 1928 brought stunning news. An old competitor announced that he would also go to Antarctica later that year to explore the continent by airplane. Hubert Wilkins, who had raced for north polar honors, explained that he would use two planes to examine the coast between the sections under South America and New Zealand, overlapping the area Byrd planned to investigate. The Wilkins party was small, with no scientific objectives. It could get to Antarctica quickly and beat Byrd to the precious honor of making the first flight in Antarctica. Furthermore, the Australian might decide at the last minute to try for the pole. Wilkins was funded by the powerful Hearst newspaper empire, which was not noted for charitably covering opponents in its publications. Byrd learned that Hearst had promised Wilkins $50,000 for beating the American to the pole. The odds did not favor Byrd. Arctic explorer Earl Hanson, the skeptical brother of the head of Byrd's radio operations, Malcolm Hanson, was sure Wilkins would best Byrd: "Commander Byrd's . . . expedition is too ponderous, too cluttered up with safety plans and specialized experts who are still absolute greenhorns under polar conditions."[4] If Wilkins got in jeopardy, moreover, Byrd might have to turn his operation into a rescue mission and abandon his own goals.

Byrd and Wilkins pledged openly to help one another, as befitted colleagues and public figures. Byrd invited Wilkins to land at the American camp and use the facilities and even offered to ferry Wilkins's planes back on the *Samson*.[5] Despite the show of conviviality, Byrd must have felt terribly dejected. For the fourth time on as many occasions, a rival had appeared at a moment of rare opportunity. Wilkins's attempt to steal the scene threatened to rob Byrd of glory, stall his career, and drive him toward insolvency. Wilkins enormously increased the pressure on Byrd to succeed without delay.

Byrd's ship, the *Samson*, also caused him indigestion. The square-rigger did not arrive in the United States from Norway in early June as expected, and the ship had no radio to explain her tardiness. As days went by with no sign of her, the fear grew that she had been lost. Much to her owner's relief, she finally hove into view on 16 June. It turned out that she had been becalmed but could not switch on auxiliary steam power because her old boiler had buckled shortly after she set out.[6]

The windjammer had been overhauled in Norway but still needed a lot of work—although Byrd told the press he found her better than expected—so he put her into drydock at the Todd shipyard in south Brooklyn. He ordered the bark-rigged ship converted to a barkentine to increase her speed. He hoped to find the money to convert her coal-burning boiler to oil, since her small bunkers could not hold all the coal she would need on his voyage. Byrd resigned himself to a five-week wait for work in the dry dock to be completed.[7]

The vessel's need for so much work was disappointing enough, but Byrd had to face another sad fact about the ship: she was simply inadequate to meet all his requirements because the expedition had enlarged since he had bought her. His roster had lengthened from fifty to nearly eighty men, for example. It was now clear that the *Samson* was too small to carry all the passengers and cargo from New Zealand to Antarctica. The large Ford plane for the polar flight, moreover, would not fit into her hold even when disassembled.[8] With only a few months to go, likely feeling that things were getting out of hand, Byrd set about locating a second ship.

Byrd had not revealed that the Fokker was no longer his lead plane. A pilot named Wilmer Stultz had flown it to Boston, where he outfitted it with pontoons and began test flights. The big plane drew crowds of spectators who thought they were watching trials for the Byrd expedition. But in fact Byrd had sold the plane to Mrs. Frederick Guest, a socialite who yearned to be the first of her sex to cross the Atlantic in the air. Her family was trying to talk her out of the dangerous attempt, so Byrd had agreed to keep the sale confidential until the flight. Mrs. Guest finally gave in to her family's wishes and decided not to make the flight herself. Promoter Hilton Railey helped her to search for another woman with the right image to sponsor. They found an unknown aviatrix who looked enough like Lucky Lindy to be his sister. Her name was Amelia Earhart. Byrd gave her pointers on oceanic flying. On 17 June 1928, with two other pilots, Stultz and Slim Gordon, Earhart took off for Europe. The crew landed safely in Wales the following day, and the world had its first transatlantic heroine. When Earhart got to a phone, her first call was to Byrd to thank him for his help.[9]

During Mrs. Guest's project, Byrd had conferred with Railey about the difficulty of raising money. The thirty-three-year-old Railey, a fellow southerner originally from New Orleans who had founded his own fund-raising company in Boston, volunteered to help out. Undoubtedly reasoning that Byrd had gotten about as much as he could from the country's multimillionaires, Railey counseled the commander to shelve the Byrd Aviation Associates and broaden his support from organizations and people who were merely well off. Edsel Ford was treasurer of the Associates and, as Railey asked pointedly, "Who wants to make a check out to Edsel Ford?" As a matter of policy, Byrd declined to solicit the general public.[10] His rationale is not known, but perhaps he did not want to ask ordinary people to make sacrifices for a project that would enrich him personally.

Since Dick Brophy, whom Byrd had made second in command after Bennett's death, could not keep up with the staggering office workload, Byrd invited Railey to be full-time assistant business manager. Railey agreed, working at first as a volunteer, then as a fund-raiser whose salary came from the donations he raised himself, and finally as a regular salaried employee.[11]

As if to underscore the polar dangers that Byrd would soon confront, an aviation tragedy occurred in the arctic. Umberto Nobile had taken another dirigible expedition north and had disappeared. Amundsen flew into the icy wastes to search for his former partner. On 20 June, Amundsen himself was reported missing. Nobile and some other survivors were found, but it soon became evident that Amundsen would never return. Byrd lost not only a revered colleague and advisor but his model explorer. The commander had written to the Norwegian, "I am following [your book] exclusively in my preparations for our expedition. . . . I am using you . . . as my ideal explorer and I am modeling after you."[12] Byrd was keenly aware that he could easily share Amundsen's fate.

Time was shrinking until Byrd's troops would have to leave to hit the narrow window between the long antarctic winters. He hoped that the slow *Samson*, which would sail mostly by the wind, could leave by the end of July. Most of the remaining members and material would sail a few weeks later on the second ship he was seeking. About the same time, the dog unit would leave from Norfolk, Virginia, after a brief stay, on a speedy Norwegian whaler, to get the cold-adapted dogs quickly through the tropics. Another whaler would take on the pilots, planes, and some supplies in Norfolk in September and sail through the Panama Canal and up to a port of call in California, where she would pick up Byrd and some others.

New York City was already broiling in mid-year heat. Babe Ruth's thundering home runs were drawing crowds into Yankee stadium. In the summer national conventions, the Democrats nominated Al Smith for president, and the Republicans put up Herbert Hoover.

The pace of business in Byrd's offices got frantic as the expedition kept growing, even as his staff began to speak of weeks rather than months until departure. Seven days a week, often far into the night, secretaries clacked away at their manual typewriters, phones jangled continually, and Boy Scouts volunteering as messengers and clerks scurried in and out. People barged in and demanded, occasionally successfully, to be included in the expedition. Byrd was still hunting additional personnel. He and his staff were buying and wheedling supplies and shipping them to warehouses in Hoboken (part of the New York port complex); Norfolk; Long Beach, California; and Dunedin.[13]

Everybody connected with the expedition was busy. The pilots were test-flying the planes. The radiomen were designing and building sets for the planes and exploring parties and planning radio experiments. The aerial photographer was checking out his gear. The scientists were doing preliminary research and gathering instruments. The doctor was supervising physical examinations for the personnel and rounding up medical supplies, and he and the cook were getting enough food to feed Byrd's company for as long as two years.[14] The chief engineer was getting machinery, fuel, and oil. The men in charge of the dogs were getting sledging and trail equipment and dog food.

Tailors were making clothing for subzero wear. Shoemakers were making special shoes and boots. Carpenters were prefabricating buildings. Others were getting all the other tools and supplies that might be needed for a long stay in isolation. Byrd, as always, was furiously searching for money to pay the bills that were pouring in.

Toward the end of July he found his other ship, a small freighter, formerly a British minesweeper, that he bought for $34,000 from the government's "rum runners' row" of ships confiscated for smuggling liquor. Named the *Chelsea*, it would be the first metal-hulled ship on an antarctic exploring expedition (though modern whalers had actually been the first steel ships in the antarctic). The *Chelsea* joined the *Samson* at the Todd shipyard for $76,000 worth of repairs and strengthening against ice. As the time-worn *Samson* was still far from ready, Byrd was forced to reschedule her sailing date to 22 August 1928, a month later than planned.[15]

Byrd could never catch up. Even the *Chelsea* left him short of cargo space for the swelling expedition. The additions included a fourth airplane, a small model made by General Aircraft, so another pilot and mechanic were necessary. Because he could not get enough money to convert the *Samson*'s boiler to oil, he would have to find space for coal where there was no extra space. In the meantime, he had become convinced that he would have to winter over, so he could not skimp at all on the amount of supplies.[16] Reluctantly, he concluded that one ship would have to try to squeeze in two 4,600-mile round trips between Dunedin and Antarctica.

The estimated cost of the expanded expedition rose to $750,000. Possibly in an effort to dramatize his monetary shortage and increase the credibility of his appeals for more contributions, Byrd disclosed an itemized budget. Furthermore, he let it be known that the accounting firm of Ernst & Ernst was donating a formal audit to assure that all cash had been responsibly disbursed.[17]

The immense scale and expense of the expedition evoked pro and con editorial comment all over the country. The Houston *Post* carped, "What a splendid educational loan foundation [Byrd's budget] would make to help deserving and ambitious girls and boys to get an education. Spent on antarctic exploration, it will return nothing of value to the world." Most newspapers praised the expedition. The Boston *Globe* declared, "No adventure in exploration in all history compares with this tremendous enterprise." Another paper concluded that just the vicarious adventure and entertainment the expedition provided made it worthwhile. The *New York Times* said Byrd's expedition promised greater geophysical and scientific results than any other, and that in fact he was modest in his financial requirements. The *Times* made two more editorial pleas for donations.[18]

Byrd kept up his promotional efforts. Gene Tunney gave $1,000 and told Byrd publicly that if the American people knew his financial difficulties "they would overwhelm you with financial support that is now lacking." Amelia Earhart risked criticism—and got it, from the *New Yorker* magazine—by endorsing a brand of cigarettes to earn $1,500 that she turned over to Byrd. Lindbergh and Lincoln Ellsworth each gave $1,000. New York's Advertising Club donated $1,000 so Byrd could "advertise 'flying America' to the world." (A collection among New York schoolchildren reportedly raised $90,000, but the figure seems high, and Byrd carried no such contribution on his books). Gimbels in New York filled two windows with expedition gear, and a ukelele-playing member of the expedition performed in the store's music department at the beginning of the display. As the promotional beat went on, Byrd's role as a celebrity grew. A new dance, "The Byrd Hop," demonstrated at the convention of the American Society of Teachers of Dancing, depicted the takeoff, flight, and landing of a plane in modified hesitation-waltz time. Byrd became ever more in demand as a dinner-party guest at the homes of the wealthy.[19]

As summer peaked and the *Samson*'s sailing date drew near, people began to say their good-byes, although the expedition's slipping schedule had made some elaborate send-offs premature. On 8 August, the Advertising Club threw a farewell luncheon for Byrd. In his address to the club, carried over the radio, Byrd announced that he would honor all the New Yorkers who had helped him and other flyers so much by renaming the *Samson* the *City of New York*. That same night NBC broadcast an hour-long special so long to Byrd over twenty-one stations. Mayor Walker, the emcee, read telegrams from notables all around the world (including one from another Virginian, signed "Nancy, Lady Astor," that proclaimed, "If men must fly, women must pray"). A New York City radio station featured several expedition members on a program broadcast two days later. The Norsemen Masonic Lodge in Brooklyn threw a going-away dinner for brother

Balchen. There were five hundred guests, including Tony Fokker and many expedition members. Byrd sent a telegram regretting that he could not attend and praising Balchen.[20]

The newly christened *New York* finally slid out of drydock on 12 August. After a few days of sea trials, she tied up at the Hoboken docks for loading. Byrd reset her departure for 25 August 1928.

On Saturday afternoon, 18 August, most of the expedition's members mustered together on the *New York* for the first time to pick up their gear and hear a talk from Byrd. The majority were young and single. The eldest, at sixty-eight, was Martin Ronne, a tailor who had been in Amundsen's band and was the only one to have been to Antarctica. Several others also came from Norway, and as the men chatted their accents bespoke origins in other countries and in every region of the United States. The members ranged from sailors who lived in seamen's homes to sons of millionaires, from soldiers of fortune to serious scientists. Many had military, particularly navy, backgrounds, and several were on leave from active duty. Most were strictly volunteers, but a third received some kind of salary, often just enough to support their families. As Byrd described them, however, all were of the volunteer type, and pay must have been one of their last considerations. Most hungered for adventure and a measure of fame. The scientists desired knowledge and professional advancement. Some—Byrd included himself—sought romance and what he called "the big kick" of seeing what no man had ever seen before.[21] Based on the records of polar exploration and aviation, the chance was high that at least one of them would never come back. The *New York Times* had prewritten obituaries on all of them.

Just two professional scientists, a geologist—the only Ph.D.—and a geophysicist, had signed on. But the two weather forecasters who would aid in flight planning would also collect meteorological data, the radio engineer would measure phenomena affecting radio transmission, and a naval officer would take soundings in antarctic waters. Additionally, Byrd classified cartography as a science and included the aerial photographer, surveyor, and topographer on his scientific staff. At the beginning of his planning, Byrd had envisioned a much larger scientific unit. He stated repeatedly that science was the most significant part of his undertaking. But aviation and survival—physical, financial, and professional—had higher priority. The expedition had mushroomed way beyond his expectations, so he had to accommodate just the top priorities. For this reason, and because of the problems he had in engaging and funding scientists, the scientific program was the only part of his venture to diminish instead of expand. Byrd's scientific staff was not the finest ever, as he had hoped, but it was about average in size and stature for an antarctic party. As the *New York Times* pointed out, moreover, this very first flying expedition could not be expected to do everything. There would be others to capitalize on the experiences of the first.[22]

Several men who had been expected to be on the rolls were not. George Noville, *America*'s radioman who had been listed in first reports as third in command, had dropped out without explanation, probably because of injuries sustained in a plane crash. One of Amundsen's top people, Oscar Wisting, had agreed to go but had subsequently pulled out to search for his friend's remains. Byrd noted that he had to give up one very good but unnamed man for demanding the exorbitant salary of $1,200 a month and a share in the media returns.[23]

All recruits had to sign contracts preventing any media competition with Byrd, thereby protecting his financial interests. The men agreed to turn over to him all of their photographs of the expedition; he would pick those he wanted and return the rest, which could not be published. No one could give news or interviews to the press until six weeks after returning from Antarctica, or publish anything for two years afterward.[24]

Byrd invited the public on board the *New York* on Sunday, 19 August, and two thousand people showed up. Souvenir hunters glommed most of the supply of paper cups emblazoned with an airplane and the legend "Byrd Antarctic Expedition." The cup factory had to go all out to replace them on time.[25]

On Monday, 20 August, Byrd announced that the winning Boy Scout who would accompany the expedition to Antarctica was Paul Siple of Erie, Pennsylvania. Young Siple had fewer than five days to get ready and travel to port in time to sail on board the *New York*.

There was no dentist on the expedition, so all members visited a New York City dentist who donated his services to fill or pull bad teeth.[26]

On Saturday, 25 August, Byrd and the thirty-three members in the first sailing contingent woke up to a gloomy day. (Until the night before there had been thirty-four members—one man's bride of four months had had him kidnapped.)[27] It was cloudy, humid, and breezy, threatening rain, with temperatures forecasted to rise into the high 70s.

During the last-minute loading, spectators joked about the barrels of alcohol put on board. Byrd piously explained that they were for "medicinal purposes only."[28]

A hungry stowaway was found behind a spare propeller in the hold, where he said he had been hiding for a couple of days. A black man, he told Byrd he was Robert Lanier, and that he had applied for the expedition but been turned down. He said he wanted to be the first "colored" man at the South Pole. Byrd liked Lanier and—minus one crewman anyway and perhaps envisioning having his own black aide, like Peary's partner Matthew Henson—officially signed the stowaway on; the ship's captain made Lanier permanent dishwasher. Consistent with the racial attitudes of the time, Siple fed the famished Lanier watermelon and recorded that "he was in his glory. . . . he sure proved his nationality." The crew members nicknamed him Sunshine. Even the *New York Times* (which did not reveal he had been made an official member) described him as a Negro "boy" in his twenties who had once been arrested for abusive language, and quoted him as saying, "I sho would like to make de rest of dis trip."[29]

Shortly after noon, the *New York*'s cargo of two hundred tons was stowed, and she was ready to sail. A crowd of relatives, friends, and well-wishers gathered with the men at the dock to hear Byrd say a few words. It began to drizzle. All hands were summoned aft. The drunken first mate and ship's carpenter tried to act sober. Standing near the wheel a little above the group, Byrd reminded the men that they were going to Antarctica for science and the honor of their countries. He told them his wife would keep in touch with their families and that their dependents would want for nothing. He said a good friend of his (an anonymous reference to Charles Bob) had promised to take care of dependents who might be hospitalized.[30]

Byrd stepped down. The men applauded and raised three cheers for him. Byrd, his wife and eight-year-old son, and several distinguished guests stayed on board for the passage through New York Harbor as the *New York* at last pulled away from the waving arms. Owen reported the touching sight of a little girl waving her doll at her daddy. Two planes flew overhead in salute, one doing acrobatics. The other held a passenger rumored to be Amelia Earhart.[31] All the boats the *New York* passed sounded their whistles. When she finally cleared the harbor, Byrd and his guests climbed off onto the *Macom*, the mayor's reception tugboat. The *Macom*'s sirens screamed as the gap between the vessels widened, and a band on board played "Auld Lang Syne" and "Till We Meet Again."

Another stowaway had been found and put off on the *Macom*. One more was discovered a little later and let ashore down the coast.

During the next few weeks, the remaining expeditioneers wrapped up their preparations. In mid-September, the dogs and a small group of drivers with their equipment left from Norfolk on a whaler, the *Sir James Clark Ross*, to get across the equator and to New Zealand as fast as they could.[32]

Before dawn on Sunday, 16 September 1928, the twenty-nine men of Byrd's third sailing contingent gathered groggily at a New York dock to finish loading their ship, the former *Chelsea*. Byrd had renamed her the *Eleanor Bolling* in honor of his mother. A bewhiskered old man holding a Bible shuffled on board and predicted doom for the expedition. The *Bolling* left shortly after sunrise but had gone only about a mile when a compressor broke down and she had to return. Repairs took all morning, and it was afternoon before she departed. She headed for Norfolk to rendezvous with the *C. A. Larsen*, a huge whaling mother ship, and pick up stores. Two stowaways turned up before she was out of the harbor, one of whom was a familiar young lady who, an officer commented discreetly, "was long interested in all of us and a great favorite of the boys during our preparations." She gave each one a kiss before a tug took her and the male stowaway back to the dock.[33]

On the following night, Commander Byrd waited to greet the *Bolling* at Norfolk with his brother, the governor; but she did not appear as scheduled. As day broke and the sun climbed with no sign of her and no radio messages, Byrd grew increasingly worried. A ham radio operator heard a broken-off message that she was in some kind of trouble. Then one of the most destructive storms in memory struck; it had already slaughtered two thousand people in Florida on the way north. Byrd desperately ordered a plane to fly south from New York to search for his ship, but the impossible weather turned the plane back. On Wednesday, when the winds finally died down, Byrd was relieved to hear that the *Bolling* had been sighted in the Hampton Roads Harbor. She limped into port at noon on Thursday.

As the harried crew related the story, the storm was just one of many woes. Although rated at fourteen knots, the *Bolling* seldom could turn more than five; most of her crew had never sailed before, and their slow responses retarded the ship's movements; many of the men were hung over on the first day, and the ship rolled so much they got seasick; two of the three inexperienced firemen were sickened by the heat in the engine room; the radio generator failed; and the creaky vessel revealed herself in many ways to be broken down and ill-suited to a voyage.[34]

Because the *Larsen* had to leave the next day and the *Bolling*'s crew had to load their ship with expedition cargo, the tired men could not stop to rest. They labored all through the night before they finally staggered to their bunks. On Friday, the *Larsen* set out for California with three pilots, the four planes, and one hundred tons of expedition fuel and other supplies as deck load.

Steamfitters went to work on the *Bolling*'s structural and mechanical shortcomings; painters redid the messroom and captain's quarters, which had flooded. Her barely rested crew restowed the cargo.[35]

Two disgusted firemen quit and had to be replaced.[36] Bill Gavronski, an eighteen-year-old who had stowed away on both the *New York* and the *Bolling* when the ships left New York City, and who had journeyed to Norfolk to sneak on board the *Bolling* there, seized the opportunity to volunteer as a legal member. Giving him credit for his spirit, Byrd took the boy on—the second stowaway to be legitimized.

On Wednesday, 26 September, the patched-up *Bolling* sailed gamely for New Zealand with three hundred tons of cargo. Byrd had more hope than confidence that she would arrive without incident.

Byrd had already gone back to New York City. He had intended to stay just long enough to tidy up last-minute business, then spend several days relaxing with his family before taking the train to Los Angeles to meet the *Larsen*. He had resolved to complete fund-raising before he left. He thought he had at long last brought his finances under control, but he was told for the first time that the cost of reconditioning the ships had escalated to an incredible seven times the estimate, throwing the expedition $300,000 in debt.[37] He also uncovered more unfinished business. Bitterly, he canceled his leave and dug in for one last fierce engagement in the Battle of New York City. His wife, Marie, came down from their home in Boston to be with him.

There seemed no end to his troubles. He was distressed to learn that the *New York* was being assaulted by a hurricane before he lost contact with her. He fretted for two days until the battered ship was able to radio that she had survived the storm.[38]

Toiling with little sleep for a week, Byrd managed to reduce the deficit to $100,000 by Friday. That shortfall was still five times as much as the debt that had greatly worried him on the way to the North Pole, but he called it quits for the time being, banking on the hope that his successes would attract more contributions. By then he had received cash from 1,600 persons and equipment from five hundred organizations, for a total value with seven figures, making the enterprise history's first million-dollar antarctic expedition. He closed down his now-silent Biltmore offices and moved what remained of his headquarters to the Putnam Building, his publisher's location, where Railey alone would handle stateside business during field operations. Exhausted, the commander returned to Boston for a weekend of seclusion.[39]

On Monday, 1 October, Byrd came back down to New York City and boarded the 20th Century Limited for a working trip to California. Making the journey with him were Marie; his fox terrier, Igloo, Byrd's inseparable companion who would "wear his little union suit and fur cap" in Antarctica, according to the *New York Times*, for which cute dog stories were a staple in the Twenties; Dick Brophy; Ralph Shropshire, who tended to business and scientific affairs; Charles Lofgren, Byrd's yeoman; *Times* reporter Russell Owen; and large, dapper Paramount cameraman Willard Van der Veer. Byrd made use of the trip to promote the expedition. He gave interviews to reporters and posed for photographers at every stop as the train clacked across America. When the group arrived in San Bernardino, California, three navy planes circled in salute.[40] On Friday the train pulled into Los Angeles.

Byrd, who seemed doomed never to have smooth going, came down with the flu. He was greeted by his transatlantic partner George Noville, who leaned on a cane because of an injury suffered in an air accident, a sight that surely did little to make Byrd feel better. Byrd, who presumably got together with the agent he had on the West Coast, Robert Breyer, stayed in Los Angeles for five days. The *Larsen* was already docked, and more supplies were loaded. The deck load stood fifteen or twenty feet high and was twice as long.[41]

On Wednesday, 10 October, Byrd released two farewell messages, one to his fellow Virginians and the other to all Americans. In both he conceded that Wilkins might make the first flight in Antarctica.

The reason, Byrd claimed, was that he was pursuing science and not racing, pointing out that he would penetrate a thousand miles farther into the antarctic than the Australian. In fact, the commander had given up hope of beating the nimble Wilkins expedition for the prize of the first flight over Antarctica. But the pole remained the most sought after trophy. It was not in Wilkins's announced plans, however, and—Byrd fervently hoped—not within reach of Wilkins's planes. Ever the southern gentleman, Byrd pledged to Virginians, "We shall try to be worthy of the standards Virginia manhood has set." Byrd also wired Secretary of the Navy Wilbur, respectfully logging his embarkation and briefly reviewing his objectives. He told the public he was grateful to the navy for giving as much help as regulations permitted and to the army for cooperating enthusiastically.[42]

Byrd left instructions for running the expedition if he should die or be unavailable for a major decision. Marie would be officially in charge, counseled by Governor Byrd, Syracuse newspaper publisher Joe Barnum, and lawyer Raymond B. Fosdick. Fosdick, manager of Rockefeller's philanthropic endeavors, was one of Byrd's closest advisors. The brother of eminent clergyman Harry Emerson Fosdick and formerly U.S. representative to the League of Nations, Raymond Fosdick had been chairman of the Commission on Training Camps during the World War when Byrd had been the commission's secretary. Byrd wrote that he especially valued Fosdick's powerful influence in Washington, D.C.[43]

Byrd could look back on an extraordinary year and a half. Starting with no experience in antarctic exploration, and despite monumental obstacles, severe setbacks, and a serious initial miscalculation of the magnitude of his undertaking, he had put together a magnificent expedition. It was the biggest and most expensive ever to invade Antarctica. It was the best equipped, best planned, and best organized. It boasted a superb core of men who would pioneer new technologies and new methods in almost every aspect of expedition operations. In an editorial, the *New York Times* bragged, "In design and scope, the expedition . . . will be the most ambitious that has ever gone south under the flag of any nation."[44] Byrd expected to advance geography and science and dreamed of making unbelievable discoveries. His spectacular flights, capped by a successful run to the South Pole, would promote aviation. His unique use of radio for operations, and a continuous stream of news about his activities and achievements telegraphed instantly around the world, would help to demonstrate the miraculous possibilities of wireless communication. His accomplishments would glorify the United States and the American way of life.

A typed, diarylike page in Byrd's files, apparently intended for eventual inclusion in his book about the expedition but in fact never published, gives his weary thoughts at the welcome end of the long preliminaries:

> . . . At last a let up! What untenable relief! What peace and relaxation! Again and again, I've struggled my last struggle and then struggled on again. Strangely, there are a few wriggles left. No doubt of it though, I'm tired—absurdly tired. Ergs and ergs of energy have gone into getting four ships and 82 men on the high seas southward—for science—glory for Uncle Sam, we hope—and, with it, high adventure.
>
> It's been a right rough fight. Drama crowded with crises subtly changing. Attack, defense, scrimmage made with all our will, spurred to it by the knowledge that the battle ahead in the unknown will win or lose their chance for victory by the battle of preparations—the lives of stout fellows in the balance.[45]

When a reporter dutifully asked Byrd his greatest emotion on departure, he answered, probably sincerely, that it was concern for his men. Antarctica had frozen and starved explorers to death, swallowed them in crevasses, and dashed them from mountain heights. Antarctica had injured men, sickened them, and driven them mad. The men whom Byrd had recruited depended on him for their safety, and Byrd was clearly determined to get them and himself back unharmed.

Back east, the Washington Cathedral initiated a prayer in its daily services for the explorers and their kin.[46]

Although each person hoped to profit in some way by participating in the enterprise, Byrd had the most to gain. A successful expedition would make his career. At the same time, he had the most to lose. Failure would break him financially and perhaps destroy his future. There were so many ways to fail: his ships could founder; the wrath of nature in Antarctica could cut him down; his new technologies could fizzle; his finely tuned, complex planning and organization could fall apart. In the adversity that was inevitable, his men—mostly strangers to him and to each other—might not pull together and could even turn against him. This last prospect frightened him the most.

Because necessity had made Byrd into a media personality and his expedition into a media event, his accomplishments had to be of more than academic interest. He knew they must create headlines. He continually had to generate a lot of favorable coverage and scrupulously had to avoid a bad press. He also had to beat Wilkins to the pole. Byrd's worries, like the other aspects of his undertaking, were grander than those of any other expedition leader.

Byrd's gala send-off on Wednesday afternoon, 10 October, was described as the greatest demonstration for a departing ship that Los Angeles had ever seen. Thousands of motorists caused a traffic jam as they converged on the Western Refining Dock in Long Beach, where the *Larsen* was berthed. The American Legion sent a farewell delegation. The mayor of Los Angeles and other dignitaries turned out for the ceremonies.[47]

Byrd's group, including a pilot and a mechanic who had joined the expedition in Los Angeles, boarded the *Larsen*. As she was casting off, Byrd impetuously jumped back on shore to hug Marie. He had married the well-to-do Marie D. Ames thirteen years before. A tall, brown-haired, brown-eyed woman, she was a Boston native whose parents kept a second house in Byrd's hometown in Virginia. Dick and Marie had four small children, their son and three preschool girls, and had established permanent residence in Boston. He once confessed that leaving his family for so long made him feel "more like a selfish sinner than an explorer going forth to conquer."[48] When he had held his wife for as long as he could, he stepped into a launch to be carried out to the ship.

The navy gave an official salute to the departing *Larsen*. A coast guard cutter bearing the dignitaries led a parade of escort ships accompanying the ship to sea. A score of private yachts and speedboats followed. The anchored vessels of the Pacific fleet dipped their flags. Ships and boats all over the harbor blew their whistles. The flotilla bobbed its way two miles out to sea, and then all vessels turned back but the mammoth *Larsen*.[49] The months of anticipation and days of celebration were over. Ahead lay a long passage to the avidly sought unknowns of Antarctica. The Byrd Antarctic Expedition was on its way.

.4.

Voyage to the Ice

FOUR widely separated contingents of the Byrd expedition were making the lengthy voyage to New Zealand: the *Larsen*, with Byrd, fourteen others, and some cargo; the *Ross*, with the dogs and principal drivers; and the *New York* and the *Bolling*, with the bulk of men and supplies.

Stretching an eighth of a mile, and weighing nearly 15,000 deadweight tons, the *Larsen* was the largest ship under the Norwegian flag. But she was not built for the pleasure of passengers: her discomforted guests had to anoint themselves with lotion every day to ward off the lice that infested the ship, she stank of the blood and gore of countless butchered whales, and the drinking water was hot and rusty. Among the expedition's members, only Balchen relished the simple, salty Norwegian food. Every austral summer, the *Larsen* hunted whales in the section of the continent-girdling Southern Ocean near Byrd's planned base. A factory ship, she was under contract to Proctor & Gamble, a U.S. company, to rend the flesh of whales slain by five killer ships—usually some eight hundred of the huge animals a year— into oil for the company's products.[1] Whales were thought of only as a virtually inexhaustible commercial resource.

Although treating the Americans politely, the *Larsen*'s polar-hard-

45

ened crew regarded the expedition as an amateur junket. Helping Byrd was something of a nuisance for Captain Nilsen, but he and Magnus Konow, the ship's owner, cooperated as much as possible, and Captain Nilsen gave as much advice as he could from his own experience in sailing antarctic waters. On 25 October 1928, he threw a party to celebrate a personal milestone for Byrd—his fortieth birthday. With Prohibition thousands of miles behind, the honoree and guests all got a little tipsy. Byrd liked alcohol, sometimes angering his wife and, he told her, disgusting himself by drinking excessively.[2]

The commander spent most of his time planning forthcoming operations. His men met with him occasionally to discuss options and occupied themselves making marker flags and sewing food bags for the trail teams. Ever mindful of his long line of creditors, Byrd queried the members about whether it would be fair for him to ask them to pay for their own meals when they got to New Zealand. They said no but agreed to pick up the tabs anyway.[3]

People thought of the romantic *New York*, fifty-six years old and one of the last working ships of sail, as *the* ship of the Byrd expedition, and she received most of the attentions of the press and public. The three-masted vessel, appropriately painted snow white, with an orange superstructure, measured 170 feet in length and 31 feet abeam. A fortress against the siege of the polar winter, she had a hull rounded and made of heavy, resilient wood to withstand the squeezing and pounding by enveloping sea ice that would sink a battleship. Byrd remarked that he knew of no other ship with sides as thick—almost three feet through. Just behind the tall center mast, rising almost a third of the mast's height, a smokestack disgorged black smoke when the *New York* burned coal for auxiliary power. The wheezing old steam engine generated a feeble two hundred horsepower, hardly more than an automobile.[4]

For those who would call the square-rigger home during the three-month passage to Dunedin, life was far from glamorous. They were always short of water. They slaved to exhaustion. Worst of all, they had to submit to the commands of a captain molded in the ways of William Bligh.

Frederick C. Melville, forty-three, was a ruddy New England sailing master who had spent most of his life at sea. Author Herman Melville was the cousin of Captain Melville's father. Gray-haired, bespectacled,

Captain Melville spoke slowly in a deep voice. Running his ship like a captain of old, adhering strictly to maritime tradition, he designated the doctor, physicist, and other professionals as officers and gave them privileged status, to the disgust of the rest and contrary to Byrd's intentions that there be no officer class on his expedition. Melville made those he designated common sailors keep watches of four hours on, four hours off—unnecessarily, they felt—so the men were never able to get more than four hours of sleep at a stretch. Siple called Melville a cruel man. The captain accused the crew of stealing supplies, most of which were later found untouched. After he flew into a rage over the unauthorized opening of a can of Klim, a brand of powdered milk, the men began referring to him sneeringly as "Captain Klim."[5]

The crew also detested the chief engineer, Tom Mulroy, thirty-one, a pretentious, unfriendly person who seemed to spend most of his energies avoiding work. The men blamed him for the always malfunctioning water-distillation apparatus and other mechanical and electrical systems that added to the crew's misery. In contrast, the physicist, Frank Davies, realizing that he would be confined with many of these men for over a year in antarctic huts, living and working together on equal terms, tried to overcome the crew's resentment of him as one of Melville's officers. Davies, twenty-four, a chubby little scientist who peered at his instruments through thick glasses, stopped eating his meals in the officers' mess and started eating with the men in the forecastle.[6] Mulroy, who would also depend on the goodwill of the others in time, acted as if he could not care less.

The *New York* docked at Panama on 16 September. Melville threw two ineffective crewmen off his ship. He also dismissed Lanier because he "lacked stamina," Melville explained. The black member resisted and begged to continue in any capacity. Melville unsympathetically handcuffed Lanier to a post and summoned police to haul him away. Another man, a constant complainer despised by the others for his selfishness, quit voluntarily; they found he had hoarded precious water in an array of cans hidden under his bunk. Melville rounded up two locals, one of whom was the estranged husband of famed aviatrix Ruth Elder, to fill out a workable crew.[7]

Byrd's first major oversight came to light when Melville discovered that he was short of cash: he had not enough money to buy coal and pay the Panama Canal's toll. A member withdrew several hundred dollars from his own pocket to cover the bills, as casually as someone might pick up a cab fare. That man was George "Mike" Thorne, twenty-six, grandson of the owner of Montgomery Ward. The Thorne family had contributed $9,000 to the expedition.[8] A square-headed, short, but rugged Yale graduate with a master's degree in forestry, Thorne flew his own plane and had spent a year skiing in Norway. He had signed on as a dog driver and topographer.

The creaky *New York* had cut across the steamy isthmus and barely resumed her voyage when engine troubles forced her to return to Panama for three more days. Delighted, her complement soaked up the heat they would miss in Antarctica and reveled in the waterfront pleasures of the sailor, including drunken brawls that got four of the men arrested and fined. Most of the shipmates showed up soused when the *New York* again sailed. Three drunks missed the departure and had to get a pilot boat to ferry them out to the disappearing ship. The patched-up *New York* headed for Pago Pago, but when her captain realized he did not have enough coal, he got Byrd's permission to make for Tahiti, where the *Bolling* would refuel.[9]

After an irritatingly slow voyage, enlivened only at the equator by the hazing of those crossing for the first time, the bored sailors came in sight of Papeete at dawn on 1 November. Sweet, sensual fragrances wafted from the beautiful, lush green island, beckoning the men to shores flagged by swaying palm trees and colored by scarlet hibiscus. Having been at sea forty days since leaving Panama—sixty-seven days from New York—the travelers could hardly contain themselves and pressed the rail as if they could push the ship faster. But the dour captain anchored offshore and ordered them to scrape the hull clear of barnacles. The men complied angrily.[10]

The faster *Eleanor Bolling* had arrived shortly before, and soon the two crews joined on shore. The *New York*'s squad learned that several among the *Bolling*'s personnel had already been thrown in jail for brawling—reinforcing Byrd's concerns about keeping his swashbucklers in line—but otherwise the steel ship's sailors were enjoying themselves.[11]

Despite their inauspicious start, the *Bolling*'s crew members were much happier than their ill-treated counterparts on the gloomy *New York*. The *Bolling*'s men liked their rusty little steamer. It was only a fraction larger than the *New York* and easily tossed about by waves, so they affectionately dubbed her the "Evermore Rolling." Her men resented the ship's standing as a secondary vessel in the public eye. The newspapers rarely mentioned her. She had received virtually nothing in the way of a send-off from either New York or Norfolk. She was a neglected stepsister to the much-acclaimed *New York*, in which Captain Gustav Brown had been second in command until Byrd promoted Brown to captain of the newly purchased *Bolling*. The name painted on her sides and life preservers and cut into her official rubber-stamp cachet read "Boling," a misspelling that symbolized her also-ran lot. But under Brown's amiable leadership, her family had a vibrant esprit de corps. Brown was a thirty-six-year-old merchant-vessel master, an immigrant who still spoke with a thick Swedish accent.[12]

The Tahitian layover further disillusioned Boy Scout Siple, already appalled by the behavior of his less-idealistic shipmates. Expecting beauty when he traveled inland through Gauguin's paradise, Siple found instead mosquitos, rats, hovels made of packing boxes, and "flabby, flat-faced" women.[13]

After three days, the recoaled ships sailed for New Zealand, their bold crews unfazed by an astrologer's published reading of the stars that foretold doom for every member of the expedition.[14]

Earlier, on board the scurrying whaler *Ross*, crisis had gripped a stricken dog unit. The huskies had begun to come down with diarrhea and distemper. Five out of the ninety that started had already died, and many of those remaining were near death. Their helpless handlers knew why: the dog food was a disastrous failure. As soon as the men got to New Zealand, they would have to junk the tons of worthless dog biscuits, work out a new formula, and somehow whip together tons of fresh chow in just a few weeks. (It was discovered after the expedition that the company that made the dog food had not followed Byrd's specifications.)[15]

No other misfiring of plans—there were bound to be others—could be more devastating. Dogs were crucial to the expedition. They were to be the engines of freight sledge-trains shuttling cargo from ship to base. The ship would berth next to unstable ice at the edge of the frozen sea that narrowly rimmed Antarctica in summer. A trail would run several miles to a base, located safely inland. The strong animals would also pull the heavily loaded sledges of the far-flung field parties. All or a major share of the burden of exploration would fall on them if the aviation experiment should fail. The dogs would back up the planes for rescue operations. Byrd even planned to take a small dog team on his polar flight in case he was forced down.[16]

Every effort had to be made to save the invaluable dogs. They had been selected as carefully as the people on the expedition. A wealthy Canadian trader had rounded up most of the candidates through his network of trading posts in Labrador, and the Washington, D.C., veterinarian who cared for the White House dogs had made the final selection.[17] Others were of a superior strain bred by the head of Byrd's dog unit. Replacement would be difficult if not impossible so late in the expedition's schedule.

The *Ross* reached Dunedin about the time Byrd left Los Angeles. The worried handlers and their dying charges disembarked onto Quarantine Island, where by import regulations the animals would have to stay until embarked on Byrd's ships on the final leg south.[18]

Arrangements were initiated—it is not clear how—to try to save the sick huskies. As a result, Dr. John Malcolm, an Otago University nutritionist, developed a formula based on beef tallow, bone meal, oil, and vitamins. The Hudson Brothers candy company magnanimously invited the handlers to use the chocolate kitchens at night to make the chow, and a dozen of the company's employees volunteered to help. In two weeks of whirlwind activity, the group managed to mix an awesome twenty-five tons of dog pemmican. The dogs loved it and, more importantly, thrived on it. Although Dr. Malcolm and the generous candy makers would never set foot on Antarctica, members of Byrd's expedition regarded them as true antarctic heroes. The Americans could not have had a more heartwarming welcome to New Zealand.[19]

The first of Byrd's troops to arrive in the country found that its odd combination of features—the best of England, Switzerland, and the South Pacific—produced a unique loveliness. The *Ross* had sailed by North Island, one of the two major land masses that constitute New Zealand, and down the coast of South Island. In the distance, the men spied South Island's mountainous spine, the majestic Southern Alps, still covered with snow in the early austral spring. Drawing into an arm of the sea that extended inland, the crew members saw Port Chalmers, Dunedin's harbor, to starboard near the mouth of the inlet, and Dunedin itself at the far end ten miles away. Later, driving into Dunedin, they thought it more a town than a city, with its neat, clean, widely separated houses and streets covering the bright hills golden with gorse bushes. The residents, called Kiwis after the country's flightless bird, greeted them hospitably in the nasally intoned, unmistakable accent of British Oceania.

The recuperating Eskimo dogs, working out on Quarantine Island to get in shape for their rigorous antarctic assignments, became sleepy Dunedin's center of attraction. A special excursion boat ferried thousands of the curious out to watch them.[20]

The group on board the *Larsen*, the second contingent to reach New Zealand, landed 5 November 1928 at Wellington on the North Island, three hundred miles from Dunedin. Byrd intended to stay about a month, mostly in Wellington, New Zealand's political and business capital, working with his local agents, the firm of Gardiner, Binnie and Halliburton. The country welcomed him as a dignitary of some standing. The mayor of Wellington received the commander and his retinue at City Hall the day they arrived, then Byrd called on Premier Coates, who kindly offered whatever help he could give. A government meteorologist briefed the American on antarctic weather. The Maoris, New Zealand's populous Polynesian aboriginals, presented him with a decorated tribal robe. He was welcomed by the city of Christchurch, where he laid a wreath at the statue of Captain Scott, the leader whose tragic mistakes Byrd prayed to avoid.[21]

The commander also managed a friendly and invaluable visit with the great antarctic hero from neighboring Australia, Sir Douglas Mawson. Sir Douglas, whom Byrd revered as the greatest antarctic authority then living, happened to arrive in Wellington on business while Byrd was there.[22] Having never met, they arranged to spend an afternoon and evening together. Always eager for good advice, and by then keenly aware of the extent of his ignorance, the innocent Yank doubtless drew as much information as he could from the experienced Aussie.

November was the time of the presidential election in the United States, and news reports carried word that Herbert Hoover had defeated Al Smith and was promising to continue the policies that were bringing ever-increasing prosperity.

Private reports presumably came to Byrd from officials in Washington, D.C., to let him know that the British ambassador had presented a note to the State Department offering the explorer "every possible assistance." As so often in politics, there was more to the offer than met the eye. The wording clearly implied British ownership of the territory where Byrd would sojourn, and documentation of the claim was attached. To accept the offer on behalf of Byrd without reservation would be to accept the claim. After taking a long time to formulate a careful reply, the State Department thanked England and added that the United States assumed the statements of claims were for information only, thus sidestepping the thorny question of U.S. recognition. Fortunately for Byrd, this high-level diplomatic dueling over his expedition had no practical repercussions, and he met no problems with either his own government or the New Zealand dominion of the British Empire.[23]

With a romanticism that belied his public stuffiness, Byrd dropped rose petals in with the letters he sent Marie. He told her self-righteously that he was ignoring the women who flirted with him.

The *Bolling* pulled into Port Chalmers on Sunday, 18 November. Predictably, she missed a formal reception because New Zealand observed the Sabbath strictly. Otherwise, the Kiwis went out of their way to make the Americans feel at home; leading citizens took in expedition members as house guests for their stay. The crew, moreover, thought the timing of their arrival was pretty good—the thirsty men were pleasantly surprised to learn that New Zealand had repealed her prohibition laws only four days before.[24] A few days after arriving, the *Bolling* made a round-trip to Wellington to retrieve the cargo from the *Larsen*.

With only a month to go until the summer sun should reach its peak and begin to descend into winter, Byrd was eager to get moving. But the poky *New York* was still drifting across the Pacific. Byrd had told Melville emphatically that he must save coal. But at one point, with the ship one hundred miles behind schedule, Byrd radioed, "Don't spare the coal that much!"[25] The last vessel of the expedition landed at Port Chalmers on 26 November 1928. For the very first time, all parts of the expedition had come together.

One man had to leave when his father died.[26] From among the many eager local volunteers, Byrd filled the total of four vacancies that had developed.

With his expedition starved for cargo space, Byrd had worked out a three-stage plan to get to "the ice," as explorers called Antarctica. First the *New York* would be equipped with sufficient supplies, including the Fairchild plane, to carry out a small-scale venture all by herself, in case the *Bolling* could not make it down. The *Bolling*, following Shackleton's example, would tow the *New York* halfway down to save the latter's coal.[27] The *Bolling* would go back to Dunedin, take on more coal for the *New York* and enough material to complete a full-scale but spartan expedition, then head for the base that should be under construction. With colder weather approaching by that time, there was a slight chance she might not get through. If she did, the iron-hulled freighter would return to Dunedin, load supplies for a dream expedition, and try once again to outrace winter down and back. Byrd realized the third stage was only a long shot. Meanwhile the *New York*, empty and much lighter, would sail on her own back to Dunedin, where both ships and most of their skeleton crews would spend the winter. They would return to Antarctica the next summer to pick up the wintering-over party.

The earlier they could start, the better. Byrd set departure for Saturday afternoon, 1 December. Everyone would have to work madly in the last few days to unload the *New York*'s original cargo and reload her according to the plan. Less than half the expedition membership showed up for the job; the rest, seduced by the pleasant diversions of the islands, were disporting themselves among the Kiwis. When the displeased commander rounded up the missing, he and Brophy gave them a stern talking to and ruled that nobody could leave the ships anymore except by special permission.[28]

Problems continued to pop up. The chief scientist, Larry Gould, found that, when the scientific equipment had been stowed, it had been put at the very bottom of the *Bolling*'s hold, which stank of decaying rats killed by shifting cargo. Much of the geophysical instrumentation and some of the geological apparatus had been damaged by water leaking from a tank. Angered at this thoughtless treatment of his scientific gear, and possibly apprehensive about what it might mean concerning the standing of science in the expedition, he growled that equipment stowage had been handled "very stupidly, to be sure."[29]

Byrd found he had some unexpected shopping to do. He realized he had somehow overlooked a necessity basic even to a weekend ski trip—sunglasses to protect the explorers against the damaging glare of the sun's reflecting off expanses of white snow.[30] Although there were bound to be mistakes in such a large undertaking, the headaches— the forgotten sunglasses, the mishandled scientific instruments, the worthless dog food, the cash shortage in Panama, the misspelling of *Bolling*—despite more than a year of meticulous planning, and before they even saw an iceberg, must have kept Byrd uneasy about being surprised by lurking calamity.

Most disturbing of all was the disintegrating performance of Byrd's second in command, Dick Brophy.[31] He had proven indecisive and grew more so day by day as the administrative pressures mounted, passing along too many decisions that he should have made himself. Byrd was forced to a painful decision: to relieve Brophy as executive officer and choose a new second in command from among the troops when he got to know them better. Byrd mentioned Brophy only in passing in later writings, so the depth of the leader's disappointment can only be guessed. He took Brophy off the ship's roster and placed him in charge of operations in New Zealand for the duration of the enterprise. Mindful of Brophy's feelings, however, Byrd did not officially demote the man but allowed him to keep the nominal title of second in command and emphasized to him the importance of the New Zealand assignment.

The loading of the *New York* threatened the expedition even further. When the Plimsoll mark on her upper hull sank below the surface, indicating that more cargo would press her dangerously low in the water, the loaders never slackened their pace as they dug away at the mountain of supplies still looming on the dock. The Norwegian consul, a veteran of an antarctic voyage, dropped by to watch and speak with the Norwegian members. Shaking his head, he told them somberly that the *New York*'s only conceivable destination was the bottom of the Southern Ocean, the informal name for the waters surrounding Antartica. Byrd, cautious by nature but seeing no alternative, feared that the old man knew far more what he was talking about than the other doomsayers.[32]

The explorers marked their departure from civilization by having a last meal together at a hotel banquet. It rained on Saturday, but a crowd of five thousand came out with umbrellas to see the expedition off. The final cargo check dragged on so long, however, that Byrd was not ready to leave until daybreak Sunday. A clutch of teary-eyed girlfriends and a thousand other diehard well-wishers were still on hand, nevertheless, to shout good-bye as the two ships cast off. The men looked back on the green island that had welcomed them so warmly, then turned to the task of breaching the cold, white-shrouded land that bid them no welcome at all.[33]

The ships began to heave before New Zealand was out of sight, starting a parade to the rails by pale, miserable-looking unfortunates.[34] Those who had learned what lay ahead knew it would, unhappily, only get worse as they moved into the belt of gales that circled Antarctica, howling around the continent's surrounding doughnut of ocean that was without any land masses to brake the wind. Those latitudes of seafaring legend known as the roaring forties, furious fifties, and screaming sixties had thrown many a sailor beneath the mountainous waves.

The overloading of the *New York* made her complement even more apprehensive and uncomfortable. The decks were piled so high with cargo that the mainsail could not be set. Even the cabins were stuffed. The only place Owen, for example, could find to sleep was a pile of soft but smelly furs crammed into his quarters.[35]

At first, Melville's harsh captaincy intensified the misery. Despite the maritime practice that a captain runs his own ship even when higher ranking officers are on board, Byrd, as the sole owner of the ships and with his fortunes dependent on them, had stated at the outset that he would exercise final authority. When he discovered how Melville's "four & four" watches fatigued the crew, and how much the men resented them, the commander decided the windjammer had enough personnel to go to three watches and allow everyone eight hours of straight sleep. His overruling of Melville was the happiest event to occur on the *New York* since she left New York City.[36]

During a storm, the quarter-mile-long towing cable snapped where it was attached to the *Bolling*. Byrd joined the gang of men who strained themselves sore pulling the heavy length onto the *New York* by muscle power alone. Siple noted that, for the first time, he felt a real expedition spirit. Epaminondas "Pete" Demas, twenty-two, a mechanic who had emigrated from Greece at the age of eleven, observed that "everyone is 100 percent Byrd."[37]

The expedition began scientific experiments during the voyage south. Shropshire charted the floor of the ocean between New Zealand and Antarctica with a newly developed sonic depth finder. Byrd talked through a radiotelephone, another technological novelty for ships, to coordinate the movements of the *New York* and *Bolling*, which was clawing the water at the front end of the restored towline to keep her heavy, bargelike sister ship moving. He communicated with New Zealand, and by relay with the rest of the world, through Morse-code radio. In an exchange that typified the modern nature of his expedition, the commander learned by radio of a public relations problem back in the States. The press had got hold of a rumor that nearly half his dogs had died. Byrd was able to scotch the story direct from the scene of the action in the churning waters of the southern Pacific. But the efficiency of radio had two sides. During the voyage south, with the crews separated from their families by long miles and months, word came over the air that Lofgren's mother and Davies's father had died.[38] While new technology eliminated some hardships, it added others.

The ships steadily ground out 170 miles a day.[39] Temperatures descended below freezing and, on 9 December, the explorers caught sight of the first sign that they were nearing antarctic waters. Far off to starboard they saw a huge, long slab of ice floating flatwise, pure white against the dark sea, the top of the frozen monolith as straight as the horizon. Soon they spotted another, and before long the flat-topped icebergs appeared frequently, often in groups. All the bergs were wide and tabular, unlike the icy pinnacles that dot the North Atlantic. The sailors passed close by one that was at least a mile across and whose level top was higher than the *New York*'s mainmast. They stared, fascinated, into fissures and grottoes carved by waves breaking against the sides. A beautiful, creamy blue light emanated from the walls, caused by the sunlight that penetrated the thick ice.

The next day the expedition officially made its entrance into the south polar region by crossing the Antarctic Circle, the farthest north that the sun ever shines at midnight in the southern hemisphere. Byrd marked the event by trying some initial exploring. Captain Scott had reported a tiny, barren island near their position, but no one had seen it since. Whalers who plied the area doubted that Scott Island, as it was called, really existed. Optical illusions and distant, weirdly shaped icebergs had caused other false discoveries. Byrd set his course through the mapped location.

About five o'clock in the afternoon the *New York*'s lookout cried that land lay far ahead. Men raced excitedly to the bow to watch as the dark speck became larger. Two hours later the island was just off to port. Two black cliffs projected from the water. One was about two hundred feet high, shaped like an elephant's head and capped with snow. The other was shorter, but the men guessed it extended a quarter mile. Ice lay at the bottom of the cliffs, and patches of moss and lichens mottled the sides. Thousands of birds, mostly swallowlike petrels as white as the snow, perched on the rocks or swarmed around the cliffs. The scientists yearned to land and collect specimens, but Byrd said he had to press on. It was not a major accomplishment, confirming someone else's discovery, but the expedition had made its first contribution to geography, however small. As Byrd surely had hoped, he had beaten Wilkins to the first antarctic headlines. Considering the natural doubts that must have oppressed Byrd since he launched his venture, the sighting was most encouraging.

Only hours later the ships came up against Antarctica's redoubtable ice pack. Byrd looked out over a vast, undulating membrane of ice, webbed by cracks, that entirely covered the southern half of the visible expanse of sea around him. Focusing on many massive individual pieces of ice that clearly weighed tons, he shuddered at the thought of what might happen to him and his crews—as had happened to others—during the three- or four-day sail through the pack if stormy seas should toss the giant floes about and pulverize his puny ships.

Byrd had read all he could and questioned experts at length on the pack and how to penetrate it quickly and safely. Glaciologists spoke of two kinds of floating antarctic ice: bergs and floes. Bergs, such as those Byrd had seen earlier, are chunks of frozen fresh water that break off ice shelves, which are essentially floating edges of the continental ice cap. The cap slowly spreads out like pancake batter over land and sea for decades or centuries, adding about as much from snowfall as it loses through calving bergs. Floes are created when winter freezes the ocean surface adjacent to Antarctica. Summer breaks the floe into pieces ranging in size from ice cubes to slabs several feet thick and thousands of feet square. The pack, which surrounds the continent, is a thick band of densely packed ice, mostly floes, penetrable only by the toughest ships when and if the ice begins to disintegrate about midsummer; there had been years when passages never opened. The formidable ice pack had prevented sailors from seeing Antarctica until a little over a hundred years before and had kept the continent pristine, as far as was known, until Norwegian whalers punched through to open water on the other side and went on to make the first landing a mere thirty-three years before Byrd's expedition. The ice jam is formed when winds and surface currents drive floes northward until they are stopped by southward-flowing air and water masses at the belt of storms. The floes pile up all around Antarctica like a giant quoit, with sharply defined inner and outer edges.

Byrd turned his ships eastward to cruise alongside the pack and keep a secret rendezvous. While on board the *Larsen*, he had cajoled Captain Nilsen into giving him a tow when the whaler plowed through the ice field, thus saving even more precious coal. Since whalers guarded their maneuvers from competitors, like many anglers who have secret fishing spots, Byrd had kept quiet about the meeting so no one could track the *Larsen* through his movements. Nilsen had confided to the American about where the *Larsen* and her five chasers planned to wait until the pack loosened; just as soon as it looked navigable they would have to go, so Byrd would have to get to the rendezvous beforehand. Byrd had worried ever since that he would not reach the *Larsen* on time,[40] but she radioed that the pack was still tight, and he was close enough to know he had made it. Because of thick weather, however, neither ship knew its exact position. The infant technology of radio displayed another invaluable benefit when the *New York* homed in on the *Larsen's* transmissions by radio wave direction-finding techniques and found her the next day.

After an exhausting day-long marathon in which Byrd's crews slung nearly one hundred tons of coal from the *Bolling* to the *New York* in five-hundred-pound sacks, the steel ship raced north to grab the second-priority supplies. The *New York* and the whalers had to wait four more days before the pack opened up enough to allow the ships to attempt a breach. Another helpful whaler, trying to aid Byrd and not knowing he was with the *Larsen*, reported on ice conditions and radioed that she had broken through the pack; Captain Nilsen found the information useful in making his way through.[41]

Ever since leaving Los Angeles, Byrd had spent most of his time wrapped up in detailed figures and schedules, trying to anticipate almost every possible eventuality for every day of the next year and a half or more. The commander realized that the man who would be second in command should participate in the planning. By 12 December, although he would have liked more time to observe the candidates, he had decided it was time to name his new executive officer.

Even at this early stage, the one person who was clearly emerging as the natural leader in matters of both intellect and action was geologist Larry Gould, thirty-two, also the expedition's geographer and chief scientist. A Phi Beta Kappa graduate of the University of Michigan, Gould was professor of economic geology at his alma mater. He had been assistant director of two summer arctic expeditions and came to Byrd highly recommended by polar experts. The commander took Gould aside and told him of the decision. Byrd began to huddle frequently with his new exec but asked Gould not to tell anyone about the promotion until the commander himself should make the announcement when the time came for Gould to exercise authority.[42] Byrd clearly did not want to upset Brophy's troubled mind or to chance any negative news coverage that would result from a shake-up in the expedition's leadership.

On 17 December, the *New York*'s crew spotted the traditional symbol of the antarctic. Posted on a floe stood an emperor penguin, identifiable by its distinctive sleek shape, black-and-white tuxedolike coloring, and three-foot height. At closer inspection, the onlookers could make out a yellow-orange throat and a long, exquisite beak edged with coral pink "lips." Antarctic literature reported that the flightless birds lived in the sea and came ashore only a few months every year to breed. Flying through the water with their flippers, they could outswim and outdive all other birds. The stately emperor penguins were considered uncommon, even rare; explorers had found only two breeding grounds of a few thousand birds each.

Minutes later the sailors came upon a flock of penguins of another kind, half the size of the emperor. The men watched the funny, pint-sized birds waddling on the floes, belly-flopping across them and jumping feet first into the water, diving, and finally popping up and landing on their feet on the ice like acrobats springing from trampolines. When the ships paused for a lead to open, some of the crew tried futilely to grab the little penguins, which yelled at their pursuers with drawn-out, rasping cries like the squawking of crows. The books identified these birds as Adélie penguins, named after Adélie d'Urville, wife of a French explorer. These penguins were reportedly abundant, breeding in numerous coastal rookeries of up to a million birds each.

Normally, the *Larsen* would have reached open water and gone off chasing whales by this time of year, but the resistant pack had proven unusually thick, and ice still ran to the horizon. Byrd, impatient but helpless, could only stand by as the delay ate into his already tight schedule.

On the afternoon of 20 December 1928, the radio brought Byrd unsettling but not surprising news. His arch rival, Hubert Wilkins, finally had beaten the American to an honor, making history by flying the first plane in Antarctica, over the continent's northernmost land, a long peninsula that stretched toward South America. Wilkins reported, moreover, that what had been thought to be a peninsula was really an island (Wilkins was later proved mistaken). Byrd, not one to publicize a competitor, never set down his reaction to the epic flight and scarcely mentioned Wilkins in subsequent publications. The American was surely not happy, fearing that the Australian might yet go to the pole. Keeping up appearances, nevertheless, the commander radioed congratulations and reminded Wilkins he would be warmly welcomed if he flew to Byrd's landing strip later.[43]

As midsummer approached and the ships climbed into higher latitudes, nights had grown rapidly shorter and then disappeared completely. The sun rose high in the sky at noon and dipped toward the horizon at midnight but never set. The crew members covered their cabin windows to sleep. Far from being unsettling, the disappearance of night was strangely comforting, calming perhaps some atavistic, inchoate fear of the dark. Unable to regulate their days by the familiar cycle of darkness and light, the voyagers relied on work and meal schedules, clocks, and the built-in rhythms of their own bodies.

At noon on 21 December, the sun reached its summer zenith. From then on it would dip lower and lower in the sky; night would appear again and overtake day, and eventually the sun would cease to rise until next summer. Byrd knew that the temperature cycle in the antarctic did not lag the solar cycle as much as it did in temperate zones, where days continued to get hotter long past the summer solstice. In less than two months, the sea ice would cease breaking up, and the ocean would start freezing again. Time was growing short for him to locate a site for a base, build and supply it, lay emergency depots, and do some exploring before continuous darkness and murderous cold shut Antarctica down.

Fortunately, the *Larsen* broke into open water that day. The whaler had taken a week, twice as long as expected, to push through the wide, thick ring of ice. Byrd led three cheers for Captain Nilsen. The *Larsen* unhitched the tow rope; her crew good-naturedly wished the

Americans luck in their race against winter, and she sailed off to the hunt. The major obstacles between Byrd and his destination had been cleared. Exuberant, he turned to face his men and intoned dramatically to Melville, "Captain, head south!"[44]

The lookouts on the *New York* spotted several whales every day as the wooden ship rode the wind toward Antarctica. Oceanographers had recorded that, for complex reasons of currents and chemistry, the Southern Ocean was a gigantic bouillabaisse teeming with plankton and other food that attracted whales. Whalers harpooned almost three-quarters of the world's catch there. Byrd reported the locations of the whales his men saw to Captain Nilsen in gratitude for his help—and in anticipation of needing further help later.[45]

The explorers celebrated Christmas 1928 with a champagne feast. Lofgren, thirty-four, looking old-fashioned and stern in dundreary whiskers, performed as toastmaster. He had served as a yeoman in the navy, including two years as secretary to Byrd, and at the age of twenty had become the service's youngest chief petty officer. He had advanced to lieutenant junior grade by the end of the great war. The year before joining the expedition he had become national director of the Fleet Reserve Association, which represented navy and marine enlisted men. Davies put on a red parka, stuffed a pillow inside, and taped cotton to his round, pudgy face to play Santa Claus. He brought each man little gifts, including cigarette lighters given in the name of Marie Byrd.[46] Owen read a touching verse he had composed for the sentimental occasion:

The penguin is a nasty bird
He shits upon the snow
He knows no better, so I've heard
And has no place to go.[47]

The commander, with his sense of the dramatic, ordered the men a special present. He told Melville to abandon fuel rationing, pour on the coal, and sprint to their long-awaited goal.

At 3:00 P.M., when the revelers were at their noisiest, a barely heard shout from the crow's nest electrified the party: "Barrier on the starboard bow!"[48] They dashed on deck, crowding the starboard rail and scurrying up the rigging. A small cannon was ceremoniously fired. Off in the distance, to the right of their southeasterly course, they made out what appeared to be a white wall stretching across the entire ocean from east to west. When the *New York* closed to within about a mile, the commander turned her due east to cruise along the face of the awe-inspiring wall, a sheer cliff of compacted snow higher than the ship. Byrd estimated its gently undulating top to average ninety feet above water. The voyagers had come to what seemed the boundary of the southern end of the earth, and they ran their eyes in wonder over its face.

Accounts reported that the wall was actually the seaward front of a gargantuan floating ice shelf at least the size of Britain, attached along all known sides but its northernmost to the continent, and covering the vast southern portion of the gulf called the Ross Sea. Sailors who had discovered the incredible partition barring their way as they voyaged toward the South Pole had named the shelf "the great barrier." No one knew its exact shape or dimensions, unknowns on which Byrd hoped to shed light. The commander and his troops were more than idly curious about the barrier—Byrd had planned that a location on its surface would be their home for the next fourteen months or so.

He radioed the secretary of the navy that they had reached Antarctica. In a message meant for the press, Byrd pointed out that the *New York* was 2,300 miles from the nearest human dwelling, as far away as a ship could get. His expedition had borne the American flag several hundred miles farther south than it had ever been. Conscious of the publicity value of his yuletide arrival at the land of snow—the extravagant expenditure of coal had not been entirely for the pleasure of his troops—and eager to begin reclaiming the public's attention from Wilkins, Byrd referred to the Fairchild in the *New York*'s hold and observed that it seemed "fitting that an airplane, that instrument of good will, should reach its farthest south on Christmas day."[49]

He ordered that the barrier be continuously sketched as the *New York* sailed alongside, the duty to be rotated among members of the scientific unit. But he kept his ship well away from the foot of the wall because of the danger of sizable hunks breaking away, as was known to happen frequently.

At noon the day after Christmas, the ship slipped into an inlet in the barrier, which looked as if a giant wedge had been cut out. Seen first by the Scott expedition and named Discovery Inlet, it had never been used for a base. Byrd had originally chosen to settle and place his stamp at that location, and knowledgeable whalers had recommended it, but he had changed his mind on Amundsen's solid advice and fixed on a site farther east. Byrd wanted to scout Discovery Inlet as an alternative, however, in case his top choice proved unsuitable.[50]

As the *New York* pulled up to the frozen ocean surface inside to set her ice anchors, Marine Captain Alton Parker, thirty-three, who had met Byrd while they were both in flight training at Pensacola and was one of the expedition's four pilots, spoiled a dramatic publicity opportunity for Byrd by leaping onto the sea ice ahead of everyone and yelling, "The Marines are always the first to land!"[51] Byrd said nothing, but another pilot, Dean Smith, sensed that the commander did not like the stunt.

The others hurried after Parker for their first experience of Antarctica, a white world as different in many respects as another planet from the rest of the earth. The men threw snowballs, chased squawking penguins, and snooped about the interesting glacial formations. Like tourists, the men gawked at the numerous dark brown, white-mottled Weddell seals sunning themselves on the ice. Explorer James Weddell had been the first to see these nine-foot, half-ton beasts. He recorded that they basked, fat and sluglike, in droves around the shore. Byrd's troops walked right up to the seals, which lifted their heads and stared back with cowlike eyes over whiskered muzzles. Having no fear of humans, whom neither these seals nor their ancestors had ever encountered, the Weddells made no attempt to flee. Made nervous by the strange, two-legged creatures, however, the gentle seals bellowed weirdly—loud, hoarse moaning as if they were in agony. Sledge-unit members, toting guns, blasted most of the seals to death for fresh meat for the dogs. The pistol cracks tolled the end of the seals of Discovery Inlet, heralding the arrival of one more raiding party, come not to visit with Antarctica but to conquer her.

Byrd and four Norwegian skiers climbed a slope to the top of the barrier to reconnoiter. They beheld a milky desert, not level but furled with gently rolling snow dunes. The snow beneath their feet was hard packed and barely showed footprints. The men scouted the rolling plain all afternoon and evening but found no stretch flat enough for an airstrip. The commander could only cross his fingers that the other location would prove suitable. The group returned to the ship around midnight, with the exhausted Byrd, a novice skier, being towed by Sverre Strom, thirty, the biggest and strongest man on the expedition.[52]

Upon returning, the commander found that strong swells were washing in and cracking the ice where the *New York* was anchored. Alarmed, he ordered everyone onto the ship immediately. In the rush to board, the men loaded only fifteen of the thirty butchered seals.[53] Half a day after docking, the smoking *New York* withdrew from the red-stained snow and stiffening bodies. Byrd headed her east again toward what he hoped would be the end of his search, less than a hundred miles away.

Early on the morning of 28 December, the *New York* arrived at her destination: the Bay of Whales. Her excited crew peered into the huge indentation in the barrier, twenty miles across at the mouth. Byrd headed the ship toward a haze-shrouded, four-mile-wide bight at the southern end. Anxiously, he tried to penetrate the fog with his gaze. He wanted to reach a special place on the east side of the bight, eight miles in. The spot was Framheim, the nearest basing site to the South Pole that could be reached by ship, the place that had given Amundsen his winning head start in the great race against Scott. Byrd coveted Framheim for his command post.

The Norwegian had highly recommended the place to Byrd, pointing out that it was also the closest accessible site to the unknown section of barrier and continent—and possibly unclaimed land—to the east that Byrd wanted to explore. Framheim also had flat terrain, with the best weather and the fewest storms of any known area, conditions that were critically important to a flying expedition. Amundsen had taken no scientists, so Byrd's specialists could break new ground in and around that location. There might even be usable remains of the Norwegian camp. Most important was that the bay area appeared to be comparatively stable, less likely than other parts of the barrier to break away and dump Byrd and all his men into the sea. Once a German expedition had been setting up camp at a similar site on an ice shelf on the other side of Antarctica when the site had calved off, forcing the explorers to retreat. The barrier around the Bay of Whales, however, seemed to be at least semipermanently attached to a hypothesized under-ice island to the south. The Americans would not be safe there—no place in Antarctica was safe—but they would be in less danger than anywhere else on the barrier. Some experts from the British Empire criticized the choice. Mawson and Griffith Taylor, a geologist from Scott's expedition, had argued that Byrd should go where the Germans had tried to enter, which was much farther from any regions that had already been explored or scientifically investigated. However, another British authority, geographer J. Gordon Hayes, published his idea of the optimum expedition, taking into account scientific, geographic, and practical considerations, and for his primary base chose the Bay of Whales. The whalers had advised against the site, nevertheless, because in their trips to the bay—named for the hundreds of whales its discoverer had seen cavorting in its waters— the whalers usually found the ocean in the bight frozen solid right up to its mouth. Shackleton had wanted to base there in 1908, but the ice had stopped him. The Norwegians thought their countryman Amundsen had been lucky the year he was able to sail up to within two miles of Framheim. The whalers pointed out, moreover, that many huge bergs floated in the bay, and unless the *New York* could get well inside the bight, she would have to cast off with every north wind to maneuver out of the way of southward-blown ice masses that would bear down on her.[54] Byrd's choice was a testimony to his faith in Amundsen.

The mist hiding the bight lifted slowly as the *New York* approached, and Byrd could see that the opening extended deeply into the barrier, narrowing as it disappeared far in the distance. His heart sank. The water inside was entirely covered with a sheet of ice.

Pacing the deck, he pondered his dilemma. He could put up with delays caused by northerlies, beginning right away to unload the cargo and haul it with sledges the whole eight miles over decaying sea ice that might soon begin to break up under the summer sun while men, dogs, and supplies were spread out on the surface. That process would require many sixteen-mile round-trips. Or he could wait for the weakening ice to crumble completely and go out, a process that might be days away or weeks—or never. He had a little while to make the decision; first he had to find Framheim and make sure it met his needs. Otherwise, he would have to seek another site.

As the ship pulled alongside the ice, a dog driver leaped the rail to be first ashore.[55] If Byrd was miffed about being upstaged a second time, he gave no recorded sign of his feelings.

Before he left on what might become an extended survey, Byrd issued the delayed announcement of Larry Gould's new position. The commander had a memo headed "EXPEDITION ORDER" mounted on the bulletin board: "Dr. Larry Gould has been appointed THIRD IN COMMAND of the expedition, which means that he is SECOND IN COMMAND at the base of operations. . . ." The move was greeted with genuine enthusiasm by virtually everyone, but the commander avoided fanfare because of the problems it might cause with

Brophy and the press. Gould's promotion was casually mentioned in the middle of a *New York Times* story on expedition activities.[56]

Byrd placed his new exec in charge during his absence. Gould's first official act was to organize Byrd's trail party and equip it for a possible week of searching.[57] At 8:00 P.M., the commander and five others set out to explore bay and barrier.

The others waited. The dog handlers killed more seals, including those of a type they had not seen at Discovery Inlet. Light brown and about seven feet long, they were slimmer than the tanklike Weddells and attacked when provoked, issuing a shrill whistling cry. The books identified the species as crabeater seals, named for their crustacean diet. Bored with being on hold, some of the intrepid explorers shot at the whales that played around the ship, killing at least three.[58] For a few people, at least, inflicting death was not a distasteful necessity but a welcome opportunity.

Byrd and his party—two dog teams and drivers, a radio operator, Balchen, and another Norwegian skier—could not find so much as a trace of Framheim, and the area had eroded and warped so much that they could not even be sure where the camp had been. Nor for two days could the discouraged scouts find any other suitable location flat and smooth enough for an airfield and reasonably close to shore. Byrd kept to himself whatever plans he had if he could not find a site. The prospects for aviation—and, therefore, the expedition—looked horribly bleak.

Finally, on 30 December, the patrol skied up a narrow, mile-long inlet on the east side of the bight about eight miles from the ship. At the inlet's head the slope rose gradually to the top of the barrier, where there was a wide basin surrounded by a snow rim that shielded the area on all sides but the west from winds. The commander said the party "recognized instantly that here was an excellent place for our base."[59] A haggard house hunter who had finally found a suitable property, Byrd could hardly have been more relieved.

Conservative, he hesitated over the hard decision of whether to unload on the unstable sea ice. The sun was swinging lower toward the horizon every night, and he wanted to lay some bases to support next year's polar flight and also to try a few flights into the map's blank spaces before winter grounded the planes. The slow *New York* had to have plenty of time to lurch out of the antarctic before the freezing ocean caught up with her. He had a crowded shipload of restless young men and whining dogs anchored with nothing to do, and he was at least as eager as his troops to hurdle the barrier and explore the mysteries beyond. Unloading and shuttling cargo would take many weeks. Measuring each precious day against its dangers, he determined that the time that could be saved by unloading the ship and immediately beginning construction of the base outweighed the risks that would have to be taken. His radio operator keyed the commander's message to the ship: "Start preparations at once to remove the cargo to the base."[60]

.5.

Little America

BYRD's first key step as chief executive of the new settlement was to delegate authority. He had originally told Gould to take charge of the unloading; but with the base much farther from the ship than anticipated, Byrd changed his mind, making Gould head of base construction, where more critical decisions were apt to arise, and assigning Ashley McKinley responsibility for unloading the supplies and transporting them to the site. Byrd had taken McKinley, thirty-two, as his aerial photographer and had put him in charge of photography overall.

Skiers laid out the best trail to the base through pressure ridges, long mounds of ice taller than a man that crisscrossed the bay, uplifted by pressure from the imperceptible but relentless advance of the barrier that buckled the sea ice in front of it. The skiers blazed the route with flags of red-orange hue, which almost had the status of official expedition color. Parkas, planes, prefabricated buildings, gasoline drums—nearly everything that moved or sat out of doors was of the same flaming color, easily visible against the white background even in bad weather.[1]

As people walked or skied about the harbor, almost all noticed the same illusion about distances. If someone judged a geographic feature, perhaps a section of the barrier cliff jutting into the bay, to be a mile or so away, he might find it no closer after a trek of half an hour because that section was really many miles ahead. If he thought a hill of ice to be huge and far away, on the other hand, he could stumble within seconds over a mound that was really only waist-high. Perceptions were distorted by the lack of common objects such as trees, houses, animals, or other people in the line of sight that normally serve as references.

Another strange optical effect, a type of mirage the scientists identified as "looming," caused distant icebergs to look stretched vertically, sometimes appearing to be on pedestals. Caused by a temperature inversion over the snow desert that bent light rays weirdly, with the same results as some fun house mirrors, the phenomenon even acted on bergs beyond the horizon, lifting their images into the line of sight and making them appear and later disappear as if by magic.

The sea ice, several feet thick and many square miles in area, was unlikely to break up and go out suddenly. Byrd expected cracks to appear and widen imperceptibly. Skiers and dog teams could even ride over the cracks until they got too wide, like the explorers who had sledged over the frozen arctic ocean during summer in seeking the North Pole. The concerned commander feared, though, that blowing snow might cover wide cracks in the decaying ice, forming fragile bridges that would collapse under the weight of the sledges. He worried, too, that dogs and drivers might become lost in snowstorms. He dictated a number of safety precautions.[2] Teams would travel in twos or threes. On departure, a radio message would alert a monitor at the destination. A lookout in the *New York*'s crow's nest would follow the teams with binoculars. Each driver would lug a sleeping bag in case he had to wait out a storm.

On 2 January 1929, the squirming dogs—eighty-four in number after one had died enroute from New Zealand—were allowed to run off the ship, and within moments they were springing at one another's throats. Amid the bedlam of snarls and yelps, the handlers waded in, cursing and screaming, kicking and clubbing with their whip handles. Once the animals had been separated, they wagged their tails and licked their masters' hands, as affectionate as lap dogs toward humans but ever wary of one another. The drivers hitched each dog to coupled sledges by tying its harness to a gang line attached to the front, with huskies arrayed on either side and the lone lead dog in front. The teams had up to thirteen dogs, depending on the driver's skill, and dragged loads of from 700 to 1,700 pounds. The handlers figured that each dog could pull roughly 150 pounds—mustering proportionately far greater power than horses.[3]

When a pair of sledges was loaded, the muscular huskies strained at their ropes and took off, the unreined lead dogs sensing their way along the skied-over trail, the demanding drivers cracking their whips and yelling "gee" to go right, "haw" for left, "yake" for straight ahead, or "whoa!" On smooth straightaways the perky dogs stepped up to a brisk trot, heads jutting forward, tongues lolling, tails held high. The six experienced drivers and one neophyte each made a round-trip. Soon all ten available teams were on the run. Driving sledges was nothing like turning a car's steering wheel or tugging on the reins of a team of horses—the new drivers worked slowly as they learned by painful experience how to control the frisky animals and keep the loads from toppling. Long after one particular team had left, it arrived back at the ship still fully loaded, the driver missing. He came walking back some time later, safe but sheepish.

On 4 January, Brophy sent a radiogram to Byrd that was probably read only by the commander and the radio operators. It has long been forgotten, yet it deserves a niche in polar history:

> Believe that you should name your base camp immediately without further ceremony as newspapers are calling it Framheim and whatnot in headlines. Still stick to my original suggestion of quote Little America unquote regardless of what Owen and others may note against it as a cheap attempt at flag waving which it most certainly is not. At any rate, do name it something right away and make it typically American and with some meaning that will ring down through the ages on the maps and in the minds of the millions who are following you daily.

The message got Byrd's attention. An unabashed patriot whose expedition promoted the American way, he relied on the financial support and potential further support of his many proud fellow citizens back home. The next day he proclaimed that the basin would be known henceforth as Little America.[4]

Byrd fretted about the low daily tonnage being sledged to Little America—only four or five tons, short of the six tons it would take to empty the *New York* by the *Bolling*'s arrival in about a month. At that time, the teams would immediately have to start hauling cargo off the brittle ship, which would be destroyed by squeezing ice if she stayed too long. Byrd wanted to assure her time to get back to New Zealand before the start of winter and perhaps even to manage a third trip. Only then could the men turn their attention back to the cargo on the *New York*. If unloading took too long, she might be stuck for the winter. The resilient ship would survive, but putting up the twenty sailors who manned her would strain Little America's measured resources.[5]

Byrd had fielded almost every husky he had, including the weaker ones meant for spares; but he had to speed up the unloading. Men— the commander included—roped themselves to sledges and dragged nearly immovable loads to a cache nearer Little America to enable some drivers to make two round-trips a day. The dogs, ears back and tails drooping, and the men, pale and stumbling, worked almost to exhaustion at unloading and hauling, no matter what a man's specialty. Byrd's physical labors and heavy administrative burdens often kept him going eighteen to twenty hours a day.[6]

Under the stress, almost half the people caught colds or flu, and at least two of them had to stay in bed, including the doctor. In a setback peculiar to polar operations, a driver got worms from his dogs seriously enough to be out of commission awhile.[7]

Nature gave Byrd his worst problems. A dangerous mass of floating ice bore down on the *New York*, forcing her to cast off and cruise back and forth wastefully for hours until it passed. A snowstorm stopped all activity for two days. A wide crack cut across the sledge route, forcing teams along a new trail that made the round-trip four miles longer. Then cracking ice required the ship to find another berth a quarter mile away. Antarctica was by no means a pushover.

Eventually, the decaying ice started to work to Byrd's advantage. A long, wide lead opened, and the *New York* slipped in two miles nearer to Little America. The edge of the bay ice began breaking away, enabling the ship to squirm even closer. Occasionally Byrd gave nature a boost by riding the *New York* up on the ice and snapping off the thinning edge. He hoped to get near enough to make two round-trips routine for each team, and maybe even to unload with block and tackle directly onto a low part of the barrier. Supplies could not be unloaded onto the crumbling sea ice any faster than the sledges could haul them off, but cargo could be dumped off the ship as fast as possible onto the thick barrier and cached safely for some time.

After he had had only a few days experience with sledging operations, Byrd wished he had more huskies. He had radioed Railey to find twenty additional dogs and a handler quickly and rush them to New Zealand in time for the *Bolling*'s hoped-for third voyage. On that final run, the *Bolling* would also carry another aviation specialist. The mechanic tending the planes still in New Zealand, an employee of the Wright Engine Company who was the expert on the engines for the polar flight plane, was returning home—officially because of "extreme seasickness" but really, according to Demas, because he had backed out of wintering over.[8] In the United States, a quick-acting replacement volunteered with only two and a half hours to get ready before boarding the only ship that could get him to New Zealand in time.

A personnel crisis heaped more complications on Byrd. Red-haired reporter Russell Owen, forty, got so ill he became delirious for several days. Byrd had gotten to know Owen well when the newsman had been attached to Amundsen's Spitsbergen expedition to cover the North Pole race for the *Times*. The commander gave up the bed in his stateroom to the sick reporter and slept on the floor of the bathroom. Officially, Owen was stated to be a victim of the expedition's flu epidemic; but the expedition's physician, Dana Coman, actually concluded that the reporter's troubles were all in his mind and diagnosed his condition as "neuropathic." In a memorandum Byrd prepared later for the record, he wrote that the problem stemmed from Owen's fear of antarctic hazards.[9] Short, slight, weak, and bespectacled, Owen was the runt of Byrd's pack and the least likely candidate for a polar mission. Byrd recorded that Owen, despite his unsuitability, had signed on because he wanted to gain fame, further his career, and gather material for books, and because the *Times* was paying him $10,000 a year. His realization that he was not fitted to life on an antarctic expedition undoubtedly contributed to his psychopathology.

Pilot Dean Smith, however, reported that Owen in fact broke down mainly because he was so "shocked and deeply disturbed" by the constraints Byrd placed on the reporter's journalistic freedom. As Smith related, the image-conscious commander treated the newsman more like a public relations agent than an independent reporter, rewriting Owen's stories and adding and deleting material in a way that, Smith recounted, "seemed to systematically build himself [Byrd] up as a heroic figure."[10] Owen seems to have regarded himself not as a regular member of the expedition but as an outsider, like a sportswriter who travels with a team but is not part of it. Byrd, on the other hand, seems to have expected Owen to function as a full member committed to the aims of the expedition and its leader.

Feeling deeply wronged, Owen carped about Byrd behind his back, thereby committing what the commander considered the cardinal sin of disloyalty. Byrd wrote in the memorandum that Owen spent much of his time "attempting to turn against me everyone he thought he could influence." The leader said that Owen went so far as to take "great pleasure in the fact that he was forcing me to sleep uncomfortably on the bathroom floor and was keeping me out of my office and cabin." Byrd angrily told Owen that, because of his disloyalty, his special permission to write a book on the expedition was withdrawn. The reporter's behavior showed, Byrd went on, that "Owen could not be normal mentally. It is unlikely that any normal person could laugh with glee at the discomfiture that person causes a supposed friend when he has given up his quarters for him." Byrd recorded Dr. Coman's diagnosis of paranoia. Coman sent radio messages to F. T. Birchall, acting managing editor of the *Times*, saying that the reporter could not stand up to the demands of polar life and would have to leave.[11] Byrd indicated that he thought the newspaper could arrange a replacement from New Zealand.

Owen, however, begged Byrd for permission to stay. Byrd wrote that Owen believed he would be ruined by leaving because he had returned from the arctic trip without completing that assignment, which had called for him to cross the North Pole in Amundsen's dirigible. Coman told the commander that Owen was so distraught that leaving would be even harder on him than staying.

Byrd relented, apparently on Owen's promise of loyalty. He wired his decision to the *Times*, referring to Owen's "surprising improvement" and "unusual recuperation." Owen, in a wire that must have raised eyebrows at the *Times*, told Birchall that he was staying because Antarctica, with clean air, no germs, and good food, was a better place to regain health than anywhere else. Owen profusely praised Byrd's generosity and said of himself that he had "made adjustments of the source of anxiety which had caused my nervous trouble."[12]

Byrd kept his wife informed about the expedition. In a letter to go back on the ships, Byrd told Marie, "Brophy and Owen were the only

ones who went haywire—but Owen has pulled out completely. . . .
Now he thinks I have been very square to him and is, I think, more
loyal than ever."[13]

On 18 January, the canine star of the expedition disappeared. The
aged dog, Chinook, twelve years old that day, had led the team that
won the first international sledge-dog derby. An offspring of the bitch
that led Peary on his trip to the North Pole, Chinook was the progenitor
of the line that his doting handler, Arthur Walden, head of Byrd's dog
unit, was trying to breed into the perfect sledge dog. Fifteen of Chinook's descendants, big, brown huskies known as the Chinook dogs,
were also on the expedition. They always carted the heaviest loads.
Too old to do much work, Chinook was a pet to Walden, who had
agreed to manage the sledge teams on the condition that he be allowed
to take his companion and bring him back; explorers often destroyed
their animals once they had done their jobs. Chinook ran loose most
of the time in Antarctica. At one point three other dogs had ganged
up on him, and Walden had to save the dog from being killed. The
saddened trainer believed the attack had made Chinook feel his life
was at its end and go off somewhere to die.[14]

At fifty-seven, Walden was the second oldest member after Ronne.
The dog handler was among the first to be sought by Byrd, who became
the man's first boss. A fast-talking New Englander, square set and
wiry, with deep-set blue eyes under bristling yellow eyebrows, Walden
had trekked to Alaska for the gold rush more than thirty years before
and later wrote a book about his experiences, *Dog Puncher on the Yukon*.
The ruddy outdoorsman remained a musher and helped to found the
sport of dog-sledge racing. He and his wife farmed and bred sledge
dogs in New Hampshire.[15]

Walden sank into depression over his loss, which compounded the
uneasiness he felt as essentially a loner on Byrd's highly organized
team. The dog handler had always driven the heaviest loads, the most
difficult to manage over the rough trail, but now took no more than
anyone else.[16]

Two days later, with the *Bolling* halfway to the Bay of Whales, Byrd
and four others went out in a boat to cruise the barrier east of the *New
York* and look for a low spot on which the *Bolling* might unload. They
came upon a good place, but access was impeded by thick sea ice.
Byrd hoped it would float out by the time the *Bolling* arrived.

On the way back the party spotted three whales porpoising through the water. The whales apparently saw the men, too, because the animals turned and headed straight for the boat. As the men squinted at the approaching parade, colors and shapes became more distinct: black-and-white bodies and sharklike fins. Byrd's people had seen members of this species near the *New York*, and some men had shot at them.[17] The occupants of the boat nearly panicked. The oncoming animals were killer whales, predators that ate penguins, seals, and other whales. None of these whales had been known to eat a man, but years ago killers had dived under a floe on which terrified explorers were standing and rammed it from below, apparently trying to deliver supper to the dining room. The explorers had hopped from floe to floe to escape. Thinking the pack might try to ram his small boat, Byrd called for full speed from the outboard motor and turned toward the nearest sea ice. The boat butted into the ice when the killers were but fifteen feet away and, although the ice looked weak, the men scrambled madly out of the boat. The whales dived under the ice while the men crouched expectantly. Nothing happened; the killers never reappeared.

When Byrd felt it was safe, the shaken crew piled back into the boat and tried to start the engine, but it was out of gas. They had to row back. Byrd's engineers had assured him he had plenty of gas; as one of the crew reported, the commander was pretty sore.[18]

As January wore on, the bay ice deteriorated, cracking extensively and turning into a jigsaw puzzle of floes, some so small they wobbled and even sank under the dog teams. One ice cake tilted and dunked a handler, who had to be fished out by his buddy. Dogs began regularly falling through snow bridges into cracks and holes.

On 24 January, driver Jack Bursey's huskies made it over one snow-covered hole, but the heavily laden sledge started to sink. They pulled until the front edge of the sledge was over the lip of the hole, but the rear kept sinking. Bursey quickly grabbed the gang line and stopped the descent, but he and his struggling team could not haul the sledge all the way out. He yelled to his companion team; his buddy, then fifty yards away, turned around and looked but, not realizing the danger, kept going. The lookout in the crow's nest saw what happened and raised an alarm. Several men raced out and tugged the sledge back on the ice.

Bursey, twenty-four, a short, wiry Canadian, grew up in a small, snowy Newfoundland village whose inhabitants drove dog teams as people elsewhere drove horses and autos. His trail companion on the Bay of Whales, handsome Quin Blackburn, twenty-nine, earned the unwelcome distinction of being the first expedition member disciplined by Byrd. Siple said the commander was sore at Blackburn for failing to stop when his buddy got in trouble. This infraction followed one on the day before, when Gould had scolded Blackburn for traveling alone. Byrd relieved the driver of his team for several days.[19]

It was an unlucky day for Blackburn, a mountain climber and geology student who worked as a surveyor, his main job with Byrd. After Blackburn gave up his dogs, he joined the crew handling cargo in the ship's hold. A gas drum toppled off a stack and fell onto him and Joe Rucker, one of the movie photographers, knocking out one of Rucker's teeth and crushing the muscles in Blackburn's left calf, an injury that would keep him off his feet for quite a while.[20]

The *Bolling* arrived three days later, flying the U.S. Mail flag (Captains Brown and Melville had received official appointments as postmasters) and bringing welcome friends, supplies, and letters.[21] Her safe passage through the ice ended the worrisome possibility that the expedition might end up ill-equipped and stunted. After handshakes and exchanges of greetings and news, Byrd had the steamer shear away 150 yards of weakened sea ice with her sharp prow, putting her within fifty feet of the low barrier section he had scouted out in the launch.

A gang erected a block and tackle on the sea ice, operated by cables from a winch on the *Bolling*, and hurriedly began transferring cargo from the ship to the sea ice and then to the top of the barrier, where the men could safely pile the supplies and not have to gear the pace of unloading to the much slower cadence of the dog teams' arrivals and departures. This procedure also got the expedition closer than ever—five trail miles—to Little America.

Byrd set one week as the target period for unloading the *Bolling* and getting her on her way, figuring the unloading could take no longer if she was to have a chance at making another trip down. Almost all other work stopped—including unloading the *New York* and sledging—so as many hands as possible could pitch into the *Bolling*. The commander himself lugged cargo.[22] They worked in two "6 to 6" shifts, creating a bustling waterfront in miniature.

In the haste, the dockworkers let a spare airplane ski slip into the ocean and dropped the crate containing the Fokker onto the ice "with an awful crash," as a witness described it, splitting the crate and slightly damaging the plane's rudder. The commander, according to one of the hands, was understandably quite perturbed. But Byrd knew he would have to deal with these exigencies throughout the expedition. It was in the nature of a polar expedition always to teeter between haste and care, danger and safety.[23]

On 29 January, just as the men unloaded the center section of the Ford plane onto the sea ice, a crack appeared in the ice next to the barrier and parallel to the ship. The dockworkers had no sooner noticed the crack than it ripped wide open, and the shock of separation split the ice platform into three floes that started to drift slowly apart. Though the floes were fortunately large enough to support men and cargo, they were wobbling. The polar flight plane, the keystone of the expedition and of Byrd's career, was in real danger of sliding off and disappearing forever.[24] Working frantically, tearing wood from crates and planking the gaps between the ice cakes, the crew slid the endangered pieces of cargo from floe to floe and yanked them back onto the ship or up onto the barrier, saving the Ford's fuselage and most of the supplies that had been beside it.

Stunned, but having to push on, Byrd resourcefully anchored the *Bolling* to the face of the low barrier, starboard side to the ice wall, and on her port tied the *New York*, so that the *Bolling* was sandwiched between the barrier and her sister ship. Working the block and tackle as fast as possible to hoist cargo to the barrier's surface from starboard, meanwhile discharging other cargo onto the *New York* from port, the men hastened to get the *Bolling* on her way. Their worry about the stability of the ice-and-snow cliff that loomed over them stimulated them to new records in the unloading.

The next evening, when Byrd was working in his cabin on the *New York*, he heard a loud crashing sound and at the same time was almost thrown to the deck by a tremendous jolt to the ship. Scampering topside, he saw that a huge hunk of the barrier had just toppled onto the *Bolling*. He watched in horror as the ship started to roll over under the mountainous weight. Her keel was just about to clear the surface when the hawsers tieing her to the *New York* stopped the roll and she came back up. Anxiously peering into the sea, he saw mechanic Benny Roth desperately clawing at ice cakes and struggling to stay afloat in the icy water. Byrd knew the twenty-nine-degree salt water could freeze a person to death in minutes. When Roth yelled, "I can't swim!"

Byrd, running alongside the rail to get closer to the mechanic, shouted back, "Hang on, Roth, old fellow, I'm coming after you." Others grabbed Byrd to stop him from jumping in and let him go only when he said he would not jump. He immediately sprang over to the *Bolling* and dived off her stern.[25]

Shropshire leaped in to help Byrd. As they attempted to make their way to Roth through the floes and bergs, someone jumped in with a plank that he paddled as a surfboard. At the same time, the chief of the radio unit, Malcolm Hanson, lowered a dinghy into the water, but so many other would-be rescuers piled in with him that he had to jump overboard to leave room for the victim. The boat got to Roth first, and he and the four others in the numbing brine were plucked to safety.[26]

Everyone's attention then turned to assistant meteorologist Henry Harrison, who was dangling in the air from a rope held by a couple of men on the barrier. He and Roth had been standing on the barrier where it cracked, and Harrison had landed on a ledge near the bottom. Companions had thrown him a rope but could not haul him all the way up. Others rushed to help and together they pulled him to safety.[27]

Miraculously, no one had been killed or even seriously hurt in the accident or the circus that followed. The ships reberthed on sea ice. Roth, thirty-six, a sergeant in the army, was the expedition's shortest man—five foot three. The commander had added Roth after the late acquisition of the General Aircraft plane, when Byrd asked the army to lend him a mechanic; Byrd had gained needed expertise as well as potentially helpful army involvement in his enterprise. Balchen characterized Roth at a "typical sergeant, kind of tough and hard-bitten." Harrison, twenty-four, a hawk-faced aerologist, worked for the U.S. Weather Bureau, which had recommended him to Byrd.[28]

The icy water had treated Byrd the worst of all. The others had had on several layers of cold-weather clothing, which at least kept the water close to their skin above freezing, but Byrd had been wearing only thin indoor garments. His legs showed the white of frostbite. Lacking rubbing alcohol, Owen massaged Byrd with brandy for half an hour till his circulation was restored and he felt warm again.[29]

Byrd's bravery once again showed his priorities. His protectiveness toward men in his charge had twice before sparked him to leap into the ocean fully clothed after them, during his Caribbean cruise after graduation from Annapolis. Congress had awarded him a silver life-saving medal for his bravery. Once, in Washington, D.C., he had been near a theater when its roof collapsed and had risked his life helping to rescue people from the still-falling debris; the navy cited him for extraordinary heroism. Even when his precious Ford's fuselage was teetering on the floe, he showed more concern for the safety of his men than for the fate of his expedition.[30] The safety of others always came first, even when he had to put his own life or fortunes at risk.

On 2 February, the *Bolling* and a crew of twenty pushed off for New Zealand with everyone wishing for, but not counting on, her return in a month, before winter arrived. At least one unlucky man who had thought he would stay was leaving; a factor in his assignment to the *Bolling* seemed to be that he fell into Byrd's bad graces for singing a song, "Ol' man Brophy," that made fun of the feckless Dick Brophy, whom the men regarded as a "nut."[31]

Although the commander could not stand for such divisive behavior, he clearly had to do something about Brophy. Radio messages from the man in New Zealand became increasingly long, confused, and querulous, and he often asked Byrd for decisions on the simplest matters. Brophy sent strange replies to requests: when Byrd radioed to send butter via the *Bolling*, Brophy said to use seal blubber instead; when asked for toilet paper, he answered, "Use wall paper." Byrd discovered that Brophy had spent a staggering amount of money on personal expenses; the loss of the money was bad enough, but news of the misappropriation would cause a public relations disaster if found out.[32] The commander could not allow the situation to deteriorate much more. Regretfully, he began to look for someone to take Brophy's place in New Zealand as a key link to the outside world, a search difficult to conduct from an ocean away. But Byrd did not immediately fire Brophy. The blow might be devastating to the unstable aide, who could precipitate the public relations problems Byrd wanted to avoid. There was no telling how much damage Brophy could do to the expedition if he were angry enough to retaliate.

To speed the provisioning of Little America, the odd snowmobile— the car with skis in place of front wheels—was added to the transport team, the first successful use of an automobile in antarctic exploration. The black hybrid vehicle, motor chugging and exhaust pipe fuming, did the work of several dog teams in dragging sledges from the cache on the barrier across the relatively smooth surface to the base construction site.[33] As efficient as it was ugly, the snowmobile left little doubt that its successors would replace the husky in moving men and supplies over the snow.

At the construction area, twenty-five men were steadily erecting the town of Little America. The site, at a vertex of a triangular basin much lower than its surroundings, was thought to be a new section of the barrier that was forming as decades of snow built up over semi-permanent sea ice. Construction foreman Larry Gould was not entirely happy about settling over the ocean on transitory ice. Little America would definitely break away from the barrier some day, and float off as an iceberg—the explorers were gambling that that calving would not happen any time soon. Gould confessed, "I must admit I'm a little nervous about the stability of Little America. Will it remain stable and stationary here the next two years?"[34] Little Americans were like people who live beside a volcano, always fearing the natural catastrophe that would send them fleeing—except that in Antarctica there was no inhabitable place to flee to.

For protection against the fierce winds and the driving snow the men expected, especially in winter, Gould's crew dug excavations five feet deep for the buildings. The snow was all crust, a hard, granular type called névé, with a consistency like loaf sugar. The men found névé as easy to walk on as concrete but unfortunately just about as backbreaking to dig into. Storms discouraged digging: the clouds dropped not light, fluffy flakes but small, dry pellets called graupel, almost like hail, that stung like windblown sand during blizzards. The dense snow repeatedly refilled the excavations, forcing the ditchdiggers to start over again.[35]

Byrd made one of his few trips from the ship to look over the site just after the gang had gouged out the excavation for one of the main structures, the administration building, adjacent to the first finished building, the mess hall. Although he had planned to group all the buildings together, he now had second thoughts because of the danger of fire. He also thought the buildings too near the edge of the barrier. He ordered the laborers to carve out a new excavation farther away and dig a tunnel to connect the buildings, wringing groans from the weary men—it "seems unnecessary," one said—and making Larry Gould angry. The total volume of shoveled snow was later calculated to be equivalent to a cube that was longer than a football field on each side and that weighed 2½ million pounds.[36]

Gould was also displeased with the prefabricated buildings, designed without nails or outside bolts that would create heat-draining cold spots. He pointed out to Byrd that the designer had not taken into account the difficulties of putting the cumbersome structures together in the cold and wind of Antarctica, making construction far more troublesome and time-consuming than it had to be. Perhaps to show his concern and head off a potential morale problem, Byrd spent an entire day laboring alongside the men to put up the administration building.[37]

During the infrequent extended breaks from their toil, mostly when they had to wait out storms, the men had a few drinks from the liquor they had bought in New Zealand. America's prohibition laws did not extend to her little namesake, and the executive officer showed himself no more of a teetotaler than the commander, passing around pints of rum and gin. Davies got drunk during one lull, taking off his clothes, jumping up on the big mess table, and entertaining the bunch like a stripper on a barroom runway.[38] With barrels of "medicinal alcohol" waiting to be dispensed, Little America was clearly not to be a dry town.

On 21 February, the sun dodged briefly below the horizon at midnight, signaling the beginning of a two-month-long dusk. The next day Byrd and Gould had to carry out one of their more disagreeable tasks. It was time to cut the squad, for the *New York* would leave that day. Of the sixty-two men there, close to half knew whether they were staying or going—they had virtually indispensable roles at Little America or on the *New York*. The others, who longed to remain, had suffered in anguish during the final days of unloading.[39] The men had sweated in the Battle of New York City, made plans to winter over, endured the hardships of voyaging to the ice and building Little America, and faced down the perils of sea and ice. These men had all sacrificed a substantial part of their lives for Byrd and science. Now, with most of the expeditions's prizes still to be claimed, twenty men— one out of every three—had to leave.

A few of the crew were lazy, untrustworthy, selfish, or incompetent—clearly unsuitable. Some just rubbed others the wrong way, ordinarily a tolerable deficiency but a serious problem in a closely confined group. Some could well have stayed, but Byrd felt they were more useful on the ship or judged that others were better suited or had more desirable skills.

The most notable cut from the wintering team was Lieutenant

Ralph Shropshire, twenty-eight, the hydrographer who had been close to Byrd during the New York phase, principally in coordinating scientific preparations, and who had charted depths in the Southern Ocean from the *New York*. Shropshire had turned out to be unreliable, in the judgments of both Byrd and Gould, and widely unpopular.[40]

Some of those called aside to get the word broke down and cried. A few were bitter, like Sydney Greason, who had been in charge of food supplies and was the cook at Little America during construction but who had lost the job as wintering cook. Byrd told Railey that Greason had gone "completely to pieces in New Zealand from drink." Greason blamed those who had brought the reports on him to Byrd: "I got it in the neck good and plenty. . . . I never in my life saw such a bunch of double-crossers. I never did 'back slap' and carry stories."[41] Byrd had to tell Bill Gavronski, the former stowaway, that the expedition's sufferance did not extend to wintering over.

Byrd had originally put twenty-three names on his list of those to board the *New York*, but at the last minute notified three happy souls that they could stay after all—Blackburn, still gimpy from the falling gas drum, and roustabouts Jim Feury and Claire Alexander.[42]

Since the beginning of the expedition, Byrd had also intended to send back one more person—the Boy Scout who had won the trip to Antarctica. Paul Siple was a favorite of the news media; the story of an extraordinarily brave and lucky boy was a natural. A typical item, in a Philadelphia paper, gushed, "It is unthinkable that a lad who possesses fifty-six scout merit badges could be found wanting in any situation whatsoever. . . ."[43] Since the scout was so much in the spotlight, Byrd feared the public relations consequences of Siple's getting so much as a scratch. The media would be just as glad to editorialize about Byrd's irresponsibility in needlessly placing a boy in jeopardy.

To the men on the expedition, however, the public's image of Siple was a laugh. It was true that he was a good scout, and he had been one of the few in the *New York*'s company to get a good rating from Captain Melville. He was no boy, however, but a twenty-year old, six-foot-one, 165-pound assistant scoutmaster about to enter his sophomore year in college. A couple of sailors on Byrd's ships were younger than Siple. He had learned to handle a dog team, driving on the supply run. One of the biggest men on the expedition, Siple almost regretted Melville's praise, thinking it might reflect on his manhood.[44]

Siple yearned to stay at least as much as everybody else and worked on Byrd and Gould to persuade them he was worth a chance. He was not absolutely sure he had won until the cut was over and he had survived. Siple had so impressed Gould that the chief scientist had gotten Byrd to keep the scout on as zoologist and taxidermist, based on his relevant merit-badge experience and education as a biology major in college. Siple would mainly collect skins of seals and of penguins and other birds for the American Museum of Natural History, a time-consuming project that Gould, the person originally responsible for the task but now burdened by new executive duties, said he no longer had the time or inclination to take up. The scout would also help to butcher seals for the hundred tons of native meat to feed men and dogs over the winter.[45]

Little Americans lined the sea ice, happy to be there but pensive, too—saddened at having to say good-bye to friends, at least until many of them returned with the ships next season. Having written off a return by the *Bolling*, the men were disquieted by the realization that the *New York*'s withdrawal irretrievably cut them off from civilization for the next year. The nearest settlement was as far from them as Los Angeles is from New York. Those who were now outsiders lined the rail of the ship, looking out toward the pristine land and its people and, we can imagine, thinking wistfully of lost opportunity. The men ashore raised three cheers for those departing, who responded with three cheers for those remaining.[46] Gangplanks were raised, men waved and saluted, and soon all that could be seen where the *New York* had been was the swell in her empty berth. As she sailed north, those who had survived the cut skied or sledged their way south to the only dwellings on the entire continent.

Far out in the Pacific, the *Bolling* was steaming south toward the thickening ice pack, her crew members determined to force her brittle, tin-can hull through the Bay of Whales to surprise their doubting comrades. Meanwhile, however, a tragedy was occurring on board the little ship. Dick Brophy was among the crew, Byrd having assented to the former exec's pleas to see Antarctica, but Brophy's mind had completely snapped. He managed to radio messages to the *New York Times*, claiming first that he was saving Byrd's expedition and then that he was taking over the *Bolling* and would sail it to Discovery Inlet to conduct an expedition of his own.[47] The *Times* ignored the messages. There is no known record of how Captain Brown handled the situation, but Brophy's tragic breakdown had no effect on the voyage. As sorry as Byrd was, he could be thankful that the mental problems had surfaced early, before Brophy was included in the wintering-over party and placed in a position to make pivotal decisions.

Bad news from the whaling ships and the *New York* revealed worse problems for the *Bolling*. Whalers who had just crossed the pack on their way home radioed that the ice was becoming impenetrable. The *New York* reported that ice forming in the Ross Sea already made sailing extremely difficult. Accepting the inevitable, Byrd ordered the *Bolling* not to attempt the ice but to accompany the *New York* back to New Zealand. Giving up, however wise, disappointed the *Bolling*'s crewmen, who hankered to chance the freezing seas, and doused whatever hope remained at Little America for supplies to make life more comfortable, secure, and productive: the fourth plane, several motorized vehicles, four houses, and extra food, fuel, scientific supplies, and other materiel. The new Wright engine mechanic and the extra dog handler and his animals were also on the ship.

The *New York* reached the all-but-solid ice pack short of coal, having used up more than expected fighting her way across the Ross Sea. Byrd asked the *Larsen*'s Captain Nilsen for a chaser to reenter the pack, locate and recoal the *New York*, and assist her to safety. Nilsen, as helpful as ever, replied that he would give aid but said the weather was so bad he would probably have to take the men off the *New York* and abandon her.[48] The news was devastating. The *New York* was half of Byrd's fleet and the expedition's only sure way of getting out of the antarctic the following year, and Byrd planned to sell her eventually to reduce his debt. But there was nothing he could do now to help her.

The *Larsen* herself and two chasers went after Byrd's ship on 25 February. Two days later a chaser from the *Larsen* was reported sunk, but it was not clear if the lost chaser was one of those involved in helping the Americans. On 28 February the *Larsen* reached the *New York*, and providentially, the weather had changed for the better. The whaler was able to transfer coal and food to the *New York* and help her through the pack and out of danger. Byrd must have wished he could get out of every jam just as easily.[49]

On the barrier, men were still hauling supplies from the seemingly inexhaustible cache to Little America. Storms and drift had buried the crates in snow, so in a kind of crazy, dreary Easter egg hunt, the men had first to locate the supplies by poking the surface with crowbars, then to shovel the crates out. On 4 March, as a blizzard raged, two dog drivers returned from a supply run and expressed alarm at not finding Blackburn at camp. He had been driving with them—his first trip since he had been suspended for disobedience. The drivers recounted that he had not been able to stop his headstrong dogs from plunging ahead out of sight when his companion teams halted on the trail. Byrd figured Blackburn had gotten lost in the blinding storm and was waiting it out somewhere; one of the others had also been lost briefly in the blizzard.[50] All the drivers had been instructed what to do in such a situation.

One of the camp's characters, Blackburn was known for his awkwardness in movement and speech. A 220-pounder, he walked with a lurching gait, frequently bumping into anything or anyone in his path. He spoke in a heavy, drawling voice, using big words whenever he could. People quipped that three languages were spoken at Little America: English, Norwegian, and Blackburnian. Byrd once took Blackburn aside and counseled him to express himself simply.[51]

The commander was not too concerned about Blackburn's disappearance until learning that he had ignored another rule, that all sledges had to have sleeping bags that would keep a man warm throughout a long storm. Byrd immediately pulled together a search party and went out to look for the dog driver, carefully flagging the trail so he could find his own way back. He returned after three fruitless hours of playing a deadly serious game of blindman's buff in the opaque storm. Now much worried, he organized several rescue groups. Not long after setting out, one of them happily found Blackburn and his dogs cozily dug into the snow a half mile from headquarters. The immediate aftermath is not recorded, but Blackburn may have wished he had not been found. Byrd must have had a little talk with the member who was thrice miscreant and barely made the roster. Probably Gould did, too; after Blackburn's last trespass, the executive officer had personally ordered all the drivers to stay together. The next day the errant driver was kicked off the sledge squad for good.[52]

Three days later, after a two-week delay because of bad weather, six bustling men got ready for a week's round-trip due south with four dog teams to lay the first two and possibly three depots for the next spring's polar flight. Byrd's idea was to place caches, primarily of food and fuel, every twenty miles along the route to the pole up to the Queen Maud Mountains bordering the barrier four hundred miles south, a distance that was halfway to the pole. The depots would serve as way stations in case the planes were damaged or grounded and the crews had to walk or sledge back to Little America. Marked with brilliant red-orange flags, the depots would also guide the Ford toward the South Pole and eliminate the need for aerial navigation with its possibilities for error until the plane crossed the Queen Mauds. Byrd reasoned that the exercise in depot laying, besides giving him a head start next season, would imbue the sledge teams with invaluable experience in long-distance trekking over the barrier. Besides, without the fuel drums now headed north on the *Bolling*, the expedition was short of aviation gas. Using dogs instead of planes to lay the bases would conserve fuel.

The four drivers were Bursey and a highly publicized group known as the Three Musketeers. Friends at Harvard, they came from Boston-area families: Norm Vaughan, twenty-three; Eddie Goodale, twenty-five; and Freddie Crockett, twenty-one. The leader of the party, Vaughan, a Harvard football player, had gotten his buddies together and volunteered their services as a group. All three men had sailed extensively, and Vaughan and Goodale had previous sledging experience, including service in Labrador with the renowned medical missionary Sir Wilfred Grenfell, who was Bursey's friend as it happened. Walden had agreed to take the Three Musketeers on as the core of the dog-driving cadre soon after he was engaged by Byrd, reasoning that they would take orders more readily and be less likely to stab the chief in the back than hard-bitten dog-punching veterans.[53] They had spent the 1927–28 winter at Walden's dog-breeding farm in New Hampshire, testing trail gear and training.

The other two in the party were navigator Joe De Ganahl and radioman Carl Petersen. De Ganahl, twenty-six, was one of those who had jumped in the water to save Roth when the barrier face collapsed. A native of Mexico, he was the son of wealthy parents who were forced out by the 1913 revolution and who moved to New York City when he was eleven. He also had graduated from Harvard—as had Dr. Coman, the expedition's physician—and had worked as a newspaper reporter. Although a qualified pilot and navigator, and a naval air reservist, he had signed on as a general hand. His parents had contributed $25,000 to Byrd's purse. Like countless others who had ever had to meet a sailing date and leave their loved ones, De Ganahl had found it painful to separate from his wife and family, especially since his year-old son was in the hospital with mastoiditis. Petersen, thirty-one, a tall, blond, owl-faced Norwegian who had emigrated to Chicago and taken out citizenship papers, was a sergeant in the army air corps. He had operated radios for a Norwegian whaler and for Amundsen at Spitsbergen where, like Balchen, Petersen had first offered his services to Byrd.[54]

Curiously, Walden, the head of the dog unit, did not go. No one had said publicly that anything was wrong, but his absence may have signified a leadership problem. The crusty old musher was not getting along with either Byrd or young Vaughan, and Walden and Byrd had little to do with one another. Exactly what Byrd had against Walden is not known, but in a letter to Marie from New Zealand, the commander had implied that the crisis over the dog food on board ship was part of the problem: "Walden has completely fallen down. His dogs have been ill ever since leaving the states. I have had to take very vigorous steps." In a radiogram to Byrd, Brophy had once reminded the commander that Walden had "completely fizzled." In a message to Brophy, Byrd had mentioned that "Walden's promiscuous giving away of dogs" left the expedition short of husky power.[55]

Vaughan had treated Walden badly, the veteran musher told Demas. Vaughan referred derisively in his diary to Walden, seeming to regard him as a cantankerous old man. Feelings between them got so bad that Walden threatened to kill Vaughan, and for several nights a fearful Vaughan took his sleeping bag to a secret location to hide out while he slept.[56] Part of the problem may have been that Walden, a lifelong loner, had difficulty adapting to an executive role in the organization.

At 3:00 P.M. on 7 March, most of the Antarcticans gathered together and gave a rousing send-off to the sledge teams. The sledgers were the most romantic figures on the expedition, conjuring images of Jack London's stories.

Nine days later the sledgers came clomping back into camp, cold, windburned, and tired. Their tale was one to excite and caution the other men. Afraid of tumbling into one of the hidden crevasses not far from Little America, the trailblazers told that they had roped up together like mountain climbers for the second day; one might drop through a bridged-over crevasse, but the others would hold him. Traveling in temperatures around twenty below, the team reached the twenty-mile point—indicated by a mileage wheel attached to a sledge—and put down the first depot that afternoon. Shortly after, a fierce blizzard pinned them in their tiny tents for a day and a half, the thin canvas fabric assaulted by winds of sixty miles per hour. "The tent rattled so violently we thought it would blow away. . . . We crawled into our sleeping bags and, as we listened to the howling of the wind and the beating of the snow on the canvas, a realization of our isolation oppressed us," Bursey related. The team established two depots and tried for three but ran out of the essential marker flags four miles from the second depot, so Vaughan radioed Byrd for instructions.[57] The commander suggested that the men carve out blocks of snow and pile them up every two or three miles as markers but let Vaughan use his own judgment. Because of the snowy weather and the long time needed to make the snow beacons, Vaughan decided to cache the remaining supplies right there, at the forty-four-mile point. Pushing it, the sledgers made the long run back home in one day.

Siple recorded in his diary the next day that Byrd and Owen argued over how much the *New York Times*'s story should praise the depot team—but the scout neglected to mention who wanted the report toned down. It was probably Byrd. The *Times* carried little about the adventure, yet it was a natural newspaper story. Demas told his diary, without stating the basis for the declaration, that Vaughan had been a failure as leader of the trail team.[58] Byrd had never stated how far he originally wanted to lay depots before winter, but he seemed to have wanted bases laid a substantial distance toward the pole. Amundsen, for example, had gone about 230 miles shortly after he arrived. The late arrival, the unexpectedly long unloading period, and the bad weather had thwarted Byrd's desires. Then Vaughan's team could not reach the wished-for sixty miles. Byrd had to hope that the dog units could get an early start the next summer.

Most of the first summer's goals for land operations had been reached—a site found, the ships unloaded and sent back, the camp built. The cancellation of the *Bolling*'s second trip and the limited depot-laying had been the chief disappointments. This was the first antarctic expedition to conduct air operations, however, and the greatest challenges were in the sky.

.6.

Beyond the Barrier

CRATES with parts for the Fairchild airplane had been unloaded on 12 January and pried open beside the *New York*. Three days later, the thirty-three-foot-long ski plane stood complete on the bay ice. The plane had a narrow black fuselage, red-orange wings on top spanning fifty feet, and big windows and ports for photography.[1] There was a seat for the pilot only, and his shoulders almost touched both sides of the cockpit. Passengers had to sit on the floor behind him. In large letters covering the rear fuselage was the legend "Byrd Antarctic Expedition," which had advertised the venture in every photo of the plane. On the nose, just behind the engine, was the name Byrd had given the aircraft, possibly anticipating that it would be the first to fly over Little America: *Stars & Stripes*.

On 15 January Byrd's aviation expedition was ready to take to the antarctic skies for the first time. When the Fairchild's single 425-horsepower Pratt & Whitney Wasp Jr. engine throbbed, it matched the nervous heartbeats of those about to fly her.

Byrd gave Parker the honor of being first up, possibly because he was least likely to be chosen for the polar mission. The aviation mechanics had cut cards to determine who would accompany him, and Roth had won. Demas noted in his diary that Byrd got sore because

Roth was taking the first ride when Demas and the third mechanic, Ken Bubier, twenty-five, a tall, skinny marine sergeant, had fought the Battle of New York City, while Roth had joined the expedition only shortly before departure. Demas said the commander promised that the *New York Times*'s story about the first flight would say that Demas had made the trip. (Owen managed to report Roth as the first passenger, however. But in a magazine article bylined by Byrd immediately after the expedition he wrote: ". . . The mechanics cut for the first flight. Bubier and Demas won. It was the least I could do to honor these men. . . .")[2] Byrd seemed to view media reports not necessarily as strictly accurate accounts but rather as tools to help him run the expedition and control his image.

With Byrd watching intently, Parker revved up the engine, and the plane slid along the ice, her skis chattering as she picked up speed. She accelerated for fifteen seconds then took off, climbing and circling. The joyful pilot and passenger took in the whole panorama of the current phase of operations, lit brightly in the glare of the harsh polar sun and the unparalleled clarity of the antarctic air. The wide, shallow slice in the barrier that was the Bay of Whales was filled with sea ice at the point and indolent seals slept beside holes in the ice. The *New York* was anchored along the line dividing the black sea from white Antarctica, and the dockside was messy with supplies and dirty snow. Dog teams moved along the trail, and men were still building the compound at Little America. Cloud shadows dappled the smooth, milky barrier that seemed to extend to infinity. After an all-too-brief flight, Parker and Roth landed and taxied back to the ship.

The other three pilots and two mechanics went up on equally short trial flights. Byrd reserved the expedition's first tentative attempt at aerial exploration for himself and two of the pilots, one serving as radioman. They crowded in and soared off to survey the area around the Bay of Whales. Hulking at the controls was big Dean Smith, twenty-nine, whose six-foot-three, 180-pound frame was enlarged by his bulky parka. He had been a pilot for the air corps, for the air mail service, and for United Airlines. Byrd had wanted a pilot with cross-country, all-weather experience and asked the National Air Pilot's Association to submit three candidates from the airmail routes. Byrd, displaying the respect for motherhood required of heroes, said one reason he picked Smith was that "when I met his mother, I knew he must have good stuff in him."[3]

Tucked in with the survival gear crammed behind Smith in the tiny cabin were Byrd and heavyset, brown-haired Harold June, thirty-three. He had been chief engineer for Harold Vanderbilt's yachts, entered the navy in the great war, and trained as a pilot, mechanic, and radioman. He stayed in the navy as a chief machinist's mate after the war and took part in the aerial mapping of the Venezuelan coastline.[4]

June had come to an interesting understanding with Byrd. At first, all four highly skilled aviators had wanted to fly as lead pilot on the major flights; in particular, each of them yearned for the glory of piloting the first plane to the South Pole. June had soon volunteered to drop entirely out of the competition. He would not fly as first pilot on any trip, but he would go as copilot and radioman on all trips. Since this arrangement gave Byrd the benefit of June's many talents while simplifying the rivalry, the commander was delighted. June traded off a chance at prime honors for the assurance of adventure and minor recognition.[5]

Byrd, Smith, and June flew over several unmapped features. On this pioneering flight, Byrd honored the transatlantic air pioneers by naming two discoveries Lindbergh Inlet and Chamberlin Harbor. He had already named the inlet leading to Little America after the French town of Ver-Sur-Mer, where he had ditched after crossing the Atlantic. All these features would disappear over the years as the sides of the barrier calved off; Byrd saved more permanent honors for his high-paying sponsors.

Halfway back to the ship, the first in-the-air crisis sprang up: the engine suddenly stopped dead, and the plane dove. As Byrd later recalled, Smith jerked at the unresponsive throttle while steering the lifeless aircraft into a long glide. Byrd glanced at the rough ice below and could not see any place to set the plane down safely. Guessing that a wing tank had run dry, Smith fiddled with a valve. The engine restarted, its deafening roar sounding like sweet music.

The adrenaline had barely stopped flowing, however, when the crew plunged into the second aerial crisis. They spied the ship up ahead but could not see the landing area because it was covered with the drifting haze or ground fog called sea smoke. With no place assuredly better to land and no gas to fly around, Smith descended toward the obscuring smoke, watching the sea surface as long as he could to judge the height of the unseen bay ice. In the haze, at what he felt was just the right moment, he leveled off—and brought the plane to a near-perfect landing. This eventful flight confirmed the precarious state of aviation in Antarctica and showed that good pilots, able to keep their heads in the face of death, were invaluable there.

A few days later, on a flight over Little America to test the aircraft's radio equipment, the radio operator established a new wireless record—the longest two-way direct communication from an aircraft, in an exchange with the *New York Times*'s radio room.[6] The feat gave Byrd reason to hope that radio might help him more than he had figured.

Wilkins had stopped pressing Byrd, at least for the time being, giving up for the year and pulling out of Antarctica, having accomplished little after the first flight.[7] He had not flown over the territory east of Little America that Byrd planned to explore, but Byrd itched to fly into the unknown territory anyway. He presumably wanted to get there as soon as possible to be sure of beating the tenacious Wilkins or anyone else who might come down next summer.

On 27 January, Bill "Cyclone" Haines, head of Byrd's meteorological unit, predicted good flying weather for the rest of the day over the Bay of Whales and the region to the east. A short, stocky, round-faced Ohioan who spoke with a heavy midwestern twang, Haines, forty-one, was chief of the weather bureau at the Washington, D.C., airport. Although Haines was not a college graduate, Balchen admired his abilities as a "very good mathematician and theoretician."[8]

Byrd jumped at the chance to explore and tapped Balchen to pilot a flight. Stocky, blond Balchen, twenty-eight, was head of the aviation unit. Exceptional gifts and experience made him almost ideally suited for the expedition. The son of a surgeon, he had the blood of polar explorers. An uncle had crossed the Greenland ice cap, and a cousin was the pilot who perished with Amundsen in the attempt to rescue Nobile. Balchen had earned an engineering degree and also won his way to the top of Norway's amateur athletic ranks as a middleweight boxing champ and international ski racer. He exhibited herculean strength. Smith, no weakling, told that when he and several others tried to lift an awkwardly shaped barrel weighing five or six hundred pounds during the loading of the ships, Balchen yelled, "Stand clear!" and, putting his arms around the barrel, lifted it himself.[9]

A flight lieutenant in the Royal Norwegian Naval Air Force, Balchen went on two arctic expeditions with Amundsen, including the north polar dirigible flight from Spitsbergen, where Balchen met Byrd. Before Byrd took off to beat the Norwegians to the North Pole, Balchen gave the American invaluable advice and assistance, to the extent that some of Balchen's colleagues shunned him. He wanted to go to the United States, where he had friends and relatives, and Byrd agreed to take the Norwegian on the return voyage. Balchen got a job as engineer and test pilot at Fokker's New Jersey operation, took out citizenship papers, and became a captain in the U.S. Army Air Corps reserves.[10]

As Balchen readied the Fairchild, designed for aerial photography, the commander told a downcast McKinley that he would not go because he and his heavy aerial camera would overload the plane and shorten its range on this probing mission. At nearly 3:00 P.M., with June and Byrd stuffed behind the pilot as in the earlier flight, the plane took off from the runway that had just been graded at Little America, climbing to three thousand feet and heading east.[11]

The radio operators on the *New York* monitored the continuous signal sent by the plane's tied-down telegraph key. Two hours after takeoff the signals stopped. Anxiously, a messenger ran to tell Gould that the plane might have crashed. Four minutes later the signals resumed.[12]

Except for the temporary radio malfunction, all was fine on board the Fairchild. About an hour into the flight, the crew had observed a large indentation in the barrier that Byrd named Hal Flood Bay after an uncle. A little while after, as Byrd later described the scene, "I saw many miles to the right a few black peaks protruding from the snow, and beyond them a single peak which invited speculation."[13] He decided to investigate the peak later.

Some two hundred miles from the Bay of Whales, the crew passed over a group of short mountains whose tops barely peeked above the snow, reaching only about half as high as the low-flying plane. This group was the easterly mountains that Scott had discovered, which marked an area he called King Edward VII Land. Shortly the men caught up to a snow squall traveling east more slowly than they, and so they turned back. After a little while, Byrd told Balchen to fly south toward the peak they had seen earlier.

As Byrd recounted, "Balchen suddenly turned and beckoned to me to come forward. I looked out over the nose of the ship, through the shimmering play of the propeller. Far ahead, but perfectly distinct, was a splendid mountain peak with the slate gray of bare rock showing.

Then as we advanced a second peak, then a third, and more lifted their summits above the southern horizon until we had counted fourteen. They lay in the shape of a crescent. This was our first important discovery. I had never seen Balchen so delighted. His splendid face was one long smile. . . . Here was something to put on maps."[14] Byrd was matter-of-fact in describing his own reactions, but he must have felt elated. The discovery fulfilled at least partly his aims for aviation, geography, and his own fame. His mood was tempered by the mountains' lying within the area claimed by Britain, and so the land could not be annexed to the United States.

Turning serious, his smile gone, Balchen wrote a note and gave it to Byrd—they could not hear over the roar of the motor—saying that gas was getting low. They had to return.

As Byrd later wrote for the public, he thought on the way back about what to name the mountains. John D. Rockefeller, Jr., came to mind, he said. Paying obeisance to the oil baron, Byrd declaimed, "He stands, steady as a rock . . . and the great power he controls is directed wisely and unselfishly for the betterment of the world." Gould commented irreverently that Byrd named the discovery the Rockefeller Mountains "after the signature on the $100,000 check."[15]

Byrd planned several more excursions to the east. As he told Gould, when the *Bolling* left and things became less hectic, he intended to sail the *New York* eastward to a coastal point near the new mountains to lay supplies and gasoline for a subbase and aircraft-refueling cache that would support longer easterly flights.[16] Gould was keen to learn how the Rockefellers related to previously discovered mountains in Antarctica and hoped to spend at least a few days exploring the new discovery before winter closed in. Mostly because of bad weather, Byrd could make only two attempts in the ship to set up the subbase, and thick sea ice prevented him from getting anywhere near the coast in that area.

By 18 February, the olive-drab Fokker monoplane brought down by the *Bolling* had been assembled and tested.[17] For her first antarctic working flight, Byrd decided to scout an easterly course for the *New York* through the sea ice and then to continue well past the Rockefellers. Bigger than the Fairchild by half, the aircraft was also powered by a single 425-horsepower Pratt & Whitney Wasp engine. Having given his first plane to fly in Antarctica a name honoring the whole

United States, Byrd, always proud of his heritage, christened the Fokker *Virginia*.

To fly the plane, the commander again picked Balchen, who as an engineer and a long-experienced pilot for Fokker was best suited to handle the aircraft. Byrd chose Lloyd Berkner to operate the radio. Berkner, twenty-four, an electrical engineer, had been working in the Airways Division of the U.S. Department of Commerce, which had transferred him to the National Bureau of Standards to prepare him to conduct research on the expedition. Representative of the modern breed of explorer, he also was a naval reserve pilot and held a commercial transport pilot's license.[18]

In case of a crash on a long flight, when it might be difficult for a rescue plane to find the downed aircraft, Byrd wanted his planes to fly in tandem when possible, with one to aid the other if necessary.[19] For this mission, he assigned Parker and June to fly alongside the Fokker in the Fairchild.

Gould hoped that he and McKinley could go with Byrd and that the commander would land the exec at the Rockefellers for some geology. Promising to let Gould have a plane when the weather was again fit, Byrd said he could not land on this flight.[20] He still felt that aerial photography would limit the Fairchild's range too much and so advised McKinley he would have to stay home again and wait for a possible flight some other time.

The plane took off at 9:00 A.M., leaving the aerial photographer standing impotent and frustrated on the ground as the photo-mapping craft took off on the third of its infrequent forays without him and his highly touted gear. McKinley soon joined the others who had gathered at Little America's radio room to follow the progress of the planes. As Smith related, McKinley, feeling ignored by the high command like specialists in many organizations, complained, "I don't understand it. Why did he bring me along if he's not going to use me? I've got thousands of dollars worth of the finest aerial mapping equipment in the world all set and ready to go. I could be making a detailed photographic record of a strip fifty miles wide along their entire flight. . . . With the kind of navigation possible in these latitudes they'll be lucky to locate any particular spot within twenty-five miles of where it actually is. I don't believe Byrd has any conception of what a mapping camera will do for him." McKinley, who was partially deaf, had been a captain in the army air corps until 1926 and had qualified to pilot balloons and dirigibles, but he had resigned to join an advertising company. He had written the textbook *Applied Aerial Photography.*[21]

Smith, discouraged that he had not made a long-distance flight (while Balchen was making his second) and afraid that he might never get an important assignment, determined to ask Byrd for permission to fly the Fairchild to Hal Flood Bay when the commander returned. Smith planned to have McKinley on board to map the face of the barrier. Expecting the commander to say no to a major flight he had not planned and was not involved in—the expedition was his show— Smith cannily gained Gould's support, reasoning that it would be hard for Byrd to turn them down in front of everybody.[22]

According to Smith, the planes again ran into snow at about the same place as on the first easterly flight, so Byrd decided to take a more detailed look at the Rockefellers. The crews found the mountains mostly hidden by clouds, however, so the commander ordered the planes to circle for home.

Byrd landed a little before 1:30 P.M., and Smith's hopeful group approached the commander with the proposal. As expected, Byrd resisted but then gave in, ordering them to fly no farther than Hal Flood Bay. Smith and McKinley, joined by Berkner, took off in the Fairchild with a spirit of victory two hours after Byrd's arrival. When they reached the bay, the clouds around the Rockefellers had dissipated, and visibility was so good that the fliers could see the mountains clearly. McKinley, making what Smith called "an extraordinary suggestion to come from the mild and conservative" photographer, proposed that the crew disobey orders and map the Rockefellers. Smith and Berkner jumped at the idea.

Smith recalled that none of them felt they had anything to lose: Smith thought he would not be flying much anyway, Berkner soon would be going back on the *New York* to New Zealand for the winter to conduct radio communications and experimental transmissions with Little America, and McKinley was irreplaceable as aerial photographer. Smith told Berkner to radio for permission to do the mapping and, if Byrd refused as expected, to report having receiver trouble. Shortly, Berkner grinned and shouted that Little America was coming through all garbled.[23]

The men flew on, McKinley happily did his job, and they were about to head back when Smith spotted a peak far away on the south-eastern horizon. They winged toward it for half an hour, gradually perceiving "a magnificent solitary Matterhorn-like mountain." Beyond, they thought they could make out a ridge of peaks disappearing over the horizon. The men were especially thrilled when they realized the location: just outside the British claim and, therefore, available to be taken by the United States. They felt "elated beyond measure . . . shouting . . . and bursting into song."[24] Low on gas, they turned back before reaching the peak and, after a flight of five and one-half hours, landed at 9:00 P.M.

Byrd had embarked on one of his easterly probes in the *New York* about the time Smith's group had taken off and did not return until the next morning. Smith described the meeting with Byrd and others for a postmortem on the flight.

> "This Matterhorn peak. . . . Where would you spot it?" Byrd asked.
> ". . . I'd put it somewhere in here," I said, drawing a circle about 30 miles in diameter on the map.
> "That's wonderful," Byrd said, speaking very seriously . . . "I congratulate you gentlemen on confirming my discovery. You have located this new land in almost exactly the place that I did when I saw it."
> "When you saw it!" exclaimed McKinley. "But you didn't say anything about it after the flight."
> "No. I wanted to be sure before I announced it," explained Byrd. "As it was so far off, and I only saw it intermittently through clouds, I decided anything so significant should have more evidence before I made my official announcement. But I did mark it on my map. Wait, I'll show you."
> Byrd got up and went into his room, closing the door behind him. We all sat mute. I caught Balchen's eye. He shrugged and rolled his eyes to the ceiling. Owen kept shaking his head gently. Gould looked amused. After about five minutes Commander Byrd returned, bearing a rolled map which he spread out on the table.
> "Here is the course of our flight," he said. . . . "And over here is where I marked the new peak."
> He showed us a heavy cross, drawn with a softer pencil than that which had been used to draw the course of the flight. . . .[25]

Smith said that, on leaving the meeting, McKinley commented, "It takes keen vision to be a great explorer. I'm afraid you and I will never be great explorers."[26]

The *New York Times*'s account of the discovery (which the paper ran at the top of page one in three columns under the triple-deck headline: "Byrd sees vast new antarctic area from his plane, claims it

for nation; names it for wife, Marie Byrd Land") is a confused narrative
that gives Byrd's side of the story:

> On the first flight [in January] he saw a mountain far to the east. On
> his next flight that way [February 18] he again saw this mountain, more
> clearly this time, and it became known as his "pet mountain" because
> of the fascination it held for him.
>
> When McKinley flew over that way . . . the visibility had improved
> so greatly that he not only saw the Commander's "pet mountain" . . .
> but also a long range to the east southeast of it which disappeared over
> the horizon.
>
> Two peaks had also been sighted due east of the Rockefeller range
> . . . peaks which were apparently as far or farther away than the new
> land to the southeast.
>
> Just before reaching Hal Flood bay . . . the Commander directed
> Balchen to turn to the southeast. They flew on this course until they
> had passed about 15 miles south of the Rockefeller range. . . . He kept
> on for some distance to the southeast. . . . Past the Rockefeller
> range, he saw the mountain he had glimpsed once before on the horizon,
> and wrote a note to Balchen: 'I think I see land to the east. Let's try.'
> They flew toward the high mountain for some time without its getting
> appreciably nearer and then turned south again. . . . The visibility . . .
> was perfect.
>
> Again Byrd turned, this time to the south, and kept on this course
> until he had penetrated more than 100 miles beyond his farthest south-
> ern point on his former flights. It was on this course that he saw the
> twin peaks far to the east and the high mountains later seen more plainly
> by the McKinley party.
>
> When the fliers turned again for home, they had penetrated so far
> to the south that another mountain range could be plainly seen far ahead
> of them, a dark streak on the horizon. This was undoubtedly the land
> faintly seen by Amundsen to the east of his polar route.

Referring to "territory which [Byrd] had declared to belong to the
United States," the story quoted him as stating, perhaps speaking
from the heart, certainly saying what his public would expect: "I have
named the land after the best sport and noblest person I
know. . . . This new land will be Marie Byrd Land."[27]

The story did not say that Byrd revealed his discovery only after
Smith's confirmation and in fact implied that the commander talked
about sighting a mountain—his "pet mountain"—before Smith's
flight.

Byrd had checked the offshore ice and weather conditions as he
flew and thought the *New York* could lay the eastern subbase, so he
sailed away in the ship soon after landing. He followed the Fairchild's

progress from the *New York*'s radio room after having readily granted permission, he said, for Smith's flight. Referring to Scott's Nunatak, a small, isolated rock outcrop near the shore east of Hal Flood Bay that the men used as a landmark, Byrd wrote, "I was rather surprised . . . when McKinley radioed a short time [after reaching Hal Flood Bay] that he had the nunatak in view, and requested permission to fly over and photograph it. I could not understand how the Fairchild had managed to cover the intervening distance in so short a time, but nevertheless gave him permission. . . . We had much fun at McKinley's expense when a message, rather humbly worded, confessed that the outcropping of rock which he had taken to be the nunatak was none other than the northernmost peak of the Rockefellers. . . ." Byrd said he soon heard that ". . . for the second time that day, the land we had discovered earlier was exposed to human gaze. . . . More than any other I might cite, the incident illustrates the great advance in modern exploration. An airplane . . . could be directed and governed by radio from a point miles away."[28]

Obviously, either Byrd or Smith told a real whopper. No one else published a description of the flights or subsequent meeting. The historical record is revealing, however. Byrd's flight was an hour less than Smith's and a half hour less than his flight three weeks before when he discovered the Rockefellers. Byrd's flight time was consistent with a flight that turned back without going beyond the Rockefellers. Upon his return, the commander had sent Marie a message that hinted nothing about a sighting: "Made another successful flight. Back OK. This is the last flight of this year so you have nothing to worry about. Much love." In the diary entry for that day, Harrison mentioned Byrd's flight but said nothing about a discovery, noting only that "low clouds forced them to turn back at 11 am." General hand Arnold Clarke, twenty-four, said in his diary that Byrd and those with him returned after "having been balked in their venture by clouds in their path." Gould wrote in his diary that Byrd had seen "nothing but white," while Smith's flight "saw a further range of mountains apparently higher and more extensive than the Rockefellers. It was claimed for the U.S. by Byrd." In a later diary entry, Gould noted that the land discovered by "the second flight" had been named Marie Byrd Land. On the day of the flights, Blackburn's diary had nothing about a discovery by Byrd. The day after, however, Blackburn noted: "Byrd announced that he himself had discovered a new range to the southeast of Scott's nunatak."[29] It was not until that second day that Owen filed his story about the discovery with the *New York Times*.

Byrd did not tell Marie about discovering land and naming it after her until three days later: "Have named a great new land after you. I have always intended to so name the biggest land we could find. Have claimed Marie Byrd land for the United States. It will, I think, be one of the biggest areas of land in the antarctic. . . . I was the first one to see the high peak of this land, and I am going to name that peak, which is a beautiful one, Helen Ames [Marie's mother]." The day after sending this radiogram, Byrd sent his wife another wire: ". . . One of the things I have most wanted to do of all was to name the biggest land after you. Take it over for the U.S. and at the same time tell the world that you are the finest person in it and deserve the credit for my accomplishments. I've done this and nothing ever pleased me so much—nothing I've done I mean. . . . I told you I'd make the world bow to you—and I'll do it again."[30]

Balchen, no braggart but not one to slight his own role in genuine accomplishments, did not even mention in the book he eventually wrote the supposed landmark flight with Byrd. Later, Balchen confirmed Smith's account.[31] No available diaries or recollections mention any such thing as Byrd's pet mountain. (Afterward, the mountain range supposedly discovered by Amundsen that had been plainly seen by Byrd on the homeward leg of his flight proved nonexistent.)

It seems beyond dispute that Smith's version is substantially correct. The question then remains whether Byrd really did see the Matterhorn on his flight. It might be expected that a questionable claim by the commander would have caused shock or at least aroused comment among the diary writers, assuming they knew all that had transpired. In fact, they write as if nothing unusual had happened. Maybe they did not know the sequence of events; when asked years later about the Matterhorn sighting, Harrison pleaded ignorance, explaining, "I was not privy to high level discussions like that." Perhaps the men did not think it mattered who saw the peak first. Perhaps they believed Byrd. It strains credibility, however, that Byrd should be the only one on the Fokker or the accompanying Fairchild to see something, or that he would not have asked someone else to take a look at the vague shape he said he saw. Smith concluded, "It was important in terms of dollars and cents to [Byrd] to concentrate the favorable attention on himself and not diffuse it among the other members of the expedition."[32]

Byrd had long intended to name new territory after Marie, honoring his beloved and following an antarctic practice of naming discoveries after wives and queens—and assuring that the name Byrd would be printed prominently on every new map of Antarctica. Christening the territory with a personal name would have been inappropriate, however, if he had had no personal role in the discovery. In Byrd's defense, he probably would have made the discovery himself on one of the easterly flights planned for later. Byrd's feelings toward Smith and the commander's need to assert himself may also have influenced his behavior. Smith, after all, had maneuvered for permission to fly—manipulation easily recognizable by the politically savvy Byrd—and then the crew had transparently disobeyed orders. Any leader who wanted to retain control of a group could not let anyone get away with that kind of challenge to command authority. In claiming credit for the discovery, Byrd characteristically chose not to pit himself directly against the challengers and possibly rend the expedition but, by depriving them of the fruits of their insubordination, to prove that defiance would not pay.

The weather was perfect for Gould's geological flight, but Byrd had changed his mind, despite having just flown himself and having recently told Gould he could fly. Byrd said he had decided it was too late in the season for the two flights that would be necessary, one to bring the scientist to the mountains and the other, perhaps many days later, to bring him out. Byrd explained that he did not want to worry about a field party that might have to hike home while he was still worrying abut the movements of the *New York* and the *Bolling* in their rush to beat winter. Clarke recorded Little America's reaction in his diary: "Well, the refusal of permission certainly affected the morale of most everyone in the camp. Gould says little, which means that he is not very pleased." Demas said that Gould was heartbroken.[33]

Perhaps Gould's support of Smith's flight influenced Byrd's decision—Smith said that Byrd had been very annoyed at Gould. The commander, however, was correct in his stated reasons for refusal. Experts agreed that antarctic weather was too dangerous for flying after mid-February. The commander took big chances when he had to, but much of his effort went into minimizing risk. He claimed the greatest difficulty he had with his men was keeping them from being reckless. Gould himself commented that Byrd's outstanding characteristic was concern for the safety of his men. As a constant reminder of the consequences of carelessness, a photo of Floyd Bennett hung in Byrd's quarters.[34]

Byrd made one more attempt with the *New York* to establish a subbase; but the floes were worse than ever, and the fresh ice of the new winter was forming rapidly, forcing him to give up for good.

On 21 February, the commander allowed McKinley to make a local flight in the Fairchild to map the Bay of Whales, intending this flight to be the last one of the year. But on 26 February, the day Byrd gave up any hope of the *Bolling*'s getting through and ordered her back, he caved in to Gould's continued pleas and told the geologist he could fly with the first good weather. Demas said Gould was tickled silly.[35]

It was not until 7 March that relatively good weather returned and gave Gould his chance, but it clearly was not the best time of year to fly away for a camping trip. The sun lingered most of the day near the horizon and spent hours below it in perpetual twilight. Stars had come out. The onset of winter was worse than normal at the Bay of Whales. It had come earlier than usual, as evidenced by the ice already forming over the Ross Sea. Little America had already been hit by as many blizzards as Amundsen had withstood in a year. Six newborn puppies froze to death in the remorseless cold. Gould knew, however, that there would be little if any time left for geological studies the next summer after Byrd achieved his established objectives. The exec felt that the importance of investigating the Rockefellers and collecting rock samples was worth the risk.[36]

Byrd let Gould choose between the Fairchild and the Fokker and gave him his pick of flight crew. Gould said he considered the Fokker the best plane and that "of course" he chose Balchen and June, describing Balchen as "the most versatile man on the expedition and one of the most generous and lovable chaps in the world. . . . I have never seen his like nor do I ever expect to again." June was also one of the most highly respected members. Clarke expressed that feeling: "I would rather receive hell from June than praise from the commander."[37]

Shortly after 3:00 P.M., while most Little Americans were at the send-off for the depot-laying sledge teams, which had also been waiting for the break in the weather, the geological trio took off almost unnoticed on a far more significant journey. They headed for the mountains, 135 miles away, for the expedition's first landing on unknown terrain and the first emplacement of an airborne scientific party in antarctic history. Less than two hours later, the radio at Little America crackled with dots and dashes, notifying Byrd that the plane had landed safely.

The radio room heard from the field party every day. When nothing came through on Friday, 15 March, the attentive operators thought the problem was probably poor signal conditions; but Byrd worried when most of Saturday also went by in complete silence: atmospheric conditions were not that bad. Nor was equipment failure likely: June had two transmitters and was prepared to make simple fixes. Little Americans grew afraid that the men had been hurt climbing a mountain or crossing a crevasse or had tried to take off in the Fokker and crashed. The feared loss could hardly have been worse: after Byrd, the people in the mountains were the three the men looked to most for leadership. As Demas lamented in his diary, "Larry, Balchen, and June are the heart of the expedition."[38]

The commander ordered Walden to mount a search with dog teams, an undertaking that would have historic proportions. The long night was coming fast—that weekend the sky lit up with the season's first aurora, advertising the arrival of winter. Byrd did not know exactly where the geological party was; Gould's report of his position was unclear because of a mix-up in the codes the expedition used to prevent any outsider from eavesdropping on the radio conversations.[39] The dog teams might have to search the entire seventy-mile-long range. Time was critical to any of the stranded party who were still alive: if they could not make their way back to Little America, they were finished once they ran out of the food they had packed (no record of the quantity is known). Counting long delays for bad weather, the rescuers figured they had to allow for as many as three spartan months on the trail, a period that would extend into the blackest, coldest part of the winter night. They had been told that if hell were cold, it would be the same as wintertime in Antarctica.

Antarctic veterans agreed that people and dogs could not live safely on the trail after mid-March, so participation in the relief effort was voluntary. Walden began putting together seven teams. Three of them, driven by himself, Siple, and general hand Chris Braathen, thirty-three, a curly-haired Norwegian sailor and veteran of Norway's

Naval Air Service, would help to haul supplies to depots twenty and forty miles east and then return. The other four teams, driven by Vaughan, who would be in charge, Goodale, Bursey, and Thorne, with De Ganahl navigating and Petersen operating the radio, would continue to the mountains. Except that Thorne replaced Crockett, ill with an ear infection, the mountain team was the same as the one that had just returned from laying the first depots.[40]

Byrd also ordered—Smith claims only at his urging—that the Fairchild be made ready to fly to the Rockefellers in the first good weather, despite the precarious aviation conditions that would endanger the aircraft and its crew. The threat to what was possibly one of only two remaining planes, if the Fokker had crashed, also jeopardized the polar flight, since Byrd had mandated that a standby plane be available for emergencies during that attempt. He ordered that the Ford be put together for another potential rescue mission in case anything did happen to the Fairchild.[41]

The possibility that his people had been killed, and that more might die in the rescue, hit Byrd hard, especially since he blamed himself for letting the three go. Talking with Owen, he remonstrated against his own decision, "I should not have given in. No plea of friendship and personal consideration should have persuaded me. I knew the flight should not be made at this time of year, but it was hard to resist when they were all in favor of it. If they are lost my work is done. And the public would never forget it, either. Is there no end to it? I have had almost more than a man can bear."[42]

Byrd felt that as the leader he had to make the flight; but he needed someone to fly him, his shortcomings as a pilot never more starkly revealed. With the radioman, that made three in the one-seater, which could hold five at most, so he could not bring everyone back at once. Byrd had to put aside whatever bad feelings he had toward the rebellious Smith, whose cross-country flying experience was a blessing in this situation, and chose him as pilot, designating Hanson to be "sparks."

The weather looked good Sunday afternoon, but Smith could not start the Fairchild's engine. Demas found that the pilot was not using the special priming technique necessary in freezing temperatures. Like automobile motors, aircraft engines were hard to start in the cold. By the time the mechanic got the engine going, it was too dark to fly.[43]

According to Smith, the flight was rescheduled for 8:30 Monday morning. The weather was good at the appointed time, and he and Hanson sat in the plane with the engine pulsating, waiting for the commander. After half an hour, Smith went to Byrd's room and found the door closed. Smith asked Owen what the commander was doing, and the newsman replied that Byrd had said he was going to pray awhile. Smith knocked, and Byrd said he would be out in a minute. The commander asked Smith to send in the doctor, who went in, came out, and a few minutes later went back in with three half-pints of brandy. It was not until nearly 4:00 P.M. that Byrd at last walked stiffly to the plane, "his face set and as white as the snow around him."[44]

Byrd told a different story. He said the weather did not clear until midafternoon, and the record backs him up. That morning, in one of the regular radio messages transmitted to the mountains in hopes that a receiver was working and someone was listening, Little America had reported that the weather was too bad to fly. When it cleared, Haines told Byrd the conditions were the best they would see, even though the meteorologist guessed there was only one chance in three the weather would remain good for the entire trip.

A reasonable interpretation for the conflicting weather accounts is that what looked like good conditions to young Smith looked doubtful to the cautious commander and Haines. In a similar situation, Byrd and his advisors had delayed *America*'s transatlantic departure for days while they waited for good weather. Tony Fokker and Balchen had thought the weather nearly perfect and had been disgusted with Byrd's postponements.[45]

Whatever the reason for the hold, Byrd clearly went through mental agony. Owen had gone into Byrd's room and revealed that "for some time . . . the commander sat . . . swinging his helmet between his legs, staring at the floor, silent." Smith was sure that Byrd feared being killed. Byrd certainly had terrifying memories: gaping at pilots falling out of the sky seemingly every day during cram courses in the flimsy planes at Pensacola; seeing the gory remains of pilots and their mangled planes when he served on the Pensacola crash board that investigated the many accidents; barely escaping with his life when he arrived too late to make an intended flight on board a dirigible that crashed, killing fifty crewmen.[46] He could remember the *America*'s crash, which injured him and resulted eventually in Bennett's death; the near disaster when the plane ditched off the French coast; and—

too pointedly—Amundsen's fatal flight over polar ice in search of missing colleagues. However much Byrd may have been afraid for his own survival, he surely also must have been sickened at the thought of the awful tragedy he might behold in the Rockefellers.

With Byrd and Hanson squatting in the back of the Fairchild, Smith taxied to the runway. He remembers that Byrd suddenly shouted, "Stop!" The commander, ever cautious, declared that the surface was too rough for a run to get airspeed, Smith related. The airmail pilot, one of the original "daring young men in their flying machines," said he argued and got Byrd's grudging consent to take off. The *New York Times*'s story—which, like all dispatches, had to be cleared by Byrd—told the events differently. The story reported that the ice on the runway was very rough, and Smith stopped taxiing to discuss the advisability of a takeoff with Byrd. The account quoted Smith: "I didn't know whether we could get off or not. But the commander said to go ahead, and we went."[47] Byrd had only to use a pencil over Owen's typing to change himself from a hesitant worrier to a bold leader, perhaps the same pencil used earlier to insert the mention of his "pet mountain."

The light plane bounced over the corrugated ice but lifted up intact. Because of the late hour and the solid layer of clouds that began to form above, the men flew in a semidarkness that made it hard to find their way. Smith was unworried, confident of his ability to land the plane safely in an emergency and unperturbed at the possibility of returning on foot if the plane were damaged: they had sufficient skiing and camping supplies.[48] The plane headed toward the southern end of the mountain chain, the party's most likely location. Smith, Byrd, and Hanson strained their eyes toward the gray snow passing underneath to try to spot anything that might be wreckage or men on foot.

The crew arrived at the southernmost peak, wheeled around it, and saw nothing. Smith took one last look back—and caught a flash of light. Spiraling down, they saw a landing "T" outlined with flags according to established procedure. Smoke bombs burned beside it, casting light on three men.[49] Byrd and Smith had agreed not to try landing if everything seemed all right. The men on the ground had been waving when they were first spotted, the established signal for a wave off. Smith remembered, however, that as the plane approached, the men stood still, the signal for landing. The downed fliers may have waved to attract the attention of the plane that was about to pass them by and then stopped when the crew had seen them. At any rate, Smith figured that the landing "T" and flares indicated that the geological party wanted the plane to come down.

According to the pilot, Byrd shouted, "What are you doing? Are you going to land?" Smith yelled back that he was and continued the turn that at one point headed the plane toward the nearby peak. Smith described Byrd's reaction:

> [Byrd] screamed, "My God! You're going to hit the mountain! You're going to hit the mountain!" Completely out of control and crying with hysteria, he leaned over me and began clawing and fighting to reach the controls, his weight forcing my head down and ramming my face into the stick. We struggled for a few seconds until I managed to unfasten my belt and wrench around so that I could hit him on the chest. The blow forced him back in the cabin and Hanson threw his arms around him and held him there. "Hold onto him," I shouted as I grabbed the controls barely in time to straighten us out and finish the landing. We landed with a loud slap of the skis . . . and I heard Byrd yell, "You've cracked us up! You've cracked us up!"

The plane slid to a safe stop. As the rescuers climbed out of the plane, Byrd grabbed his sleeping bag, placed it on the ground, knelt down, and bowed his head for a few moments before joining the joyous group.[50]

Byrd's account of the landing, like that of the takeoff, differed. He mentioned seeing the landing "T" and then wrote: " 'Shall I land? asked Smith. . . . I nodded my head. He . . . made a wry face and then throttled down. . . .'"[51]

It seems to be a startling truth, nevertheless, that Byrd, one of the most famous aviators of his time, was phobic about flying. Harrison admitted later that "there seems to be little doubt [that Byrd] was afraid to fly."[52] Smith and Harrison agreed that this fear made Byrd's flights all the more remarkable.

The stranded Rockefellers trio reported that on their first full day there, Friday, 8 March, they had triangulated the positions of the peaks they could see and collected rocks. A hurricane then struck, keeping the men in their tents until Wednesday, the best day of the trip, when Gould essentially completed his geological inspection. The next day another storm hit with such ferocity that it blew the trio off their feet. The wind came straight at the nose of the tied-down Fokker with as much aerodynamic lifting force as the plane would have if it were in full flight. The men could not anchor the plane as securely as they wished because the area had only a shallow snow cover over glare ice, which they could see as green patches where the wind blew the snow completely away. Crawling around, battling winds the crew estimated at 150 miles an hour at least, they piled snow around the Fokker's skis to secure it. The men tried to radio Little America about their predicament but could not get through. Finally, at night, the fierce hurricane lifted the Fokker, which had the main transmitter, and smashed it to the ground, virtually demolishing the plane and radio. The party found the Fokker the next morning about a mile away, the fuselage and propeller wrecked. June never could get the emergency transmitter to work.

The standby receiver was good, however. That morning the three men had heard that the weather at the Bay of Whales was still bad, so they were jubilant when they tuned in at 4:00 P.M. and could hear that the Fairchild was enroute. They had lit the smoke bombs before the plane flew overhead; but as the plane turned and the men on the ground realized with shock that they had not been seen, they waved to attract attention, and Balchen broke open a bomb and poured its contents over the flame of another to ignite the flash that caught Smith's glance.[53]

There was not room in the Fairchild for everybody, but neither Byrd nor Gould wanted to leave while anybody was left. The two decided that both of them would stay, along with Hanson. The plane would make two more trips to retrieve the men and the equipment. The Fairchild took off easily shortly after 6:00 P.M., and a couple of hours later landed safely at Little America on a runway lit by gasoline flares and flashlights.[54]

Owen wrote the story of the adventure as June told it shortly after the landing:

> "How it blew!" June moved his head solemnly as he told of the 150-mile wind which wrecked the plane. . . . "I never heard such a sound," he added. "When it stopped it was so quiet that it hurt."
> He and Balchen were sitting in what we call our library. . . . Dean Smith, his long legs stretched out, sat near them listening. It is a small room, the walls lined with books, with a desk in the corner and a stove roaring on the other side. But it was quiet and comfortable.
> "It will linger a long time in my memory," said June. "I can hear that wind and feel the flying blocks of snow hit me yet. And how we wrestled with those shovels! We had to lie on them to get them down."
> He chuckled. He is a man without nerves, with eyes like blue ice,

which twinkle merrily when he laughs. He was wearing his heavy fur parka and the leather helmet with the radio earphones, for any moment the plane might go back to get the commander.

". . . Once [Balchen] slid away so far that he had to take his knife and dig it into the ice to crawl back. . . . We went out to hold onto the ropes [tieing the plane down] again, for the plane was trembling and lifting on the shock absorbers. Once Larry . . . who was holding the rope on the wing was blown out straight like a flag. After that we lay down on the ground to hold the ropes. . . .

"We crawled into our bags for a while to try to get warm, and the ice under us was jarring. It was probably from the plane. She was lifting up and down. The skis did not lift—they were stuck fast—but she moved up and down on the landing gear and on the shock absorbers. . . . We could see her dimly from the tent opening, swaying and tearing at her fastenings. About 11:30 the sound of the wind suddenly changed from a roar, and the sound became thin and higher. There was a little shake, and we looked out and saw that the plane had left. She went straight up and sailed away."[55]

Byrd radioed Owen not to mention the prayer on the sleeping bag in the news story, perhaps realizing, ironically, that this display of genuine emotion would have seemed phony.[56]

Off in the mountains, the conversations between Byrd and Gould hunched side by side in their tent went unrecorded, but they must have had serious and perhaps emotional discussions. The loss of the Fokker was the first major blow to the expedition, a severe setback to both men. Of itself, the incident on the initial scientific flight undercut a major goal of the expedition: to demonstrate the practicality of aircraft and radio in antarctic research. Now that the aviation unit was down to two aircraft out of the original four, there were no extra planes. Since by Byrd's rules a plane could not fly without a standby for rescue, he would have to baby the aircraft he had left. As it was, the Fairchild could not make it over the polar plateau for a tandem flight or possible rescue, as the Fokker could have, so the wreck had made the polar attempt in the Ford that much more dangerous. Byrd would have to use the planes sparingly, when the expected payoff from a flight outweighed the risk. The sturdy, reliable dog teams would have to do much more of the depot laying and exploration than had been envisioned. With the high priority of the polar flight and other nonscientific aviation missions, the geological objectives would suffer the most.[57]

The dangers had been known. Griffith Taylor, the British antarctic authority, had prophesied that Antarctica's sudden, fierce blizzards would blow aircraft off the ground, so he believed that aviation would not work on the continent. Byrd himself had said of the planes, "We shall be extremely fortunate if we bring them all back."[58]

Each man blamed himself, Gould for requesting the trip and Byrd for allowing it. Gould had written in his diary after the Fokker sailed off that he felt he let Byrd down because the commander had been kind and generous to the executive. The geologist was sure, he wrote, that Byrd would take "a fine and generous attitude toward the whole affair."[59] (Having seen how committed Byrd was to his self-interest, however, Gould may well have been sarcastic.)

Bad weather closed in again the next day. With no way of knowing when or if a break in the skies would allow the plane to come for them, Byrd radioed instructions to McKinley, the senior man at Little America, to send the dog teams. The weather continued bad for one day after another, with the marooned men laying plans to ski west and meet the dog teams. On Friday morning, 22 March, to everyone's joy, winter relented long enough to let Smith and June fly to the mountains. When the Fairchild's door opened, Hanson, Byrd, and Gould all wedged themselves in. Gould had to leave behind most of his equipment and specimens; since another flight was beyond hope, they were lost for good.[60] Almost too heavy to fly, the overloaded plane lumbered back to Little America.

The brave sledge teams, then sixty-three miles out, turned around and, pressing hard to get off the cruel trail, made the snug camp in thirteen hours, beating by one mile the antarctic record held by Amundsen for a nonstop sledge journey.[61] The fangs of winter had frostbitten the sledgers and caused the collapse of a lead dog who had to be trundled home. No one regretted the cancellation of the rest of the planned epic journey, any more than soldiers regret the withdrawal of orders to charge into heavy artillery fire.

Byrd, an executive who liked to have everything in writing even in his small antarctic organization, and who could not simply pass off the devastating loss of the Fokker, fired an austere memo to Balchen and June: "Please write out for me a joint report of your efforts to prevent the 'Virginia' from blowing away. I particularly would like to have your reasons for not lifting the tail of the 'Virginia' and for not freezing the skis to the ice. The object of this report is constructive, to avoid a similar occurrence, and there is no desire to attach blame."[62]

Balchen took the workhorse Fairchild on one short last flight for the season. He and Owen soared off the barrier and out over the Ross Sea to look at ice conditions. The ocean was entirely frozen except for a few leads, issuing sea smoke, that would soon close and lock up that whole part of the ocean for the winter.

When the Fairchild returned it was drained of gas, the wings were folded, and the only operational plane was placed in its winter cocoon, a hanger made of snow blocks covered with a tarpaulin. Then the Little Americans, with Byrd himself pitching in, dug a huge pit and slid the partially assembled Ford inside. The men roofed the pit to form a chamber where they could work on the engines over the winter.

In New Zealand, the ships went into drydock for overhaul during the winter, with most of the crews staying on at subsistence wages. Twelve men left the expedition, including a hard-to-replace mate who, Brown said, had colluded in Brophy's mad attempt at mutiny. Byrd would have to find substitutes by next season. Captain Melville asked that another man be sent back to the States because he had taken some girls on the ship, but Byrd refused that request. Robert Lanier, the tenacious black ex-member, showed up by surprise in New Zealand and pleaded to rejoin the expedition. Byrd refused this request also, telling a minister who interceded for Lanier that "members of his own race" had declared the young man morally unfit and that his previous employers would not give him good references.[63]

One of the returned men sold photographs of Little America to Hearst, breaking his contract with Byrd and threatening Byrd's own exclusive contract with the *New York Times* feature affiliate.[64] Incensed, Byrd could not find out who had sold the pictures, but he convinced the feature syndicate he had no fault in the matter.

New Zealand's government waived regulations to allow Byrd's fifteen adult dogs and nine pups on the mainland. Their handler arranged for them to keep in shape and earn money for the expedition by serving as transport for construction work at a resort at Mount Cook.[65]

Brophy was hospitalized for what Byrd called a nervous breakdown. A magistrate ruled that Brophy was suffering from paranoia and ordered him returned to the United States. Much of Byrd's time was taken up (and would be for many months) by almost daily discussions with advisors in the United States and New Zealand about how to handle Brophy for his own good and the good of the expedition. Byrd, loyal to those who devoted themselves to him, said he would stick by Brophy and defend him, if necessary, from charges of misappropriating the expedition's funds. The commander, who kept Gould informed of all post-expedition intentions in case he should die in the antarctic, told the geologist he would give Brophy another job if the former exec recovered from his neurasthenia. Railey was moved to wire Byrd: "Nothing you have ever done . . . has made me respect you as much as your loyalty to Brophy." To replace Brophy in handling all the expedition's New Zealand affairs, Byrd retained his politically influential Dunedin shipping agent, the Honorable Harold Tapley.[66]

Little America went on daylight saving time to conserve the waning hours of brightness.[67] With virtually all the first summer's rush jobs completed, Byrd changed meal hours to the winter schedule, with dinner at 4:00 P.M. instead of 5:00 P.M., effectively shortening the working day.

The prolonged sunset often painted a beautiful sky. Demas once gazed at a red sun and yellow moon near each other on the horizon and gushed that it "was a sight I'll never forget." Owen described another spellbinding evening: "There was a mass of mottled clouds in the southern sky above a streak of olive green and below that a thin line of gold. The clouds were pink or rose . . . and looked as though they had been splashed against the sky and taken on solid form. To the north, directly opposite, the sky was dark green above the horizon and purple above. And in the east hung an elongated moon, shaped like an egg."[68]

The sun rose and set for the last time on 17 April, deserting them until August. Byrd had to give up the crowbar search for the remainder of the cache on the barrier, claimed by the deepening snow. Their days of going forth ended, the Little Americans withdrew into their compact orange containments to hibernate for nearly seven months. They snapped from a life of high adventure to a simple, steady existence dominated by isolation. The men would view no changes in scenery, watch no changes from night to day, and feel no changes in weather except from one degree of below-zero cold to another. The men would eat no fresh food. They would see no new faces and have no contact with the outside world except by radio. A criminal in jail would lead a more thrilling life. The expedition's members would save themselves from total monotony mainly by planning and preparing for the coming summer and by working at science, other specialized jobs, and housekeeping. Visions of the stirring polar flight and of other thrusts into the unexplored continent at the end of the winter confinement would keep the men going.

During the winter, a man would face the unknown not on the plains of ice or on the far-off mountains but in his own mind as he tried to hold out against maddening boredom and oppressive crowding by forty-one strangers.

.7.

The Warren

BYRD and most of the other leaders lived in the administration building. The prefabricated building intended as a bunk house for most of the men had been on the *Bolling* during her aborted trip, so the construction detail had remodeled part of the administration building to serve as sleeping quarters. Two rows of double-tiered beds were lined up against opposite walls, the feet just far enough apart to leave a narrow aisle. The administration building housed seventeen men total: commander, pilots, journalist, cameramen, scientists, doctor, engineer, secretary, and—in consideration of his age—tailor Martin Ronne. Tellingly, Walden was the only unit head who lived elsewhere. The library, in a corner of the administration building, had a door that opened into Byrd's combination office and bedroom, which measured about ten feet by six feet. The other rooms, all small, were the special laboratory for radio research, the workshop for all the scientists, and the dispensary. There would have been several individual work and bunk rooms had the *Bolling* made two trips. The walls and ceilings were all covered with greenish gray cardboard, with orange-yellow tape stuck here and there to repair cracks.[1]

To leave the building, one put on a reindeer-fur parka, fur pants, muskrat cap, mittens, and boots or reindeer-fur mukluks, the calf-length soft boots of Eskimoan design.[2] The exit was a vestibule whose double doors conserved priceless heat. Off the vestibule was the entrance to one of the camp's two unheated, four-seater outhouses—not places for leisurely reading. A ladder led to the surface from the partially buried building. Outside nearby were the white, slatted shelter for the thermometer and hygrometer, the meteorological supply hut, one of two shelters for geomagnetic measurements and, an eighth of a mile away, a large cluster of buildings and towers, all flaming orange. A tunnel connected the administration building with the cluster. The sides of the tunnel were lined with supply boxes that left an aisle barely wide enough for pedestrians to squeeze past each other, and the low roof made them stoop.

At several places along the tunnel were entrances to rooms dug out of the snow. These side rooms, roofed with snow-covered tarpaulins, were the medical storehouse, the general storehouse, the gymnasium, and the other geomagnetic lab. Halfway to the cluster another tunnel, lined with fuel cans, led to the radio supply room.

The main tunnel ended in a large, supply-filled vestibule that served four connecting or abutting rooms. Directly ahead was the entrance to the bunkhouse called sometimes by its official name, the Biltmore (after the hotel that donated offices in New York), and other times by its Norwegian-language nickname, the Norge ("Norwegian," in English) house, because it had been prefabricated in Norway. Eight men, including most of the dog drivers, slept in double bunks arranged sideways against the walls of the eleven-foot by fourteen-foot room, which had been intended as a machine shop until sleeping space became a problem. A large box in the middle served as a table, and smaller boxes were used as chairs.

Left of the Biltmore was the coal cache. Immediately right was the machine shop, a dugout lined with airplane crates, that held Little America's power plant, a small farm generator—the first electric plant in Antarctica. Far to the right was the mess hall, the camp's second main building, which also served as a workshop, recreation room, and bunkhouse for fourteen men. In one corner was the radio communication room. At the other end was the darkroom. A telephone on one wall was connected to the administration building. The rooms were poorly illuminated. To save generator fuel, the inhabitants had strung just four light bulbs, which lit the kitchen, machine shop, darkroom, and Biltmore. The men had forgotten extra mantles for the bright gasoline pressure lamps and so could use them only sparingly. Light, weak and yellowish, came mostly from kerosene lanterns that had been intended for hand use.[3]

Another ladder extended to the surface, where the wind carried the wolflike howling of the huskies when they were outside. Byrd described other outdoor sounds: ". . . from afar would come perhaps the distant rumble of the barrier breaking, or from nearby the terrifying reports of contracting ice, like a burst of rifle fire. Once or twice I heard a snow quake—an extensive rumbling and shaking under foot as the crust of vast snow fields to the south settled to a more solid level."[4]

Against an outer wall of the mess hall was a snow-covered extension with sides of boxes and a roof of boards and canvas. Inside was a tent surrounding a cot and a table.[5] Blackburn had built the doubly insulated sleeping shelter to get away from the crowd in the main building.

Not far from Blackburn's lair were storage sheds and an adjacent nine-by-twelve hut, made from aircraft-engine crates, that was used as living quarters by two other refugees from the crowd, Braathen and the reclusive Walden. Called Mooseheim or Blubberheim ("-heim" is Norwegian for house), it was heated by a stove that burned seal blubber so as not to take scarce regular fuel from the main body of men. The co-owners were always lightly coated with pungent seal soot, and the others could smell the two coming.[6] Outward from these buildings ran two parallel tunnels where some dogs were kept and exercised.

Arranged about the mess hall in a triangle fifty yards on each side were three sixty-five-foot towers, with the radio antenna strung atop them. A light on one tower served as a beacon for those who might wander in storm or darkness. Nearby was the snowmobile garage, a lifeboat, and a small cluster of enclosures for the aviation unit, housing the planes and gasoline and a workshop wallpapered with pinups.[7] Not far from the aviation cluster was a hut the weathermen used to make giant box kites.

Between the kite house and the mess hall, in the center of the area called dog town, were the seal cache and meat chopping room. Most of the dogs lived in three long, branching tunnels that radiated from the butchering facilities. Visitors had trouble seeing—the frosty breath from the panting animals coalesced into a fog that restricted visibility to twenty feet. The dogs lived in crates set in niches spaced every ten feet along the tunnels. The animals were tied to leashes that kept them apart and peaceful, and during winter were allowed to exercise individually by running up and down the corridors. When visitors entered the tunnels, the huskies yelped and squirmed in delight, but underlying the licks and wags was a still-wild nature. As winter set in, two males had been killed in a fight over a bitch, so bitches and males had been segregated to prevent further carnage. A "maternity ward" had been carved out of the snow after adults bit the heads off some newborns. Eighteen pups were born during the expedition. They were allowed to roam the camp, and the men played with the youngsters until they raided the meat storehouse and ate the turkey, chicken, and veal that had been set aside for special occasions. The pups were jailed for the rest of the winter in the maternity room.[8]

On the barrier's surface near the mess hall there was a sharp, putrid, but fortunately weak aroma composed of exhausts from the kitchen and from burning coal, blubber, kerosene, and gasoline.

Overhead, when it was clear and dark in winter, the sky was decorated with vivid stars, a brilliant moon—with an upside down man-in-the-moon because of the southern-hemisphere vantage—and often the beautiful aurora. The southern lights were not as spectacular as those up north. Demas said they were not generally as bright as the aurora borealis he had seen when he worked in the Hudson Bay region. Gould described how fascinating the display was nevertheless: "Most often it was manifested as huge greenish white curtains or arches. Sometimes these would be quite still for some seconds, but more often they were dancing—sometimes with the complete ecstasy and abandonment of jazz and again with the slow, writhing motion of the oriental dance. From a dark center overhead I have seen streamers shooting outward in all directions, like the spokes of a wheel, until they disappeared below the horizon on all sides. I have watched a great wave of faint red to purple light boil up over the dark rim of the night, way off toward the northeast, and then rise higher and higher until the whole heavens were filled with the 'wondrous light,' and even the great patches of snow all about me shimmered with a pale abalone glow."[9]

If the time and conditions were just right, there appeared what many agreed must be one of the most beautiful sights in nature, the moon and "moon dogs"—patches of light on either side of the moon and some distance from it, caused by ice crystals high in the atmosphere—shining through the gossamer auroral curtain. Owen was also enraptured one night by an unusually beautiful moon halo: "There were two complete spectrum rings—red, then yellow on the inside, then green and purple, and then red and yellow again. It was hard to distinguish some of the colors, but it was of exquisite beauty."[10]

When clouds covered the sky, and especially when snow was falling, the possibility of getting lost made going outside treacherous. Once, walking from the mess hall in a snowstorm, Harrison carelessly wandered several hundred yards beyond the administration building. When he realized his predicament, he fearfully peered about for the tower beacon, spotted it, and followed it back. Still disoriented, he had a hard time finding the drifted-over entrance before he stumbled on it and descended to safety.[11] In any weather, the icy wind frequently caused frostbite, and those who ventured topside had to be alert to white frostbitten patches on faces or hands.

The forty-two-man group was the largest ever to winter in Antarctica. Because of the expedition's modern nature, the group included four pilots, three aircraft mechanics, an aerial photographer, three radiomen, an engineer, and a machinist, not to mention Byrd's secretary, a newspaper reporter, and two movie cameramen. To fill the more traditional occupations were five dog drivers, three surveyors, four scientists, the cook, the doctor, the tailor, the carpenter, eight general hands, and, of course, the leader. The average age of the men was thirty-two. Six were college graduates: Byrd, Balchen, Coman, Davies, Larry Gould, and De Ganahl. Five were Norwegian citizens: Balchen, Braathen, Petersen, Strom—all blue-eyed and fair-haired— and the dark-eyed Ronne. (Hanson was the son of Norwegian immigrants and spoke fluent Norwegian.) Eleven are known to have been Masons: Byrd, Balchen, Blackburn, Bubier, Lofgren, McKinley, Parker, Roth, Rucker, Strom, and Tennant. (Brophy and Captains Brown and Melville were also Masons.)[12]

The men lived adequately in their warren but hardly in the deluxe style that some newspapers had inferred from Byrd's budget. Breakfast—canned fruit, prunes, mush or oatmeal cakes, molasses, sometimes ham and eggs—was served from 8:30 to 9:30 A.M. on the big table in the mess hall, which seated twenty; at every meal, only half the patrons could be served at one time. Indoor thermometers read a comfortably mild seventy degrees or so at head level, but only about twenty-eight nippy degrees at shoe level.[13]

Each man did his own work and often assisted others. All but the older men and those with full-time duties, such as the cook and radiomen, took turns at dishwashing, hauling coal, shoveling snow into the melter, and performing other household jobs. Haines showed a talent with scissors and usually served as barber.[14] The men had fun acting for Paramount's cameras, dramatizing some actual events and faking others.

Byrd had forbidden Owen to post his dispatches on the camp's bulletin board, pointing out that they naturally tended to focus on the few explorers who did exciting and newsy things. With unusual candor, Byrd commented that "I suppose of all the men here I have the least right to talk depreciatively about the value of getting one's name in the newspapers," but he said he felt that posting stories starring just a few would arouse dissatisfaction and jealousy among the many neglected members. At the same time, maybe Byrd did not want the men to notice the occasional discrepancies between what was reported and what actually happened. Because everybody was curious to know what the *New York Times* was reporting to the world about the expedition, Byrd relented and allowed the stories to be posted. As if to prove Byrd's point, one man, fearing he was losing stature in his girlfriend's eyes, pestered Owen for more coverage.[15]

There was no scheduled lunch. The two weathermen regularly left the administration building around 1:00 P.M., reportedly to "take an ob"—take a meteorological observation—but actually sneaking over to the mess hall for sandwiches. Others began to join the weathermen until light, make-it-yourself lunch—usually sardine or salmon sandwiches, sometimes with cheese—became a routine meal, called "the ob."[16]

The official work day ended at 4:00 P.M., and dinner was served from then until 5:00 P.M.: generally soup, either canned or made from leftovers; mutton, beef, whale, or seal meat; dehydrated or canned vegetables; and custard or pie. The whale meat—two tons of it, donated by the *Larsen*—had hung in the *New York*'s rigging to cure in the funnel smoke. The men liked the whale meat best cut thin and fried or chopped and rolled with onions into meatballs. It tasted like hamburger or, when cold, like lamb. Weddell seal was black and had a gamy taste. Once the cook served crabeater seal fixed with breadcrumbs, tomato sauce, and onions, which Owen liked and said tasted like beef. The scraps most often left on the plates were the dehydrated vegetables, World War surplus of vile taste and consistency. Relative to previous antarctic parties, the food was not bad. Owen thought that "no expedition ever had as good food as we have."[17]

The cook, distinguished by his flaming red beard, was toothless George "Gummy" Tennant, forty-six. So devoted to the commander was Tennant that, after the north polar flight, he tried to give back his wages when Byrd had trouble eliminating his debt from that venture. At Little America, when he once took a holiday from cooking, others cleaned up his kitchen and were almost sorry they did—they found it filthy, with stinking pieces of meat in various nooks and crannies and green particles in the crevices of the meat chopper.[18]

After dinner on most nights, half the men attended class at the Biltmore in what they called Antarctica University. The specialists taught subjects such as geology, aeronautics, navigation, and radio telegraphy. Dr. Gould, whose pipe smoking, shorn head, and Vandyke beard made him look like the stereotypical scientist, held the most popular lectures. The professor gave his University of Michigan geology course and made attendance a duty for the five others who would sledge with him come summer. He wanted all who had the opportunity to do so to collect scientifically useful rocks, something not always done by other parties.[19]

Men exercised mostly by walking or skiing—if they could get skis. Byrd had not expected such hard-packed snow and had brought snowshoes—unneeded, as it turned out—for each man but few skis, which the expedition could have used in quantity.[20] Some dedicated exercisers worked out in the icebox dug out of the snow that served as a gymnasium. Balchen gave boxing lessons, and weekly matches between him and Strom, two of the best fighters in camp, became a popular event.

In the evening, some readers went to the library in the administration building to peruse the three thousand volumes that Gould had collected. The book the men liked most was the tropical mood piece *Green Mansions*, a love story about a beautiful, fairylike girl in the Venezuelan jungle. The book took them by imagination as far away as possible from their hard life at Little America. Byrd removed the adult and juvenile biographies about him to his own room, explaining, "I don't want the fellows to think they have to read the books."[21] (On the other hand, he could keep track of who was devoted enough to request a biography—a ploy not out of keeping with his ways.)

Someone usually turned on one of the two hand-cranked record players. Blackburn played "The Bells of St. Mary's" over and over all winter on the library Victrola, a torture the others endured silently. Strom, the only active musician on the ice, sometimes played his accordian. In the administration building, Haines usually popped corn for the gang. Most of the off-duty explorers gathered in groups to talk and play cards or dice. Bridge, hearts, blackjack, and poker were the most played card games. Acey deucey, a backgammonlike favorite of sailors, and craps were the dice games. The gamblers usually played for cigarettes—almost everyone smoked.[22]

Cliques formed, mostly along the lines of specialties. The dog drivers talked sledging and the aviators talked flying; arguments over the best kinds of sledges and planes raged for months. On many nights, the five Norwegians gathered at Blubberheim to socialize. Activity time was over at 9:00 P.M., but usually men sat on their bunks and continued bull sessions long past then, the men in the upper bunks a bit too warm in the stratified heat, those below a bit too cool.[23]

The bunks were each individual's private chamber in the close confines of the winter burrow. Most of the men decorated their spaces with wall hangings. Some built elaborate shelves and arrayed privacy curtains. The beds were sometimes refuges during free time in the always-dark hours the clock said was day. After lights-out at night, men lit candles on shelves over their bunks and for an hour or two read or wrote entries in pocket-sized, leather-covered diaries that had been provided.[24]

At the beginning of winter, men—Byrd included—took turns on the evening and night watches from after dinner until lights-out, and from lights-out until morning. The duties were rotated alphabetically. The watchmen had to be especially alert for fire, which had devastated several camps in the dry antarctic. The men on watch also regularly noted weather and auroral conditions for the scientific record.[25]

Byrd believed that stale air and fumes from burning coal had contributed to the physical deterioration that most members of previous expeditions had experienced. He ordered the fires to be allowed to die and the doors to be opened at 11:00 P.M. Fog rolled over the floor as the cold air met the warm air in the hut. The Little Americans slid into sleeping bags that kept them warm even as the temperature dropped to well below freezing. Those scheduled to sleep out on the trail had bags insulated with reindeer hair. The others had eiderdown bags. With voices and activities silenced, the men fell asleep to the low, melancholy keening, seemingly far away, of wind blowing organlike over the ventilating pipes.[26]

The night watchman closed the doors and relit the fires in the morning. Those men in trail bags were covered with fine reindeer hairs that they brushed away from their eyes and noses upon rising. A morning temperature of about 15° encouraged fast dressing.[27] For indoor wear, one put on long underwear, a wool shirt, ordinary pants, two pairs of wool socks, and moccasins or lightweight sealskin mukluks.

Day's end on Saturday gave the men something to look forward to. At 4:00 P.M. they gathered around loudspeakers in the administration building and mess hall to hear the special programs beamed to them on alternate weeks by General Electric's station WGY in Schenectady and Westinghouse's KDKA in Pittsburgh. A different newspaper or other organization produced each program. The programs established a milestone in radio history: the farthest that voice or music had ever successfully been transmitted. Reception was poor; the sound had an echo because signals take paths of different lengths around the earth. Music never came through well, and a third of the time the men could not hear anything.[28]

When they could hear voices the men loved the shows. Celebrities performed and talked to the expedition. Harpo Marx, the mime who never talked in his regular performances, spoke for one of the few times in public. Distinguished personalities and politicians from cabinet officers on down spoke. A young WGY announcer named Jimmy Wallington, working at his first job in radio (and later to become one of the best known voices of the airwaves), read letters to supplement the limited personal messages the men were able to get through the routine code transmissions. Best of all, sometimes relatives and friends came on to read the radio mail themselves. A whole program might be dedicated to one member, as on "Paul Siple Day," for example. The radio mail was on short wave only; the rest was broadcast over commercial stations to a national audience.[29]

The programs did cause some problems, however. Some of the mail was personal enough to embarrass the recipient. The voice of Siple's mother drew tears to his eyes. A few lonely souls were pained and embarrassed by rarely or never getting radio mail. Once Vaughan was shaken by an unusual radiogram telling him to be sure to listen for a message to be delivered by his mother the next day on the weekly radio program. He was glued to the loudspeaker when Mrs. Vaughan, plainly trying to contain her emotions, told him his brother had died. He broke down and sobbed.[30]

Westinghouse had prepared for the programs by transmitting experimental signals to radio hams in New Zealand, but WGY's programs came in clearest. The antarctic consensus was that WGY also put on better shows and that KDKA's were self-serving. The men told Byrd they would like WGY to do all the programs, but by then it was too late to change the arrangements. While serving the commercial interests of the stations and producers, the novel programs promoted the expedition, helped to advance wireless technology, and, overall, proved invaluable to the expedition's morale.[31]

Reception of New Zealand's radio improved during the long night so much that Little Americans could hear long wave from Wellington, which they tuned in whenever possible. It was to the New Zealand station that the explorers turned when they wanted to hear a new popular tune that seemed written for them. Apparently after allusions to the ditty by friends and families, Byrd sent a message to the station: ". . . we have heard repeated references to a new American song hit entitled quote Button Up Your Overcoat, You Belong to Me unquote. . . . The boys would like to hear it some night."[32]

Sunday was honored as a day of rest. Somewhat surprisingly, given Byrd's religious feelings, the civic piety of the Twenties, and the practice of other antarctic parties, Byrd held no prayer services. Most likely, few would have wanted to attend but many would have felt constrained to go, and Byrd always went to great lengths to avoid coercing his volunteers.[33]

After Sunday dinner, the men usually saw one of seventy-five old movies donated by the National Film Review Board, the censoring organization. The board had culled the films to eliminate any suggestive movies that might titillate the celibate explorers. *Nanook of the North* and Charlie Chaplin comedies were favorites. The men ate popcorn, chocolate bars, and Eskimo pies made by lanky ice cream manufacturer and former bootlegger Jim Feury, twenty-seven. The audience whistled and shouted like kids at a Saturday matinee. One Sunday, Demas interrupted the movie to introduce a surprise skit, with the boys from the Norwegian house dressed as girls in dish-towel skirts and rope wigs, a schoolmaster, a tough guy, a sissy, and a Negro named "Rastus." Demas had made himself up as a caricature Semite for the part of Abie Jew, a thinly-disguised taunt at the party's only Jewish member, Demas's fellow mechanic Benny Roth, whom Demas did not like.[34]

After the weekly movies, the men played special poker games to determine not winners but the four biggest losers, who had to take care of the crystal palaces—the pits beneath the seats of the two latrines. Excrement piled up in frozen columns that almost reached the seat holes by the week's end. The unlucky ones stuck with the duty had to reach way down into the area beneath the seats and break up the nauseating brown columns. Davies, who had never played poker, studied and practiced harder than he ever had for a physics test. Smith said, "You never saw closer-to-the vest poker played anywhere."[35]

The men did not bathe or do laundry often, although they did not have to in the cold, relatively clean snow desert. Besides, all water came from melted snow, and a lot of snow reduced to only a little water, which was used sparingly. In a practice they called dry washing, the explorers put clothes away without laundering them until the clothes the men were wearing were even dirtier. Then they put on the stored clothes, which seemed clean by comparison. The men tended to go too long before filling up the small round tub to take baths, which were neither comfortable nor convenient, and so suffered frequent boils and rashes. Byrd followed an unusual bathing routine, washing a different third of his body every night. The climate, as dry as the Sahara, occasioned other minor inconveniences—cuts took a long time to heal, hangnails and raw throats were common, and everybody was always a little thirsty. Many did not shave, taking advantage of the opportunity to see what kind of beard they could grow. Some, trying to make hair care easier, followed a shipboard custom of shaving off all the hair on their heads.[36] Byrd did not grow a beard, but he and many others cut their hair to the scalp.

The men missed the companionship and civilizing presence of women. However, except for occasional discussions of conquests— June, for one, like to reminisce about his extramarital flings—and the crude jokes that went the rounds, the explorers seldom spoke of women, whose absence kept libidos quiescent. A repartee that occurred between Gould and Owen exemplified the level of talk about sex. The reporter said he liked the sex in Balzac. "Hold up your hand," Gould requested. Owen did. "Now pull yourself out of the gutter," Gould jabbed. Byrd liked to say the thing the group missed most was temptation.[37]

Byrd had a lonely position as the commander. He was the only one who had a private room. Imbued with the tenets of naval tradition, he was convinced that a leader had to maintain distance from his men to assure them that decisions were impersonal and unemotional. A degree of Olympian isolation also strengthened his aura of authority. He conveyed most orders and rebukes through Gould and the unit heads, avoiding possibly undignified confrontations. Few Little Americans called Byrd "Dick"—he was usually addressed as "Commander." In the formality of name he was alone. Even Dr. Gould was always "Larry," if not "Simon," an affectionate reference to Simon Legree. Byrd took himself very seriously and, except when drinking, was humorless and ill at ease in the barracks environment. Once in a while he joined awkwardly in the games, such as craps, of those who on other missions would be the enlisted men. The fun was too obviously contrived: the men appreciated his efforts, but he could never be one of the boys.[38]

Byrd developed a formal way to keep in touch with his men. Every day he would invite one or two of them for a walk. He asked them what they were doing, answered questions, inquired about problems, counseled each one on work or personal difficulties, determined how particular men felt about the expedition's happenings, and when appropriate offered reassurances. After Blackburn came back from one of these walks, he told his diary admiringly that Byrd "certainly takes a very kindly interest in all of us. What a man!"[39]

Although resolute about his own authority, Byrd felt the best way to govern a community of private citizens was to democratize it as much as possible. On board ship he had rebuked a man who was a military officer for pulling rank on another who was an enlisted man. The commander declared firmly that an expedition allowed of no social differences and that special privileges would not obtain.[40]

Owen said that Byrd would be generous with others at times but extremely difficult at other times. With generosity, for example, Byrd gave one of his parkas to Clarke ("The kindest man I have ever known," Clarke inscribed in his diary). Byrd gave up his personal loudspeaker to the Biltmore so the boys there could enjoy Wellington's daily music broadcasts. Everybody at Little America witnessed or experienced his explosive temper, however. Although he rarely used profanity, when he was in a bad mood he could fly into a rage over a little thing like a dirty dish or a messy table. He did, however, give praise when it was due. During the last-minute rush in New Zealand, Clarke had written in his diary, "The commander, despite all his cares and worries, finds time to commend meritorious service."[41]

In Byrd's leisure hours, he liked to read Dickens and detective stories while smoking cigarettes in a holder, with his terrier, Igloo—who looked like the dog listening to his master's voice in the RCA trademark—curled up in his lap. When Byrd was asked his favorite music for a radio program dedicated to him, he listed pieces by several classical composers as well as "Dixie," the "Stars & Stripes Forever," and "The Star Spangled Banner."[42]

Most of the commander's limited socializing was with the equivalent of the officer class. He was devoted to bridge, which had become widely popular since it had been introduced in its modern form two years before. Byrd played the game night after night and was the best on the ice. Four of the expedition's southerners—Byrd of Virginia, Harrison of North Carolina, McKinley of Texas, and Joe Rucker, forty-one, of Georgia, a toothy hillbilly-faced Paramount cameraman—played a nightly game in Byrd's room. "He plays a daring, clever game . . . [and] discusses every point repeatedly, usually arguing against the [convolutions?] of play," Harrison, Byrd's steady partner and one of the best card players himself, scribbled in his diary. Byrd took the game so seriously, Harrison said, that the commander "seemed to get quite peeved and almost huffy when I begged off from bridge to take a geology exam." Harrison told his diary there were times he found it tiresome to be so chained to the nightly game, "but on the whole I enjoy it."[43]

Byrd sighed that he was in poor trim because of the hard life he had led since becoming a polar explorer. To get in condition, he walked five miles daily by going back and forth fifty times on the surface between the administration building and the mess hall. He also worked out in the gym every day, lifting weights and doing calisthenics. Demas said that, although without clothes Byrd appeared to be a weakling, the commander was stronger than he looked. Getting into shape brought back the former acrobat's pride in his strength and agility.

Once, the commander showed Siple how he could chin himself with one hand. Another time he boldly challenged Strom, the huge Norwegian sailor, to an Indian-wrestling match. Byrd, however, had overestimated his ability—Strom flexed his bulging muscles once and the commander went flying, cutting his head on a stove so badly it had to be stitched. Strom felt terrible, wriggling and apologizing over and over.[44]

One of the best and most popular decisions Byrd had ever made was appointing Gould executive officer and, after Brophy's departure, second in command. (Brophy had retained the title of second in command until he left the expedition.) Brown-haired, brown-eyed, average in height and weight, Gould somewhat resembled crooner Rudy Vallee. Byrd praised his executive, calling him brilliant. With Dr. Coman and Owen, Gould was considered one of the camp's three intellectuals. Balchen said the executive was a natural leader.[45]

Gould and Byrd exhibited opposite personalities. Gould was even-tempered and good-humored, with no trace of pretense, according to Owen. When the executive did get angry, the reporter noted, Gould "could swear strongly without ever using a single cuss word." Gould felt at ease in the give-and-take camaraderie of the masculine world. The dog handlers named their scroungiest animal "Gould," delightedly anticipating cursing and berating it on the trail. When the exec objected, the men rechristened the animal "Simon."[46] None would have thought of naming the dog "Byrd" or "Commander."

Gould had originally planned to fly with his party to the likely junction of Carmen Land and the Queen Maud Mountains. Amundsen had discovered the mountains stretching across his route on his way to the pole and named them after Norway's monarch. Since only two out of four planes were left, Gould's party would have to travel entirely by dog sledge. He would coordinate his mission with that of the party that would use sledges to lay emergency bases along the polar route, and he would start his investigations due south of Little America instead of southeast at Carmen Land. The geological party would grind out some 1,300 miles, making their journey one of the longest sledge trips on record and, according to the *New York Times*, "one of the greatest enterprises ever attempted in the antarctic."[47]

Committees of those men involved in the two ground parties—almost everyone in camp—investigated all alternatives and what ifs and recommended plans and equipment. Gould spent most of his time arranging logistics under the ambitious new plans, and he directed the preparation of a comprehensive report describing the operations. The planners frequently looked up information in the collection of polar literature Byrd and Gould had gathered, which they considered one of the top polar libraries in the world. Gould, like Byrd, believed that Amundsen's trek to the South Pole had been the best-run sledge operation in polar history, and the executive based his plans on what the Norwegian had written in his book.[48]

Some of the tasks with highest priority involved correcting errors in equipment planning. The sledgers had realized during the freight runs from the ships to Little America that the big sledges were too heavy and cumbersome to use on the trail south. Strom redesigned them, lightening them by half. The trail stoves were another mistake, proving too heavy, much too complicated, and dangerous as well—one of them blew up when tested. Machinist Vic Czegka, forty-nine, made new cookers and other trail equipment out of supplies he had selected back in New York for all emergencies. Czegka, born in Austria but said to have lived in Czechoslovakia, came to the United States at the age of twenty-four and enlisted in the marines. One of several brawny men at Little America, he could lift 650 pounds off the floor, but a chronic bad back often crippled him with pain.[49]

Byrd wrote a memo to the sledgers, suggesting that they practice falling down crevasses while roped together, using a deep, gaping crack near camp. Bravely and with humor, he volunteered to lead the way: "I will be glad to take the first fall, with Strom, Siple, Van der Veer and a half dozen other huskies on the other end of the line."[50]

Byrd and the four pilots got together regularly as the polar-flight planning committee; the three mechanics sat in on the sessions and gave advice. Byrd encouraged discussion in all meetings of the flight and sledging committees, although he had a tough time keeping his clubby aviators from turning their meetings into general bull sessions. The loss of the Fokker required the pilots, too, to change their plans because of the impossibility of a tandem flight and the diminished rescue capability. The major change was a decision not to risk a takeoff and landing on the unknown polar surface to plant the flag, or to fly fifty miles beyond the pole into unseen territory, as Byrd had intended. When he arrived at the South Pole, he would pivot around in the air and hurry back. Byrd tried to resurrect his full flying program by arranging for another big plane to be donated and shipped down on a whaler early in the flying season, but he was unsuccessful. As usual, having learned from the success of Amundsen and the failure of Scott, Byrd wanted to plan for every contingency during the flight. "It is my practice to leave nothing to chance," he said. He directed that schedules allow for estimation errors of twenty percent.[51]

The pilots were the highest paid of the members on salary. Smith said that the first pilots to join the expedition, Balchen and June, had been paid only about $250 per month until Smith negotiated the handsome monthly figure of $500 to join. Balchen, as head of aviation, felt he should get no less, so Byrd gave the Norwegian a raise. Byrd allowed June to seek a sponsor to supplement his salary. June turned successfully to his former boss, Captain Vanderbilt.[52]

Wintering over was not all routine. Noteworthy events occurred, many never revealed to the world because they so mocked the upright image of Byrd and his antarctic comrades.

.8.

Days of Night

At the beginning of winter, ten men were jammed into two double bunks and two triple bunks in the Biltmore. In mid-April, after Walden and Braathen moved from the mess hall to Blubberheim, Byrd ordered Alexander and Feury to move from the overcrowded Biltmore to the mess hall and take the vacated bunks. This innocent order precipitated an episode that revealed a division among the Little Americans. The Biltmore's residents included the three musketeers from Harvard, who would drive dogs for the geological party that would explore the mountains, and Bursey and De Ganahl, who would drive dogs for the supporting party that would lay bases along the route to the mountains. Byrd had wanted to keep the sledge teams together, but for unclear reasons, the three musketeers did not want to associate with the other two drivers. The Harvard trio wanted Bursey and De Ganahl to vacate the Biltmore instead of the two men Byrd had tapped. The musketeers garnered the support of most of the Biltmore's other residents and approached Byrd, who acceded to the will of the majority and told Bursey and De Ganahl to move out.[1]

In May, Byrd reached a major decision about the nature of his expedition: to extend it for at least one year by leaving a scientific party of volunteers to continue research. He clucked to Railey that "it seems a pity to lose the chance for scientific results" at the scheduled end of his expedition. Byrd did not want to run or support a continuing expedition himself, however, and asked Railey to try to find a governmental or private organization to take over. Railey responded enthusiastically to the idea, pointing out that ". . . it would react greatly to your advantage."[2] The business manager tried for months but never could find a taker, however, so the concept died aborning.

On Thursday, 9 May 1929, to celebrate the anniversary of the north polar flight, Byrd's men surprised him with a turkey banquet at which he and the fourteen others who had been with him at Spitsbergen were the guests of honor: Black, De Ganahl, Feury, Charles Gould (no relation to Larry), Haines, Hanson, Owen, Parker, Petersen, and Van der Veer, as well as Balchen, Demas, Mulroy, and Tennant, who had also worked on the transatlantic flight. Alexander put on blackface and worked as the "darky" servant. Coman broke out the alcohol and mixed it with lemon powder to make a potent drink called Blowtorch. Byrd ordered plenty for everyone, and the men slaked thirsts deep from months of extraordinary toil and stress. Davies, who had emigrated from Wales to Canada and like so many other Welshmen abroad was nicknamed Taffy, proclaimed that no Yank could outdrink a man from Wales. Entering an elbow-bending bout with fellow scientist Gould, Davies drank himself under the table. Only six men abstained: Siple, Demas, Vaughan, Bursey, Mason, and Van der Veer. According to Siple, "A few others drank as gentlemen." Afterward, half the group adjourned to Blubberheim, where Gould got carried away and ordered everyone, in his words, "to get cock-eyed drunk." The men drank and partied till 4:00 A.M. in what Harrison described as "a spectacular and riotous drunken orgy." One by one, most of the revelers passed out, and many were too ill to get out of bed the next day. When Byrd called his bridge foursome together the following night, McKinley, still sick, fainted and fell out of his chair.[3]

Shortly after lights out that following night, 10 May, Bursey felt restless and decided to visit the other Canadian, Davies, who was then posted in the darkroom as night watchman. Davies was a Ph.D. candidate in geophysics at McGill University in Montreal when he joined the Byrd expedition. Bursey noticed that Davies's greeting was groggy, but then most Little Americans were still in a fog. Strangely, the playful puppy that was kept there lay still and did not greet Bursey at all. He bent over and found the pup out cold and barely alive. Bursey roused Coman. Just when the doctor came in, Davies started shaking violently and collapsed. Figuring there was something wrong with the air in the room, Bursey and Coman carried Davies out and stretched him on a table and then retrieved the pup. Both recovered in half an hour. Investigation revealed that a blizzard had filled the room's ventilator with snow, allowing carbon monoxide from the kerosene stove to build up to a toxic level. Davies, who apparently had sat through the poisoning thinking he was only hung over, would probably have died but for Bursey's timely visit. Carbon monoxide remained a danger. When the Biltmore's residents felt headachy and faint one day, they recognized the symptoms and cleaned out their ventilator before any of them were overcome.[4] Explorers did not escape danger when they stored their planes and sledges—Antarctica could get men even as they hung around doing nothing.

The unconstrained north polar celebration awakened the desire for liquor at Little America. The day after, lanky, tobacco-chewing carpenter Charles Gould, thirty-two (who like many ship's carpenters bore the nickname "Chips"), and Thorne felt they had some catching up to do, so they broke into the fifty-gallon drums of pure alcohol in the locked storeroom. After lights out, when the commotion over Davies's poisoning was over, these two met with Black and Feury in the Biltmore "against [most of the] inmates' wishes," Siple scrawled angrily in his diary. The boozy get-together featured an all-out battle in which the drunks threw everything that was loose in the room at the nonparticipants and themselves.[5]

The rowdy parties became a nightly event. Siple, who was getting little sleep, complained to Byrd, who promised him on 13 May that the parties would end that night. Nevertheless, on they went. Once, when a violent argument broke out, a drunken Feury got raving mad, nearly wrecking the place. Repeatedly punching Demas in the mouth, Feury stopped only when hit on the head with a heavy ski boot and knocked out by Thorne. Byrd normally allowed peer pressures to control behavior, but there were too many drinkers and too high a tolerance for drunkenness. Byrd and Gould sought a nondivisive way to stop the parties. Byrd did not want to give anyone a tongue-lashing or punishment that would corner him into a position of defiance, a position that would seriously undermine the commander's authority over his civilian volunteer force and split the expedition. Byrd was stalemated and reacted by turning testy.[6]

Almost three weeks after the celebration that started the problem, the drinking climaxed in a particularly wild party lasting till 5:00 A.M. The drinking bout was "like a tornado," Harrison said; "a decided brawl," Gould moaned. Thorne and Chips Gould got inebriated again the following afternoon. Remorseful, the two drunks staggered to Byrd and confessed they had stolen alcohol and instigated the parties. The two men detailed their problems, which dated back to servitude under Captain Melville on the *New York*, and promised to sin no more. Byrd absolved the men. With relief, Siple wrote in his diary, "Thank goodness it was all smoothed over. . . .The commander surely is a diplomat."[7]

A few days later, Larry Gould recorded that "there has been so much to do these past few days getting the boys of the recent drunk back into proper line and proper frame of mind toward this very compact society. . . . [It] was a bad thing and it came nearer demoralizing camp than anything that has happened heretofore, and it can in no sense be tolerated again."[8]

In mid-May, Demas had been granted permission to take the watch every night for the rest of the winter. Demas, who had enrolled at New York University to major in engineering when Byrd asked him to delay matriculation and come along to Antarctica, wanted to use the quiet hours to study in preparation for college.

At 5:30 A.M., Thursday, 20 June, night watchman Demas let out what Harrison described as "ungodly screams," jolting everyone in the administration building awake. "The barrier's breaking! The barrier's breaking!" Demas yelled, looking terrified and confused. "All hands on deck! A crevasse has opened up and is threatening to separate the camp." Everybody leaped out of bed, donning whatever clothing first came to hand and rushing outside. The men had feared this catastrophe since the voyage down, when they had seen enormous sections of the barrier floating by. Recently, cracks had formed around the camp, feeding the fear that Little America would become an iceberg that in summer would drift out to sea and melt away, and that the United States would have to mount a desperate rescue mission. Demas's alarm meant that the men would have to move supplies and quickly relocate the camp much farther south on the barrier. It would be difficult at best in the cold and dark of winter, and perhaps impossible if the base drifted away faster than expected. The incipient castaways wondered why Byrd had not come out of his room. Then they saw Gould laughing.[9]

Alone during the night, Demas had cooked up the prank, which he had discussed with Balchen, Byrd, and Gould. Gould advised against the idea. The commander warned Demas that the joke was pretty serious but let him use his own judgment. The main target was fearful Owen, who worried openly about disaster and had taken a lot of kidding about his fears. Owen said good naturedly that he and others were "trying to think of some way of getting even with [Demas]. Boiling him in oil would be satisfactory to me." Demas related that for a week after, in fear of retribution, he jumped at every sound.[10]

The bored shut-ins played practical jokes all winter: a door handle was wired to give shocks, for example, and a stove pipe was stuffed with rags to choke Owen as he started a fire. Jack O'Brien, thirty-two, a surveyor who had prospected in Mexico and Canada, wired a toilet so he could set off a charge of flashpowder inside when someone raised a seat lid. The Welshman, Frank Davies, was the selected victim. After the prank, a mock news story appeared on the bulletin board. The item—one suspects it came from Owen's typewriter—referred to features of auroras the physicist had taught the watchmen: "Coronas, streamers, arches and many other phenomena were brought home vividly to Professor Frank as he sat on the crapper this morning planning his day's magnetic work and disposing of Great Britain's food problem. A FLASH, A FLAME, AND SMOKE GALORE, SCORCHED HIS BOTTOM FOREVERMORE!"[11] The shenanigans served as a safety valve to vent the hostilities that winter living engendered.

Silliness seemed to infect everyone as the confinement began to wear. The burly Dr. Coman ran the two hundred yards from the administration building to the mess hall in fifty-two-below temperatures, brandishing a walking stick and wearing a pith helmet and socks—and nothing else. (Later, Haines and Hanson also made runs in the nude.) Because of a neurological disorder, Coman never shivered or felt normally cold, and always wore light clothes.[12]

Assistant resident surgeon at Johns Hopkins University Hospital, Francis Dana Coman, thirty-three, whose friends at Little America called him by his middle name, was among several members who had served with the Grenfell mission in Labrador. Before college, during the great war, he had spent three years as a private in the French infantry. His expedition duties included dentistry, but he lacked either the skills or facilities to do good dental work. After he pulled a tooth from Demas, the mechanic jotted in his diary, "It sure did hurt!" Coman did not have any anesthetic to use, Demas complained, but he was not clear whether he meant during the extraction or afterward to kill the pain. Coman's patients were glad that he had a backup for emergencies in the form of the Radio Consulting Medical Board, organized by several New York physicians who had copies of all the explorers' medical records.[13]

Midwinter day, 21 June, was the blackest day of the antarctic year, and at midnight the radiant sun was as far as it would go below the horizon. At noon, when the sun was closest to the horizon—comparable to an hour before dawn in New York—only a pale yellow line showed on the horizon. The absence of daylight was as vaguely unsettling as the absence of darkness had been comforting, as if the lingering terrors that had nightly threatened mankind's ancestors had become permanent. Byrd said he considered midwinter the most dangerous part of the stay. In a message to Railey, the commander wrote, "I wonder if you realize the personnel difficulties of a winter night not generally known by any but explorers who do not tell about them. . . . Almost without exception, the veteran arctic explorers have told me many tales in order to warn me about this phase of the winter night. . . ." Indeed, as winter had deepened, chronic depression overcame some men. Insomnia kept many awake, yet they hated to get out of bed— Chips, for example, probably depressed, earned his second nickname, "Horizontal" Gould, for spending so much time in his bunk. Even thinking seemed too great an effort. Men became absentminded, staring vacantly and having difficulty concentrating on anything. Discussions usually did not stay on one topic for long, and talk tended to become assertive and unresponsive. Conversation turned more and more to badinage—the language salty and the banter ribald.[14]

The men got on one another's nerves and were literally driven to distraction by petty idiosyncracies. Owen, for example, related how maddening he found De Ganahl's panting way of breathing, his belief in dreams, and his frequent use of the phrase "I'm sorry." The cultural disparities that made the camp a melting pot—and which Byrd said had inspired him to call it Little America—contributed to the friction.

Byrd, for instance, had to tell New York Irishman O'Brien how infuriating others found his wisecracks. As a result of the petty conflicts, Czegka became so morose he threatened to kill himself. Doubtlessly referring to the machinist, Byrd wrote that he "had walked for hours with a man who was on the verge of murder or suicide over imaginary persecutions by another man who had been his devoted friend."[15]

Perhaps Byrd's own mind was affected. Harrison observed that the commander was "dabbling in philosophy more intensely than ever," an inward-looking trait associated with mental strain when that study is motivated more by emotional needs than intellectual curiosity. Byrd thought a lot about the riddles of creation and the meaning of life. He had always injected philosophic reflections—usually jejune and often unclear—into his writings and had written an unpublished book of his personal philosophies. He read works on philosophy and copied passages that interested him. In conversation, he often remarked on the philosophical and psychological aspects of the matters at hand. He would pump Davies for explanations of the nature of matter and energy. Byrd committed some of the philosophical ruminations that he considered especially incisive to a winter diary entry: "There has just taken definite form in my mind a great psychological truth. It is this: That our unknown, untouched, unsuspected, enormous, deep, cosmical, almost unlimited mental resources can be called upon and utilized by a certain type of idea which may spring from a number of different stimulus [sic], such for example as asceticism—the denying of one's self the gratification of natural desire. . . . Here lies one of the deepest and most profound truths of life."[16]

After dinner one Sunday, Byrd invited Harrison in for one of the discussions about philosophy that the commander had held with others. For three hours, Byrd ran on about theology, relativity, eternity, evolution, atomism, and the never-ending processes of change in the universe. "He may be worrying too much over these matters for the good of his mind," Harrison commented.[17]

Although the solstice was winter's turnaround point, the cloistered men still had weeks of debilitating darkness to endure. Serious trouble broke loose again on the Fourth of July. The holiday began innocently enough with bugle calls and gunshots at reveille. At the end of the workday, moved up to 2:00 P.M. for the holiday, the dormant explorers enlivened their winter hutch with an all-out party. It started with a turkey feast and cocktails. Some of the more creative members staged a show afterward with a chorus line and vaudeville skits. Blond, beard-less, fair-skinned Crockett looked so pretty in his chorus-girl costume that the hall resounded with wolf whistles. The broad comedy made fun of everyone and everything, from the volumes of words and film that Owen and the so-called Paramount twins, Rucker and Van der Veer, were generating, to the promiscuity of the dogs, to personal quirks and foibles. (Straight man: Was Owen the first one out when he thought the barrier broke? Comedian: No, he was way ahead of the first!).[18] The audience laughed long and hard, releasing much of the winter's tension.

Despite the lessons of the first party, alcohol flowed freely. Gould vowed to keep sober and patrol the compound all night to make sure no drunks passed out and froze to death in the sixty-below cold. Byrd, in contrast, seemed totally unconcerned about drunkenness and even encouraged it. The commander collared his young bridge partner, Harrison, and forced four glasses of high-proof punch down his throat, getting him thoroughly intoxicated. As a drunken Haines stumbled around, swinging wildly and inviting all comers to fight, challengers approached and allowed themselves to be "knocked out" before the guffawing crowd. Byrd passed each fighter a drink as he stood up, then offered one to Haines. Before the weather chief could take it, Byrd pulled it away and swallowed it himself. The commander got falling-down drunk, and Gould and others had to help Byrd to his room. As they were carrying him, Byrd confessed that he was ashamed of being drunk and asked them to keep his condition quiet. Unaware of who was holding him, and pathetically desperate to maintain his holy image, he pleaded, "Don't tell Simon about this. Don't tell Owen. And, above all, don't tell Igloo."[19]

Some of the men drifted off to Blubberheim for serious drinking. During the bout, Smith sought out Mulroy, who was in charge of fuel and mechanical equipment. Mulroy was generally disliked. Those who had sailed all the way on the *New York* blamed him for the poor condition of the water distillation and other systems on the ship that had helped to make the voyage miserable. A self-important person, Mulroy had refused to clean the crystal palace when he lost the weekly poker game, and he had flared up about being kidded in the show. With almost everyone else who broke a rule, or whose behavior was excessively annoying, the group's razzing or unfriendliness was usually sufficient discipline. Peer pressure was especially effective in Antarctica because the guilty party had no one else to turn to and even had to rely on the others for physical survival; but Mulroy seemed oblivious to the pressure to be more cooperative. Smith quizzed Mulroy about his claim to be a member of the Quiet Birdmen, a select aviation fraternity to which Smith belonged, because Mulroy did not fit the fraternity's mold; under the persistent questioning, as the room quieted and all eyes turned to him, he had to admit he had been lying. He was embarrassed, angry, and inebriated when something about McKinley, who was sitting drunkenly nearby, set him off; the usually mild-mannered McKinley, who got arrogant and belligerent when under the influence, may have said something. Mulroy walked over to McKinley and, without warning, slugged him on the jaw, drawing a river of blood from his mouth. The group, enraged, their pent-up hostilities exploding, converged on Mulroy like caged animals released, pummelling him viciously until Gould pulled them off. Gould and Smith took Mulroy to his bed.[20]

Feeling that the despised Mulroy had gotten off too easily, the supply officer Black, thirty-two, a sandy-haired little navy veteran and former prize fighter who had the thick-featured face of a boxer, slipped off to the bunk room in the administration building. Demas, on watch, tried to stop Black, but he slapped the young mechanic and demanded that Mulroy come back to Blubberheim. Fearfully, Mulroy followed. Black shoved Mulroy through the door right in front of a surprised Thorne, who reacted instantly by swinging and knocking Mulroy down. Several people challenged him to get up and fight, but he cringed and begged loudly for mercy. Gould again intervened and, with Smith's help, got Mulroy once more to his bunk.[21]

The next morning at breakfast, the mess hall fell silent when Mulroy walked in. Never looking at anyone else, he sat alone. Later that day, to escape from the hell of isolation, he volunteered for the distasteful crystal-palace detail every week for the rest of the winter. Only after performing this task faithfully and taking on other unpleasant duties did he win acceptance back into the group.[22]

Byrd, "very bashful and sheepish," Demas wrote, queried the mechanic about the night before. "[Byrd] thinks his conduct was very bad. I said 'no.' I personally think he helped morale by joining the boys," Demas said.[23]

The chagrined commander soon had other reasons to regret setting demon rum loose again. Two days after the bash, a gang broke into the alcohol supply once more and held a wild after-hours drinking bout. Harrison thought the tippling had its merits; as he noted, "Parties like this are good for morale. Under the influence, men seem to understand one another better than when sober." But as Demas noted, Byrd seemed most disturbed. The commander had to think of the consequences, so he reprimanded the men and asked them to end the parties. Byrd said he was afraid that drinking would lead to fighting and, with fatherly rectitude, admonished his troops: "Harmony on the expedition is the most important thing. . . . I'd rather be able to say we acted like Americans than fly over the pole."[24]

The drinking continued, however, resulting in Byrd's first overt confrontation over discipline and arousing his fear of disloyalty. On 12 July after taps—when quiet individual activities were allowed—the commander ordered O'Brien, one of the drinkers who was still at it, to turn in. O'Brien, a hatchet-faced Irish-American who had played professional football, objected to the order, apparently feeling he was being singled out unfairly. Byrd immediately ordered a general curfew, with everyone to be in either his bed or the library every night after 10:00 P.M. The commander announced that the night watchman would enforce the rule and told Demas to use his judgment to handle and report offenders. Byrd wrote darkly in his diary the next day, "The first real indication of a mutinous heart was when O'Brien openly criticized my order to him last night, taps being at 10 o'clock. As there are no favorites, I issued the order. At the breakfast table he tried to get Blackie to stand with him. . . . All the trouble comes from four people. Probably three out of the four are OK at rock bottom, but on the surface they are constantly criticizing and attempting to make trouble."[25]

Demas was uneasy, finding himself between the restive men on one hand and Byrd on the other. "I must be on the good side of both," he wrote plaintively the night of the order. The fears of the mechanic-cum-monitor were well-founded. Two days after the order he wrote, "There has been quite a bit of criticism caused by the taps order. The commander and I to a certain extent have made a few bitter enemies. I have been referred to as 'the messenger' and 'the aide de camp' and so forth. [But] duty is duty." Two days later, Demas quoted Byrd: " 'Demas, old boy, don't let what happened the other night worry you any. Larry and I have talked the whole thing over and we have found that all are behind me, like yourself, but two;' " he did not name the two.[26]

Byrd once said that "[Loyalty] is a quality which I value higher than merit."[27] Byrd surely prized loyalty so highly because he had no legal or economic power over his men—no direct way to compel them to work for his goals or follow his orders. He could offer no raises or promotions; he could threaten no firings or courts-martial. These limitations were a severe handicap for a leader of a quasi-military operation involving aggressive, active, largely uncultured young men, especially during the long periods when the group was confined in close quarters without much work or play to absorb youthful energy. The commander had to rely on extraordinary faithfulness in his troops.

On 15 July, Byrd told Demas he was "very much pleased with the loyalty of the gang," and Demas inscribed in his diary the commander's assurance that the mechanic would never regret their "mutual compact"—Demas wrote no explanation—in years to come.[28]

Five days later Byrd's dread of subversion led him to write an extraordinary document. A fourteen-page memorandum intended for those close to him in case he should die, the document concerned what he saw as Owen's disloyalty.[29] The document read: "I am glad that there has been (so far as I know) only one member who has been uniformly disloyal. . . . It has been tough that the one I have treated far kinder than anyone else should be the one who is against me. . . . He has threatened that he will show to the world the inefficiency of the expedition—that he will ruin the leader with the public. . . . It is therefore advisable that I give the facts in the case so that my friends and family will have them—solely, of course, for defense."

Accusing Owen of hating Amundsen and Lindbergh when the reporter worked with them, Byrd wrote, ". . . it appears to be congenitally difficult for Owen to be loyal to anyone he is detailed to serve with. . . ." Byrd described Owen's psychosomatic episode in January and mentioned Dr. Coman's diagnosis of paranoia. "Should I get down he would most certainly jump on me, so I must bring his enmity out in the open." Without being specific, Byrd wrote that Owen had criticized him behind his back, noting that Demas had written an attached statement (now missing).

Byrd continued, "Owen had told me that I was one of the best friends he ever had," referring to Owen as his closest friend on the expedition. But Owen, Byrd wrote, tried to turn the men against him. "Very fortunately, however, the loyalty of the men to me was of such a nature that I soon learned all about Owen's treachery in much detail. . . . Everyone but himself is loyal."

Byrd complained that in New Zealand Owen had not reported two events that Byrd felt should have been publicized: a speech that Byrd gave and the arrival of the *New York*, when the entire expedition had merged for the first time. (Byrd was surprised to find after the expedition that Owen actually had reported the speech.) The commander criticized Owen for ceasing all work except his reporting duties (although a duty roster for the housecleaning detail at the end of the winter included Owen's name).[30]

Byrd claimed that Owen "had a free hand in the writing of his stories for I never saw them until they had been given to the radio operators, unless he brought them to me to show me some particular part of them. . . . I discovered that he was supersensitive and vain about his stories, so in order to play the game with him I decided not to read his stories until several months after they were written. . . ." This statement implies that Byrd had been reading the stories after Owen gave them to the radio operators and had made changes that offended Owen's sensitivities. The implication also appears in an entry in Byrd's diary on 30 April 1929: ". . . I decided a month ago not to read Russell Owen's stories. I do reserve, however, to myself the power to regulate mentions of personnel. . . ." The reservation gave Byrd plenty of room for censorship, of course, since most of the stories were about the activities of personnel.

Smith recounted one of Owen's first experiences in radioing a story from Antarctica: "When Owen attempted to dispatch his story, the radio operators explained that it must first be reviewed and approved in writing by Commander Byrd. Although Owen protested vigorously in a long session with Byrd, the commander insisted then and throughout the expedition on personally censoring all news dispatches before release." Balchen later told a writer that Smith was right.[31]

In a subsequent addendum to the memorandum on Owen, Byrd wrote, "Owen showed great surprise that I know so much about his criticism of me behind my back." Byrd said Owen stated that the reason for his attitude was "the manner in which I at times look at him. He said that it was not what I did or said but that my eyes penetrated him and lacerated him terribly." The commander recorded that Owen promised to reform. "I requested him to put his promise in writing, but he said he would rather not do so."

In messages to Railey, Byrd also complained that Owen would not give credit to the expedition's supporters in his reports. The commander apologized by radio to the man for whom Little America's library was officially named (David Lyman) when Owen did not mention him in a story about the library (which Owen used as his workroom).[32] Byrd said he had not seen the text until it had been sent.

Confiding distrust of the reporter to Demas, Byrd implied that he wanted to be kept abreast of what Owen was up to. The mechanic, reflecting on what the commander had said, wrote in his diary that Owen "has a mental disease. He thinks himself above the others not actually but mentally. He has quite an important position on the expedition. We have to put up with him and watch him carefully, for he can do a lot of damage if he chooses by giving false facts."[33] Demas frequently wrote about others whose behavior he disapproved of and named those he did not like or respect, but he never criticized Owen's behavior before or after this entry.

Byrd had tried earlier in the winter to circumvent Owen's monopoly on news coverage by getting the *Times* to routinely accept reports from others at Little America. The commander wired a message to Railey, apparently not the first of its kind: "Strongly suggest to *N.Y. Times* that others (besides Coman, Davies, McKinley, etc.) write stories. It would give a more comprehensive picture of the expedition to have more than one man telling the public about it. This suggestion must come from you and I must not be brought into it." The members Byrd mentioned occasionally wrote special articles or features, mostly about individual projects. Railey responded: ". . . matter . . . has troubled me greatly for two months. Have already skirted subject with Sulzberger [*Times*'s vice president] who privately sympathizes with our point of view. Don't ask me to explain, but take my word for it that different and varied interpretations greatly needed and will help tremendously if it can be brought tactfully." Byrd replied, "In matter you are taking up with Sulzberger, it may be well to get all the backing you can from Fosdick and others. It is entirely wrong to put so much power in one man, Owen."[34] (Despite these efforts, however, Owen remained the only regular reporter on the Little America beat.)

Siple, who had been asked before sailing to write a boy's book about the expedition by Byrd's publisher, recorded sketchily in his diary,

"The commander spoke again about a book to me—as Russell O. has been asked to write a boy's book."[35] Perhaps this book was the one Byrd had earlier rescinded permission for Owen to write; the edgy commander may have wanted to be sure someone he trusted beat Owen to the book stores with a volume on the expedition.

Owen's side of the story is not known. In the books he wrote later, he did not seriously criticize Byrd, and none of the expedition's other authors or diary writers revealed a trace of suspicion that Owen was crazy or out to get Byrd, or even that the reporter was a troublemaker. After the expedition, Owen told other newsmen that Byrd had re-written the *Times*'s stories to make himself look better. Smith said that this rewriting was really the root of the problem and that Owen was severely distressed and angry that his professional integrity was being compromised.[36]

Besides having to contend with Byrd and the physical hardships, Owen also had to put up with the sneers of many of his compatriots. Demas recorded in his diary that Owen "is small in stature and weak physically (the weakest here). He has not participated in any of the work of the expedition other than his line to any extent." The reporter always seemed to have something wrong with him and could not do the heavy work that everyone else did, although at least for a time he served as the permanent housekeeper for the administration building. Some in the machismo-oriented society despised him for avoiding strenuous physical duties and taunted him, calling him names such as "diarrhea," "ringworm," and "step and a half," from a limp due to chronic arthritis in his right knee. The men callously christened one of the heads "the Russell Owen House."[37] O'Brien had originally intended Owen instead of Davies as the victim of the flash powder in the head, but Dr. Coman heard of the plot and beseeched O'Brien to switch targets—Owen was too often the butt of cruel humor and was near the breaking point from all the stresses on him.

Owen surely had himself in mind in describing the scramble for places at the long dining table, not big enough for everybody at once, when dinner was called: "There is a football scrimmage in getting places on the bench, and one is apt to be seized by a strong arm and lifted bodily. [Antarctica] is no place for a little fellow." As Mulroy met the psychic needs of the men to have a target for their hostility, Owen met the need to have a target for their contempt, whom they could belittle to make themselves seem superior. He served in the role of the palace fool, winning general acceptance only by joking about his weaknesses.[38]

The reporter once got some laughs at O'Brien's expense. O'Brien was to test a sleeping bag Gould had designed for the long summer trek by bedding down in a tent but called off the trial when the temperature dropped to a forbidding minus fifty-five. Owen, who liked O'Brien but had often borne the brunt of his Irish wit, surprised everyone by declaring that if O'Brien was too much of a pantywaist to go through with the test, the reporter would have to take over. Owen later waddled out the door, wearing so many clothes he could hardly move, and carrying what seemed to be two sleeping bags tucked one inside the other. Next morning, when he flung open the door and shuffled in to breakfast, the crew cheered a new "hero." When O'Brien slunk in, they booed. Still the men regarded Owen's performance as the cavorting of a fool; their opinion of him was no higher. Demas, as tough as Owen was weak, reached over and seized O'Brien's coffee cup. When O'Brien remonstrated, Demas taunted, "If a thing like Russell Owen treats you like that, I certainly can take your coffee away from you."[39]

In Owen's books, his severest criticism of Byrd was that the commander was somewhat secretive and suspicious.[40] Owen did not know—or tell—the half of it. The day after Byrd wrote his splenetic diatribe against the newsman, there occurred one of a series of meetings between Byrd and a few selected members that may be unique in the annals of expeditions and similar enterprises anywhere. The meetings bespoke Byrd's intense preoccupation with potential disloyalty.

The commander asked Siple to come for a walk-and-talk session out on the gloomy barrier.[41] Presumably, Byrd looked dead serious and spoke in a rehearsed manner. He talked of the waning of the winter night, which on other expeditions so affected some men that their loyalty failed their leaders. Then he declared, "I have a proposal to make to you . . . I cannot, however, make this proposal to you unless you agree on your solemn word of honor not to mention in writing, by speaking, or in any other way, the matter I am about to propose." Siple gave his word. At this point, the pair probably went back to Byrd's office and closed the door.

Byrd had composed a five-page script with twenty-nine numbered paragraphs for what he had to say.[42] Likely picking it up and glancing at it, he went on, "I am now free to invite you to join a fraternity, the purpose of which is to ensure, as far as possible, that neither now nor in civilization any person or persons in the expedition be permitted to be disloyal or mutinous. In other words, that you join with me in trying to prevent the spirit of loyalty of the expedition from being lowered by disloyal, treacherous or mutinous conduct on the part of any disgruntled members. . . . Until you agree and become a member of this fraternity it will be nameless, for its name must not be known by anyone but its members. . . . No one but myself will know who the other members are until we return to civilization, when at some suitable time, in my home, they will be made known to each other."

The ritual was undoubtedly influenced by Byrd's experience in the Masons. Every so often he paused and asked the awestricken scout if he still wanted to proceed. Getting "yes" answers every time, Byrd administered the oath of the secret brotherhood:

I solemnly swear on my word of honor and by all that I reverence and hold sacred, and without hesitation or mental reservation, that I will divulge to no one in any way and in no manner anything whatever in connection with the Loyal Legion . . . that whenever you call for my assistance in the name of the Loyal Legion . . . I will take such action as you request; that I will not divulge the request to anyone, just as I will hold as confidential and sacred matter anything whatever connected with the Loyal Legion, nor will I, by any act whatever, make an effort to learn the names of the other members of the fraternity; that in case of disloyalty displayed in a crowd when you are present, I will act in response to a predetermined signal and a predetermined course of action; that I will strive just as faithfully after the expedition ends to maintain its spirit of loyalty and will oppose any traitors to it then, as now. In short, I . . . will protect this expedition against [traitors] from within. . . . To all of this I swear, so help me God.

Then Byrd swore his own oath to Siple:

I . . . solemnly swear, by the same oath that you have taken, that I will hold your pledged loyalty as a sacred trust, and will pledge you my loyalty; and I will also, in evoking through you the spirit of the expedition to help save it from malcontents, agitators or traitors, that I will at the same time do whatever is practicable to save these men from themselves and from ruining their own lives.

(Byrd continued his ultrasecrecy about the Loyal Legion after the expedition, when he implored his anointed acolytes to destroy correspondence that mentioned the group.)[43]

That night, Siple recorded ecstatically in his diary: "[Byrd] has one grand idea and ideal which puts more pep into me for the expedition, and that if my opinion of the commander had not yet reached the sky it surely got there today."[44]

A week after inducting Siple, Byrd tapped another impressionable young man, Pete Demas. In a diary entry headed "The Loyal Legion," Demas wrote joyously: "The greatest honor that I could attain on the expedition was bestowed on me tonight. The commander has made me one of his chosen few of his most loyal or 'loyalest of the loyal,' as he put it. This he told me was formed in 1926."[45]

Other known Loyal Legion initiates were two more youths, Crockett and De Ganahl, and the unsophisticated carpenter, Chips Gould. Byrd may also have tried to recruit Clarke. The young general hand noted mysteriously in his diary: "A surprise came . . . when the commander asked me to go for a walk. . . . He had a proposition to offer me which I refused. Then we discussed future plans and incidental politics."[46] Based on their known devotion to Byrd and their level-headedness, other likely candidates would appear to include Bubier, Goodale, and perhaps Lofgren, who probably typed the neat pages of the induction ceremony and of the memorandum about Owen.

The overwhelming insecurity that prompted Byrd to form the Loyal Legion was apparent to many people who knew him. Larry Gould said of Byrd, "I think I have never known a more unhappy man or a man less secure, a man more suspicious of the motives of those around him." Vaughan noted that Byrd was unsure of himself. Byrd's insecurity poisoned his relationships. Balchen often spoke in exasperation of his difficulty in getting to know Byrd. General Billy Mitchell had said that "[Byrd] is very well known, but no one knows him very well."[47] The commander's reserve was a matter of personality as well as policy. He seems not to have had a close friend at Little America, no one with whom he could unburden himself, nor to have taken anyone fully into his confidence, even Gould. Given Byrd's extreme fear of mutiny, he must have felt he could not fully rely on Gould's abilities as exec to keep the men in line.

Every so often, when Byrd felt almost overcome by events, he repeated a phrase that revealed his emotional isolation. He would tell people that his problems were "more than any one man should have to bear alone." In a winter message to Captain Brown in New Zealand, for example, the commander said plaintively, "I have had more worries and apprehensions than any one man should have to bear alone."[48]

A verse that Byrd took the trouble to find, copy, encode, and radio to Marie reflected both his insecurities and his loneliness:

> Someone like you who stands steadfastly near me, knows me, likes me for just what I am. Someone like you who knows just how to cheer me, someone who's real without pretense or sham. Someone whose fellowship isn't a fetter binding my freedom, who's loyal all through. Someone whose life in this world makes it better. Blest to me, best to me. Someone like you who's the same day and morrow, firm as a rock and square as a clock. Someone who's steadfast in joy or sorrow. Someone who's dearer each day that goes by. Fortune is fickle and hope is deceiving. There's only one thread that runs all through the weaving. Fair to me, square to me. Someone like you.[49]

Byrd continually tried to find out all he could about what was going on among the men by encouraging everyone to come to him with information and by approaching individuals in private about what they knew. Those who cooperated with him were taunted as apple polishers or flag wavers by the rest. Byrd once told Demas that some men were working against the expedition and, through accusations of apple polishing, keeping the others from showing maximum loyalty to the commander. Demas, perplexed, told his diary he had no idea who Byrd was talking about and did not think the assertion was true.[50]

There were some legitimate grounds for Byrd to worry, however. For one thing, he could assume that the aggressive Hearst organization, which had already published contraband photos from Little America, might buy off someone else—and perhaps already had—to get the inside story of the expedition, embarrassing and possibly ruining Byrd. On the other hand, he seems to have felt much more insecure than was warranted. The paranoid side to his personality led increasingly to misunderstandings and bad feelings between him and many of his associates. Byrd's obsession with loyalty colored his relationships with his men. Even one of Byrd's most devoted, Demas, had speculated in his diary about the commander's motives for asking who was willing to stay another winter if he could arrange a continuing expedition. Demas wondered if Byrd "may be trying to find out how many will still be loyal to him." Most of the men probably never considered loyalty to be a questionable issue. Years later, Davies commented to Harrison that Byrd had "the quite mistaken notion that the expedition was divided into loyal and disloyal groups. This is nonsense." Harrison replied, "I heartily concur."[51]

Someone proposed that the Little Americans reassure the commander about their loyalty. Siple thought the suggestion came from Balchen, and Harrison thought it came from Black. Given Byrd's manipulative ways (including his role behind the scenes in getting signatures for another loyalty reaffirmation after the expedition), it is conceivable that the defensive commander himself planted the suggestion for the pledge with a devotee. All the men at camp agreed to present Byrd with a plaque, signed by everyone, expressing appreciation for his governance and pledging their loyalty. Bubier wrote the words. Balchen, a talented artist who used his scanty free time to paint local scenes, sketched the design, which pictured the camp, the *New York*, dogs, the Ford, and an aurora. Gould presented the plaque to Byrd in a little ceremony after dinner one night.[52]

The next day Byrd told Demas that he felt loyalty at camp was one hundred percent, except for Owen. To Byrd's displeasure, the cynical newsman did not report the affirmation of loyalty to the *Times*. The commander badly wanted that story published, probably to strengthen his hand against Owen and any other "traitors" who might make charges against Byrd's leadership after the expedition. Frustrated, Byrd had Lofgren send the text of the plaque to Railey, clearly indicating that he was to get the text into the newspaper (the messages had to be subtly worded, since they were received by the *Times*'s radio operators). Railey succeeded "after taking greatest precaution avoid appearance publication was inspired by you," he told Byrd, and even persuaded the newspaper to run an editorial extolling Byrd's leadership. Lofgren, one suspects on Byrd's orders, radioed the text of the testimonial to the expedition's contingent in New Zealand and suggested that they also have the text published.[53] They complied.

Besides Owen, there was another key person whose attitude seems to have irked Byrd: Bernt Balchen. The Norwegian might have been expected to be among those closest to Byrd; in fact, a *New York Times* report during the early planning stages listed Balchen as fourth in command of the enterprise. Balchen was in charge of the technical aspects of the flying program, and Gould praised Balchen for the splendid aviation equipment. A versatile worker, he designed a light sledge that Byrd wanted the Ford to carry for man-hauling supplies in case of a forced landing and helped Strom rebuild the sledges for the summer treks. With Ronne, Balchen designed a tent especially for antarctic conditions. A marvel at making things, he improvised items ranging from doorknobs to airplane parts. Although the Norwegian's loyalty was then unquestioned, Harrison noted that "[Balchen] seemed to be in the bad graces of Byrd" all during the expedition without any reason obvious to the others—nor, Balchen said, was the reason obvious to him. Balchen's opinions about the commander may have shown through and contributed to Byrd's frostiness, however. From the tone of Balchen's writings, it seems clear that he felt himself a better man and explorer than Byrd. The Norwegian was bigger, stronger, and physically superior overall. He was mechanically talented and Byrd was not. Unafraid to fly, Balchen could fly much better and knew more about aviation technology than Byrd. Like his hero Amundsen, Balchen was skilled at the outdoor activities he felt natural to explorers—hunting, fishing, camping, skiing—and Byrd had little interest or experience in them. Without Balchen's help at Spitsbergen, Byrd might not have been able to take off for the North Pole. But for the Norwegian, Byrd's transatlantic flight might have ended disastrously. There is no indication that Balchen told anyone his opinions abut Byrd, but the Norwegian's feelings may have been too evident. According to Smith, Balchen's chief failing was that "he tended to underrate men whose talents were different from his own, and was a bit too ready to look at them with contempt."[54] Byrd diminished himself further in Balchen's eyes by shamelessly manicuring a public image.

Balchen also resented Byrd's dealing directly with the members of the aviation unit and bypassing the unit chief. Once Demas and Roth got into a shouting match over responsibilities for mechanical work on the Ford's engines. When Balchen stepped in to calm them down, both Roth and Demas claimed to have received responsibility for the engines from Byrd. They both revealed that Byrd had asked each of them to report to him if the other mechanics did not do a good job. Balchen told them they reported directly to him, not to Byrd, and should take orders only from him. Balchen then confronted the commander, insisting that as head of the aviation unit he could not have Byrd or the men going around him; Balchen did not reveal Byrd's reaction. Byrd's treatment of Balchen was not unique—Byrd had also bypassed his ship captains in New Zealand, appointing, over their objections, a crew member as "personnel" officer to have responsibility for the men of both ships and to report to Byrd. Balchen also said he thought Byrd used his walk-and-talk sessions with individuals as much to manipulate as communicate. Byrd seemed to string the pilots along, for instance, hinting to each of the hopeful contenders that he would fly the polar plane.[55]

Balchen's main winter chore was to work on the Ford's performance figures, charting the effects of variables such as weight, altitude, speed, and temperature, singly and in combination. He also had with him extensive data on Byrd's north polar Fokker gathered from the records Balchen compiled while working in New Jersey as a Fokker engineer and from the cross-country promotional tour he and Bennett had made in the plane. Balchen related that he once went on one of Byrd's walks. "I said just in passing that now [that I'd completed the Ford's performance chart] I had been thinking of making up one on the [north polar Fokker] if [he] would like to have it. Well, that was the wrong thing to say . . . because he flew into a rage and told me that if I ever at any time monkeyed around with the figures of [that plane] , he would sure teach me something else, and for me to forever stay away from any of those figures."[56] There was no expedition-connected reason for Balchen to spend time on figures related to the north polar flight. He seems to have raised the subject just to needle Byrd. Getting the expected reaction, Balchen became certain what the calculations would show, but he let the subject drop, perhaps not wanting to antagonize Byrd too much before the commander announced the pilot for the south polar flight.

There were other personality clashes among the men. Siple had his own list of members he did not like, for example. In the privacy of his diary, he drew up what would be the antithesis of the Loyal Legion, under the quotation, "If he is a devil in his heart, and though he makes his way to a seat on a throne, he will fall hard." The names were Shropshire, Melville, Brophy, Coman, Mulroy, Feury, and two sailors on the *New York*. At the bottom under the subheading, "In lesser ways," Siple added the names of Thorne, who with Feury was one of the problem drinkers, and Walden, who not only had not worked out as head of the sledge unit but who Siple thought was also neglecting his dogs. (Interestingly, Siple did not list either Balchen or the top name on Byrd's black list, Owen.) Coman was standoffish and not widely liked. He had made himself unpopular on the voyage down by taking advantage of the privileges Captain Melville bestowed on his officers and by helping the cook to chloroform the crew's sick pet dog, which the cook did not like. Byrd had designated Coman Little America's biologist, but the doctor had ignored Siple's proposals for studying seals and would do no biology himself (although Byrd may never have given the doctor the support to pursue biology).[57]

Despite the personality clashes and other strains of wintering over, the men generally got along well together, and some, such as Gould, "had a great time," as he put it. He felt that intellectual and cultural interests were the best protection against mental deterioration. Loyal Legionnaire Demas ascribed the high morale to another cause: "Our love for our leader is one of the things that has kept us in a fine spirit."[58]

The Bay of Whales was the coldest place men had ever based in Antarctica. Amundsen had recorded minus 74.4 degrees at Framheim. On 28 July 1929, the temperature descended to a record low for Little America of 72 below (which would remain the coldest).

The world was different when the temperature sank below minus 60. In the unheated sections of Little America, antifreeze froze. The telephone wire connecting the two main buildings got brittle and broke when handled. An iron pipe made into an axe handle cracked at the shock of a chop. Carpenter's nails had to be warmed to withstand hammering. Batteries would not work, candles would not light, and kerosene congealed—making it harder to overcome the dark. Breath froze into tiny crystals, and if a breeze blew it past one's ears, it sounded "like the rustle of a woman wearing silks," according to Demas.[59] Touching cold metal was almost like touching red-hot metal—it gave a frost burn that felt, looked, and eventually peeled like sunburn.

The men who operated delicate equipment—Davies, the meteorologists, the Paramount cameramen—spent a lot of time keeping their instruments working in the extreme cold, when metal parts overly contracted or failed, and especially when moisture got inside and condensed or froze on moving parts and lenses.

Temperature swings were so violent that, only three days after the record low, the reading rose to 15 above. "That makes a range of 87 degrees—as much as the *annual* range over most of the eastern U.S.," Harrison observed.[60]

Although confined by the oppressive cold and darkness, Little

Americans reached out to the world by radio. The wireless operators would talk with Byrd's representative in New Zealand in the morning but had to wait until afternoon—when it was dark in New York's longitude far to the east—for signal conditions to be good enough to contact the United States. The operators would exchange news and official messages first and then personal messages to and from members. If time and conditions permitted after New York signed off, the operators would talk with hams, who would also relay personal messages. After something said to a ham was passed on to the rival Hearst papers, however, the *Times* made Byrd forbid his operators to discuss anything newsworthy.[61]

The nightly news from the *Times*, and often other radio news sources, was typed on "Radiogram—Byrd Antarctic Expedition" letterhead and drew a crowd when snapped onto a clipboard that hung on a nail outside the radio room. The isolated explorers were even hungrier for personal news; in midwinter, the number of personal messages ran twice that of official ones. The expedition, however, was short of fuel to run the generator that powered the transmitter; even Czegka, the machinist, limited his use of power tools to two hours a day. Byrd realized he would precipitate a crisis in morale if he arbitrarily rationed personal messages, so he formed a committee of members to set procedures. As a result, each man was limited to sending one message every two weeks, and form messages were composed that could be sent simply by specifying numbers. Message number six, under this businesslike regime, for example, read, "Have enjoyed receiving your messages that came by voice from stations KDKA and WGY. Appreciate your kind thoughts and send best wishes from Little America."[62]

Radio continued to bring bad news as well as good. In August, Dick Brophy, who had returned to the United States months before, disappeared while swimming. He had left a suicide note saying he would drown himself, and his clothes had been found in a seaside bath house at Brooklyn's Coney Island after everyone had deserted the beach. Railey softened the announcement by informing Byrd that circumstances indicated that Brophy had faked suicide so he could disappear, but Byrd told Marie he believed Brophy had killed himself.[63] The news must have been unsettling to the commander since the burden of responsibility for his associates always weighed heavily on him, although there is no record of his emotional reaction.

With sunrise approaching, the horizon began to show a rosy color at noon. As the sky brightened, so did spirits at Little America. Gould noted in his diary that "there is an increasingly genial attitude of the various men toward each other."[64]

Byrd, who Harrison noted had "added a few gray hairs" over the winter, could hardly wait to see the dawn. On 20 August, with sunrise officially two days away, the commander climbed a tall radio tower at noon to try to peek over the horizon. He reported just being able to make out the refracted image of the upper limb of the longed-for sun. Gould wrote joyfully, "Not long now until we shall have a midnight sun and then light, light, light—brilliant, blinding, dazzling light for weeks and months on end."[65] Sunshine never meant more to tribes of sun worshippers than it did to the deprived Little Americans.

At official sunrise on 22 August, the joyful commander staged a flag-raising ceremony, with the Victrola playing a scratchy bugle call to arms. The meteorologists initiated a season-long series of measurements to show how much heat arrives directly on the antarctic snow from the sun.[66]

Gould had promised to celebrate sunrise with a *real* party because it was also his thirty-third birthday. The camp decided to turn the event into a festivity for all members with birthdays around that time and to commemorate the sailing anniversary of the *New York*. The celebration started with a dinner emceed by Byrd, who presented Gould with a certificate of appreciation signed by everyone, again drawn by Balchen and showing dogs, a whip, a pressure ridge, and Gould sighting mountains. In Byrd's writings, he commented—and Owen agreed in his own commentaries—that Gould had been the one who held the expedition together over the winter.[67] The exec kept morale high and maintained a sense of group purpose under circumstances that had torn apart less well managed expeditions.

Despite the bad experience with alcohol at parties, and perhaps seduced by wishful thinking, neither Byrd nor Gould seemed convinced that drinking would inevitably cause problems, indulgently allowing the party to become "plenty wet," as Gould put it. No doubt under the influence, the commander, giving an incredible after-dinner performance, appeared "rigged up as a perfect dollar waterfront whore, and his takeoff nearly started a riot," Harrison recorded. Someone got the idea to hold a football game in the mess hall. "Then things became rough. The mess table, glassware, and a blackboard were wrecked,"

Harrison said. Gould, in a carefree mood, was the first to pass out and be carried to his bunk.[68]

As might have been anticipated, the next evening a half dozen weak-willed members resumed drinking and kept at it on and off for days. "Those few who drink to excess have been taking advantage of the commander's good nature of overlooking a lot of things. . . . The commander and all the rest are thoroughly disgusted with it," Demas entered in his diary.[69]

Finally, Gould summoned all the problem members to the library. Demas wrote, "Larry gave the boys quite a talk, which the commander seconded. [Larry] commanded them to stop drinking. If anyone drinks again without permission he will be sent back as a passenger." Byrd again placed Demas in charge of enforcement, promising to help in any way. The mechanic had a talk with the drunks.[70] They assured him they would stay sober, and impressed by the lectures and threats, they did.

The sunrise, days long, was as gorgeous as the sunset. Gould wrote in awe: "It was as though the sun had been storing up over the four months that he had been gone for the great splashes that colored the early days of his return. And it is when the sun is near the horizon that the snow takes on its richest colorings, shading from the pale blue of celestite to the deepest purples where the shadows are heaviest. It is a kind of giant fairyland, for in the flat oblique rays of the sun everything casts long skeletal shadows that give an effect of only semi-reality."[71]

By then, all the buildings had been buried by drifting snow, with only the stove pipes and ventilator shafts snorkeling above the surface. Because of the weight of snow on the roof of the mess hall, the supporting beams had begun to give way. Chips braced them with six stanchions that made the hall look like a New York subway station, and the building's residents decorated the columns with mock subway signs.[72] Byrd gave the long-awaited order: start digging out for the new season.

Signs of the approaching summer abounded. On 16 September, the whalers *Larsen* and *Ross*, carrying provisions for Little America, left the docks at Los Angeles for the antarctic hunting grounds. On 18 September, the temperature went up to minus five degrees. The handlers took the dogs out for exercise in the "balmy" weather, and many people went for walks. Thorne sighted the season's first antarctic petrel—Siple called it "our robin of spring"—and Balchen and Strom spotted the first baby Weddell seal. Penguins and skuas appeared, and a few of them wound up on the dinner table, the diners enjoying the scavenger bird more than the fishy-tasting penguin. Blackburn moved back out to his summer sleeping shelter.[73] After the aurora observers recorded southern lights on 26 September, Davies ended the program. He had collected 7,412 observations. From then on, the sky would be bright enough even at midnight to wash out the dim displays. The increasing sunlight provided some spectacular displays. Sun dogs, or false suns on either side of the real one, appeared. Byrd, captivated, described the ethereal phenomenon: ". . . the canopy of clouds overhead was rent into feathery fragments. . . . The air suddenly became charged with ice crystals, which fell like rain. The sun broke through the shattered cloud fabric which turned yellow and opalescent in its growing power, then an arch more beautiful than any rainbow I have ever seen swept upward, curved, and in a moment the sun was crossed by two great shafts of brilliant light, in the center of which it burned with leaping tongues of flame. On either side could be seen the trembling halos of the mock suns, each impaled on its shaft of prismatic light. Directly opposite the sun was the antehelion, the reflection of the outstretched reach of the cross, a luminous gray pillar rising from the snows of the Barrier. For nearly an hour we watched this gorgeous display, while the ice crystals that formed it fell in sparkling showers."[74]

As sunlight penetrated the barrier, the walls in Little America's tunnels glowed a milky blue, and sunshine filtering through the tarpaulin roofing suffused the rooms dug out of the snow with a yellow radiance. The camp went back on daylight saving time. Breakfast was changed from 8:30 to 7:30 A.M. and dinner from 4:00 to 5:00 P.M. to lengthen the working day. The whaler *Kosmos* set out from New Zealand, carrying supplies for Little America.[75] As the low-voltage activity of winter switched back to the high-voltage frenzy of summer, a new work order was posted, taking those busy at key jobs off the house-tidying detail and assigning that duty to a rotation of thirteen men. Demas ended his stint as permanent watchman so he could resume his regular duties as mechanic; the watch would be rotated among six people not directly connected with flights or field parties.[76]

Byrd pushed his workers to go all out in their jobs because every second had become more important than ever—competitors were again horning in on the antarctic adventure market. Mawson announced he would lead an expedition that would include a small seaplane. Byrd probably also got word that the Norwegian Hjalmer Riiser-Larsen planned to explore a portion of the coast with a seaplane.[77] Neither foreigner could try for the pole, nor would they approach the territories Byrd was exploring; but their activities, and especially any discoveries, could steal the world's attention from his exploits.

The worst news, which had come in a series of messages throughout the winter and climaxed in September, concerned the "interloper" who had dogged Byrd throughout his career. Harrison recorded that the expedition heard "that Wilkins plans to invade our territory." Siple, indignant, reported that Little Americans received the news of Wilkins's disruption "in a spirit of rage." Wilkins had declared that he would return to his base under South America to fly over the territory east of Little America, and he promised to drop in on Byrd's group for Christmas dinner. Demas noted that Byrd turned grouchy the day he heard the news. "There is no doubt that [Wilkins] means to race to the pole," Demas stated, noting that the announcement had everybody at Little America "talking of the possibility of Wilkins beating the commander to the pole." Byrd really was worried about that possibility and was peeved that Wilkins revealed few details of his venture, Harrison reported, although it appeared to be a small, limited expedition like the one Byrd himself had originally intended.[78]

Gritting his teeth, Byrd told Wilkins, in a radio message released to the press, that he would be welcome at Christmas and quipped that Little America would save a penguin leg for him. Wilkins offered to leave his plane for Byrd, but the image-conscious commander, even though short of aircraft, told Railey, "You can well understand that we would not want to use Wilkins's plane." The Australian sent an audacious radiogram to Byrd, asking permission to ship gas and other supplies to Little America on the *Bolling*'s next voyage, and stirring up much consternation, according to Clarke.[79] Byrd agreed to the request.

Wilkins had once more sold news, photo, and movie rights to Hearst, which Demas called a bitter enemy. The publisher, through its King Features Syndicate, would try to beat Byrd into the papers with the first pictures from Antarctica in the forthcoming season. Byrd reacted by initiating discussions with whaling companies about chartering a whale chaser to get his photos to New Zealand and thence to New York ahead of Wilkins's. Byrd also declared he would try again as soon as he could to sail east in the *New York* and set up a depot, apparently to explore as much more of the coast as he could before Wilkins could fly over.[80]

Byrd explained his predicament to Railey: "You must not forget that Wilkins is out to lick us. I wish to impress upon you that the flight he proposes is even more important than a flight to the south pole. He is flying over the area that we are most anxious to explore and which is most important to science. As he starts much farther north than we do, he can start early and he is going to make every effort to beat us to it. Don't forget that he was offered $50,000 by Hearst to beat us to the south pole and that he will now possibly fly here by way of the south pole. He will have a big advantage in that his material comes fresh from the states with the latest design and he has not had his material subjected to the cold seventy below temperatures. In spite of this we have got to be sports and have got to be square with him, but do not give any information as to when we start flying. If he thinks we are going to start early he will naturally hurry the more and make it very difficult for us. . . . We must be very careful not to do anything that is lacking in sportsmanship. . . ."[81]

On 15 September, a fretful Byrd told Railey, "Have repeatedly asked Wilkins for his plans, which he does not give me. All he says is that he is going to fly to us December 15. Since we are publishing our plans, it is only fair that he should give us his. If he is going to fly to the south pole, I want to know it. Please make urgent request to him for his plans." Byrd made similar behests of his sponsors at the American Geographical Society and at the *Times*. Ten days later Hearst's San Francisco *Examiner* carried a report, radioed to Byrd, that Wilkins intended "to penetrate much farther south" and expected to have his planes ready to fly about mid-November—disturbing to Byrd, who had not planned on flying until December.[82] Shortly after, Wilkins give his plans to Railey and the *Times*. The key point was that the Australian said he did not intend to go to the pole. Whether Wilkins was really aiming for the pole or not, Byrd had to get there as soon as possible so he could turn early attention to the east.

The time he had had in surfeit during the depths of winter was gone. He could not dally. He had the advantage of already being crouched at the mark and set to sprint for the pole when flying weather returned. No project, however, had ever gone smoothly for Byrd, and no leader in Antarctica could count on the steadiness of either man or nature. As the summer days grew longer, the commander's patience grew shorter.

Byrd in 1927 at the age of thirty-nine, when
he began to form his first expedition to
Antarctica. (Wide World Studio)

Bill Haines, chief meteorologist, takes the
wheel of the *New York*. All expedition
members worked as seamen when sailing on
Byrd's ships. (National Archives)

Bernt Balchen, chief pilot and world-class skier, prepares to accompany two dog-team parties and another skier scouting a site for the expedition's base at the Bay of Whales on 28 December 1928. The *New York* is docked alongside the dog teams. (National Archives)

The Fairchild, specially outfitted for aerial photography, stands by the *New York* shortly after assembly on 15 January 1929, waiting to make the expedition's first flight. (National Archives)

The *Eleanor Bolling*, the former minesweeper named after Byrd's mother, shows why the crew called her the "Evermore Rolling." (National Archives)

Henry Harrison, assistant meterologist, is hauled back up on the barrier after a section broke off and fell on the *Bolling* on 30 January 1929. (Ohio State University)

A dog team rests by the edge of the barrier. Byrd relied primarily on dogs for ground transportation. (National Archives)

Laborers build Little America. A worker calculated the total weight of all snow shoveled during construction to be 1,250 tons. (National Archives)

(L–R) Mac McKinley, Byrd, and Larry Gould—the three top officers—enjoy a lighthearted moment during a conference at Little America. (National Archives)

The Fokker takes off during the first summer at Little America. (National Archives)

Ready to be flown back to Little America in March 1929, the Fokker waits at the camp in the Rockefeller Mountains before a storm destroyed it. (National Archives)

Little America offered scarce elbow room. Here, airplane mechanic Benny Roth, Paramount cameraman Joe Rucker, and pilot Harold June work at a crowded table. (National Archives)

The dining table was not large enough to serve all Little Americans at the same time, so the men had to eat in shifts. (National Archives)

Since the Little Americans had to melt snow for wash water, they seldom used the tub. Here, pilot Dean Smith takes one of the camp's rare baths. (National Archives)

During the long winter night, card games helped to pass the time for players and kibitzers alike. (National Archives)

Someone (Christoffer Braathen?) and Byrd (right), who had cut his hair to the scalp, look over a model of the *New York* made during the leisurely winter hours. (National Archives)

The aviators met regularly in the library to plan the polar flight. This conference includes (L–R) Dean Smith, Alton Parker, Byrd, Bernt Balchen, and Harold June. (National Archives)

Posing by the Ford Trimotor, the polar-flight plane, are the three aviation mechanics: (L–R) Pete Demas, Ken Bubier, and Benny Roth. (National Archives)

The men stow cargo on board the Ford Trimotor in preparation for a flight during the second summer. (National Archives)

Little Americans hoist the just-landed polar-flight crew to their shoulders in jubilant celebration of the historic achievement that had been the expedition's primary goal. (National Archives)

Byrd (center) talks with supporting party leader Arthur Walden (left) and Joe De Ganahl before the group sets out. The supporting party left caches of food and supplies for the geological party and the polar-flight crew, in case the aviators had to land and walk back to camp. (National Archives)

Byrd's snowmobile, a model "A" Ford on skis and caterpillar treads, was the first motorized vehicle to operate successfully in Antarctica. The snowmobile showed that mechanized travel over polar snows, though not yet perfected, was feasible. (National Archives)

The geological party prepares to start for the Queen Maud Mountains, halfway to the pole, to explore the range and aid the polar fliers if their plane should have to come down. (National Archives)

Exploring from this campsite and others in the Queen Mauds, the geological party found that the range links with other ranges to form the world's longest fault-block mountain system. (National Archives)

In the Queen Mauds on 21 December 1929, at the end of the geological party's outward journey, the explorers claim Marie Byrd Land for the United States. (National Archives)

Byrd congratulates members of the just-returned geological party on 19 January 1930. Recognizable are Byrd (second from left), Eddie Goodale (far right), and Norm Vaughan (next to Goodale). (National Archives)

Bill Haines holds a box kite near the motor the meteorologists used to reel in the kite string. The kites lofted measuring instruments over a mile high for weather studies. (National Archives)

General hand Arnold Clarke (left) and geophysicist Taffy Davies record a measurement of the earth's undulating magnetic field. Their work helped science better understand the nature and behavior of geomagnetism. (National Archives)

Chief radio engineer Malcolm Hanson works on an instrument. Hanson was the first to study radio conditions in Antarctica. (National Archives)

Larry Gould (L) and Dana Coman. Gould led the geological party and served as chief scientist and second in command of the expedition. Coman was the expedition's physician. (National Archives)

Bernt Balchen headed the aviation unit and was the pilot for the flight over the South Pole. (National Archives)

Henry T. Harrison, weatherman and Byrd's constant bridge partner at Little America, kept one of the expedition's most detailed diaries. (National Archives)

Russell Owen, the reporter for the *New York Times*, was continuously at odds with Byrd. Owen won a Pulitzer Prize for his dispatches from Little America. (National Archives)

Paul A. Siple was the lucky Boy Scout who won a trip to Antarctica with Byrd. Byrd selected him for the wintering-over party when he proved one of the most able men on the expedition. (National Archives)

Byrd introduces June to President Hoover at a reception at the White House for the expedition's members on 20 June 1930. (U.S. Naval Institute)

City after city acclaimed Byrd for his achievements when he returned from Antarctica, as in this ticker-tape parade in Chicago on 11 July 1930. (Ohio State University)

.9.

Breaking Trail

BYRD was in a bad humor on the last weekend in September. One of the geological party's dogs had pulled its stake out of the snow and unwisely challenged and been killed by a tougher dog. This incident was just the latest in a series of deaths and maimings from dog fights. Byrd emphatically told the dog handlers they had to stop the drain of essential dog power. "It can and must be done!" he thundered. The trail parties themselves, of course, depended on dogs, and Byrd did not have as many huskies as he wanted for rescue purposes and re-loading at season's end, with far too few in emergency reserve. The unnecessary casualties were making the situation worse. Byrd had ordered his dog handler in New Zealand to come down with his charges on the whaler *Kosmos*, and they were then on their way to Little America, but the whaler would not pull in until long after the trail parties had left.[1]

Byrd chewed out Hanson for falling behind in putting together the radio sets for the trail. The sets would be the sledgers' only means of communicating with Little America—for three months in the case of the geological party. Malcolm Hanson, thirty-five, a short, pockmarked naval reserve lieutenant, was a radio engineer at the Naval Research Laboratory. He had been in the arctic with Wilkins, for whom he had

159

built the first shortwave radio for aircraft. The procrastinating head of the radio unit had to work day and night to get the sets ready and tested by October 7, the departure date for the first trail party.[2]

The sledging committee had worked up a twenty-four-page plan calling for a supporting party of four men and twenty-seven dogs to start out then and haul supplies two hundred miles—halfway to the mountains—through the difficult crevassed area south of Little America. This party would establish four depots at fifty-mile intervals for the larger geological party. Later, Gould's group of six men and fifty-four dogs would speed along the trail the supporting party had made and continue all the way to the Queen Mauds. There Gould would establish a base for his own group's operations and to support the polar flight by relaying weather reports and standing by for possible rescue of downed fliers. Byrd wrote the geological party a glowing memo: "I am greatly pleased with the report of the plans and preparations of the geological party. Heartiest congratulations."[3]

Byrd had placed Walden in direct charge of the supporting party and asked him to prepare a detailed plan for that party's operations. As head of overall dog team activities, however, the commander had replaced the failed manager, Walden, with Gould. The Klondike veteran's reaction is not known, but he could hardly have been pleased. He dragged his feet on the report. On 27 September, the restive commander leaned on Walden with a memo: "I am anxiously awaiting some report of your plans. Please turn in in rough form some time today your plans for daily marches. . . ."[4]

Byrd turned Gould down on one point. During the winter, Gould had asked Byrd to let him have Siple for the geological party. The executive had argued that the Boy Scout was more mature than many older members and had the poise of a much more experienced man. Siple badly wanted to go, but Byrd had already bent further than he intended in allowing the scout to winter over and would yield no more for an assignment that held much more danger for Siple's health and Byrd's public image. Siple, knowing that when dogs were no longer needed they would be killed and fed to the others, complained bitterly to his diary, "Because I am a little Boy Scout they will not let me go on the trail next summer. It is very hard to keep quiet when I hear the plans they are making. Not a thing is being said to me, and I say nothing. . . . As I see it, O'Brien will take my team—after I have fed them all winter—and use the dogs just as dog food on the way back. . . . Why wouldn't I boil??? For I have grown to love those dogs."[5]

Joining Gould on the geological party were Thorne, O'Brien, and the three musketeers—Vaughan, Goodale, and Crockett. To shake down the little-experienced geological party's sledge teams and hasten their long journey, Gould and his companions planned to accompany the supporting party and come back after having dropped their loads at the second night's campsite or after they had reached at least the twenty-mile depot laid down the summer before, whichever point they reached first. After four or five more days of preparation, the geological party would leave for the mountains.[6]

On Saturday, 5 October, Gould passed his duties as chief administrator to McKinley. Hanson, however, had not yet finished the field radios when Monday arrived, so the start had to be postponed. To make matters worse, the sledgers found, upon tieing up the sledge tanks—big canvas bags that held the supplies—that the orange dye had rotted the fabric, which would require extensive repair. "It was a very disquieting revelation," Gould commented in his characteristic understatement. Byrd's wrath must have been awful, although no one recorded his mood. Departure was rescheduled for Thursday, but then the weather became unbearably cold for traveling. Gould got sick, moreover, and Walden would not start without the exec.[7]

On Friday, Byrd blew up at McKinley during the nightly bridge game, his black mood surely due less to misplayed cards than to his sputtering attack on the pole.[8]

Gould was too sick even to think of leaving until Saturday, but the weather remained impossibly cold, with bitter temperatures hitting minus 60. The sledgers had no choice but to stay put and wait for suitable temperatures—minus 20 at the lowest.[9]

Byrd desperately wanted to get things moving. Since the dog units had not laid many depots the previous summer, they had little time to spare. Early on Sunday, his frustration and seeming conviction that the waiting sledgers lacked determination may have gotten the better of him. He summoned both sledge parties to a meeting although, curiously, he later wrote that only the supporting party was involved.

Accounts of the meeting are sketchy, but it was clearly acrimonious. Byrd apparently thought that the draft dogs could actually begin the mission despite the cold and sought to force the drivers to leave at once. The sledgers were split in their opinions, and some superstitious drivers did not want to leave that day anyway because it was the unlucky 13th. Gould and Harrison recorded that most of the nine drivers disagreed with the commander, although Byrd wrote that only one or two men disagreed with him. Byrd turned down a hopeful suggestion that the groups would not need to worry about an early start if he would use the idle planes to help lay the depots. He was not willing to risk either the polar craft or the standby rescue plane for the sake of the dog teams, and aviation gas was in short supply. The sledgers were unhappy about bearing the whole burden. Given Byrd's suspicious nature, he may have felt they were stalling to force him to support them with planes. When the drivers continued to balk, Byrd suggested that they haul their waiting loads some seven or eight miles through the difficult pressure ridges in the arm of the frozen sea that lay across the route to the pole and the Queen Maud Mountains. He argued that this trek would give the men a head start when they began their long journeys, but mainly he seems to have hoped to get them going. Gould saw nothing to be gained by a premature foray.[10] After a long meeting, however, all but O'Brien, who continued to rebel, did as Byrd wished.

The teams carried only half loads to make the trip easier, except for Thorne's, which carried a full load to prove to Byrd that the dogs could not pull in the low temperatures. Thorne's huskies tried but failed to pull their burden unaided over the dry, sandlike snow. Because it was too cold for the pressure of the sledge runners to melt the thin layer of ice, a process that enables sledges and skis to glide over snow, it was like sledging along a beach. None of the teams did well, "naturally vindicating Larry," according to Harrison. The beleaguered men returned to Little America for another conference, during which Byrd agreed that they could wait for warmer weather. He also decided to break out the feeble snowmobile and perhaps give it a try at depot-laying.[11] He placed McKinley in charge of snowmobile testing and operations.

Some of Byrd's troops evinced shock at his overbearing behavior. Clarke confided to his diary that "the farce reached a chaotic condition today. If there is one here who still respects [Byrd], it is because there is something wrong with him." Harrison wrote in his diary that his bridge game with Byrd that night broke up "in a disagreeable and insulting fashion," commenting, "Under stress or at close range, the idol usually topples from his pedestal." Wailing about the disappointment and disillusionment Byrd caused, the young weatherman said he felt like a "child who has just discovered that there is no Santa Claus."[12]

O'Brien reluctantly gave in Monday and drove his load across, but only so he would not be behind when the long march began.[13] The temperature rose above the minus 20 minimum the teams had established; and the warmth held on Tuesday, so the supporting and geological parties decided to leave about noon. The sledges groaned under half-ton weights. The unhappy huskies, gulping in the piercing cold air, strained to their utmost to drag the cumbersome burdens, and the drivers often had to push or even pull with the animals to keep the sledges moving.

Walden, Bursey, Braathen, and De Ganahl drove teams in the supporting party. Vaughan, Goodale, Thorne, and O'Brien drove in the other party, with Gould skiing along. Petersen went along to break De Ganahl in on radio technique, and Rucker went to take movies; both would return with the geological party. For unexplained reasons Crockett, the third musketeer, stayed home. Byrd was worried about De Ganahl's suitability as a radio operator—he had failed his winter training, but none of the others knew anything about radio.[14] Like a mob of sports fans sending their team off to a game, a crowd led by Byrd escorted the sledgers to the end of the Bay of Whales to say good-bye.

That night, the trail parties radioed that, following announced plans, they had camped only a few miles from where they had bade farewell. Infuriated that they had not gone farther, Byrd complained sourly in the hearing of others at headquarters that the sledge mission was not being run efficiently.[15]

The geological party notified Byrd on Wednesday, when they reached the twenty-mile depot, that they would leave for home the next day as planned. Byrd, openly worried that the trail parties were failing, pleaded with Gould not to come back but to continue to the one hundred–mile depot. The commander promised to send Crockett to help them and a dog team to bring back Petersen and Rucker. The hapless members of the geological party were having a lot of trouble, however: a sledge had run over Gould on his first attempt at driving and badly bruised his left arm; the teams had bogged down in deep snow; the cooker was not working; and, most of all, the men were convinced "beyond any question," according to Gould, that they did not have the time to carry out their established mission without the help of a plane.[16]

Defying Byrd, they drove back to Little America the next day, figuring on staying a week before leaving for the mountains. Byrd wrote later that he was "anxious that the geological party continue according to plan," but all evidence shows that the party was proceeding exactly according to plan.[17]

The next morning the discouraged group met for a long time with the stone-faced commander. Gould tried mightily to persuade Byrd to use the Fairchild to fly supplies for the geological party to the mountains, or at least to a depot enroute. Byrd was planning two flights in the Ford to check it out and establish a refueling and emergency supply base for his own special mission. But the spectacle of the polar attempt and the flights of discovery had such high priority that Byrd would not suffer the slightest threat to their success, emergencies aside. For the safety of the crews, he had ruled that a rescue plane must stand by. The Fairchild had to be in good shape, and Byrd felt the risk of disabling the craft on an always-chancy antarctic flight, especially one involving a landing and takeoff on an unknown surface, was too high. Gould seems to have disputed the commander vigorously on the degrees of priority and risk but could not move him. As Byrd later related, however, he promised to give the hard-pressed explorers extra time by not sailing for home until 10 February instead of at the beginning of the month and, if necessary, to charter a whale chaser to pick them up as late as 25 February.[18]

Gould wrote that Byrd also promised to leave dog food for the geological party at his own flight depot if he could, so the sledgers would not have to kill dogs. Plans called for the men to slaughter huskies at each depot as they dropped loads and did not need as many animals for the remaining loads. Otherwise, the teams would have to lug food for dogs that were not needed. Most of the depot goods and half the sledge loads were dog food, and the sledges were already overloaded. Byrd never mentioned a promise later; he wrote that he had secretly determined to leave food for the sledgers if he were able but did not want them basing plans on the possibility.[19]

Gould observed that everyone in Little America without exception was concerned that his party might not be able to complete its geological and geographical objectives. The Little Americans hotly debated the question of whether Byrd should or should not allow a flight to help Gould. In the tiny community where violating the "one for all and all for one" ethic was a mortal sin, Byrd's loyalest supporters had trouble defending the leader's insistence on taking care of one of his own aviation projects to the total exclusion of the geological party.[20]

Byrd never questioned the significance of the scientific effort compared to what he termed the "purely geographic investigations" of the aviation unit; indeed, he emphasized the geological study.[21] He focused his objections on the danger of using planes when he thought dogs and skis would do, but it was clear that his was really a dual conflict: showmanship vs. science—a spectacular flight against ho-hum geology—and caution vs. daring. In the world of the practical in which Byrd was master, showmanship and caution had to win.

By contrast, Byrd enjoyed recreational gambling. Shortly after the supply runs from the ship to Little America had begun, for example, he bet Thorne $100 that the snaking route covered a total of eight miles; Thorne guessed twelve miles. (The winner was unannounced, but Byrd seems to have been closest.) Harrison recorded that during the winter Byrd had expounded on a casino gambling system he believed in. In earlier days, Byrd had argued the other side of the care-vs.-risk debate. Eight years previously, the young officer had officially requested his military superiors to allow him to try a solo, nonstop transatlantic crossing in a navy plane that did not have sufficient range, counting on tail winds and perfect weather to see him across. His request was denied. Only four years before he had had a confrontation with Donald MacMillan similar to Gould's argument with him. On the MacMillan-Byrd expedition, Byrd wanted to keep trying to fly despite the worsening weather as winter approached. MacMillan would not allow the flights, thinking the younger man rash; Byrd made it clear he considered MacMillan uncooperative.[22] In the past, however, Byrd had had much to gain and little to lose by taking chances. At the present stage of his career, he had everything to lose and virtually nothing to gain by a geological flight.

Bowing to the commander's continued entreaties, and accepting that the obstinate Byrd would never provide airborne support, Gould agreed that the geological party would leave for the one hundred–mile depot in two days. The sledgers would then return to Little America for a week of further preparations before their final assault.[23]

On Sunday, 20 October, the geological party left on its second preliminary trip, without Gould, as there was no navigating to do on the marked trail and no geology to study. He remained behind to let his arm heal and to try to work out a plan to salvage the program for which he was sacrificing two years. Byrd failed to appear to say good-bye to the team but apologized for his absence by radio the next day.[24]

Byrd sent a peculiar memo to Strom that day, sounding more like a garden club's president than an expedition leader. Apparently related to Byrd's considering Strom for the snowmobile team, the memo was another example of the commander's passion for recording those matters that he, and sometimes he alone, considered important and sensitive: "Dear Strom—A week ago I asked you what your feelings were in regard to going on the trail. Evidently someone who heard this question carried a malicious tale to Larry Gould and told him that I had said to you that the fact that you were not on the trail was Larry Gould's fault. I could not possibly have said that as I did not of course even think it. I therefore request that you make a statement as to exactly what I did say to you. Sincerely yours, R. E. Byrd." Strom replied: "Commander Byrd—October 3 you asked me how I would like to go on the trail. My answer was,' Very much, Commander, and I am willing to go whenever you send me.' You didn't even mention Larry's name. Sincerely, Sverre Strom." (Strom probably meant 13 October, when Byrd decided to try the snowmobile.)[25]

On Tuesday, 22 October, the first midnight sun of 1929, when temperatures were getting mercifully warmer, ambitious snowmobile drivers Black and Feury, dreaming of beating the dogs to the mountains, tested their lurching vehicle. It was really not up to a rough journey, and no field radio was available for the machine. The two motorists had never been alone in a wilderness before and had no experience in snow travel. At McKinley's urging, and against Byrd's better judgment, the commander commissioned the vehicle to go out the next day along the southern trail, towing sledges loaded with additional food for the depots. He assigned cross-country skiing expert Strom to go along with the New York City boys and take care of them in any emergency. No one else gave the clumsy snowmobile much of a chance even to get past the big pressure ridges that blocked the way, so the vehicle delighted everyone when it actually maneuvered across and, cranking along at eight miles an hour, disappeared over the horizon. The pall of disappointment that the dog-team operations had cast over Little America lifted slightly, as when a winning sports team boosts the spirits of a city. The men "needed a success to stimulate them," as Owen observed.[26]

On 28 October, the geological party returned from its depot-laying chores to rest a week before the final run. The men and their Eskimo dogs had sped the 110 miles back in three days. More than ever, the sledgers felt bitter about the lack of air support, asking what the planes were for. "Have you got any airplanes here? Heard a rumor about it," one of them jibed. "Yes, but they don't fly," someone responded. Vaughan grumbled that he could not understand why Byrd was down on this party.[27]

The commander felt that the members of the geological party were quitters. He told his diary on 29 October: "I am greatly astonished that the boys in the Geological party wanted to give up so easily. If this should get around the camp it would undoubtedly be very tough on them with their shipmates. However I feel about it, I must protect them in this matter. That is why we are publishing daily bulletins on the progress of the trail parties, withholding from the bulletins that sort of information."

On Thursday, the supporting party radioed unsettling news. The sledgers had passed excruciatingly slowly through a region of dreadful crevasses, which they believed to be the most treacherous area ever crossed in the antarctic. As snow bridges collapsed under them, men and dogs frequently dropped into invisible crevasses until halted by ropes that tied them together. They sometimes found themselves tightrope-walking narrow ridges between yawning chasms. De Ganahl radioed: "It was a restless sleep for all last night, for every few hours we were awakened by thunder announcing the birth of a new crevasse and shaking the hollow snow beneath us." Byrd congratulated the group for the near-impossible crossing, which he said he considered "the best piece of work done by the expedition." He was also pleased at how well De Ganahl was doing after all as a radio operator.[28]

The next day the supporting party announced it had established its last depot and was on the way home. In a diary entry, Byrd wrote admiringly of the supporting party—and, by implication, disparagingly of the geological party: ". . . . the way these fellows carried on without a single murmur speaks well of them." Demas observed that the supporting party did better than expected, whereas the geological party, which he noted had the pick of the dogs and was going to do wonders, could be a washout. Siple remarked that Byrd and Gould both wanted the geological party to leave very soon, but the three musketeers insisted their dogs needed more rest.[29]

At 1:30 in the afternoon of Monday, 4 November—two weeks after the originally planned departure—the geological party readied the dogs. The party had forty-five huskies, nine fewer than planned. The three musketeers claimed, moreover, that half their animals were only second-rate haulers because many good dogs had to stay behind for use at the base; Siple, with even O'Brien in agreement, said the party "had all the best dogs."[30]

Few Little Americans came to see the party off. Dog-team departures had become almost routine, the mood of the unhappy party was depressing, and the three Harvard boys had few admirers. These three often gave the impression of having little use for anybody but themselves, even vexing their trail partners Thorne and O'Brien. Harrison said that, nevertheless, they were "really fine boys at heart," and Gould told his diary that his trail mates were "amazingly fine men. . . . I like them all." Leaden skies, threatening a blizzard, matched the spirit of the forlorn men, who would have to endure the rigors of three months on the trail with probably little time to accomplish planned scientific aims, the trip having been shortened by fourteen days. Even the dogs were unusually quiet, seeming to have caught the melancholy of their masters.[31] Byrd bade them farewell, his parting words the same as always when a field team left: safety first, nothing is more important than the well-being of the men.

Gould, the only one of the six not driving a team, sat on Vaughan's lead sled. When they started to move he turned to wave good-bye, lost his balance, and toppled off.[32] As he ran to catch up to the sled, his watching supporters could only hope that in the months ahead luck would finally catch up to him.

Later, Coman typed a note to be sent in the air drop that Byrd would make on the polar flight as he flew over the geological party. In the letter, Coman told Gould that at a general discussion, when a pilot had brought up the issue of a geological flight, "everyone reacted against him," apparently wanting to bury the divisive controversy. The doctor wrote, "There are a few of us who KNOW that on you alone the scientific value of this expedition will be judged." He urged Gould to stay in the mountains to get his work done even if he had to miss the return ship, assuring the geologist that many members would stand by him.[33]

The first night on the trail, Gould radioed that he had met the snowmobile trio hiking home about fifteen miles south of Little America. The troublesome vehicle had stripped its differential some eighty miles out.[34] The failure of the freaky car, though expected, must have pushed the morale of the geological party even lower.

When the weary hikers marched into Little America early the next afternoon, the lighthearted citizenry greeted them with a mock celebration. Welcome home signs were hung on the buildings. People climbed the radio towers to strew confetti. Others set off flares. Czegka cranked a mock movie camera. The returning "heroes" wailed their disappointment, but Byrd assured them they had done well enough to prove that a vehicle could eventually be designed for long-distance travel in Antarctica.[35]

The trail-worn members of the supporting party dragged themselves back into Little America on Saturday, 9 November, rubbing their eyes to ease the flaming pains of snow blindness—the term for sunburned eyeballs—that afflicted them all. Walden's crew recounted how they had battled intense cold, fog, blizzards, and awful crevasses. They reported meeting the outward-bound, downcast geological party and having to tell them a discouraging tale. The supporting party had given two of their best dogs to Gould's party and taken his worst.[36]

The return of Walden's crew marked the end of the first phase of summer operations. The next major activities, waiting on good weather, would be the first flights of the new season.

A couple of noteworthy events had happened while the trail parties were shuttling to and fro. On 25 October, Byrd had turned forty-one. The gang usually recognized a member's birthday with celebrations ranging from simple decorations in his bunkhouse and humorous presents to the big blowout held for Gould. There was no party for the commander, however, following his request that all summer birthday parties be postponed until after the polar flight.[37]

Big news came on Tuesday, 29 October, via radio from New York: the high-flying stock market had plummeted to a terrible crash. Few Little Americans felt that Wall Street happenings held any meaning for them, but the bulletin sent Smith reeling—before leaving, with visions of making a killing, he had sunk his considerable savings from his fat pilot's pay into Chrysler stock. It had plunged from $100 down almost to $30. Byrd generously advanced Smith $2,500 to finance a stock purchase plan the pilot devised to prevent being wiped out. The same day, the commander sent a radiogram to Railey revealing a high sense of duty toward the men: "I realize that in making this advance to Dean Smith I will probably lose his friendship in the end on account of it as I have always done in the past. . . . Whenever a member of my expedition gets into trouble it is up to me to do all I can to help him."[38]

The crash must also have affected Byrd and his family, as well as those who had pledged him money, but he said nothing about it. Personally, he had had a stroke of luck. Earlier that month, Marie had radioed her husband that she had sold several of his securities at a big profit and that the rest of his holdings were safe and conservative.[39]

On 9 November, the day the supporting party returned, there occurred an emotion-laden conflict that none of the participants or observers later talked about publicly or more than alluded to in their guarded writings, even in diaries. Owen revealed in his book that it was "one of those trying incidents in human relationships which occur on every expedition . . . and . . . it centered largely on me. . . ." Harrison confided to his diary that Owen had been given "the gate." Coman typed elliptically in his note to be airdropped to Gould that "Russ finally gave a written guarantee" but that Byrd kept all the "signed statements." The doctor wrote that in the evening Byrd and Owen made up in "a love feast." Owen reported that the rift "was overcome finally with the aid of some rather melodramatic atmosphere, and when I told my bunkmate (Parker) it was all right, tears rolled down his cheeks, his face trembled, and it was all he could do to keep from sobbing. . . . Later [McKinley] came along and he said, 'Thank God.' " Harrison recorded that Owen was "completely reinstated."[40]

Evidently Byrd had discovered Owen talking behind his back again and collected written statements of proof. Feeling it was the last straw, the commander fired the hated correspondent. Byrd might have waited to ac: until the supporting party returned with loyal legionnaire Joe

De Ganahl, also a newspaper reporter and a possible replacement. Owen must then have won his job back by apologizing and producing the written promise of loyalty and good behavior that Byrd had requested earlier. The reporter wrote that the situation around him had been so tense that it was several days before an air of relaxation returned to camp.[41]

Coman seems to have given one of the statements, maybe a declaration of Owen's "insanity" that Byrd wanted for when he would inform the *Times* of his action. Later, Coman apparently regretted his part in the affair and asked Byrd's secretary, Charlie Lofgren, to retrieve the document. Lofgren, who knew how the commander handled such matters, wrote the boss a memo: "[Coman] feels he can never practice medicine as long as the written statement which he signed for you is out. I mean the one about R. O. I guess the doc would draw a sigh of relief if he could get this back; but if you send it to him, or think of doing so, it would be well to have it photographed without saying anything to him about it."[42]

Two days after the ice-shaking confrontation between Byrd and Owen, the reporter wrote a letter to the commander, which has been lost, explaining that the situation was not as bad as Byrd thought and trying to further straighten their relationship. Byrd replied, in a tone that evokes a picture of him with jaws clenched: "Dear Russell—I am delighted to get your letter . . . and in answer I want to tell you that I am very glad indeed to learn that you have frequently commended my actions as leader. I am very glad to learn . . . that you have many times upheld my acts and viewpoints. I am naturally happy to know this and wish to thank you. I also thank you for your . . . earnest expressions of good will. I assure you that I am equally anxious to straighten out the situation, and will continue to do what I am able to bring harmony. Sincerely yours, R. E. Byrd."[43]

Byrd's nemesis, Wilkins, gave Little America more to worry about. He had arrived in the Antarctic, and Byrd learned to his discomfort that his arch rival was getting ready to fly. The bad weather that had kept Byrd's ground parties back had also prevented any early flights, and so the lead over the hated Wilkins-Hearst expedition, gained by staying the winter, had almost vanished.

All the men at Little America feared the Australian would fly to the pole first, spoiling their own efforts to play a role in the first south polar flight and rendering meaningless the heavy sacrifices they had made solely to help make aviation history. Spirits slumped. Coman broke out a dozen records he had squirreled away over the winter, and the new music helped to take everybody's mind off the threat while the Little Americans focused on the attempt for the pole.[44]

.10.

The Pole

SUNDAY, 10 November, finally brought weather fit for flying. The workhorse Fairchild was ready, so the elated pilots took it up and soared over the Bay of Whales for the first time in nine months. The fliers made several successful test flights before Balchen's turn. Normally proficient, on this run he angled the craft so steeply on its ascent that the gas flow was interrupted and the engine quit. The onlookers gaped as, with luck and skill, he made an uneventful dead-stick landing.[1]

The big polar plane was proving far more difficult to make ready for its maiden antarctic flight than the Fairchild or the lost Fokker. The mechanics were preheating the engines for a test when flames leaped from a carburetor, apparently from an excessive accumulation of gas. The blaze spread to the fabric hood that covered the engines the mechanics were working on, but the men were able to put the fire out before it did serious damage. The shaken mechanics lost a day to make repairs. Dirty fuel lines then caused further problems and delay,[2] and then bad weather again shut the fliers in. The black cloud that had always hung over Byrd seemed to be dogging him again.

Thursday, 14 November, was beautiful, so Byrd gave the go-ahead to fly the Ford, named *Floyd Bennett*, assigning Parker as test pilot. The whole camp helped to tug the gigantic plane out of its sunken hangar, its blue aluminum-alloy body, with orange wings, gleaming in brilliant sunshine against the white backdrop. Dwarfing the Fairchild, and reportedly the largest plane ever to fly on skis, the Ford extended fifty feet from nose to tail and had a wingspan of seventy feet. A row of four celluloid passenger windows ran along the corrugated fuselage that had earned the plane the nickname "the flying washboard." It had a 525-horsepower Wright Cyclone engine in the nose and two 220-horsepower Wright Whirlwinds on the wings. The enormous center engine had caused endless trouble. The engine had caught fire on its acceptance flight, and in the air pilots had to pay special attention to keep it turning smoothly.[3]

At 3:00 P.M. Parker climbed up into the raised cockpit and sat down at the pilot's controls. Unlike the Fairchild, the Ford had side-by-side seats and dual controls for the copilot. Balchen stepped in to Parker's right, and eight riders crowded into the bare passenger compartment that had been stripped of trim and seats to save weight.

For some reason Byrd did not know the moment when the plane was ready to go, and he was in his office when he heard the engines roar at full power to herald a takeoff. He scampered outside to the runway and, as the plane sped by, was horrified to learn only then that almost a fourth of his expedition was chancing the risky trial run.[4] With still vivid memories of mistakenly loading his entire transatlantic crew on a plane that crashed on a test flight, Byrd must have sweated even in the 14-below cold as he waited for the heavily laden plane to come down. Forty-five minutes later, to his relief, the Ford landed with no hitches. Byrd did not radio news of the milestone to New York for fear the report might spur on an eavesdropping Wilkins.

All the pilots flew the Ford that day. On the last flight the left wing engine started to miss, so the mechanics took the plane in to work on the troublesome carburetor. The problem turned out to be so thorny that they worked feverishly all night and the next two days on it.[5]

When the mechanics finished their fixes, Byrd deemed the plane ready for its initial major flight: laying the gasoline cache where the Ford would have to land and refuel during the polar run, and stocking the depot with emergency provisions in case the crew had to walk back. He announced that Smith would be the pilot, having tentatively made another decision that he told only to Marie: Balchen would probably pilot the polar flight.[6]

Atmospheric conditions caused a radio blackout that delayed the undertaking for several days, however, showing once again that explorers would have to put up with the curses of modern technology to enjoy its blessings. The airwaves cleared on Monday, 18 November. At 9:40 A.M., the Ford sailed into the southern sky. June copiloted as always on key flights, and McKinley manned the aerial mapping gear for the swing Byrd wanted to take along the front of the Queen Mauds. The commander had decided not to take an emergency dog team on this or the polar flight, probably to save weight. The mission was essentially a dress rehearsal for the polar attempt, with the probable exception of the pilot.

Byrd was nervous as always. If the problem-plagued plane should have an accident and be disabled to any great extent, the polar flight was off. In a serious crash, if weather or other conditions prevented a rescue by the Fairchild, the geological party would have to rush to the scene and cancel its mission. No one wanted to think of even worse possibilities.

Trouble began right away. The tachometer for the center engine broke, making it difficult for Smith to control fuel consumption. Disgusted, Smith and June did not tell Byrd, who was back in the passenger bay, so as not to make him any more worried and risk what they felt might be his overreaction. After about an hour out, the hand fuel pump under Smith's seat sprang a leak. June patched the pump with chewing gum. Again, the men did not inform Byrd who, Smith said, had taken a few nips from a bottle and fallen asleep.[7]

Following the trail made by the ground parties, the quartet had flown a couple of hours when they came upon the struggling sledge teams a little over two hundred miles from Little America. The dogs, taxed to the limit, were belly down as they strained at their heavy loads, and the determined men were pulling with the animals, toes digging into the barrier's crust. The comfortable fliers circled and dropped the bag of mail, gasoline, and equipment that Gould had requested.

A couple of hours later a ragged line appeared on the horizon ahead. As the Ford flew on, the line grew clearly recognizable as the Queen Maud range—the majestic ramparts of the polar plateau. Smith looked for Heiberg Glacier, which Byrd had chosen as his route to the plateau, and picked out a wide glacier that matched Amundsen's description of Heiberg. The men flew around until they spied a likely spot several miles north of the foothills, dropped flares, turned into the wind, and came down.

Byrd presumably was at least as anxious as he had been when Smith was about to land the Fairchild at the Rockefellers to rescue Gould's party. Pilots had a hard time judging the smoothness and consistency of unknown snowy surfaces: bridged-over crevasses might be hidden anywhere. Even telling the location of the surface under Antarctica's unusual lighting conditions was tricky—fliers faced the danger of "landing fifty feet up." Byrd's aviators had realized in the first flying season, moreover, that the struts and landing gear on their planes were not as strong as they should have been for the rough takeoffs and landings on the bumpy ice. These lessons had strongly influenced Byrd's decision to cancel plans to land at the South Pole.[8]

The Ford hit snow that was hard and rough, and it battered the skis and shook the plane as the *Floyd Bennett* skidded to a stop. Everything and everybody remained intact, and one more milestone on the way to the pole was behind the expedition.

The crew took off uneventfully after laying the depot, and the commander had Smith head east along the range to search for Amundsen's hazily seen Carmen Land and northward-trending mountains. The men flew fifty miles and could see for fifty more miles but could make out no sign of either claim far past where the discoveries were supposed to be. Nor had the crew (nor the sledge parties) seen any land to the east on the way south. Byrd had to conclude that probably neither of Amundsen's discoveries existed—contradicting the commander's own claim to have clearly seen Carmen Land on the flight when he supposedly discovered Marie Byrd Land.

Byrd knew the negative finding would be great news for Gould. The geologist could cancel his planned journey eastward from depot #5 on the way home to what apparently was only an apparition, thus saving enough time to investigate the Queen Mauds thoroughly. Without mountains barring the way to Marie Byrd Land, Gould could probably even make his way far enough east to step foot on it and plant the flag, to bolster an official claim by the United States to the territory.

Byrd wanted to continue east to explore farther, but June shouted

over the engine noise that his long dipstick—the only way the crew
had to tell how much gas remained—indicated they were burning up
gas much faster than expected and already had barely enough to get
home. They turned and ran straight for Little America. About the
time they passed over the geological party Smith realized they were
not going to make it. He apparently did not tell either Byrd or Little
America of the plane's plight, perhaps so as not to raise a furor that
might be uncalled for, counting on stretching out the fuel to a landing
at the stranded snowmobile, which had a large gasoline supply.

But Smith miscalculated. Abut 130 miles south of Little America
and some 1,200 feet in the air over a rough, wavy area, June was
radioing to headquarters when the engines sputtered, indicating they
were almost out of gas.

Back at Little America, the radio operators were translating transmissions from the plane for a knot of intent residents gathered around
the receiver. June's message stopped in midsentence, and the suddenly fearful listeners heard nothing but static. Harrison noted in his
diary that the time was 7:00 P.M.[9]

In the absence of the first three in command, it was up to Haines
to decide what to do. Byrd had appointed Haines fourth in command
and placed him in charge of Little America for the duration of the
flight. At 10:00 P.M., with the Ford overdue by an hour, Haines sent
Balchen and Petersen, a qualified pilot as well as radioman, in the
Fairchild with one hundred gallons of gas in case the Ford had run
out.[10]

At 11:00 P.M., Petersen radioed simply that he and Balchen were
ninety-five miles south, could see the Ford, and were landing, making
no mention of the condition of the plane. For a suspenseful hour and
a half the waiting audience heard nothing more, then Petersen radioed
that he and Balchen were in the air again and gave the gist of the
story.

When the engines had sputtered, June immediately stopped transmitting and cut off the two outboard engines, turning off the radio
since it was powered by those engines. The plane started to drop.
June dove at the emergency hand pump and began working it furiously
to force all the remaining gas into the coughing center engine. Byrd

looked at the rippled surface below and, he later admitted, thought to himself, "Here's where we get it."[11]

The plane had dropped four hundred feet when the center engine picked up and began turning normally. Smith nosed the plane back up to cruising altitude. He kept flying with the center engine, struggling to reach the snowmobile fifty miles away.[12]

When they were still fifteen miles from the snowmobile, the last engine went dead. Smith exclaimed that he had never heard of a big, three-engine plane landing with absolutely no power, but the four men were about to see if such a landing could be made. Byrd and McKinley scrambled to the rear of the plane to keep the tail low. There was no time to drop flares and head into the wind. Handling the Ford like a glider, Smith brought the plane down, turning it parallel to the ridges. The expedition, the men's fortunes, their very lives depended on how the Ford would hit. Its skis smashed heavily against the barrier's surface, and the plane careened across the frozen corrugations. Miraculously, it slowed to a stop, and "everything held," as Byrd phrased it. Byrd noted the landing time as 7:29 P.M. For this safe landing and the one at the depot, both on rough surfaces that would have torn apart ordinary aircraft skis, Byrd and Smith gave credit to the special wide skis that Balchen and Bennett had cleverly designed.[13]

With hearts still pounding, the downed fliers jumped out and immediately started the messy job of draining the oil so it would not congeal. Smith complained that Byrd did not help but put up an emergency tent, crawled inside, and went to sleep. The other three men got the dirty oil out, much of it squirting on them and soaking their parkas, and tied the plane down to prevent the wind from destroying the Ford as it had the Fokker. June tried to raise Little America on the emergency radio, but the transmitter was broken. The men could only wait for Haines to send the Fairchild for them when they were overdue.[14]

Before long the rescue plane came in for a landing and taxied over. The men unloaded the twenty heavy five-gallon gas cans and laboriously poured them into the Ford. When the fueling was completed, Byrd indicated he needed no more help, so Balchen and Petersen took off. The Ford's crew started manually cranking the engines, but Smith claimed Byrd quit after a little while with complaints of a bad back. The straining men labored long at the huge center engine but could not get it to start. So again they drained the oil and, embarrassed, lay down to wait for Haines to realize they were still in trouble and send Balchen and Petersen out again.

If Smith's memory is correct about Byrd not helping to drain the oil or start the engine, it is unlikely that Byrd was physically not up to the efforts. He had exercised himself into athletic fitness through gym work, long walks, and, for the past two months, regular sessions of hauling a sledge loaded with 150 pounds of simulated emergency supplies to prepare for the possibility of having to land during the polar flight and march back to Little America. Byrd did not disdain menial labor—he had pitched in several times during the expedition when hands were needed, and he took turns sharing some of the camp's routine chores.[15] Perhaps Byrd was still feeling the effects of the liquor that Smith said the commander had been drinking. Or his anger about the plane's running out of gas and his being kept in the dark about the fuel problem might well have disposed him not to help those responsible.

Eventually the Norwegian pair came back, put more gas and oil into the Ford, heated the center engine, and started it up. Byrd wrote later that a frozen booster had caused the initial failure to start the engine, while Smith implied that the crew might have started it if Byrd had helped.[16] This time the rescuers waited until the cantankerous Ford was in the air before they took off. It was midnight before both planes were back.

Most of the camp stayed up late talking with the aviators about their adventures, but Clarke revealed that Owen had been practically in tears because he could not get a straight account from the fliers upon their return.[17] Presumably they disagreed about the details of the forced landing and balky engine, and probably Smith and June did not want to say much publicly about their contretemps. Byrd may have been too disgusted to talk. He may also have been embarrassed about what seems to have been a foolish decision to keep flying on one engine and not come down as soon as possible while the plane still had power to maneuver for a relatively safe landing.

The incident raised some awkward, unanswered questions, most notably about crew coordination. Why was the decision made to keep flying, and who made it? If not the commander, why not? Whatever Byrd's role, he always claimed afterward that all three engines had stopped at the same time without warning, forcing them down immediately, and he never mentioned trying to reach the snowmobile.

By the account Owen wrote later, the crew flew on the center engine alone for thirty-five miles and fifteen minutes. Demas recorded in his diary that he was also told fifteen minutes although, given the loss of most of the plane's power, that time seems short if the reported distance was correct. The difference in time between the interruption of June's message and the landing was twenty-nine minutes, if Harrison's and Byrd's watches were accurate, a flying time more consistent with the indicated distance.[18]

The entire incident depressed Balchen. As the mechanics discovered, a broken fitting and excessively high pressure had caused both the leak in the gas pump and leaks in a couple of the gas lines. The broken tachometer and—probably most significant—a carburetor malfunction that the men could not understand also contributed to the excessive fuel consumption. The aviation mechanics, who were supposed to see that such things did not happen, were under Balchen, so he felt that the mechanical problems hurt his chances to make the polar flight. Not knowing Byrd's mind, Balchen reasoned, furthermore, that Smith's assignment as pilot in the rehearsal meant he would be playing the lead role in the actual performance.[19]

Byrd, not at all in a good humor, took Balchen for one of his walks the morning after the flight. Byrd was all business, wanting to know why the fuel consumption had been so high. Balchen explained the mechanical problems and promised to go over the engines thoroughly. He said he would also double check his figures on what the fuel consumption should be. Apparently not wanting to miss the chance to take a jab at Byrd, Balchen waved his pocket slide rule and said he had been keeping careful track of mileage and consumption, just as he had on the north polar plane when he had accompanied Floyd Bennett on the plane's triumphal U.S. tour. Balchen related that Byrd, his eyes full of cold fire, interrupted, "Forget about that slide rule. From now on you stick to flying. I'll do the figuring."

As they continued walking, Byrd shook his head moodily and grumbled that the other pilots had not learned to handle engine problems caused by the cold. He cited the fiasco of the day before and the first summer's trouble in starting the Fairchild's engine for the rescue of the stranded party in the Rockefeller Mountains. According to Balchen, Byrd then exclaimed in exasperation: "How is it you always manage to do the right thing? Why do I have to come back to you? I made up my mind a long time ago you would never be my pilot, but now I have no choice. You will fly to the South Pole with me."[20]

Byrd's feelings may have had their roots in Balchen's tour in the north polar plane with Bennett, whom Balchen as well as Byrd counted as best friend. Balchen had kept records of speeds, distances, and gas consumptions and noted that the plane seemed too slow to have made the round-trip to the pole in the time Byrd and Bennett had been gone. Balchen mentioned his observation to Bennett. Balchen had confided Bennett's response to only a few persons, including Smith. As Balchen related to his confidants, Bennett had confessed that he and Byrd had never even come close to the pole. Bennett and Byrd had discovered an oil leak shortly after takeoff, and Byrd ordered Bennett to fly back and forth between the coast and horizon, out of sight of the base, for fourteen hours before returning.[21] Balchen seems to have acted smug with Byrd ever since Bennett's revelations. Byrd was too perceptive not to sense Balchen's contempt toward him for this reason and because of what the Norwegian thought were Byrd's basic deficiencies as a person and an explorer. Additionally, from Balchen's two mentions of his calculations, the commander may have picked up a hint of blackmail aimed at ensuring the Norwegian's choice for the south polar flight. It stands to reason that Balchen's attitude triggered Byrd's dislike.

The Wright Engine company radioed advice on the Ford's fuel-consumption problem—another benefit of radio—and the aviation unit worked frantically to ready the plane for the next base-laying flight.[22] It is not clear whether Byrd intended to build up the first depot or lay an alternate depot. Considering the inauspicious first trip, he probably wanted another test flight to make sure that the problems had been fixed, that nothing else was wrong, and that the plane could stand up to prolonged operation in subzero weather. Aircraft engines had a hard time running in freezing temperatures. Byrd's mechanics had insulated and cowled his engines to conserve heat, but cold remained a constant threat, especially for the extralong polar flight into the most frigid part of Antarctica.

On Saturday, 23 November, Byrd made what was for him an unusually bold decision: to forgo another shakedown mission and concentrate all efforts on getting to the pole as soon as possible. He was undoubtedly concerned about his competitors, and the unplanned total of four hundred miles flown by the Fairchild in aiding the downed

Ford had eaten into the already-low gasoline supply, which an extra flight would drain further. On the other hand, he would have no opportunity to prove that the mechanics had rid the bedeviled plane of its many bugs, so he would be chancing a misfortune such as a misadjusted carburetor, a cold-induced malfunction, or an oil leak of the kind that had occurred on the north polar flight. Byrd told Balchen and June to check up more closely on the mechanics' work.[23]

The news brought reminders that even the best pilots could meet disaster. Little America surely got word that Wilmer Stultz, who had been identified as a "Byrd Expedition pilot" during the secret preparations for flying Amelia Earhart across the Atlantic in what had been Byrd's original plane, had died in a plane crash.[24]

On Monday, 25 November, Wilkins announced he had made a short flight, his first of the year, from his antarctic base. Jolted, Byrd checked his expedition's readiness for the polar flight.[25] The mechanics said they felt sure the Ford could make the pole and back. The geological party was not yet at the Queen Mauds but was close enough to report on weather near the mountains and was positioned to attempt a rescue if necessary. Byrd decided to go for the pole when the cloudy weather broke up.

All eyes scanned the overcast sky for a sight of blue, and everyone hung on the latest weather reports from Gould. Monday, Tuesday, and Wednesday morning went by with the whole barrier still socked in and nerves increasingly on edge. Work came almost to a standstill, and only the scientists went on with their daily routines.[26]

Balchen developed painful boils on his arm but kept quiet about them for fear he would be bumped from the historic flight.[27] Wednesday afternoon Gould radioed that the clouds over the mountains were beginning to disappear. At noon on Thursday, 28 November—Thanksgiving Day—he reported perfect weather as far as he could see from his position sixty miles from the Queen Mauds. Some clouds still cast shadows on Little America, and the winds could have been more favorable, but Haines pronounced the weather overall to be as good as Byrd could ever expect. The commander ordered the turkey dinner postponed: it was time to go.

The aviation unit loaded an extra one hundred pounds of gas into the Ford because of the bad experience on the earlier flight, and at the last minute Byrd nervously ordered the ground crew to stow an extra 250 pounds of emergency food—supplies perhaps intended for the depot until the second flight was canceled. Balchen argued that the extra provisions piled on too much weight and warned Byrd to keep the excess in a handy position to throw out if the plane ran into trouble.[28]

Byrd considered bouncing McKinley to compensate; the only area worth mapping was the pass through the mountains, and Amundsen had reported generally on that pass already. McKinley probably feared this possibility. Byrd had asked McKinley and Gould for reports on the value of aerial photography on the polar flight and the possibility of having a pilot do the job. When Owen's story about the plans for the snowmobile mission had appeared on the bulletin board, mentioning McKinley's role as the enthusiastic mentor, the acting exec had approached Owen in private about the report. The reporter revealed that McKinley was worried to death the vehicle would fail and he would be associated with the debacle.[29] He surely had noted that the commander seemed to have written off the sledgers of the geological party when they displeased him. Presumably, McKinley wanted to stay on Byrd's good side and not make it easy for the commander to leave the aerial photographer out of the south polar flight as he had been left out of the first year's flights.

Byrd chose in favor of mapping photography. Along with the instruments Harrison put in the plane's tail to take weather readings automatically every minute, aerial photography placed a scientific cachet on the flight that made it more than a stunt. None of the remaining crew knew enough about aerial mapping to do McKinley's job; besides, manipulating the one-hundred-pound camera demanded the photographer's full attention when mountains were in sight, just at the time the rest of the crew would be busiest piloting and navigating. Additionally, June would be functioning as a cameraman for Paramount, besides copiloting and operating the radio. Byrd decided to keep both McKinley and the extra weight.[30]

A bag was placed on the plane containing souvenirs belonging to expedition members, as well as flags and other insignia from numerous governments, institutions, and organizations, most of which had requested the favor for what they had done for Byrd or could do for him.[31] He had also packed many small American flags to present to friends and persons of influence.

The day was so special that each of the crew members performed the rituals, rare at Little America, of bathing and changing underwear.

Byrd gave sealed messages to Lofgren to hold in case the crew did not return. Nobody could totally suppress doubts and fears kindled by the expedition's experience: plans had been formulated or carried out wrongly; items had been forgotten; weather, planes, and people had often not behaved as anticipated; judgments had turned out faulty; confidence had occasionally proven baseless; security had been shattered by the unexpected. Even as thoroughly prepared as the men were for their trial, an almost infinite variety of natural traps, mechanical flaws, and human errors could ruin the mission and, at worst, take the lives of all four. A special radio code devised for use on the flight contained signals for "crashed," "seriously injured," "starving," and "dead."[32]

The crew members took their positions in the Ford—a type of plane that had been introduced only in 1926, which Byrd had taken for political rather than strictly technical reasons. Balchen revved up the engines, the plane skied down the runway for half a minute, and at 3:29 P.M. the men lifted off and headed south. As Byrd looked out a passenger window, he saw the well-wishers dancing, jumping, shouting, and throwing their hats in the air, "wild with joy that we were off for the pole."[33]

Because of strong easterly winds, Balchen nosed the plane a few degrees east of the course to compensate, so the Ford crabbed its way sideways toward the pole some 800 miles away. The plane followed the southward trail uneventfully until the crew had the Queen Mauds in sight and passed over the geological party faithfully standing by at the seventh depot. Byrd dropped a bag that included McKinley's photos of the mountains from the earlier flight, as well as chocolate, cigarettes, and messages.[34]

The crew had come to the most difficult part of the flight and had to make a crucial decision. The mountain peaks reached higher than the Ford could fly, so the men would have to follow a glacier up a pass to the immense, Tibetan-like polar plateau, two miles high, that the plane could barely surmount. The winds in the pass might be tricky, possibly turbulent; the passageway would be too narrow to maneuver much; and there would probably be no safe landing areas. Byrd had tentatively selected Heiberg Glacier as his first choice and Liv glacier, twenty-five miles west, as his second.

The crew left the comforting sledge trail and approached the towering range, peering along both channels. The men could not make out much beyond the mouths of the glaciers, but there seemed to be clouds at the top of Heiberg and none over Liv. Liv appeared to be lower and wider besides. The airmen did not have enough fuel to reconnoiter. A "white knuckle" flier who was probably in the grip of fear now that the worst moment was at hand, Byrd had to say he liked the looks of Liv better. The stolid Norwegian pilot nosed the Ford in that direction, climbed to 9,000 feet, and followed the glacier's ascent at eighty miles per hour.

The Ford gradually ascended to 9,600 feet, and all went well until the craft got to the south end of the pass. It had narrowed so much that there was not enough room to turn—they had to go ahead. But in front of them the glacier rose steeply and was split by a peak several hundred feet higher than the plane. There was no space to go around the peak. They had to get over it.

Balchen pulled back on the stick, but the Ford did not respond: the plane had gone as high as it could for its weight. He ordered the food dumped, so the men pitched out one of the extra 125-pound bags as well as all the five-gallon gas cans that had been emptied into the tanks during the flight. Balchen yelled, "More!" and the men tossed out the second bag.[35]

The plane shot up a few hundred feet but not quite enough to clear the mountain. The Ford was bucking violently in the downdraft spilling off the plateau. Balchen figured there might be a backlash of rising air along the cliff wall to the right. He swung over that way, the wing tip almost touching the rock face. The pole was forgotten—staying alive was all that mattered to anyone.

Balchen found his updraft. The craft hurdled the mountain and cleared the pass to emerge over the white plateau some hundreds of feet below. They had survived. Euphoric, as only they can be who have faced down death, the fliers again seized the vision of the pole and turned due south.[36]

Their goal was now what should be an easy three hundred miles away—supposing all the engines could maintain their energetic exertions at the cold, oxygen-scarce altitude of 11,000 feet—1,000 feet above the plateau. If even one engine should quit over the high plateau, the plane would have to come down: two engines could not keep the heavily loaded plane up in that thin air.

Suddenly the right engine backfired and began missing. June grabbed the lever that would dump all the gas, to avoid a fire upon crashing.[37] Balchen shouted that he had just leaned the fuel too much, and he adjusted the choke slightly to make the power plant purr again.

Midnight brought a new day, although, of course, the Ford was still flying in bright sunshine. An hour later the pole was within the horizon. The focus of years of toil and worry, of over a million dollars worth of expenditures and donations, and of the devotion of scores of people, the South Pole was, ironically, an imaginary point—a mathematical location on the vast blank plain beneath them. Balchen passed Byrd a note saying that by dead reckoning they should reach the pole in fourteen minutes.[38]

Fourteen minutes later, at 1:14 A.M., Friday, 29 November, one of the happiest moments of Byrd's life, he wrote the historic words on a note he passed to the pilots: "We have reached the South Pole." He opened the hatch and dropped a flag weighted with a stone from Floyd Bennett's grave—the closest the commander could come to his original goal of planting the Stars and Stripes at the pole. June tossed out a flag of the American Legion.[39]

Although most pleasing for all of them, the moment was not at all electrifying. The ice cap looked no different than it had for hours, and the plane felt and sounded no different. Calculations showed that the Ford must be at the pole, but it was an achievement the men could appreciate only intellectually. The accomplishment was as sterile as everything else about Antarctica.

Byrd gave the word to head directly back to the Queen Mauds, and the crew flew smoothly to the mountains. Starting from a high altitude and with the plane much lighter than before because it had spent most of its fuel, the men faced a much easier return passage. The commander ordered Balchen to head down Heiberg Glacier east of Liv, the shortest route to the depot site.

Smith says he was told later that the crew flew to the site—but there was no depot there. Assuming they had marked its location wrong, Balchen handed the controls over to June, who had been on the depot-laying flight, so the copilot could fly around and try to find familiar landmarks. Byrd did not record the incident, but he must have dreaded a repetition of the forced landing and the Fairchild's relief flight. June recognized terrain nearer Liv Glacier and, presumably to the gratification of all, spotted the depot about twenty-five miles northwest of where the crew had thought it was.[40]

Smith explained that he had landed at the wrong place on his flight.

He claimed that Byrd had given him no navigational instructions and that, left to his own devices, he had simply picked out the wrong glacier—one between Heiberg and Liv.[41] (The geological party, also headed for Heiberg, made the same mistake, although they soon realized their error; when viewed from due north, the glaciers to the west apparently fit Amundsen's description of Heiberg better than Heiberg itself.)

June brought the Ford safely down. Balchen reported later that on the way from the pole to the depot Byrd had pulled one of several pints of cognac out of his flight bag and begun draining the bottle. As the Norwegian described the scene on the ground, Byrd staggered around the depot yelling, "We made it! We made it!" while the others wearily lugged seventy ponderous five-gallon gas cans to the plane and hefted them up to the fuel intake. Balchen said June whispered that they would have to get the bottles away from the commander if he got into them again. Byrd did break out another pint and left it for the geological party,[42] but, according to Balchen, did not drink any more on the flight and sobered up during the easy four-and-a-half-hour trip to the Bay of Whales.

As the Ford approached Little America's landing strip shortly after 10:00 A.M., the crew could see everyone clustered at the end. When, after eighteen-and-one-half tense hours, the plane taxied to a halt by the group and opened the doors, excited comrades lifted the crew out, hoisted the victors to their shoulders, and paraded them into the mess hall for a celebration. The crew, exhausted but elated, rehashed the flight and answered questions all day long.

McKinley confessed that he had had qualms about his presence on the flight when they were fighting for height over Liv Glacier. Commenting on the mission for the public, however, Byrd declaimed sanctimoniously that "it was for [McKinley] and the camera he so sedulously served that the flight was made. The mapping of the corridor between Little America and the pole was one of the major objectives of the expedition."[43]

Smith had to put up with some ribbing about misplacing the depot, but the embarrassment was really Byrd's. The commander was supposed to have navigated to a precise spot and checked its location carefully once on the ground, since there were few landmarks and he would have to find the spot again during the polar flight. Discussing the cache-laying flight later, he wrote, "It was absolutely necessary that I know exactly where we were when we planned to land for the base" and "We had to trust entirely to navigation." Owen's story in the *New York Times* about the cache-laying flight reported that Byrd had used his sextant to determine the position, which "checked perfectly with their dead reckoning, so that they have no doubt as to where the base lies. The entire flight was a splendid test of navigation under flying conditions down here, and Commander Byrd is quite satisfied now that his calculations will work out as expected. The course was kept perfectly with the aid of the sun compass and checked with the navigation done on the way out. . . . The flight . . . enabled the commander to use the methods he developed this past winter."[44]

These boasts contrasted sharply with the message about the location of the polar plane's base that Byrd had sent to Gould upon returning from the flight that put the base down. The geologist had requested that Byrd give the location "as accurately as possible." The navigator had replied, "It is impossible for us to judge distances from those mountains by eye but our base appears to be about ten to 15 miles west of Axel Heiberg. Distances as estimated may be very much in error." Gould then asked Byrd to transmit the latitude and longitude of the base on the next radio schedule. Byrd did not do so. Instead, on the polar flight he airdropped a message to Gould, saying, "I can't tell you the latitude and longitude of the mountain base as I got my sight at the wrong time." The commander told Gould to use the accompanying photos to help locate the base, although admitting they were confusing. Later, even after visiting the base site a second time on the way back from the pole, Byrd made the most damning indictment of his navigational claims—he asked Gould to send the latitude and longitude when the geologist reached the base.[45]

After the expedition, Byrd contradicted what he had told Gould about the general location of the base. The commander wrote that on the base-laying flight the crew had found the area fifteen miles west of Heiberg impossible for a landing and had to look near Liv. But in neither the *New York Times*'s story about the flight bylined by Owen nor the follow-up personal account in the paper bylined by Byrd was there any mention of having to seek out a site closer to Liv.[46]

Byrd wrote later that he wanted to swing east on returning from the pole to expose more territory to the aerial camera and to verify the conclusion, made during the first Ford flight, that Carmen Land did not exist. Those reasons were strange ones, especially for the supercautious Byrd. The plane was low on gas, and prudence called for the fliers to try to locate the depot as soon as possible. Moreover, the men had been in the air about twelve hours and had gone the night without sleep; the Ford was not entirely trustworthy; and expedition members had already been east on the depot-laying flight.

According to Byrd, his crew had flown far enough east after exiting Heiberg Pass to satisfy themselves about Carmen Land and then had tried to find the cache. He described later that the others on the flight, "who evidently had not been watching the course carefully," thought the depot was near the foot of Heiberg and that he directed them to the cache's actual location nearer to Liv.[47] He claimed that June took the controls as the plane approached the depot only because the copilot was familiar with the landing surface.

Smith charged that Byrd, save for once giving a compass heading, had never passed the pilot navigational information on any flight, always letting the competent Smith fly by visual clues and dead reckoning. Balchen said essentially the same thing, claiming Byrd had not given any navigational directions on the transatlantic and south polar missions.[48]

Byrd admitted he was not sure how near he had really come to the definite spot of the South Pole. He told Railey he bent over backward not to claim flying to the exact pole but only to the vicinity of the pole because scientists who looked at the navigational records might decide Byrd had not gotten close enough to the precise geographic point. "The plane was rocking so much that I could not get accurate astronomical sights at the pole and had to go by dead reckoning," he radioed. (A committee convened by the National Geographic Society in 1931 examined the records of the south polar flight Byrd presented and confirmed that navigation was almost entirely by dead reckoning, concluding that Byrd had gotten within at least four miles of the pole and probably closer.)[49]

After the expedition, when McKinley disputed Byrd over using antarctic flight data for making maps, the aerial photographer wrote an intriguing, unexplained letter to Byrd concerning the records McKinley had kept on the south polar flight and on a flight or flights to the east: "Dick, without going too deep into either the polar or eastern flights, you know that my polar records, while kept with all possible precision, were asked to be destroyed and not used as they were, and that I was never furnished with complete navigational data. . . ."[50]

Byrd nevertheless drew a picture of himself as the masterly navigator on whom the success of his flights turned. In a passage in the commander's book that must have caused Balchen to hit the ceiling, Byrd described his navigation of the south polar flight: "From the navigator's table aft, where my charts were spread out, a trolley ran to the control cabin. Over it I shot to Balchen the necessary messages and courses. On receiving them, he turned and smiled his understanding. . . . I would steady Balchen on his course . . . first shaking the trolley line to attract his attention, then waving him on to the new course."[51]

If the pilots' memories are better than Byrd's, then the commander played up the importance of his navigation so that he would be seen as the active leader of the flights rather than as merely a distinguished passenger, in Smith's words. Owen, who had written most of the story about the polar flight from the plans, before the actual event, noted in the book he wrote later that he had put the navigation section off until the last—presumably expecting that Byrd would have much to write himself.[52] (Interestingly, Byrd said that on the 1,530-mile north polar round-trip he had had no problems guiding the flight mainly by celestial navigation.)

Little America held its delayed but appropriately timed Thanksgiving dinner following the regular Saturday broadcast on the day after the return of the big flight. Siple said grace before the meal, the only occasion on which a public prayer was ever offered on the expedition. Once again some of the group put on a vaudeville show, lampooning the snowmobile excursion and the polar flight. McKinley asked Byrd to break out the alcohol for the party. In a mood to celebrate and overlook the possible consequences, the commander agreed. Blackburn noted that "McKinley and Haines and Black furnished a comedy element as usual, and even Demas loosened up." The straitlaced mechanic, moved to imbibe alcohol for the first time in his life, drank himself sick. Some of the athletic revelers wrestled and played football in the snow. Fortunately, none of the chastened problem drinkers tried to turn the event into a days-long binge. Clarke called the party the best ever.[53]

In the days that followed, the radio operators were at their busiest, decoding the cascade of dots and dashes—five times more than usual—

that brought praise and news of reaction from around the world. Messages from President Hoover and Congress topped the stack of congratulatory telegrams. The Smithsonian Institution awarded Byrd its rarely given Langley Medal for aeronautics.[54]

An editorial in California's *Long Beach Sun* recommended Congress "honor itself" by promoting Byrd to admiral for his contributions to science and country and for serving youth "as a hero worthy of emulation and as a stimulus to ambition." Senator Swanson of Virginia sent word that he would try to get a bill passed awarding Byrd the promotion. By radio, Byrd and Swanson corresponded on the wording of the bill. Byrd thoughtfully tried to have the bill include citizenship for Balchen, early retirement from the navy for June, and at least an army promotion for McKinley, but the commander withdrew his request upon being advised not to overload the bill and hamper its chances for passage.[55]

Ecstatic and flushed with success, Byrd charged toward further prizes in aerial exploration. On Monday, 2 December, he ordered the aviation unit to make general preparations for a flight to the unknown area to the east, although he did not set a definite date for the mission. He had originally intended to fly southeast to investigate Carmen Land; because that territory proved chimerical, Byrd could now explore elsewhere. The president of the American Geographical Society, one of Byrd's key advisors, had radioed a suggestion that the explorer make another flight eastward to try to discover the barrier's eastern boundary and locate the coast of Marie Byrd Land, which would "establish an indisputable basis" for a U.S. claim to the territory. Byrd radioed Marie that if he did not make an eastern flight, the "expedition will be severely criticized by scientific bodies."[56]

.11.

A First-Class Discovery

At breakfast on Thursday, 5 December, Byrd surprised the flying unit by almost impulsively ordering Parker and June to take him and McKinley far to the east in the Ford that very day, without going through the usual protracted discussion and planning for such a major flight.[1] Byrd later explained he had planned the flight quietly to avoid the kind of tension that had gripped Little America while everyone was waiting for the weather to clear for the polar flight; but the polar flight had been the expedition's great goal, and no tension had ever accompanied any other flight.

He may have been goaded by the insinuations of a Norwegian member of Scott's expedition, Trygve Gran. Two days before, Gran had criticized the American expedition to the press as nothing but sensationalism.[2] As Clarke noted, the commander was highly incensed when he learned of the aspersion. Byrd had probably also learned of the impending flights of Riiser-Larsen, who had taken a seaplane to the waters off the other side of the continent. The commander knew that Wilkins was attempting to get a major flight off. In high spirits over the polar conquest and assured promotion, and excited that the long-range Ford was available for the first time for exploration, Byrd may have wanted to try for more headlines before antarctic discoveries lost some of their news value.

The hurried crew took off shortly before 11:00 A.M. and pointed the big plane along the shoreline, which ran northeast from their base. Describing the flight in his book on the expedition, Byrd wrote that they had followed the desolate coast for almost two hours when, in the distance where Marie Byrd Land was, they dimly saw a long range of mountains angling across their path from the right. Even before he could make them out clearly, Byrd felt he had made "a first class discovery." The crew raced ahead at one hundred miles per hour, and about twenty minutes later the mountains, which ran north and south, stood out clearly. Byrd gazed at the peaks and "beheld one of the sights a man will go to the end of the earth to find and risk everything for. A range of mountains of great extent. . . . Here was the romance of geographical exploration."[3]

When the mountains were still sixty miles away, the commander excitedly ordered Parker to turn north, and the plane flew parallel to the mountains and coast for about sixty miles. Not having come to the north end of the chain, the aviators flew east a few miles to bring the mountains a little closer and then turned south to find the end of the chain in that direction. At about the time they had retraced the sixty miles of the range they had seen, Byrd saw what looked like islands to the northwest in the Ross Sea. He ordered the plane to veer that way, but when it became clear the islands were much farther off than they looked, he put the Ford back on the southward course.

Byrd's exuberance continued: "Of all the flights I have ever made, none was so full of excitement and profit as this one. . . . One could only gape at [nature's] handiwork and say 'Holy smoke!' " He stated that some of the glorious peaks were "surely 10,000 feet high." Byrd said that, most important of all, he saw a white plateau behind the range, which he thought might be a counterpart of the polar plateau. The aviators kept on without finding the southern end of the range until the coastline swept to the west. Byrd noted that McKinley had photographed two hundred miles of the new range and that they had seen farther with binoculars. Byrd said that, with the Ford low on gas, he ordered Parker to fly past the Matterhorn mountain discovered the previous summer so that McKinley could photograph the peak, and then to proceed home.[4]

Byrd treated the historically significant Matterhorn oddly after the expedition. His profusely illustrated book did not even include the peak's picture, and he did not officially give any mountain the name Matterhorn (or Ames, as he had told Marie). The book did not refer to the newly discovered territory as Marie Byrd Land in the chapter on the Matterhorn sighting, when the christening actually occurred, but rather in the account of the 5 December flight. In a detailed report on Marie Byrd Land that Byrd wrote for *The Geographical Review*, he did not even mention the discovery of the Matterhorn, and in fact implied that he discovered Marie Byrd Land on the 5 December flight.[5]

In numerous references, Byrd clearly identified the Matterhorn with the mountain he officially named La Gorce Mountain, after the vice president of the National Geographic Society. But there are two problems with that identification. First, La Gorce Mountain is not in Marie Byrd Land. The peak lies west of 150 degrees longitude and within the British claim. If La Gorce really is the Matterhorn, then Byrd's headline-making announcement of the discovery of Marie Byrd Land in February 1929 was premature and, had the mountains seen on the 5 December flight not existed, would have been monumentally embarrassing. If Byrd really came to believe that La Gorce Mountain was the Matterhorn—thinking that its position had been misjudged in February—then he might have misplayed the Matterhorn's discovery to avoid ridicule. The second problem is that the location of La Gorce Mountain does not square at all with either Smith's or Byrd's account of the Matterhorn discovery. La Gorce is northeast of the Rockefellers and less than fifty miles away. When in his book Byrd tells of discovering the Matterhorn, he describes it (echoing Smith's account) as so far away from the Rockefellers that "to our chagrin it did not appear to be nearer, although both planes were advancing toward it at the rate of about 100 miles per hour." In the *New York Times*'s account of the Matterhorn discovery, Owen wrote: ". . . the new hinterland, the beginning of which [Byrd] has seen, is well outside the limits of the British claims."[6]

The morning after Smith, McKinley, and Berkner had arrived back from sighting the Matterhorn on their February flight, they radioed an account of their discovery to Byrd, who was enroute to Little America after exploring the ocean to the east on the *New York*: ". . . We could see from the Rockefellers a range of mountains which we agreed must be more than a hundred miles to the east southeast of the Rockefellers. This range was headed by a very high peak with a lower peak to the north and what appeared to be a high ridge disappearing into the southeast, with indications of other mountains on the horizon. Also due east of the Rockefellers were two peaks equidistant or further than the range seen to the east southeast." Berkner added his own note to the joint message: "Range we sighted to ESE must be eight to ten thousand feet high to be visible at the distance. It stood out like a sore thumb and not a cloud that way so it was clearly visible for more than an hour."[7]

There is a large mountain east southeast of the Rockefellers, about one hundred miles from the northern end of that chain and well inside Marie Byrd Land, that Byrd named Mount Grace McKinley, after the aerial photographer's wife. It is at the southern end of the range Byrd saw on 5 December, and exactly where the Matterhorn was described to be when it was discovered.[8] (On the rough map at the end of the book Byrd later wrote, the Matterhorn is shown approximately at the site of the mountain now known as McKinley Peak.)

It seems likely that Smith and the others on his flight were actually the first to see the new mountain range. If so—and if Byrd knew it—then he might have misidentified the Matterhorn to ensure that he himself would be regarded as the indisputable discoverer of Marie Byrd Land and the new mountains.

Owen commented that he found the track of the 5 December flight, "to say the least, puzzling." He pointed out that Byrd could easily have gone all the way to the mountains to get good, cartographically and geologically significant pictures of the range, but did not—and in fact flew away from the mountains at one point to look for islands that, Owen stated, could not have been nearly as important. The pictures would disappoint Gould. On being informed of the discovery by radio, his first reaction was to express his hope that McKinley's photos would show enough detail to tell if the mountains were like the Queen Mauds. The geologist declared that there was "perhaps no sector of the antarctic where the discovery of new land was of more interest to me."[9]

Byrd explained that he kept a distance from the mountains "to enable McKinley to keep the coast line in his survey photographs, a most important consideration in the discovery and mapping of a new area." The commander clearly gave mapping and establishing a claim higher priorities than geology. Byrd may also have thought it more important to determine the extent of the range—equally significant to him and to Gould—than its details; flying all the way to the mountains (and back) would have cost him about an hour of gas. Or perhaps he was not thinking clearly at all. The account of the 5 December flight is Byrd's; no other crew member ever wrote about it. Many people, however, who had gathered to hail the returning explorers revealed the ending of the flight. Siple told his diary circumspectly that "the commander was very happy—and celebrated." Harrison wrote that Byrd had been under such a nervous strain in the preceding weeks that he had become run down and tried to pick himself up with ' alcohol on the flight, arriving back "in anything but a dignified condition." Smith revealed that the commander had been slugging down brandy and could not walk without help. Balchen reported that, when the Ford's door opened, he saw June and McKinley sitting on Byrd, who was flat on the floor struggling and cursing. He suddenly went limp, Balchen related, and the welcoming committee hauled the commander to his bunk.[10]

Despite the impulsive beginning, controversial flight path, and ignominious end, the flight meant a lot to geographers and geologists. In later writings, Byrd commented, "[It] was more successful than I had dared to hope. . . . It proved the existence of land in that area— an immense landfall." He pointed out that the discovery extended the coastal outline and provided Marie Byrd Land with coastal access. He proclaimed that he considered "the results of this flight far more important than the results of our flight over the pole." Smith, who had no illusions about Byrd, admitted to being convinced the commander really did prefer such exploratory flights to the polar project and like stunts.[11]

In the days following, the American Geographical Society informed Byrd that he would be the first recipient in five years of its Livingstone Medal for important scientific achievement in geography. The prestigious American Association for the Advancement of Science, the coordinating body for U.S. scientific societies, sent congratulations to the expedition for "making a great America greater."[12]

For some reason—perhaps to bargain for a larger contribution from a donor—Byrd did not immediately name the new range. (Despite his announcement after Floyd Bennett's death, Byrd never named any major new land after his friend.)

Two days later Riiser-Larsen flew to the Atlantic section of Antarctica and charted a portion of the coastline. Then Mawson made coastal discoveries by seaplane in the Indian Ocean littoral. Byrd enjoyed the satisfaction of achieving two major goals: making discoveries and beating his competitors into print.

Byrd had been planning three more flights to the east and perhaps one to the west. There was talk at Little America of another flight to the new range to map it as far southward as possible. The commander, however, decided not to make another major flight. He announced in the *New York Times*, in a story dated 12 December, that he felt the purpose of his expedition had been accomplished. He stated that, although he might make short flights, he planned no more long ones because flying weather deteriorates after early summer in the polar regions. But this reasoning is weak. The sun was still ascending and would not touch the horizon again for two and one half months. The summer before, Byrd had not even begun flights of exploration until 27 January, and Marie Byrd Land was not discovered until the long flights of 18 February; on the same date a year before he had not even reached Antarctica. He also explained that if a plane were forced down three hundred miles away, for example, the fliers could not walk back in time to meet the ships. The ships were not expected to depart for home for seven more weeks, however, and surely could have been delayed a while if necessary, so there seems to have been plenty of time for such a contingency. Besides, Byrd had a standby plane and dog teams to expedite rescues. If the gasoline shortage was a factor, Byrd did not mention it. He had radioed Gould enigmatically the day before the announcement, "Am not sure we are going to be able to fly out to the mountains again for operational reasons which I will explain to you when you return."[13]

Marie Byrd's attitude could have been instrumental. She frequently begged him not to take chances. After the south polar flight, she had radioed him, "Do rest on your laurels and come home." The calculating explorer did not say it, but he may also have been thinking that he had little more to gain personally by more discoveries on this expedition and much to lose if anything should go awry. In Smith's judgment, "Byrd felt that he had achieved his purpose and he did not want to take any chance that something might go wrong on a subsequent flight and tarnish his perfect record."[14] Byrd was already talking confidentially about his next expedition, moreover, and might have wanted to save something for future headlines.

(In his book, Byrd wrote nothing about deciding to end major flights early and, in fact, stated that only bad weather prevented a flight to the east of the Queen Mauds before the expedition had to get ready to leave.)[15]

The day of Byrd's announcement, the geological party missed one of its alternate-day radio transmissions. When last heard from, the sledgers had been in an avalanche-prone area, and Byrd feared they might lie buried under tons of snow and rock. After two more days without contact, he ordered planes and dog teams made ready for a rescue, soliciting fifteen volunteers for another winter and preparing for another year of operations. Much to everyone's relief, Gould came through on the night of 14 December and reported no trouble whatsoever. No one recorded the reason for the missed transmission. Byrd, who must have been more than a little irritated, scolded Gould that day, "For heaven's sake keep me well posted and play the game carefully. You mustn't mind my saying this for I can't help from being greatly anxious."[16]

With the successful flight to the pole and the discovery by air of the long mountain range to the east, the expedition's major remaining goal was in the hands of the six men who, far from the sanctuary of Little America, were battling to explore Antarctica in the old-fashioned way.

.12.

The Queen Maud Mountains

THE trail sextet—leader and geologist Gould, surveyors and drivers Thorne and O'Brien, and drivers Vaughan, Goodale, and Crockett—usually began their day at 6:00 A.M. They dressed lightly in woolens and windproofs—made of aircraft fabric for these modern explorers—since the day's exercise would keep them warm. For breakfast they had hot oatmeal, biscuits, and tea. They made juice by mixing water and a fruit powder that Byrd had had developed to prevent scurvy.

About 8:30, after breaking camp and packing up, they hitched up the dogs and skied along behind them, or pulled with them when they had heavy loads. The men drove single file, about a quarter-mile apart. Although they followed the supporting party's trail for the first two hundred miles, Gould practiced navigating. He admitted with embarrassment that he really "dropped the ball" one day when he led his teammates due north the whole morning; by day's end, they had advanced only two miles. Gould did not mention how the others reacted but, with time so dear and the loads so weighty, it is doubtful that anyone laughed it off.[1]

The group traveled until noon and stopped for lunch, typically cold pemmican, Eskimo biscuits with butter or peanut butter, a chocolate bar, and tea, cocoa, or malted milk. The brown Eskimo biscuits were shaped like large Graham crackers, but thicker, and were made of wheat, vegetables, and some meat compacted into a hard material, like dog biscuits, so the rough handling on the trail would not crumble them.

The men typically went on after lunch until 5:00 or 5:30 P.M., when they stopped for the day, usually having traveled about ten miles at first when they were heavily loaded and twice that distance later when they were lightly loaded. The campers erected three-man "A" tents—like big pup tents—for sleeping, with three-foot-long funnels that the men tied closed after them. They also put up a pyramidal cooking tent, like a teepee with a square bottom. The tents had white bases and orange peaks.

The men got out of their work clothes, arrayed them so they would air out and dry overnight, and bundled up in warm furs. The sledgers had to be careful to avoid moisture problems: their clothes became soaked with perspiration, which intensified the cold when the men rested.

For the first dinner course, the men buttered Eskimo biscuits and laid two strips of bacon on top. Then they heated half-pound blocks of pemmican with snow and added pea-meal sausages to make a rich, greasy brown stew. Byrd had gotten the pemmican in four-inch-square, one-inch-thick blocks from Amundsen, who had had them made from finely ground dried beef and fat with a little seasoning. The stew had the look and consistency of fresh wet concrete. Drinks were the same as at lunch.

The dog handlers fed their charges the superb pemmican Dr. Malcolm had formulated in New Zealand. For dinner, each husky got a pound-and-a-half block of the special food, which continued to prove itself the nearest thing to canine ambrosia.

The drivers chained the dogs for the night so they would not eat the leather harnesses and lashings or get into fights. The tough animals curled up on the surface to sleep. Sometimes drifting snow covered them over, but the explorers said the dogs did not seem to mind.

Every other night Crockett raised Little America on the shortwave set. His trail buddies would be almost too tired to crank the stiff hand generator that provided power for the set but, delighting in the contact with others, would often gossip awhile with an amateur operator such as Smith after the official transmissions.

For relaxation, the weary explorers would read—erudite Professor Gould, for instance, had a volume of Shakespeare's works—or play cards, usually hearts or bridge. Gould, Thorne, and O'Brien slept in one tent, and the three musketeers shared the other.

When only five days out, the sledgers began to feel the searing pain of snowblindness. Thorne complained that it felt as though "someone had thrown hot sand" into his eyes. In addition, Gould was so poor on skis that he had become tired and blistered to the extent that he seriously doubted whether he would last.[2]

A little more than a week after the party left, they gazed at what looked like mountains dead ahead. Although the men knew they had not traveled far enough, they did not immediately realize they were fooled by a mirage caused by the looming of the terrible crevassed area that the supporting party had found. Walden's group had drawn the sting from the area by marking a safe trail, so Gould's party crossed easily.

The antarctic oddities they encountered included disorienting white-outs, when an overcast made the big sky look the same as the barrier's surface, blurring the horizon. A person, feeling suspended in an infinity of whiteness, might peer all around futilely for another person, only to look up, see his companions "floating in space," and realize he had been looking downward instead of scanning with eyes level. Another characteristic of the trail was the unexpected settling of the ice. The men would often hear a muffled roar, and the surface would drop slightly beneath them. Gould said the settling gave him a sickening feeling until he got used to the phenomenon. He explained that it was caused by sudden compression of a deep layer of snow under the weight of the overlying burden.

On 18 November the group reached depot four, their halfway point and also the terminus of the supporting party's march. From then on, Gould's men would have to break trail and carry all the food and supplies to establish four more depots. They stacked eighty pounds of dog food from the depot onto each of their already groaning sledges, hoping to discard much of the food that same day after the Ford's flight that would lay the polar mission's base, which Gould thought might include a load for them.

That evening, assuming Byrd had returned, Gould radioed him at

Little America: "Will you please tell me how much dog food you deposited for us? . . . Several dogs will probably have to be killed within a few days and our present plans call for cutting to eighteen dogs when we arrive at the mountains. We like our dogs very much and hope we won't have to kill so many." Gould wrote in his diary that night, while unknown to him Byrd's plane was out of gas and stranded: "We hope they landed some dog food and supplies for us so we can lighten our loads here. It is so important."[3]

When Byrd returned to Little America, he fired back a reply stating that the plane had been greatly overloaded and declaring peremptorily, ". . . You had better not depend on us at all. Left no dog food. . . . Please give us daily . . . weather report." Gould, in scientific understatement, wrote later that "we of course derived but little comfort" from Byrd's message.[4]

Byrd would not even air drop dog food for the party, even though a drop would not involve a risky landing on and takeoff from an unknown surface. Perhaps the commander's implacable attitude can be laid to supercautiousness or to a threatened shortage of gasoline. He may have intended to carry dog food on the canceled second depot-laying flight. On the other hand, knowing how Scott's aversion to killing dogs had been a cause of his failure, while dispatching huskies had been an integral part of the success of Byrd's model explorer, Amundsen, the commander may simply have steeled himself not to go out of his way in the slightest to save unneeded dogs.

Harrison thought it possible and Smith thought it likely that Byrd was also willing to trade off the advantages of aviation in this case for a publicity advantage. The dramatic story of men and animals struggling on their own in the great tradition of polar exploration would garner more newspaper space than if the parties relied on mechanical aid. Clarke, apparently assuming that someone had explained the situation to Gould the evening he radioed his plea, had commented in his diary that night, "The man who is probably trudging wearily southward must be bitter at heart tonight."[5]

The men were exhausted and tortured by snowblindness, and the dogs were dragging the heaviest loads of the long journey, but the demoralized party willed itself onward for the dual missions of polar-flight support and geology. Every morning the sledgers dutifully delayed their start for an hour to report the weather for the polar attempt that might be made any day. Then Thorne, the best skier, led the way. The huskies, with no reins to guide them, traveled better when they had someone to follow. Gould drove Thorne's team right behind him, watching a boat compass mounted on the sledge and yelling directions as necessary. The men planted small flags every half-mile, erected permanent beacons at every rest stop, and planned to lay down depots every fifty miles. At each depot, Thorne and O'Brien would ski out five miles left and right, placing flags a quarter-mile apart to make the caches easier to find.

Gould calibrated his navigational watches with time checks he heard on the radio from Arlington, Virginia. He pointed out that this time reference enabled his party to chart positions far more precisely than earlier expeditions—another major contribution of wireless to exploration.

To everyone's surprise, a bitch gave birth to two pups—and promptly ate them. A short while later three more were born to her and froze to death. A sixth was born on the trail and had to be killed. The well-trained mother never stopped pulling, but her pitiful whimpering that night kept everyone awake.

The sledgers established the first of the new depots, number five, on 22 November. The men were over the hump—as they dropped food and supplies at this and subsequent depots, the loads would lighten. Although the journey had been grueling, the men had found unimagined inner reserves and had forced themselves and the dogs to keep to the pace originally planned. Gould had been surprised at his own powers of recovery. Nature had helped: temperatures had risen; the men had not yet lost a full day to bad weather; and after leaving the blazed crevasse field, they had encountered no other crevasses.[6] The explorers were doing much better than anyone had expected when they had left camp three weeks before.

No one was smiling, however, and in fact the frowns were deeper than ever. The men had dreaded this horrible milestone since they had first planned it in the dark of winter, when their dogs had been simply petted and playful companions. With smaller loads, the sledges required four fewer huskies. Ironically, the animals to be killed had to be culled from those who had exhausted themselves the most pulling and sacrificing for their masters. But whose teams to cut? Which individuals—Lady or Spy or Packy—to kill? And—worst decision of all—who would kill them? In a discussion dominated by long periods of silence, each man volunteered unenthusiastically. Vaughan, the only one who never used cuss words on his dogs, argued that the responsibility was his as head driver. Gould, who later admitted feeling guilty that he might have abdicated responsibility as overall leader, gave Vaughan the nod.[7]

The men built an execution wall of snow about fifty feet from the tents. As the others hunkered in the tents, Vaughan dragged the marked dogs one by one behind the wall. Gould wept in his diary, "The crack of the revolver as Norm shoots the dogs makes a dull sound, yet I hate to hear it and try to keep myself as busy as possible doing something else." Stifling their emotions, the grieving sledgers cut up the steaming carcasses and stashed them in the depot to feed the remaining dogs on the way back.[8] The grisly chore would have to be repeated several times as the supply of dog food ran down.

About noon three days later, Thorne topped a small ridge and began waving wildly, pointing his ski pole toward the southwest horizon. When the others caught up with him, they got the first glimpse of their long-sought destination, still one hundred miles away but already distinct—the immense Queen Maud Mountains.

The men's spirits soared. With the near-certain cancellation of the trip to Carmen Land after neither they, the supporting party, nor the crew of the depot-laying flight had seen the reported highlands, the expedition was just about back on schedule. Byrd's refusal to help had put Gould's party through hell, and they might have been far behind schedule had they not been so lucky. Fortunately, they had not absolutely needed Byrd's planes. Because of grit and good fortune, the men could anticipate completing their mission successfully.

They stood by on 27 November for a possible polar flight until it was called off, resuming their trek at 3:00 P.M. Then, seeing what they thought was Heiberg in the distance a little to the right of their planned course, they made straight for the glacier. They sledged until 11:30 P.M. O'Brien described the vista as they sledged toward the snowy mountains, lighted from behind by the sun: the "most awe-inspiring and glorious sight that any of us had ever witnessed . . . the snows assumed the most marvelous combinations of delicate color. . . . Pale gray, pink and blue . . . We [stood] around while making camp just watching the ever-changing shadows on the slopes as they turned to lavender and purple tints, while above the peaks glowed rose-pink in the brighter light."[9]

The men realized after a while, however, that they had picked the wrong glacier—they were headed for Liv, not Heiberg. Heiberg looked smaller than they had been led to believe by Amundsen's descriptions. No one in the party knew that Smith had made the same mistake from the air nine days before. Gould decided impulsively to keep going to Liv and begin work there.[10]

On Thursday, 28 November, Byrd flashed word that he was about to try for the pole. As planned, the sledgers stood by to monitor the plane's transmissions to Little America in case the dog teams were needed for a rescue. But the messages Byrd sent out over the airwaves during the flight were in a new code to be sure the news was safe for the *New York Times*. In another understatement, Gould admitted that he and his partners were "just a little piqued" that no one had thought to give the code to them. Byrd had given the code to the radio unit in New Zealand because, he explained, of their natural desire to know what was going on. Despite the geological party's sacrifices for Byrd's attempt, the commander left Gould's men in the dark when the polar flight took place. Because of the bureaucratic foul-up, they never had any idea during the long flight what was going on, and did not even know for sure when or if the plane had reached the pole. This latest in the series of real or seeming slights and slams did little to endear Byrd to Gould. The angry geologist sent Byrd a message of congratulations in a nonsense code.[11]

On Saturday, 30 November, the sledgers beheld a glorious peak that they hoped was Mount Nansen, the tall, layered mountain that was their most important goal. As they drew closer they were delighted to find that indeed it was. Gould could hardly wait. He hoped to find evidence confirming that the Queen Mauds and the ranges to the northwest all constituted one long chain.

A photo dropped to the sledgers from the polar flight purported to show terrible crevasses right in their path. The black lines in the picture were so straight and neatly spaced, however, that the men were all convinced they were scratches on the negative. The men's belief that Little America could send them a photo so obviously flawed, or touched up as a prank, betrayed their state of mind and trust in those back at the head office.

They made not the slightest alteration in course; but as they discovered to their chagrin and endangerment the next day, the crevasses were real, the worst anyone had encountered so far. Luck was deserting the men—as they entered the crevasse field, the wind picked up and blew straight at them. In his book, Gould described their grueling passage through the area, whose surface was glare ice dusted with snow:

> Little pellets of hard snow in the teeth of the heavy wind felt like gravel being hurled into our faces, and the wind was ever on the increase. . . . [Soon] even [Thorne, the best skier] could no longer ski against it. He had to fall back and be helped along beside a sledge like the rest of us.
>
> Safety precautions were difficult to devise for this kind of travelling. With the surface so slippery, it was out of the question for us to rope ourselves together and still attempt to manage the dogs and sledges. We . . . decided that the safest procedure . . . was to tie long ropes onto the rear of the sledges. We hung onto the free ends of these ropes and drove the teams ahead of us. If they cleared the roof of a crevasse with their loaded sledges it seemed a pretty safe bet that it was strong enough to support us. Hanging onto the rope, we slid across on skis, swinging out to one side so as not to cross the roof in the exact spot where it had been weakened by the dogs and sledges. We reasoned that if a roof collapsed with us upon it, the team on the other side would support us until we could be hauled out. . . .
>
> Our route continued across great partially covered crevasses that stretched away to the right and to the left as far as we could see. . . . Many were at least 100 feet wide. . . . We were able to slide over these because of our long skis, but it was not so easy for the dogs. Individuals were always partially breaking through the thin roofs or falling in bodily to hang suspended in their harnesses until the forward surge of the team dragged them out. As we went on, the surface became more icy and slippery; it was increasingly difficult to manage ourselves on skis. . . . Just as O'Brien and I cleared an especially big [crevasse] the whole surface fell away behind us. Where we had crossed but a second earlier was now a yawning chasm, large enough to have swallowed our entire party. . . . (It was) a frozen inferno. . . .[12]

It took the group until 9:30 at night to get past the crevasses to a safe area, only a mile from the foothills of Liv. Although almost totally exhausted, the men managed to make camp and cook dinner. Gould depicted their fatigue: "One of the boys with his spoon half way to his mouth suddenly dropped off to sleep. His bowl of pemmican slipped from his fingers and spattered over the man beside him."[13]

The next morning the men covered the last mile and reveled in the sight and feel of rocks, the first encountered in a long time. The dogs that had been born at Little America had never come across rocks. When the sledges drove up to the boulders, the young huskies did not know what to make of the funny things, gingerly circling, sniffing, and licking them.

The explorers stayed three days but were disappointed to find no significant or datable rocks. Gould and O'Brien spent a day trying to climb Liv to reach Mount Nansen but found the glacier too steep and crevassed. Since Byrd had flown over both Liv and Heiberg, Gould asked the commander by radio if Heiberg was better. Byrd replied that Liv was impossible but Heiberg was good. (Although there is no record of Gould's reaction, he may well have been irritated by Byrd's not reporting this evaluation before the geologist had wasted a day.)

On 4 December, the group camped at a large glacier between Liv and Heiberg. The glacier seemed to offer a smooth path to Mount Nansen, and the campsite was excellent, so Gould decided to establish his base of operations right there. He named it Camp Strom in honor of the magnificent sledges Sverre Strom had built during the winter. Gould declared that his arduous trek would have been impossible without Strom's sledges and called them the most important material contribution to the geological party's success.

The surveyors Thorne and O'Brien began mapping the mountains while Gould investigated their geology. The sledgers killed several more of their stalwart dogs and were scheduled to kill three others the next day but did not have the heart. So as not to reduce food for the others, the men put two of the pardoned huskies on a diet of human excrement, from which the dogs extracted nourishment and which, according to Gould, they relished anyway.[14]

On 6 and 7 December, the party sledged up the glacier toward a section of Mount Nansen, over a mile above them, that looked like geologically interesting sedimentary rock. On the way, Goodale spotted scaly patches on some rocks that turned out to be the primitive plants called lichens—the farthest south that life had ever been found.

On 8 December, with the rock layer only a short distance away, Gould, Thorne, Crockett, and Goodale climbed the rest of the way on skis, herringboning and sidestepping up the steep slope. When the men neared their goal, Gould raced ahead, bent over, picked up a few yellow, crumbly stones—and rejoiced. He exclaimed that these "amazingly interesting rocks" were just what he "had come all the way to the antarctic to find." Only sandstone, but more valuable to the geologist than gold, they were part of a stratum that the geologist identified as "the beacon sandstone formation," typical of the mountain range in Victoria Land at the northwestern corner of the barrier.

Gould's discovery confirmed that the Queen Maud and Victoria Land ranges were really part of one chain more than one thousand miles long. The chain was a horst, formed when a section of the earth's surface tilted upward, as if two shoeboxes had been pressed side to side and the inner edge of one had been raised. Gould declared that his rocks revealed the horst to be "the most stupendous fault block mountain system in all the world."

Gould was sure the sandstone finding would lead to another major discovery, and only a day later he spied it—a black seam in the upper part of the beacon formation. Inspection revealed the black seam to be low-grade coal, like the identical seam in Victoria Land. The coal meant the mountains held one of the longest coal fields on earth, and Antarctica must have rich deposits, second only to the United States.[15] In Gould's Antarctica University lectures, he had explained that coal was the fossilized remains of plants that grew in warm climates eons ago, and its presence in the horst showed that—for reasons not fully understood—Antarctica had once been as steamy and lush as Florida's Everglades.

The geologist was as happy as the aviators had been when they reached the pole and probably had a greater feeling of satisfaction— at least he had acquired something tangible, if only lowly sandstone and coal, for his efforts.

The climbers had a scare on the way down Heiberg. Gould told Byrd about it by radio: ". . . we came to a suspiciously steep slope and decided to turn back and changed our course. As we came on we saw that we had been near the brink of a great ice cliff some 100 feet high."[16]

Before leaving the Heiberg area, Gould wanted to find the polar flight's cache, which held food and supplies his party could use now that the flight was safely over. After crisscrossing several miles over the reported site and wasting many hours, he radioed Little America that the directions Byrd had given after the polar flight must be wrong. After conferring with Byrd, the geologist found the depot with little trouble.[17] It may not have been happenstance that Gould missed his regular radio report to Little America that night and stirred up so much consternation about a possible rescue mission.

On 13 December, the sledgers began the trip eastward to Marie Byrd Land, their first venture into unexplored territory. Mapping the mountains along the way, the men ended their uneventful excursion on 21 December some one hundred straight-line miles from Camp Strom and about ten miles past 150 degrees west longitude, the border of the new land.

Gould planted a small American flag, then the men doffed their hats and observed a moment of silence. Afterward, all but Crockett, who minded the dogs, climbed the tallest nearby peak, which the men named Supporting Party Mountain, and built a cairn. Inside, Gould placed a tin can containing a note saying that "in the name of Commander Richard Evelyn Byrd [we] claim this land as a part of Marie Byrd Land, a dependency or possession of the United States of America."[18]

The party's surveys had proved that the Queen Mauds trended due east from Heiberg Glacier instead of southeast as Amundsen had reported. The mountains got lower and more rounded in the east, and the beacon sandstone was missing, as if it had been scraped off. Gould felt that the scouring ice cap had once ridden over the eastern part of the range. The party had mapped 175 miles of the north face of the horst—equivalent in length to the entire Vermont section of the Appalachians—and discovered in the passes and valleys some of the largest glaciers on the planet. The sledgers had extended by more than a hundred miles the known easterly reach of the Queen Mauds' side of the barrier. These explorations, together with the aviators', had enlarged the known extent of the barrier to a quarter-million square miles.[19]

From Marie Byrd Land the men thought they saw the mountains turning north far in the distance, indicating that the peaks Byrd had discovered running north and south on his last flight might be part of the same great chain. Gould yearned to continue east to see what happened to the chain but had neither time nor supplies. The sledgers headed back to Camp Strom to rest the dogs for a few days before turning toward Little America.

On Christmas, the party camped by Mount Betty, where Amundsen had erected a cairn marking his journey and discovery of the South Pole. Before starting east, Gould's party had searched in vain for the monument. During their Christmas rest, the sledgers decided to investigate what looked like a lone rock near the mountain. As they approached, they gradually discerned that it was really a pile of small rocks. Growing more excited, they skied up to the isolated pile and found that indeed it was the historic eighteen-year-old cairn. Gould got "the greatest thrill of my life" when he dislodged some of the rocks and reached the hallowed contents, which included kerosene, matches, and a can containing a note describing the Norwegian's accomplishment.[20] Gould and the others built their own cairn beside Amundsen's. The surveyors appreciated the lucky find because it gave them the only definite point that both they and Amundsen had mapped, enabling them to tie his less precise observations into theirs.

At the beginning of the trip back to Little America across the barrier, the group heard the alarming rifle-shot sounds of crevasses forming, and Gould guessed the weight of his party was triggering cracks in the stressed ice. The trip, however, was mostly uneventful. The men traveled through whiteouts and sunny weather. One day was so warm that Vaughan spent the afternoon traveling in what Gould called Olympic style—naked except for his boots.[21] On some days, on the other hand, the weather got so bad the party wanted to stop; but prolonging their time on the trail would deplete the scarce dog food to the extent that they would have had to kill more huskies, so they pressed on.

Byrd proclaimed to the public that the "resourceful and stubborn" members of the geological party had "exceeded expectations." He declared that he "could not speak too highly" of the geological survey, and called it "the outstanding feat of the whole expedition."[22]

Harrison noted in his diary, with his mind on the popularity of aviation and also, perhaps, on his "toppled idol's" personal publicity machine, that Gould's journey "should stand out as the expedition's greatest accomplishment—yet there are several reasons why it probably won't."[23] Like most researchers, Gould and the expedition's other scientific personnel would never bask in the public recognition accorded to figures like Byrd. People who were interested in science and nature were nevertheless intrigued by Gould's work and the investigations going on at Little America.

.13.

Science and Nature

THE scientific aspects of the expedition drew commendation from many antarctic experts. Even the British, keen on south polar matters since Scott's trip, and unbiased—or, if anything, negatively biased—toward the Americans, spoke well of the non-English expedition. For example, Frank Debenham, a geologist on Scott's expedition, declared to the Antarctic Club in London as Gould's party returned to Little America that "Byrd's men are doing extraordinarily good work in a scientific way." J. Gordon Hays, English antarctic geographer and historian, called the U.S. enterprise "the most efficient antarctic expedition in history." Griffith Taylor, Scott's Australian geologist, pronounced Byrd's "one of the great expeditions of the antarctic."[1] Taylor's only criticism was that the scientific staff was too small. Taylor, who had initially quarreled with the location of Byrd's base, admitted the site had turned out to be the best since it favored aviation. Taylor concluded that proving the effectiveness of airplanes had been one of Byrd's greatest contributions.

The major question for antarctic geology was what the land looked like under its shell of ice. The part that lay in the eastern hemisphere was mostly a continental plateau, but the western section was a mystery—it might be a continuation of the continent or a separate continent, or might once have been a sea bed, perhaps dotted with islands. If there were more than one land mass, the ocean beneath the barrier might flow between and continue across Antarctica as an immense, buried strait.

In the Rockefeller Mountains, Gould had found only characterless granite and no sedimentary rocks. He guessed that the peaks had been formed by the erosion of the land around them rather than by the mighty forces within the earth that had pushed up the two major antarctic chains: the horst Gould himself had just explored, and the folded mountains running down the Antarctic Peninsula that were known to be a continuation of the Andes. He concluded that, if the ice cap melted, the Rockefellers and nearby peaks would probably be a group of islands in a shallow portion of an expanded Ross Sea. Likewise, the geological party had passed a large hill in the barrier, which Gould thought to be a buried island, near the crevassed area not far south of Little America. The geologist was sure the crevasses were caused by the slowly spreading barrier's grounding on the island, which, by holding back the steady glacial flow, must also be responsible for the semipermanent features of the Bay of Whales, like a river island that has relatively still water off its downstream shore. He guessed that the horst and the mountains Byrd had seen a few weeks before might all be part of one incredible, U-shaped chain rimming an ice-capped plateau.[2]

Taylor agreed with Gould's interpretation of the expedition's geological discoveries, calling the seeming plateau an entirely unexpected and scientifically important feature. (The significance of Byrd's discovery was later diluted, however, with the discovery that the mountain chain extended no farther in either direction than he had seen—it did not link to the horst—and that there was no continental plateau behind the chain. Furthermore, the peaks were only half as high as Byrd had estimated.) Taylor also noted that one of the expedition's most important contributions lay in not making a sighting—proving that Carmen Land did not exist.[3]

While journeys by plane and sled beyond the barrier created most of the expedition's excitement, routine scientific observations taking place on the barrier at Little America also contributed to the expedition's enduring worth. Members studied weather, geomagnetism and auroras, radio conditions, birds and seals, and the characteristics of the barrier.

The weathermen made complete observations every six hours during the day, and these observations were supplemented by the night watchman's readings. Byrd's men were the first to launch weather balloons in the antarctic. These balloons, launched once or twice a day to about 30,000 feet, enabled the men to study upper air movement. As the aerologist and junior half of the meteorological team, Harrison had to stand outside and follow the balloons with a theodolite for thirty to forty-five minutes, telephoning the readings inside to Haines. These readings continued through the worst of winter's cold, when Harrison had to hang bags with lighted candles from the balloons to see them in the dark.[4]

Harrison also used meteorographs to record temperatures, pressures, humidities, and wind speeds in the upper air. One method of sending these graphs aloft was to place them in the tails of aircraft that were going flying. The primary way of hoisting these graphs, however, was to fly them with huge box kites. These four-celled or six-celled kites were shaped like giant cigarette packs, the top part white, the bottom black, and were about as tall as a man. Harrison tied the kites at half-mile intervals along a wire with meteorographs attached. Unfortunately, the kite program never seemed to go right. Since the box with the sticks never showed up and was presumably among the lost supplies in the snowed-over barrier cache, Harrison had to improvise substitutes from planks; it was not until mid-October, after weeks of trying, that he got his first string in the air, the top kite reaching more than a mile high. The strings stayed up a long time—Harrison had trouble getting a line down on one of the first launches, and it flew all night; four men had to pull it down. He tried to fly the kites every few days and once got them as high as 9,000 feet. He was nevertheless expending much more time and effort on them than he had planned. The aerologist grumbled to his diary that the type of kite he had been given was wrong for the job, wishing he had been consulted ahead of time. He and his helpers spent most of their time hauling in the lengthy train of kites and wire. Czegka had connected an outboard motor to a big kite reel, but that arrangement soon failed. Ice would coat the kites and drag them down to the surface, straining the patience of the kite team and forcing them to use a dog sledge to follow the chain and gather everything up.[5]

The kite wire snapped during the fortieth or so run on 22 December, and the whole string blew out of sight. Harrison asked Byrd if a sledge team could conduct a search for up to three days for the equipment. The commander refused the request, saying the search area was too dangerous for dog teams but again seeming to give a low priority to science.[6] Thus the fitful kite program concluded prematurely, ill-fated to the end.

Atmospheric phenomena fascinated the men. In Owen's report in the *New York Times* of 20 April, he described a strange display of nature. When the sun was just below the horizon, right after having set for the winter, ". . . a tiny speck of light flared up on the hillside of the barrier north of the camp. A second after it went out a bright green glow burst forth and a whole section of the barrier flamed as if with an internal green light."

The intriguing spectacle and a similar happening half a year later may have been related. Late on the evening of 16 October, when the sun was rising and setting every day, Hanson strode into the administration building and called to the meteorologists that the sunset was strangely green. Haines and Harrison, along with Davies and Coman, hurried outside to take a look. They saw that the sun was mostly below the southern horizon, shining through notches in the undulating line where the barrier met the sky. The sunset was cycling through an array of vivid colors—red and orange as well as green—that sometimes flashed briefly, sometimes lasted for seconds. Haines found he could see different colors just by moving his head around, and commented that the effect was like a changing traffic light. The striking display went on for over half an hour.[7]

Haines declared that what the men had seen was an unusual phenomenon called "the green flash," never before reported in the Antarctic and rarely seen elsewhere. He explained that the green flash was caused by sunlight passing at a critical angle through a temperature inversion, an atmospheric condition wherein temperatures rise with increasing altitude instead of decreasing as usual. In lower latitudes, where the sun sets more quickly, the unique green color lasts only a moment.

Another study concerned the effects of cold weather. Dr. Coman, with a deep interest spurred perhaps by his pathological inability to feel cold, ran experiments on the combined chilling effect on the skin of wind and temperature, measuring heat flow from the body under various conditions. (Years later, Siple greatly extended Coman's work and developed what became famous as the windchill factor.)[8]

When the winter sky was clear, Davies and six others he recruited took turns observing the aurora every half hour and recording its characteristics by standard classifications. Davies explained to his helpers that the aurora seemed most vivid after sunspots appeared and when the earth's magnetic field was disturbed. The celestial glow was apparently caused by the interaction of electrical radiation from the sun with the geomagnetic field and the atmosphere. Scientists sought a detailed explanation.[9]

Davies told his assistants that the earth's magnetic field continuously undulates, and every so often it shakes violently as if disturbed by a storm. He explained that these magnetic storms light the aurora, make compass needles swing erratically, and induce air and ground currents that disrupt radio, telephone, telegraph, and even power transmissions. Scientists of the time were not sure of the cause of the geomagnetic field's movements. Data such as those Davies collected would help to answer those questions about how magnetism affects telecommunications. His program was planned and supported by the Carnegie Institution, a geophysical research organization in Washington, D.C.

Davies was first to make geomagnetic measurements near the South Magnetic Pole during a peak in the eleven-year cycle of sunspot frequency, when the intensity and frequency of magnetic storms on earth also increases. Beginning in May, he made continuous records of the varying strength of the earth's magnetic field and the changing directions of the magnetic lines of force. Compass declination, or the amount by which the needle varied from true north-south, sometimes changed three degrees in a single day.[10]

Davies measured geomagnetism with two sets of instruments, each of which had its own makeshift, unheated hut; a comfortable hut specially made for his measurements lamentably had been on the *Bolling*'s second, aborted trip. In one shed, the apparatus made continuous photo recordings of the back-and-forth, up-and-down fluctuations in the magnetic field. In the other enclosure, a large igloo, Davies painstakingly performed a five-hour ritual every week or ten days to determine the precise strength of the field at that particular time.[11]

Sometimes Larry Gould helped out, but usually Clarke aided Davies. Clarke frequently served as the camp's laboratory assistant.

During one Saturday's radio show, two of Davies's colleagues from McGill University had made one of the first scientific uses of global telecommunications, asking him to report strong aurora by radio for immediate correlation with North American observations. These colleagues further requested that he collect aged glacial ice whose entrapped air, possibly thousands of years old, "might have blown over the earth in the time of the Egyptian kings."[12]

Davies also regularly sampled the concentration of dust in the air for a project aimed at understanding atmospheric electrical phenomena. He had started taking the measurements on board the *New York* and was the first to make such recordings in the Pacific and in the polar regions. These readings showed the crisp antarctic air to be so pure that it was twice as clean as the air over the middle of the Pacific.[13]

Hanson's radio studies were closely related to Davies's work. Hanson was primarily interested in how the phenomena Davies studied affected or otherwise related to wireless communications. Hanson's work at the southernmost part of the world would contribute to a general understanding of global radio communication and the factors affecting it. In particular, his data would help to improve the many radio-transmission paths that would cross the polar regions. The poles were known to be hard on radio signals, distorting or drowning them for reasons not fully understood.

Writing later, Howard Mason, the third operator in the radio group, described a peculiarity of antarctic communications: "Sometimes when things started to fade we would look outside and see a beautiful aurora starting to appear on the horizon between us and New York. As it slowly rose the air would be completely dead until, after maybe an hour, the aurora would have risen overhead and died out. Signals would be back strong then." Mason, twenty-nine, with glasses and a young face that made him look like a schoolboy, had been on two arctic expeditions with Wilkins.[14]

Hanson worked closely with a far-away partner—Lloyd Berkner, who was living comfortably with his wife in New Zealand for the winter and working in a facility provided by a Dunedin radio station. He beamed experimental signals southward from a transmitter on a mountainside facing the Pacific. Hanson recorded static and wave characteristics over various frequencies, noting changes in the data hour by hour, day and night and in all seasons. The National Bureau of Standards sponsored the research.[15]

To complete another major project, Hanson had to journey out on the barrier into winter's blackness and coldest of cold to record at different times the height and behavior of a mysterious layer of the high atmosphere that was known to reflect radio waves. Several times, with two dog drivers who volunteered to accompany him, he sledged ten miles away and camped for two days. Petersen transmitted test signals to Hanson from Little America. A couple of times, after regular Saturday programs, KDKA also broadcast special signals to Hanson from Pittsburgh. Hanson had taught his Antarctica University class that the atmospheric layer, called the Kennelly-Heaviside layer after its discoverers (and later renamed the ionosphere), makes long distance communication possible by enabling radio waves to skip along earth and sky instead of passing into space. He noted that the layer's height and reflective properties change from place to place and time to time, and scientists at that time were charting its vagaries around the globe. Hanson was the first to take measurements in a polar region. He used an instrument that was sensitive enough to measure the brief instant that elapsed between the time he received the direct signal and when he heard its "echo," a time lapse that enabled him to calculate the layer's height. The U.S. Navy sponsored this work.[16]

In his spare hours, Hanson—who seemed always to be whistling a low, meaningless tune—supplemented Davies's work by recording the spectra of sunlight and moonlight for what the rainbowlike patterns could reveal about the condition of the atmosphere the rays had passed through.[17]

Commenting on Hanson's radio experiments, Taylor said, "We are led to expect . . . very valuable data regarding conditions of wirelessing over long distances and under the handicap of six months of darkness. Curiously enough, the long winter night seems to break up the mysterious Heaviside layer."[18]

Radio operations using Little America's pipsqueak one-and-a-half-kilowatt transmitter were at least as important as radio research, and most people who followed the expedition found the radio transmissions much more exciting. In its wrap-up of world news for the year, the *New York Times* unabashedly, but with good reason, pronounced the greatest marvel of 1929 to be the newspaper's own radio communications with Antarctica. In one melodramatic example of the wonder of telecommunications, Byrd starred in true Hollywood style. He keyed a signal that blew an automobile horn and drew curtains to reveal a big picture of himself before a gathering of ten thousand people at the National Radio Exposition in Los Angeles, which honored him for promoting the revolutionary technology.[19]

In a ceremony broadcast on a Saturday radio show from the Radio World's Fair at Madison Square Garden, RCA's Vice President David Sarnoff presented Mrs. Hanson with her husband's Radio Operator of the Year Medal, awarded by the Veteran Wireless Operators Association. Hanson's radio unit and the New York Times's radio group exceeded their objectives, and Byrd's effort to advance short-wave technology was counted a phenomenal success. Owen transmitted an average of four double-spaced pages of news copy a day to his paper, and Railey spent every night in the New York Times's radio room exchanging like amounts of information with his far-away boss. No one had expected the technology to allow such a steady volume of long-distance communications. Another RCA executive said the expedition's outstanding contribution to radio was the discovery of the extraordinary reliability of the medium. Owen wrote later that Hanson had really established short-wave technology.[20]

Astonished that the New York Times had received a radio transmission directly from Byrd's plane as he announced he had reached the pole, Lee De Forest, whose key wireless inventions led him to be called the "father of radio," wrote, "It is not too much to classify the achievement of Byrd and his associates with radio communication, especially during the south polar flight, as the most astounding example in the history of the art of transferring intelligence. . . . Constant use of radio by Byrd . . . has proved its reliability under conditions more trying than could have been produced artificially. It means infinitely more than if communications was merely established between two fixed radio stations far apart on the earth's surface, such as New York and London."[21]

Byrd's boost to radio was the same as what he, Lindbergh, and others were giving to aviation.

Several expedition members tested the nature of the barrier. Gould, Davies, and Coman probed mysterious snow formations called haycocks, which were blisters, about twenty-five feet high, on the barrier.

The men dynamited one and found it hollow. Gould agreed with his counterparts on Scott's expeditions that the haycocks were caused by gases arising somehow from under the ice.[22]

With Clarke replacing Coman, the trio descended into crevasses to snoop around. Davies, with Clarke's help, returned repeatedly to the frozen depths to photograph ice crystals and measure the temperatures, densities, and electrical conductivities of various layers for clues to the history and behavior of the seaward-moving barrier.[23]

Some of the expedition's laymen explored the crevasses for the emotional experience. Byrd described being lowered into a crevasse at the end of a rope during winter:

> It was perhaps three feet across. . . . The beam from the searchlight fell on immense ice crystals, some of which were from five to eight inches long, which festooned the walls and burned like myriads of gems. The walls themselves, when I glanced back, had in the light of the searchlight turned into emerald green and blue and purple, and seemed transparent. Preceded by a shower of crystals, I descended slowly. . . .
>
> About 40 feet down I touched bottom, and found myself standing in a grotto, with the domed walls curving in above me, and the refracted illumination from the searchlight falling through the slit rose in a glorious rainbow. Here and there a few thin columns of vapor rose trembling from the floor. . . . What fascinated me most were the ice crystals, which littered the floor of the crevasse. They were extraordinarily large and perfect in structure. These antarctic flowers are formed by the vapor from the warmer sea water rising, condensing and freezing, the successive droplets forming long, pendant crystals.[24]

Owen described an ice cave that he entered through a crevasse: "It is in some ways the most beautiful spot I have seen here. . . . The most marvelous thing . . . is the millions of crystals which cover its sides and form the under side of the roof. . . . A ceiling so beautiful in civilization would be one of the wonders of the world."[25]

Blackburn began a survey of the Bay of Whales during the spring, helped by Coman and occasionally others. Siple sounded the depth of the ocean beneath Little America to be 1,600 feet. The camp was on ice one hundred feet thick.[26]

A while after the last long-distance flight, June and McKinley flew in the Fairchild to map the barrier's face between the Bay of Whales and Discovery Inlet. Byrd decided to go to the inlet himself, perhaps thinking ahead to his next expedition and trying to be luckier in a plane than he had been on skis in scouting an alternate basing site. With Smith piloting and McKinley taking photographs, the plane flew a triangular course, first west one hundred miles to the inlet, then south 140 miles, and then back to Little America. Byrd searched for land that might protrude above the barrier or for signs of islands buried beneath it near Discovery Inlet; he averred that "land must be around somewhere" because, like the Bay of Whales, the inlet was semipermanent. The crew, however, saw nothing unusual on the foray, the expedition's last flight.[27]

Isaiah Bowman, president of the American Geographical Society, stated that the expedition's aerial photography, combined with the ground mapping, produced more important topographical results than any other effort in polar history. Taylor, of Scott's expedition, proclaimed that the aerial photography of the Queen Mauds on the south polar flight was a major accomplishment, and that the aerial photography of the barrier's face and top was of great importance.[28]

As the time to go home approached, Byrd detailed Siple to capture twenty penguins to bring back to zoos. With the help of others, Siple dug out a pen in the ice and rounded up twenty struggling penguins—fourteen emperors and six Adélies. When the birds got out of the pit by climbing over one another or hacking out steps with their beaks, the man on mess clean-up duty was assigned to penguin watch, with orders to report any signs of escape activity.[29]

Ironically, Siple, whom Byrd would not allow in the geology party for fear of injury, severely pulled the chest muscles attached to his left shoulder in the spring upon trying to heft a frozen seal that had been stored for dog food; the scout had to wear a sling for several months. The ambitious Siple nevertheless managed to start a scientific project of his own, regularly recording the growth of ten bleating Weddell seal pups that were born on the sea ice about a mile from camp. He also found a way to participate in the expedition's geologic efforts, passing pebbles he found in the stomachs of the penguins he skinned to Gould, who scrutinized the stones for clues to the geology of unexplored coastlines.[30]

Numerous whales swam into open water just a mile from Little America during the second summer, and many of the men trotted down to see them. The vapor the animals spouted smelled vile, and someone commented that they had halitosis. Standing on the edge of the ice and exhibiting surprising streaks of cruelty, Byrd, Balchen, and Strom amused themselves by whacking and poking the unsuspecting whales with ski poles and a spade, drawing blood. De Ganahl wanted to dynamite a whale. Byrd at first gave permission but then, perhaps realizing there was no way to haul the unfortunate beast onto the ice, changed his mind.[31]

The expedition's biological activities expanded when the aptly named John Bird, who had been a student at Harvard with the three musketeers, joined the crew of the *New York* to study birds during the relief voyage.[32]

Byrd and his recruits had successfully met the challenges they had sought and, although the scientists' work would keep them absorbed every day they were on the ice, the excitement of the expedition was virtually over after the last major flight. Before establishing Little America Byrd had had no experience in dealing with the antarctic or leading troops on a long-term expedition. A more seasoned explorer might have perceived that Byrd's greatest problems were only now appearing.

.14.

The Prison of Ice

DECEMBER 1929 brought a couple of pieces of good news from home. The first was a bizarre twist to the Brophy affair: Byrd's former exec was discovered alive if not completely well in Omaha. Describing himself as a nervous wreck, Brophy said he had intended to drown himself but backed out and hitchhiked to Nebraska.[1]

Secondly, on 21 December, President Hoover signed a special bill that had been rushed through Congress as a Christmas present for Byrd. The bill, approved by the Senate without debate or roll call, then by hand-clapping members of the House, skipped Commander Byrd over the rank of captain and promoted him immediately to rear admiral. The nation had done the same for Peary after he announced reaching the North Pole. At forty-one, Byrd became the youngest living rear admiral and one of the youngest in American history—he had risen from lieutenant to admiral entirely with political promotions in only six years. He modestly asked his men to keep calling him "Commander" since he was commander of the expedition. He said he would feel self-conscious if they began calling him "Admiral."[2]

As the sun shone from near its highest point, the outside temperature at Little America rose to the mid-twenties. The sunlight was so intense that it melted snow on top of the administration building, and the roof leaked. Some people moved from the oppressively crowded huts into tents. At work, the men sometimes stripped to the waist, and several took to nude sunbathing.[3] Pallid winter complexions turned tanned and even sunburned, as the direct rays of the sun passed through the clear antarctic air and bounced off the ice cap, the world's largest solar reflector.

On the sly, Owen and Haines tapped the doctor's alcohol supply Christmas eve and threw a quiet little party for the boys in the administration building. Owen confided that he "was afraid the commander would raise Cain if anyone got into the alcohol again," so the reporter and Haines kept out of Byrd's sight.[4]

On Christmas day, Davies again made himself up as Santa Claus and handed out trinkets; the men had decorated a pathetic mock tree with cotton, cough drops, and cigarette papers. Drink was rationed, and when the glasses were emptied the still-dry revelers hauled Byrd before a tribunal. He pleaded guilty to now-forgotten charges and paid the fine of one bottle of alcohol, which he claimed was all he had left.[5]

As the sun started its slow downward spiral into another winter, Byrd began winding down his expedition and packing for home. He put McKinley in charge of demobilization, letting him work out alternative schedules for knocking camp down and sledging gear to the waterfront, depending on how many ships would get through and when. McKinley would gradually have to shut down operations and assign priorities to all equipment in case Byrd could not take everything back.

The only remaining excitement at Little America was expected to come from Wilkins's arrival some time soon. Since Byrd had won the big trophies he and his antagonist had contested, Little America was now relaxed about the Australian's flight. Admiral Byrd could be warm indeed in his hospitality.[6]

On the morning of 30 December, all hands were called for a work detail, but only six men showed up. Like short timers in school or the military, most members no longer cared about the expedition now that the main jobs were done and the men were essentially just waiting to go home. As Clarke complained to his diary, "this volunteer status is all wrong." Several bored men had slipped back to their wintertime drinking habits and begun to meet frequently at night in the Biltmore for booze sessions. That evening, the gregarious Harrison dropped in for a few snifters and noted that the drinkers had a nearly inexhaustible supply—they were tapping the great one hundred–gallon drum of medicinal alcohol.[7]

At 8:00 P.M. on New Year's eve Byrd asked if anyone was going to give him a drink. Feury tapped the drum, toasts were exchanged, and the party began. After midnight, Byrd and a bunch of others adjourned to drink and snack at the Biltmore, where he helped to cook pork chops. Feeling convivial, Ken Bubier, a camp wisecracker, called the new admiral "Dick." When Byrd acted pleased, the men gave him three cheers. The leader said that back home they would have to call him "Dick" all the time.[8]

Everybody yearned for the relief ships to arrive. The big Norwegian whaler *Kosmos* and a chaser from the *Alonzo* were scheduled to visit early in the season with additional food and other items that Byrd wanted to make the last weeks and the evacuation easier and to provide a more ample cushion in case he had to stay longer than planned.[9] A new center engine for the Ford was in the cargo. The *New York* and the *Bolling* would come later to reclaim the expedition.

The whalers were late getting through the unusually dense ice pack that—ominously for Byrd's own ships—was reported to be the worst in history. Byrd began discussions with the whalers about their taking his expedition out if his ships could not get through. The *Alonzo* finally cleared the pack two weeks later than anticipated, after the grinding ice had sunk one of her chasers. Another whaler, the *Ross*, also managed to break through. Last season's record whale catch had attracted five whaling companies to the Ross Sea in 1929–30 instead of the usual two, and yet there were fewer whales south of the pack, so competition was fierce.[10] Probably to make up for lost time, the *Alonzo* did not immediately dispatch the chaser with Little America's cargo as expected.

Sadly, the *Kosmos* reported the Antarctic's first aviation tragedy. The seaplane used to scout for whales had been lost, and the pilot and his passenger, the ship's doctor, were missing. The captain asked Byrd if he would allow Dr. Haldor Barnes, the *Bolling's* Danish physician, to leave the expedition and join the *Kosmos*. She was carrying new dogs as well as supplies for Byrd and would take back his planes. The indebted explorer assented. He arranged for the *New York*, which would leave New Zealand before the *Bolling*, to rendezvous with the *Kosmos* and transfer Barnes.[11]

The *New York* left Dunedin on 5 January 1930, but the whalers reported that ice conditions were far worse than Byrd's ships could handle. The *Southern Princess* announced that the extremely rough pack ice had sunk one of her chasers.[12] The reports reminded Byrd's men of what they were—prisoners in a jail of ice, little better than Siple's captive penguins, dependent for release on the whims of nature. Knowing that, in the past, seven other antarctic exploring parties had been stranded for a year longer than planned when the freezing ocean had blocked their relief ships, the Little Americans began to fret about being stuck on the ice for another year.

The commander got word that Wilkins had scratched his long flight to icebound Little America.[13] The Australian claimed he could not find a stretch of flat sea ice for his takeoff. He may well have been scared off by the possibility of being trapped at Byrd's base.

On 14 January, the *Kosmos*, which had not yet entered the pack, sent a message saying it was doubtful the ship could get to Little America until the next month—"if at all."[14] Giving up on the ship, Byrd resignedly asked her captain to transfer Little America's dogs and supplies to the *New York* when the whaler picked up Dr. Barnes.

Harrison reported that the heartbreaking message from the *Kosmos* "created a real sensation" at Little America.[15] If a big whaler could not find a way through the ice, how could the weakly *New York*? The threat of being stranded had become distinctly more possible, if not probable.

It did not take Byrd long to reach a tough decision—to clear out of Little America with the whalers if things did not get better soon. Byrd implored the *Alonzo* and the *Ross* to send chasers to pick up all his men and the Fairchild if the ice had not broken up by the time the whalers were ready to try pulling out; the whalers had indicated they might leave any day. The thought of soon going home electrified the camp.[16]

Harrison called the next day "the most hectic yet." The *Ross* announced she had begun her trip north and was not turning around. Although none would admit their reasons, the whalers did not want to commit time to a rescue mission because it would lose the companies too many whales and profits and cut into the earnings of the crews. Stockholders in the company that owned the *Larsen* had severely criticized management for helping the expedition the year before. As Owen observed, Byrd may have blown any chance for help by asking the whalers to save the Fairchild as well as his men. Byrd's equipment was certainly important to him; he might need some of it for his next expedition, and cash from redeeming or exhibiting other equipment was vital to his strained treasury. The whalers, however, were not so magnanimous as to give up $30 thousand per day to rescue a plane so the American would not lose money.[17]

Frantic, Byrd hastily sent a message to the *Alonzo* that, Harrison observed, amounted almost to an SOS. The message stated that the expedition was not prepared to stay another year and that there were "several men who need medical attention." Harrison, in that night's diary entry, underlined "medical attention" in disbelief. Clarke also recorded his dismay at Byrd's claims of illness and inability to spend another winter. As Byrd himself later admitted, while his expedition would not be able to live very comfortably over another winter, the group had enough food and supplies to survive. As far as the men could tell, there were no serious medical cases at Little America. Byrd in fact confessed to Railey that no one was seriously ill but pointed out that ". . . there must be some real emergency to get whaling ships south."[18] The commander added, however, that some men had medical problems that might become serious if they had to stay another winter. He cited Owen's run-down condition, Siple's shoulder, Czegka's suicidal depression, and symptoms of mental instability in the embittered Walden and of appendicitis in McKinley.

The *Alonzo* replied that she could send one chaser to leave food and pick up as many as ten "sick men"—again underlined in Harrison's diary—but no equipment. Analyzing the "sparring messages," Harrison, the card whiz, wrote, "Starting as a chess game, it wound up in a hand of poker in which the bluff was called."[19]

Unfazed, Byrd brazenly besought the big factory ship itself to come down and pick up his entire outfit. She did not acknowledge Byrd's plea, acting as if she did not hear it, until another ship relayed it to her. The *Alonzo*'s captain then said he could not reply that day because he wanted to confer with her owners.[20]

Byrd grimly asked for volunteers to remain if the whalers could not take the entire contingent. He notified the geological party, then 104 miles away on the homeward trail, that a whaler might arrive in two days, urging Gould's group to "please hustle all you can."[21]

In messages to Little America that day, *Ross*, *Alonzo*, and *Kosmos* all said, "Don't worry." The phrase, easy for them to say but unreassuring to the Americans, quickly became a running joke at camp.[22]

The next morning, "everyone was in a fever heat awaiting the *Alonzo*'s reply," according to Harrison. When her answer finally came at 10:00 A.M., "we were absolutely turned down cold," Harrison related. The *Alonzo*'s pressured captain radioed that he was on his way north and did not have the time to divert his ship to Little America. Clearly beaten, Byrd notified Gould that the whalers "will be unable to come for us so you can take things easy the rest of the way."[23] Ironically, Byrd was playing the same scenario with the whalers that Gould had played with him: desperately needing transportation, pleading for help from others with superior resources, and being rejected.

Later that day, the expedition's old friend the *Larsen*, for which the *New York* was carrying a load of harpoons, and for whose captain Byrd had judiciously named a mountain, predicted that Byrd's own ships would break through sooner or later and indicated the *Larsen* would come for the men if the *New York* or *Bolling* could not.[24] Byrd feared that by then it might be too late.

The next day was another hectic one, according to Harrison. The *Ross* reported that she was stuck in an awful pack of ice three feet thick. The situation had never looked bleaker—Byrd revealed later that he worried about this crisis more than anything else during the entire expedition. He wrote that he felt the *New York* had one chance in ten of making it and the *Bolling* had none.[25] To avoid panic in the United States, however, he did not for the moment reveal to the public the jam he was in.

Some expedition members declared that they would not mind staying another year, especially if they could conduct a scientific program, but most wanted badly to get home, including Byrd. He had to think of retiring his huge debt and financing future expeditions. In another year his polar flight and other exploits would be stale news, diminishing the amount of money he could rake in from appearances, cinema, and publications. If he or any members of his expedition were marooned until 1931, the long-running saga of their plight would detract from his accomplishments.[26]

The commander called a conference with McKinley and Haines (third and fourth in command), Strom (a licensed ice pilot who had worked on whaling and sealing ships), June, and Owen, presumably about the tense situation and how to handle the release of any news. By radio, Byrd conferred with Railey in New York City, telling him to "bring all possible pressures to bear" on the whaling companies to send their ships to Little America, and agreeing that approaches should be made to the British ambassador (one of the whaling ships was owned by the British Lever Brothers) and Norwegian minister in Washington, D.C., to enlist their aid in applying pressure.[27]

The stress began to tell on the stranded men. The unity of the expedition, which had withstood the severe trials of winter, started to crack. Smith revealed that a half dozen or so men were disgusted by Byrd's desperate pleas for outside help and tried to get the radio operators to tone down the messages considered hysterical. "Those whalers must be laughing themselves to death," one of them spat, knowing that from the beginning the flinty whaling crews had considered the expedition a joke. Others, Byrd himself admitted, suspected that their situation was worse than he was letting on and believed that he was withholding bad news from the men, although he denied it.[28]

At the beginning of January, Feury and his drinking buddies had established a club to meet in the Biltmore regularly and discuss their views on Little America's policies and politics. This group's founders called their organization the Harbor Board, after the body in Dunedin that governed port activities. When Byrd met with his advisors, the Harbor Board also convened, "to combat with the commander," as Siple put it. The members of the Harbor Board felt the expedition's personnel were not getting all the news on the ever-changing evacuation developments, or not getting it fast enough, so the group planned to follow closely all radio messages concerning the ships—when the transmissions were not in secret code—and to give out bulletins on their own. Smith described the camp as "up in arms."[29]

Like the *Ross*, the *Alonzo* got stuck in the ice pack as she tried to go north. The *Bolling* left New Zealand on 20 January, with no more real hope of reaching Little America than on her unsuccessful final trip the previous season. Byrd somberly began working out the details for spending another winter on the ice.[30]

Already hospitalized for a short time because of exhaustion from working for Byrd, Railey worked himself beyond his limits again. He held discussions with Gilbert Grosvenor, president of the National Geographic Society; Governor Byrd; Senator Swanson of Virginia and the Naval Affairs Committee; the secretary of the navy; and the acting secretary of state. State Department officials, in turn, communicated with their counterparts in London and Oslo about help from the whalers.[31]

The U.S. Navy pointed out that, unfortunately, its nearest ship was 8,000 miles away. The coast guard stated that it would be willing to send an icebreaker if necessary, but there was no real chance it could get to Little America in time.[32]

Railey and Byrd's other advisors worried that with so many people and organizations aware of the sensitive situation, and radios all over the world monitoring and possibly deciphering the expedition's messages, the news media would blow the dramatic story all out of proportion. The advisors wanted to avoid sensationalism and panic by letting the word out in a controlled, factual way through a statement given to the press, but Byrd wanted to sit tight. The acting secretary of state pointed out, however, that political pressures would not work unless the public was aroused, so Railey, using his own judgment, wrote and released a statement straightforwardly describing the situation. The *New York Times* helped with an editorial insisting that the expedition was in no immediate danger but that Byrd's taking precautions was only prudent.[33]

The reaction of other newspapers was worse than the advisors had expected and just what Byrd had feared. The stranding of the forty-two heroic men became a sensational national story. Friends and relatives of expedition members pressed for immediate official action. The matter got entirely out of hand, embarrassing Byrd and his men. The commander was furious with Railey. The communications between governments that had, in the commander's view, escalated the matter into an unwelcome international incident further incensed Byrd; he had told Railey all pressures were to be directed solely to private interests. By radio, the commander flayed his business manager: "Everything has been done just the opposite to what I requested and urged, and I never dreamed that it would be necessary to get one government to call upon another one. . . ."[34]

The men on Byrd's southward-bound ships were among those mortified by Railey's press statement, which they presumably picked out of the air when the text was radioed to Byrd. Those men had never believed the situation warranted Byrd's calling for outside help. Thinking the statement had been Owen's idea, Lloyd Berkner, acting as a radio operator and *New York Times* correspondent on the *New York*, sent the reporter a message saying the crew had not seen much ice and thought chances favored getting through. In words thick with sarcasm, Berkner said the statement made the ships' crews look afraid of the ice and concluded, "So Russ, old boy, have a heart and don't let the newspapers make us feel so damn foolish." Berkner's radio upset Byrd, who declared that if it got "picked up in the States, it would appeal mightily to the yellow journals." Owen sent a blistering reply; despite Berkner's apology the next day, Byrd wired Captain Melville to appoint another correspondent for the *Times*.[35]

Recognizing the need to communicate with the affected men, Byrd wrote a memo to the Little Americans that explained the situation and then described further efforts to get help: ". . . Ex-Secretary Charles Hughes obtained the cooperation of J. P. Morgan and Lamont, the great international financier; the Chairmen of the Foreign Relations Affairs in the House and Senate, who are great friends of the expedition, have helped to obtain the friendly assistance of the diplomatic representatives. . . . I am still strongly of the opinion that at least the *New York* to (*sic*) get through. . . . There seems little doubt that we will get out this year. . . ." To contain the ferment among his personnel, the commander followed good management practice by instituting an open-door policy: "If any one at any time wants any information about the situation, don't hesitate to question me, as there are no secrets in this proceeding."[36]

Despite Byrd's reassurances, however, most Little Americans agreed that prospects for escape looked bleak. Demas wrote, "It looks like another year down here. Everyone is beginning to say he will go crazy next winter." Little Owen, who had dropped thirty pounds he could ill afford to lose while most of his comrades gained weight during their largely sedentary time on the ice, declared that if they had to spend another year, "there will be a lot of sick men around here by spring and I'll be one of them." Smith predicted that, without an inspiring goal, a second year would be bitter, with many fights.[37]

Byrd, showing how hard he could be when defending his interests, decided to supplement the political efforts with blackmail. He radioed Railey to tell the Norwegian minister that the *Alonzo* refused when she could have helped while she was south of the pack, and that this information would have to be made public if the expedition could not get out. Byrd instructed Railey to tell the minister that the commander was trying to protect the sea captain. "Do you get the point here?" Byrd asked Railey conspiratorially.[38]

The whalers would not budge, sanguinely promising again and again that they would come to the rescue if they were clearly needed. Byrd responded, with concern, that it might be too late by the time the Norwegians agreed that he was in real trouble. Railey, confident he could raise any amount of money for national heroes in an emergency, encouraged Byrd to promise the whalers he would reimburse them for evacuating the expedition. Nearly despondent, the commander finally agreed.[39]

Railey got busy quietly rounding up the money. One of his first calls was to Charlie Bob, already among the largest contributors, and for whom Byrd had named a newly seen section of the horst. Bob promised $600,000 more if it were needed. The Harvard and Yale committee organized by well-to-do parents of expedition members pledged a large sum. Reginald Bird, wealthy father of the *New York*'s ornithologist, virtually demanded that he foot the $1 million bill the Norwegians might submit for a rescue.[40]

On 28 January, Byrd asked Railey to transmit a message hinting at impending tragedy to the secretary of the navy and to all newspapers: "If we should not get out this year, the only emergency of a serious nature that would face us would be from several possible hospital cases and one or two men who have been going down hill physically. . . ." Railey and the advisors beseeched Byrd not to insist on this ploy, and he backed down.[41]

That same day brought some good news. Both the *Ross* and the *Alonzo* had wrenched themselves free of the ice and worked their way north and out of the pack. The *New York*'s ice pilot, Bendik Johansen, conferred with the *Alonzo*'s captain and with other whalers about ice conditions and trends. Johansen radioed that he "firmly believed" that the *New York* could slowly work her way through. Railey, encouraged by that word and by his progress in contracting for the whalers' services, sent a letter to the distraught families of the members saying that there was no cause for alarm and that Byrd expected to get off in February, with or without aid. Because the expedition's escape was not yet absolutely certain, and because Railey did not want to fuel the rumor mill, he asked the relatives to keep the message confidential and especially not to give it out for publication.[42]

The prisoners of the antarctic jail were reprieved on 29 January. The U.S. and Norwegian governments both notified Byrd that the whalers had firmly committed themselves to send ships to Little America when and if requested, provided they were reimbursed. The big item would be insurance, costing as much as $250,000; the total might run to $500,000.[43] Railey had secured sufficient funds, and Byrd agreed to the costly but necessary deal. He did not say how much if any of his equipment the whalers had agreed to take if they had to come, but he told his men he would have to leave the big polar plane behind. Wanting to maintain good relations with his potential rescuers, he indicated to the public that the deal was reasonable and assured everyone that the whalers were fine men and not mercenary. The English government sent word that it would help the expedition, if for some reason the whalers could not. The camp was jubilant.

Now that relief was virtually certain and the financial onus was on him, Byrd was in no hurry to summon the whalers until he lost all hope in his own ships, even though the evacuation was behind schedule and the season was getting late. Byrd had originally expected his two ships to arrive about 20 January and planned to leave around 1 February. Nevertheless, he decided to wait and see if ice conditions would improve.

While the crisis had been raging, at mid-afternoon of 19 January, the six sledgers of the geological party had returned. A festive crowd turned out to welcome the mountaineers home, banging pots and skillets and setting off signal flares. Lean and tan, but filthy from the accumulated soot of two-and-a-half washless months, the sledgers had covered a total of 1,525 miles on the main and preliminary trips, about the same as the distance from New York City to Austin, Texas. The excursion was one of the longest dog sledge journeys in history and certainly the longest ever made in the name of science. Gould and his men were delighted to get home to baths, clean clothes, real food, and soft beds, even if these amenities were somewhat limited. The sledgers' return brought fresh faces and tales of adventure to a group that badly needed a lift.

Furthermore, as Harrison observed, "The camp is a new place with Larry back and a better feeling of peace and security prevails."[44]

Siple lamented that greeting the geological party "was one of the saddest experiences of my life." As he had feared, every one of the dogs that he had trained, cared for, and loved the previous summer and winter—and then had to turn over to the party—had been shot.[45]

The party did not return as one big happy family either. O'Brien, odd man out, complained to Demas about getting a "dirty deal in the moutains." Gould informed Byrd that O'Brien "was the one member of the geological party who failed to do his job." No one committed either side of the story to paper, so whatever happened concerning O'Brien remains a tantalizing fragment of gossip. (In an odd discrepancy, Gould wrote in his diary at the end of the journey that throughout the sledge trip he had "had the most splendid cooperation of all the men with him"; perhaps he was already drafting his public statements.)[46]

Shortly after the party returned, Gould, backed by Coman, approached Byrd to resubmit the idea that the commander had broached during the winter: that a party remain another year to extend the scientific program. Nothing explains why Gould felt the idea might then receive support when it had failed only a few months before. Perhaps the geologist tried to persuade the commander to provide funds, or maybe Gould was encouraged by his own connections among potential supporters. The geologist proposed that he himself head a fifteen-man scientific group to stay on. He would sledge to the mountains Byrd had discovered in December to determine their nature. Gould declared that this exploration was now one of the two highest priorities of antarctic geology; the other was to follow the great horst to its end—or to its hookup with Byrd's mountains.[47] Others in the party would investigate the barrier further, study birds, fish, and seals, and double the volume of meteorological, auroral, and geomagnetic observations. The scientists felt the accomplishments of another year, given the extra time and the experience they could now apply, could be scientifically monumental.

Harrison said he doubted the commander would OK the plan. After giving it some thought, Byrd did turn Gould down because, according to Siple, who was among those wanting to remain, "he [the commander] felt responsible for us and feared that the ships would have just as much trouble another year."[48]

On 29 January, the day Byrd finally settled the distressful evacuation crisis, Demas wrote that the commander was in a good mood. He reported happily to the Harbor Board on the relief arrangements but did not attend the party that followed. Demas noted that the good news inspired an all-night celebration with chops, drinks, and "wild talk." McKinley, still acting exec, got drunk, went to bed, and then came back later without his pants. Evidently the party was too wild, setting off the explosive tensions accumulated over the month. The Biltmore was a wreck the next morning. Clarke reported that the party had "caused a lot of uproar around camp" and had disturbed Byrd, who "had a face as long as the clock." Demas noted that the commander was "quite peeved." Harrison recorded that the Harbor Board was "in bad graces today because of last night's fracas." He noted that they had purloined bread and biscuits from the mess hall for the party. Tennant, the teetotal cook, refused to bake bread for a week unless the disruptive parties stopped. Harbor Board members retaliated by going on a bread strike and putting on red bandanas to symbolize their resolve.[49]

Clarke wondered how long Byrd would tolerate the Harbor Board. Demas hoped that the commander would put a stop to the meetings, many of which the mechanic felt were "uncalled for." He complained that he was disgusted with the Harbor Board's members who, he said, bellyached about everything, criticized everyone, and ran Byrd down. He claimed they hated Byrd and that many of them were "far from being loyal." They bragged that Byrd was afraid of them, Demas wrote, and the mechanic felt they were taking advantage of the commander's liberality.[50]

Most of the men had no reason to remain in Antarctica any longer, and they could hardly stand marking time. The ball was over, and they wanted to go home. Gould murmured that "it is hard to get used to the deadening lethargy that pervades the atmosphere here." Harrison's evaluation of the camp was apt: "This month has been the toughest of the whole expedition between uncertainty, lack of discipline and disciplined work, rumors and counter-rumors about ships and getting home, packing up one day and unpacking for a second year the next, all of which has resulted in a general loafing and probably a little too much 'free thinking.'" Grousing and drinking were not confined to the hard-core Harbor Board members. People mixed antiscorbutic powder with alcohol to make hooch that Davies said tasted like liquid marmalade. Haines, for one, spent several days in bed either drunk or hung over. Smith reported that the overall mood turned tense and ugly, and the camp went into undeclared mutiny. Balchen affirmed Smith's observation, recording that some of the "drunk and disorderly men" threatened to "get [Byrd]. . . . [But] with the help of my Norwegian friends, we stood up for Byrd and offered to tangle with anyone who made a move against him." The besieged commander may well have regretted finishing the exploration program so early, failing to provide the energetic men with goals to occupy idle hands and minds during the remaining months the men were deprived of civilized diversions.[51]

When Gould officially resumed the position of exec on 30 January, Demas noted with satisfaction that the Harbor Board's meetings would probably end. Curiously, however, Gould seems never actually to have seized authority again. After the sledge journey, the man who had held the men together over the trying winter and who had run many of the expedition's crucial operations was never again mentioned prominently in accounts or diaries. He had no visible role in closing down Little America or attending to the serious personnel problems. Perhaps he no longer cared to do any more than absolutely necessary for a man who would do no more for him. As Goodale came to understand, the geologist felt he owed no loyalty to Byrd since Byrd had been unfair to him. (After returning home, when Gould learned that on Byrd's second antarctic expedition he planned to spend the winter alone at a subbase away from Little America, the exec hinted at more strife between himself and Byrd than ever publicly revealed. Gould wrote to Balchen: "That, of course, will be a godsend for the rest of the expedition.")[52]

Contrary to Demas's expectations, the Harbor Board continued to meet in the Biltmore "tavern" to moan and groan two or three times a week on the average. Siple, vexed but powerless, usually tried to sleep elsewhere to get away from the noise and rowdiness. Demas often skipped out, too, but sometimes sat in and defended Byrd. At least half the camp attended the drink-and-talk sessions at one time or another, but the mainstays were Feury, Black, Thorne—whom Demas thought were the worst offenders—Rucker, Owen, Harrison, Smith, June, and O'Brien.[53] (Consistent with Balchen's remark about resisting the "drunk and disorderly men," he seems never to have attended a meeting, and the other Norwegians infrequently did.)

Whatever the feelings and expressions of some individuals, however, clearly not all attendees opposed Byrd. McKinley, a frequent participant, and June remained among the commander's trusted advisors and helpers. Owen concluded later that really "we were all in the Harbor Board. I think it was a good thing." Harrison, although disillusioned, bore no animosity toward Byrd. As the weatherman described the meetings, furthermore, he did not believe the crabbing was at all as serious or anti-Byrd as some others thought. Whatever seditious words were spoken seemed to Harrison to be just talk, of the kind common to barracks and dormitories, although he admitted that the agitation was "potentially dangerous." He declared that Black in fact was "one of the true believers in [Byrd]—I feel sure he would have given his life for Byrd." In private communications much later, Harrison asserted, "As a charter member and regular attendee at Harbor Board meetings, I never saw or heard of any organized disloyalty to Byrd. . . . This little underground . . . group served a valuable role in permitting a dynamic and vocal collection of men to let off steam when it needed letting off."[54]

During one meeting, at 2:00 A.M. when the talk "was really heating up," as Harrison recounted, Byrd suddenly appeared in the doorway. There was a stunned silence. Then one member spoke up, trying to sound casual: "Commander, won't you come in?" Byrd walked in, sat down, and, Harrison noted, "fell in completely with the atmosphere (I think) and appeared to enjoy himself immensely with the help of our pure grain alcohol borrowed from Coman's medical house."[55]

Byrd seemed to treat the rambunctious Harbor Board lightly most of the time. When he was explaining a policy or decision in a general discussion, he would sometimes ask, "What does the Harbor Board think of it?"[56] Losing control of his men was always one of his biggest fears, however—he still had handcuffs at the ready. He never commented about the Harbor Board publicly, and his true feelings, which were often masked and in many less-justified cases tinged with paranoia, are unknown.

While the Harbor Board was flirting with revolt at Little America, Byrd had to confront a manifestly genuine challenge to his authority out at sea.

On 28 January Captain Brown had radioed Byrd that the *Bolling* was in the northern edge of the pack and recommended taking the ship through. Byrd replied: ". . . Sorry I cannot permit you to attempt to force the pack in its present state. It would in my opinion be suicide. . . . I note you are in the pack. I am surprised at that. Is the *Larsen* in the pack? If not, you will get out of the pack immediately. . . ."[57]

Meanwhile, the *New York*, steaming back and forth along the northern edge of the ice pack, had run short of coal for the second time. The *Larsen* and the *Kosmos* generously transferred some of their low supplies to the *New York*. (Earlier, Byrd had been shocked to learn that Captain Melville—for reasons "that are beyond me," said Byrd— had left New Zealand fifty tons short of enough coal for even an undelayed round trip. The *Bolling* had had to load the rest of the coal and carry it to her sister ship.)[58]

The commander now ordered the faster *Bolling* to go back to New Zealand to get more coal for the *New York*, whose thick wooden sides gave her a much better chance to steam both ways through the floes. Byrd directed the *Bolling* to come back down to the edge of the pack and wait to transfer the coal to her sister ship when she emerged on her way north.[59] Byrd now had to pin his hopes on just one small old vessel for the chance to get out on his own.

On Wednesday, 29 January, Byrd must have learned or discerned that Brown intended to ignore orders and continue pushing south through the fearsome pack to rescue the Little Americans and reap the glory so long denied the *Bolling* and her twenty-three–man crew. The commander radioed Brown crisply: "I order you not to attempt to break through the ice pack." A little later in the day, deeply worried, Byrd sent a lengthier, more impassioned message: "As commander of this expedition who is responsible for the safety of all men on the expedition I order you not to attempt to break through the ice pack. You will probably lose the lives of the men with you for no useful purpose because we are in no danger whatever and are certain to get out later. For the sake of the men whose lives are in your hands, I urge you not to make the terrible blunder of disobeying my commands. Stop and think a moment and then answer me."[60]

On Thursday, the *Bolling*'s first and second mates, Charles McGuinness and Harry Adams, jointly sent an unprecedented wire to Byrd: "Aware of contents of recent radios. Wish to inform you that we do not in any way concur in any disobedience of your orders and ask you to now respectfully order captain to obey them. Your information on ice conditions is correct."[61]

That same day, Brown answered Byrd: "Will obey orders. Sorry." Byrd seems to have worried that Brown had not really changed his mind. The day following, Gould and McKinley, as second and third in command, and clearly at Byrd's behest, together signed a message telling Brown to obey orders. Like Byrd, the two men followed this message with a longer, more compelling radio stressing that the people Brown was trying to help did not countenance his actions: "If the important orders given by Admiral Byrd . . . are not obeyed, not only he but every member of the expedition at Little America will be hurt and thoroughly disappointed in you. . . . We at Little America ask of the captain of the *Bolling* for compliance with any orders given by the leader of the expedition."[62]

On Friday, Brown responded sardonically to the radios. He told Byrd: "After receiving radio from Larry and Mac, I hope you and all of you do not think I would disobey my leader's orders." He sent a separate reply to Gould, McKinley, and "the rest of the bunch": "Surprised at your telegram as we are headed full speed to Dunedin according to our leader's orders. You should know I never would disobey the leader's orders."[63]

On the evening of 6 February, Captain Melville signaled that he and his twenty-seven crewmen on the *New York* were about to plunge into the pack and attempt the passage.[64]

Siple had noted in his diary the night before that Mason had not been feeling well the past day or so. Dr. Coman diagnosed appendicitis. He asked Siple to help with an operation if necessary and outlined the appendectomy procedure. The Boy Scout's experience with dissecting penguins had made him the best qualified assistant.[65]

(When writing later about having pleaded for the whalers to rescue the "sick men," Byrd gave in to the temptation to make himself look better by rewriting history. He placed the onset of Mason's illness in early January—a month before the radioman felt any abdominal pains.)[66]

On Thursday, 6 February, Mason's appendicitis worsened, and he begged Coman for morphine. A Harbor Board meeting went wild that night, apparently spilling over into the mess hall and keeping Mason awake all night. Siple clearly felt it was time for Byrd's secret elite corps, the Loyal Legion, to act against the Harbor Board. Siple recorded in his diary, without explaining what he meant, that early Friday morning, "I gave the commander the confidential letter I have held for some time. It more or less took him off his feet and he called me in for a conference."[67]

The conference, held later that morning, ended abruptly with a dramatic interruption: Byrd got word that the *New York* had broken through the ice pack into open water and hoped to reach the Bay of

Whales in five or six days. The bars of ice had suddenly broken, and Little America was free. The commander worried about the public repercussions of his ship's passage after all the fuss about being imprisoned by a nearly impenetrable pack, but if anybody noticed the seeming discrepancy, nobody rubbed it in.[68]

Overjoyed at the word they had been anxiously awaiting for weeks, the residents immediately began to break camp. Coman warned Byrd, however, that if Mason's appendectomy had to be done at Little America, the patient could not endure the rough passage through the antarctic seas during recuperation. Volunteers would have to stay with him until ships could get through again in a year; but the doctor thought the radioman could hang on until New Zealand before having his appendix out.[69]

Over the weekend, in a reversal of the prior year's construction period, nine men were sent to establish a loading camp near the docking area at an inlet called Floyd Bennett Harbor, ten miles from Little America. The crew set up tents and a rudimentary mess hall less than a mile from open water, next to caches of cargo that had been hauled out optimistically a month before. Because most of the nine felt they were in disfavor with Byrd, they called their isolated bivouac "Detention Camp." The inmates were Balchen, who was placed in charge; Harbor Board stalwarts Feury, Black, and Smith, who were thus out of Mason's hearing; Mulroy, who had been ostracized; Blackburn, who had been disciplined; and three who had avoided controversy, Parker and Loyal Legionnaires Demas and Chips Gould. Clarke, in the main camp, jotted in his diary that "it is a source of great pleasure to those of us who will do the work that Balchen and June will have a large part of the supervisory end to look after."[70] One of Byrd's strengths was knowing how to pick good lieutenants.

Haines and Harrison wrapped up their balloon runs on Sunday, 9 February, with the 415th launch.[71]

A sign-up sheet was hung on the bulletin board for anyone who wanted to take home a dog. On Tuesday, because there would not be enough room on just one ship for the pets and all the other dogs, Vaughan sadly began slaughtering the weak huskies and puppies that could not help in the loading operations. Ironically, when the new dogs coming down on the *New York* finally reached their destination, they would not be needed. With dog-team operations concluding, the commander resolved a personnel problem. As Harrison noted, Arthur

Walden, the original head of the dog teams, had aged ten years during the expedition. Presumably to spare him public disgrace because of his demotion, Byrd graciously gave Walden nominal charge of the dogs for the trip home and promised that he would get credit in publicity as leader of the dog unit.[72]

Byrd had yet to resolve the problems with alcohol. Demas confided to his diary on 11 February: "Bernt tells me that the commander has been under the influence of liquor. I hope he snaps out of it, for if anyone lets it out in the States he will be ruined." Three days later, Siple set down in his diary without explanation that "the commander took the final step to quell the rum ring—they were over at Walden's last night." Smith reported that Byrd, tugged one way and then the other all during the expedition by his liking for drink and fear of it, finally ordered all the remaining alcohol to be dumped. According to Smith, Thorne, however, hid a supply and kept everybody's glass full.[73] Byrd never really brought the problem under control.

Byrd invited Harrison in for a chat one evening. Harrison described the meeting: "We talked over some intimate details of the year. He told me of his persistent and repeated efforts in preserving harmony among our group; discussed the Harbor Board and possible far-reaching effects of it; and thanked me sincerely 'for sticking by me and never affording me the slightest cause for worry.'" Later, Byrd had a similar debriefing session with Clarke. The commander apparently had many such debriefings with his troops toward the end for his own education and to resolve any dissatisfactions. He asked Clarke point blank what the young man thought of the expedition and of the commander's running of it. A reticent person who had mixed feelings, and who may have suspected that Byrd was looking for a snitch, Clarke penned in his diary that night that Byrd "knows no more than he did yesterday."[74]

Byrd posted a notice on the bulletin board reminding the men of the commercial restrictions on them. The notice stated that because of the contract with the *New York Times*, everyone had to turn in all his photos and negatives. The pictures would be used not only for the *Times* but also for Byrd's book and other purposes, and would all be returned in four months (thus preventing anybody from publishing the photographs ahead of Byrd). A worried Paramount executive radioed Byrd to warn him that, upon returning, no one from the expedition should grant interviews to the new "talking newsreels," as such interviews would "take the edge off exclusivity of films to a very serious extent."[75]

The cruel antarctic seas showed Byrd they were not yet through with him. The *New York* had a terrible, stormy trip across the Ross Sea. The gales coated her with two to three feet of ice—200 tons— and weighed her two feet deeper in the water. The crew had to toss some nonessentials overboard to prevent her from sinking. She did not face clear sailing until 16 February when, Byrd later wrote, she found that the violent winds had blown her off course to Ross Island at the western corner of the barrier, a 2½-day cruise to the Bay of Whales.[76]

Ralph Shropshire was on board to do oceanographic work. After the expedition, in a letter to the cartographer who was drawing a chart of ocean depths based on Shropshire's soundings from the *New York*, he cautioned that what he was about to write was "extremely confidential." Then he warned: "Don't use the log book of the *New York* for the trip through the ice pack in 1930. Byrd radioed orders to Melville to go through the pack in the vicinity of the 180th meridian. I'll explain further when I see you." The mysterious message was probably related to a series of radiograms from Melville in which he had striven unsuccessfully to persuade Byrd to let the *New York* try a more westerly route through the ice pack than the one Byrd wanted. In denying the requests, Byrd had countered that ice conditions to the west were always more dangerous than those in the designated route. The 180th meridian is halfway between Ross Island and the Bay of Whales. Melville may actually have taken the forbidden western route. The captain had often spoken of his desire to see Mount Erebus, the majestic snow-covered active volcano that dominates Ross Island. The *New York* passed within sight of Erebus when she was "blown" 300 miles to the west of her intended course. Byrd himself confided in a letter to the cartographer, a friend named Harold Saunders, "I certainly did pick my men very poorly . . . in many cases. Melville was one of those."[77]

The cloud that seemed to be following Byrd blackened on Monday, 17 February, when McKinley crawled into bed with what almost unbelievably looked like another serious attack of appendicitis.[78]

On Tuesday, with the *New York* scheduled to arrive in the evening, Little America's mood was dominated by the odd mixture of joy and sadness that accompanies departure. Davies took his last geomagnetic reading, the 240th. Petersen made a ceremonial final transmission to the *New York Times*'s publisher Adolf Ochs. In small groups during the afternoon, the residents of the base drifted away to the edge of the sea. McKinley, happily well enough to get out of bed, lowered the flag as the commander stood rigidly in lonely salute.[79]

The expectant voyagers gathered to wait for their agent of deliverance. New ice cakes in the ocean showed that it was already beginning to freeze over. Another week and the men would be trapped. Sea smoke hugged the water, and they could not see the horizon. At about 7:00 P.M. one of them pointed to something above the smoke in the distance. As they watched, the vision formed into ship's masts, and slowly the ghostly hull itself materialized out of the gray fog. As Owen wrote, the arrival of the *New York* was a sight none of them would ever forget.[80]

The *New York* tied up, and the people from the ship and those ashore greeted each other with as much display of emotion as such men ever allow themselves. Eager to be off, everyone got right to work loading the *New York*.

By next morning, when the men had loaded all they could, there were still fifty tons of equipment piled on the sea ice, inventory that would disappear into the ocean when the ice eventually broke up—a sickening sight for the debt-ridden commander. There was room for only sixty dogs on the ship, and they had seventy-seven. After each sledge driver's final trip to the *New York*, in what was mercifully the last of this horrible rite, he had to hand some of his dogs over to Vaughan.[81] As the men marched up the brow, the last sounds they heard from Little America were the seventeen pistol shots.

At 9:30 A.M., 9 February, the *New York* cast off and sailed slowly toward the real world, carrying off the antarctic continent's only human inhabitants. Little America shrank gradually out of sight, becoming only a memory. Except for the long voyage still ahead of them, Byrd and his men had survived all the hardships and dangers they had bargained for when they had committed themselves to the pioneering expedition. In one form or another, Antarctica had been a career investment for most of them; but they could not then appreciate that the prosperous world they had left in 1928 was but a memory, too, and that they were returning to a shaken world where investments of all kinds were turning sour.

.15.

Welcome Home

As the ship began the homeward trip, which would prolong the expedition for four more months, Byrd pleased the men of the ice party by granting them a holiday for the first twenty-four hours of sailing. Many used the free time just to read the sacks of mail that had piled up in New Zealand during the previous year. The sacks included fan mail, of which popular Paul Siple got the most and poor Chips Gould the least—one postcard.

The Paramount twins surprised their buddies with a special treat. Rucker and Van der Veer had arranged for the motion picture company to film relatives and friends of the explorers a couple of months before and rush the movies, along with footage taken on the ice the year before and developed in New York, to the *New York* before she left New Zealand. The showing was particularly poignant for Hanson, who saw the son born shortly after the expedition had sailed. The Little Americans would have enjoyed themselves thoroughly had not heaving seas made most of them seasick.[1]

The *New York* reached the ice pack in a week and, to the delight of all, forged through the astonishingly weak floes in little more than a day. Like Gould, Byrd got by without the help he had pleaded for.

The wooden ship was welcomed to the outside world by two vessels that had rendezvoused earlier: the *Bolling* and the whaler *Kosmos*. The ailing Mason was transferred to the *Kosmos*, where Dr. Barnes could take care of the patient and even operate if necessary as the big whaler rushed to Wellington. Byrd wired the anxious families of all the members that the men had come through safely, finally allowing Owen to report to his newspaper the danger to the radio operator's life, news the commander had suppressed presumably so as not to worry people back home who could do nothing to help, and to avoid the inevitable pressures on himself.[2]

Several dogs, apparently those that were to remain in New Zealand, and their caretaker were also slung on board the *Kosmos*. A crate with two pups fell out of the sling between the two rolling ships; ironically, after the slaughter of dogs in Antarctica, Bursey and a couple of the ship's company bravely risked their lives to save the pups. The other dogs and the penguins, along with their caretakers, went on board the *Bolling* for ferrying to the *Larsen*, which would take them back to the United States after a layover in Dunedin. A few men who had to return quickly also boarded the *Bolling* enroute to the *Larsen*. The Paramount twins, for instance, had to help ready their documentary for release during the welcoming-home hoopla. Several others of the ice party switched from the overcrowded *New York* to the *Bolling* to even out the billets.[3]

When Byrd's ships reached temperate latitudes, the men who had wintered over marveled at the warm breezes and the first normal rhythm of day and night the group had experienced in more than a year. As the ships approached New Zealand, Byrd had everyone sign new statements promising to attend the reception hosted by the mayor of Dunedin, and promising not to say anything for the talkies, release any photographs, or tell anything new to reporters.[4]

On Monday, 10 March, as the vessels sailed together into Port Chalmers, the voyagers crowded the rails to drink in the harbor smells, the sights and sounds of horses and cars and trains, the green vegetation, brown soil, houses, buildings, and people, scores of people, especially the women. Thousands had gathered to greet the polar heroes. Byrd, Gould, and Davies—the British Empire's flagbearer on the expedition—all spoke at the reception at the town hall.[5]

Afterward, Byrd gave members of the ice party forty-eight hours shore leave and doled out $100 to each of his men for necessities and fun. The New Zealand government presented them with free railroad passes to tour the lovely dominion.[6]

Few men kept notes about what they did on resuming normal lives, but Harrison faithfully recorded in his diary that on the first day he and his friends got the best affordable hotel rooms and then hopped from pub to pub to drink beer. To catch up partially on the rapid progress civilization had made in the men's absence, they dropped into a movie house and saw their very first talkie. Siple, despite his twenty-one years and recent life with the hard-drinking Harbor Board crowd and Byrd's other worldly adventurers, remained the Boy Scout. He wrote: "I spied some late summer [flower] varieties blossoming on the other side of a fence and I leaned over to inhale their fragrance deeply. Then I hurried to a field where I flung myself on the ground and lay daydreaming in the soft warm breezes until my body cried out for a glass of milk and some fruit." Smith observed that, contrary to what might be expected, most of the crew first sought the ordinary, licit pleasures of civilized life. It cannot have been long, however, until most of the men reached for comfort in the arms of the sympathetic Kiwi women who vied to console the long-deprived expeditioneers. Owen, debilitated in mind and body, checked into a hospital to recover his health. Smith observed that Owen "had a hard time of it, much worse than anybody else."[7]

Smith wanted to leave right away to resume his lucrative pilot's job and recoup the nest egg he had lost in the Wall Street crash. Byrd told the pilot the newspapers might misconstrue his separate return months ahead of the expedition. Although several others left immediately for personal or business reasons, Byrd may possibly have been worried about competition from Smith. Little America had joked about the encyclopedic diary that the pilot spent long hours writing. The commander might have suspected Smith was actually composing a book or material for articles that could preempt Byrd's own publications. Smith revealed that the commander offered inducements to remain with the party: $500, free hotel accommodations, and first class passage on an early commercial ship departure to Panama, where Smith could get in flying time at an army base while waiting for the expedition's ships to arrive and pick him up. Smith agreed.[8]

Byrd put his ships into drydock, set up headquarters at the Grand Hotel, and again took on his role as the lionized celebrity, attending receptions, performing ceremonial functions, and giving speeches. Rusty at fielding questions from the press, he carelessly blabbed to a reporter that the expedition was on the verge of bankruptcy. Byrd moderated his alarming statement after it appeared in print, explaining he had been half joking and that, although still in debt, he would be able to pay his creditors.[9]

Byrd managed to create other headlines during his interlude in New Zealand by holding a radio conversation with publisher Adolf Ochs, who spoke from the *New York Times*'s building. The dialogue was broadcast to the public. Two-way voice transmission over such a long distance was big news, even if the conversation was largely garbled, especially since it involved a charismatic figure like Byrd. Even the competing *New York Post* was impressed with the expedition's demonstration of radio capabilities, running an editorial noting the marvel of Byrd's communications with the *Times* throughout the expedition. The event, however, bared the commander's insecurities. To prepare his answers, he asked what Ochs was going to say, nervously telling Railey: "I am a total loss when it comes to speaking extemporaneously over the radio and would feel comfortable about the matter only if I had a chance to prepare my talk ahead of time. It is . . . very risky to talk over the radio extemporaneously."[10]

The commander tried to round up his frolicking, long overdue troops on Tuesday, 18 March, to get ready for the return voyage. He wired Coman, who was with a group that had gone to the resort at Mount Cook, "Collect the boys and return immediately. Sailing Sunday." The vacationing boys, deciding that "immediately" could mean as long as two days, stayed until Thursday. In their absence, Byrd apparently had to dig deeper into his pockets and hire longshoremen to load his ships.[11]

Byrd had intended to take home only Walden's Chinook dogs and those that had become pets, leaving the rest to work at the Mount Cook glacier until he returned on his next expedition. Since nearby ranchers complained that the fierce huskies and their progeny might escape and kill sheep, Byrd arranged to ship all the dogs back. (None of the penguins made it to the States, however. Most died when they accidentally drank a caustic cleaning solution on the *Larsen*, and the ship's crew, who considered the squawking, defecating birds a nuisance, let the rest go.)[12]

The *Larsen* sailed for the States with the dogs and their handlers and soon turned up a stowaway—Claire Alexander, thirty-one, a general hand who had been assigned to Byrd's own ships. Byrd told others he was afraid Alexander might have sneaked onto the speedier ship, which would arrive in the United States in only a month, to make a deal with the Hearst people. Alexander, once a circus acrobat, radioed that he had to rush back because of an opportunity in vaudeville.[13] Other expedition members resented Alexander's deserting them.

Byrd wrote Marie a long letter commenting on men who had given him trouble. Owen was uppermost on his mind: ". . . Owen has been the only consistently disloyal one. But for the past four months he has made a supreme effort and has done very well indeed. He has the same thing Brophy got only not anything like so badly. He is a weakling and I'm sorry for him. He has bad megalomania so I guess he's not sorry for himself." Then Byrd rambled about some of the others, confused about their loyalty: "The least loyal of the men are coming back aboard. Alexander, Black. The latter may be intensely loyal. Has always seemed to be. But I don't know. There may really be few disloyal ones. But Alexander is disliked by everyone for a stunt he pulled. . . . But I've always got along with him. Anyhow, these fellows threaten my contract by coming back ahead. . . ."[14] In the same letter, Byrd, the loner, provided a surprising revelation about how much the comradeship with his men meant to him: "Next to you and my family, I guess the spirit of this expedition is one of the biggest things that has ever come into my life."

Byrd showed another face to Railey. About the same time as he wrote the letter to his wife, he radioed to his business manager a message that sounded as nasty as ever. It concerned Owen's passing up an international story: "Want you understand extraordinary success expedition creating goodwill people New Zealand. Before fleet arrived, strong anti-American feeling. Expedition did more than fleet to eradicate this animosity. It's outrageous that Owen did not give this credit to expedition in America. . . . Take [New York Times publisher Arthur] Sulzberger into confidence. Owen should be reprimanded for his neglect in this matter."[15]

Byrd was particularly sensitive to international relations because he had won Rockefeller's support on the basis of advancing amity among nations; Rockefeller's policy then was not to support pure science or exploration. Byrd had been angry with Owen in New Zealand on the way south, thinking (mistakenly) that the newsman had not reported the commander's speech honoring England's Captain Scott and promoting internationalism. Owen had aroused Byrd's ire at Little America by reporting neither the raising of the British and Norwegian flags at the sunrise flag-raising ceremony, nor Byrd's associated messages to the families of Scott and Amundsen; Byrd himself had gotten the stories into the *Times* through Railey.[16]

Byrd's attitude and actions against Owen are especially interesting when contrasted with a message the commander, while in Antarctica, had sent to Lloyd Berkner, then the expedition's correspondent in New Zealand for the *New York Times*. Byrd suggested that the radioman give New Zealanders credit in his stories: "I am not asking you to write these things. I am suggesting them because I make it a policy to try not to dictate the stories written by any member of the expedition."[17]

The international side to the expedition broadened when the commander accepted a friendly offer from the Canadian government to transport, for free, the materiel that he had no room for on his own ships.

On Sunday, 23 March, ten thousand New Zealanders swarmed to the seaside and bid adieu to their famous American friends who were leaving on the *New York*. With the Yanks were three Kiwis whom Byrd was giving passage in return for their service on his ships. Byrd himself was not on board. While at Little America, after hearing the plaintive tales about Captain Melville, the commander had told his men he would go back on the *New York*. Subsequently pressed for time, however, he decided to book passage on a faster commercial ship, bidding "bon voyage" to his flagship. He wrote Marie, "I don't like not crossing the Pacific with them (my men), but there's a very great deal of business to clear up with Tapley."[18]

The *Bolling* sailed a week later, no more glamorous for her antarctic adventures than she was before—only a few hundred people came to see her off. A stowaway was found and had to be kept on the leg to Tahiti, where the *Bolling* would meet the *New York* and tow her the rest of the way. Byrd and his immediate staff left a month later, and the commander made a point of saying "au revoir" instead of goodbye.[19] Byrd's party would rendezvous with the crews of the *New York* and the *Bolling* in Panama.

The *New York* once more sailed in gloom. Having tasted freedom and luxury, the crew had a hard time getting used to shipboard discipline again, especially Captain Melville's variety. The vessel was seven short of a full crew, so the thirty-one remaining had to work all the harder; those members who had left early with weak excuses were not thought of kindly. As on the voyage down, the dispirited men divided into two distinct and sometimes inimical groups—not "officers" and "men" this time, but those who had wintered together on the ice and those who had not.[20]

The *New York* arrived at Papeete, Tahiti, on 12 April. Difficulties in getting money for coal stalled the ship there for five days—with few complaints from the crew. The *Bolling* pulled in and used all of her money to bail the *New York* out. The wooden ship left, returned shortly to eject four stowaways, and then sailed again.[21] The *Bolling* had to wait five days herself for more funds to arrive. She caught up to the *New York* again on 30 April and threw a towline; like Siamese twins, the sister ships slowly made their way to Panama.

Byrd and his retinue got to the isthmus first, on 14 May, and were greeted with what was reportedly the biggest celebration since the canal's opening day. The busy commander requested that all the entertainments that had been planned in his honor during the following days be canceled, except for a few obligatory functions. He explained pretentiously that he was heading to the quiet of the mountains for two weeks to "work up important scientific data," as well as to straighten out the expedition's affairs, to write, and to rest. Down from the States to work with him were Railey; an editor from the *National Geographic* magazine, which had reserved most of its August issue for reports on the expedition; the Paramount twins, who, five weeks earlier, had been the first members to get back to the United States; and Charles J. V. Murphy, the reporter from the *New York World* who had accompanied Floyd Bennett on the trip on which he died. Murphy, a Harvard man, had written a biography about Byrd that came out shortly after the commander left on the expedition. The two had become good friends, and Byrd had been best man at the reporter's wedding. Officially, Murphy had come to Panama to help the explorer "update his biography." In fact, Byrd had chosen the reporter as a ghostwriter to compose his book about the expedition.[22]

A plane flew down to meet Byrd's ships and fly his commercially valuable movie film—20 miles of it—and photo negatives back to New

York as fast as possible.[23] The long-distance flight, which took several days, was in itself unusual enough for the *New York Times* to run stories almost daily about its progress.

The *Bolling* sailed alone into port on 22 May, having released the *New York* 700 miles out after running low on coal. The flagship was battling contrary winds, so Byrd asked the Navy Department for a tug. The navy classified the *New York* as a commercial vessel, however, and so refused. Admiral Byrd began contacting friends; just in case, the *Bolling* coaled up and headed back. Two days later the secretary of the navy reclassified the *New York* as a scientific vessel and countermanded the offensive ruling. Byrd said the help would be too late, but he would accept an offer to tow his ship for a few days after it passed through the canal. The *Bolling* returned with the old windjammer behind on 31 May.[24]

The expedition's dentist had traveled to Panama to check and fix teeth. He reported that most of the men's mouths were in unusually good shape under the circumstances, and he found no signs of scurvy or other vitamin deficiencies, which had afflicted past explorers.[25]

Acting for Byrd, Railey had some kind of showdown with Owen. Railey referred to it subsequently in a letter to the commander, but the details are unknown. The business manager wrote that in Panama he had taken care of a matter regarding Owen "as finally as it can ever be done." He mentioned how crucial Byrd regarded Railey's intervention, quoting the commander's own words of gratitude back to him: "If you never did another thing for me in all your life, I could never repay you for this one act." The mystery invites speculation. Perhaps, using the signed statements against Owen that Byrd had gathered, but acting ostensibly on his own to give the commander deniability about being associated with blackmail, Railey had coerced the reporter into not making public any criticisms or revelations about Byrd.[26]

On 3 June, the *Bolling* and the *New York* with its navy tug sailed northward. To stage a triumphal entrance into New York harbor, Byrd shipped on his romantic square-rigger for its final leg. Byrd, who always milked a good thing, tried to get the tug to pull him all the way to New York; the navy refused, so four days out of Panama the *Bolling* took over.[27] The ships made such good time that Byrd ordered them to slow down so as not to reach New York before 19 June, when the city had scheduled celebrations to welcome the expedition home.

On 16 June, while the ships were killing time off New Jersey, an unknown member committed the only flagrant crime that occurred within the group during the entire enterprise. Smith, discovering with shock that his locker had been rifled, found that his antarctic diary case had been opened and the thick stack of pages had been taken. As Harrison recorded, Smith had been offered $15,000 by the Hearst syndicate for the detailed diary. Smith asserted, however, that he had not written it with thoughts of publication (but later admitted he had received a subsequent offer from Hearst). The pilot reported the theft to Byrd, who ordered a thorough search of the ship. The diary was not found. Owen, having feared a similar theft of his property, had radioed his girlfriend that if he did not padlock his belongings on ship, things would be taken. Smith was not surprised that Byrd did not turn up the diary—the pilot knew Byrd dreaded literary competition and possible publication of the dark side of him and his expedition: the mistakes, deceits, pretenses, and conflicts, and the drinking and fighting, all of which Smith had graphically depicted. Byrd knew that the diarist was disappointed for having had little of the expected opportunity for personal flying in Antarctica and was not devoted to the commander. Smith figured the culprit was the commander himself. (In 1954, however, Byrd wrote to Smith: "I want to herewith give you my word of honor that I don't know who stole your diary. I know that was awfully tough on you. I am going to ask certain members of the expedition to help me find out, in the hopes it hasn't been destroyed." Smith claimed that, years after the expedition, Harold June confessed to having taken the diary on Byrd's orders and given it to the commander. Smith also declared that Charlie Bob confided to having seen the stolen diary at Byrd's home.)[28]

On Thursday, 19 June, Mayor Jimmy Walker, accompanied by relatives of the expedition's members, including Marie Byrd and eleven-year-old Dickie, sailed out in the reception tugboat, the *Macom*, to meet the ice-scarred ships as they pulled into the harbor. Two of the best known radio announcers in the country, Graham McNamee and Jimmy Wallington, were on board to broadcast the first greetings direct from the ships to the nation and to as much of the world as shortwave could reach.[29]

Byrd leaped from the *New York* onto the *Macom* to reach Marie and Dickie. An undated letter from this period written by Marie to her husband shows the anguish she felt at his absences: "Darling—I am wondering . . . if the time will ever come when we can be like human beings and have a real home. . . . Glory and fame may be all right, but we certainly have paid well for them." Byrd had also received a card from his lonely little boy with a heart-wrenching message scrawled in pencil: "Dear Daddy—I love you very much and I miss you very much. I wish you would be home more. I think I would get along much better in school if you were here."[30]

Because of his absences and faults, the explorer had grown increasingly worried that he might have lost Marie's love. He had radioed her from Antarctica, ". . . I have often felt that I have done a poor job as a husband." From New Zealand, on the way back, he had sent a letter apologizing for once breaking a promise by drinking, and concluded forlornly, ". . . You haven't used 'dearest' in your radios for a long time." In another letter written at about the same time, he had declared, ". . . Long separations are *over*. But maybe you don't care now." (Byrd wrote reassuringly despite his intention to launch the second antarctic expedition shortly. In a radiogram planning his next expedition, he had warned the recipient not to let Marie know he was preparing to return to Little America.) Apparently even his beloved wife's loyalty was not exempt from his suspiciousness. Just a few days before reaching New York City, he seems to have told her by radio that he had heard something that made him doubt her. She had replied plaintively: ". . . There is so much, Dick, that I can't write or radio as I can't run risk of ever being decoded. But, dearest, always take things you hear with a grain of salt and remember the old song, 'Have a Little Faith in Me.' My one and only longing is to be together again way off in peace and quiet with no more heartache and loneliness."[31]

He rushed to Marie standing on the deck—and shook hands. A man of his times, he would not put on an unseemly display of emotion before the watching and listening world. He did give young Richard an acceptable hug, calling him "Dick, old fellow."[32]

The ships docked, and the triumphant members boarded an automobile caravan that plowed through a snowfall of shredded paper, in one of the city's biggest ticker-tape parades, to reach City Hall, where five radio stations had set up mikes. In welcoming remarks on the front steps, Mayor Walker proclaimed that Byrd was "one of the finest human beings ever born into the world throughout its entire history." Speeches by other dignitaries and responses by Byrd and other members followed. All the guests were then feted at a huge banquet.[33] The next day, the first six pages of the *New York Times* had little but stories about the great expedition and New York's welcoming. *Collier's* magazine, in an editorial, opined that the magnificent reception would "long be remembered in history."[34]

On Friday, 20 June, Byrd, his family, and the members of his expedition traveled to Washington, D.C., on a special train provided by the National Geographic Society. President Hoover received the group at the White House; the National Geographic Society gave them a luncheon banquet; and they were received by Congress. When Byrd was introduced to the House, a representative from Virginia let out a rebel yell, which was taken up by many other sons of the Confederacy. Next, Byrd called on the secretary of the navy, and then the explorers went to Arlington National Cemetery to place wreaths at the graves of several people connected with exploration. That evening the National Geographic Society put on a reception attended by Hoover, Vice President Curtis, and almost everybody who was anybody in Washington, D.C. The society's auditorium held only six thousand people, and fifteen thousand ticket requests were turned down. Hoover bestowed a "Special Gold Medal of Honor" of the society on Byrd because he already had the Hubbard Medal, the organization's highest established award. Gilbert Grosvenor, the society's president, pronounced the expedition "one of the most comprehensive, dramatic, and productive explorations of modern times." When Byrd stood at the rostrum and described the discovery of Marie Byrd Land, stating "it was . . . claimed in the name of the United States," the patriotic audience issued its loudest and longest applause.[35]

The government's machinery was swayed by no such emotions. As Balchen had walked out the White House's gates shortly after noon, a man had stepped up and handed the pilot a subpoena. With bureaucratic pettiness, the document stated that the United States was deporting the alien explorer, who had taken out citizenship papers, for breaking residency requirements by not applying for permission to leave the country and return. At his hotel room later, the downcast Balchen received a telephone call from feisty New York City Congressman (and later mayor) Fiorello LaGuardia, who was screaming that the inane deportation order was "a Goddamn outrage." He bade the Norwegian not to worry and promised that he and Minnesota's Senator Shipstead (who had a large Norwegian constituency) would get the order rescinded. Later, Byrd wrote to the commissioner of naturalization to plead Balchen's case.[36]

The train returned to New York City the next day, but Byrd stayed south to be honored by Richmond and his home town of Winchester over the weekend. The commander gave his men money for new clothes and transportation home and said good-bye. Assuredly, no words or ceremonies seemed adequate to the moment. Like a school class breaking up or a military unit disbanding, personal events that seem to happen with a disappointing fizzle instead of some kind of appropriate bang, the Byrd Antarctic Expedition simply ended.

Like all the work between the harvest and the meals, much business and science remained to be completed. The commander and his scientists had yet to capitalize on the raw material produced by the expedition. Byrd had to find money to pay off his mountainous, six-figure debt and to fashion the stories he would tell through various media. His take depended largely on how well the stories would sell. The scientists had to study the specimens; sift, analyze, and digest the data; and publish the results. Individual expedition members had to pick up their lives, capitalize on their unique experiences, and most of all find jobs as the stricken economy sank deeper into depression.

.16.

Cashing In

ADMIRAL Byrd went back up to New York City on Monday, 23 June. At a Chamber of Commerce luncheon, he chatted with Charles Lindbergh and congratulated him on the birth two days before of his baby boy (who would be kidnapped and killed two years later). The next day Byrd and nine of his men went to Albany, which celebrated their arrival with what was reportedly the largest demonstration that had ever taken place in New York's capital. Governor Franklin D. Roosevelt, whom Byrd had served as aide when the governor was secretary of the navy, presented the explorer with the state's gold medal, only the second ever given to a non-New Yorker (the first went to Lindbergh). On Thursday, 26 June, Byrd went to Brooklyn to dedicate an airfield named in honor of his dead companion Floyd Bennett. The next day he traveled to Boston, his adopted hometown, for what Mayor Curley promised to be "a welcome such as has never been accorded any other American."[1]

On and on the celebrations went, for months after Byrd's return, as place after place, organization after organization, hailed the conqueror of the south polar skies. Many groups in the United States and abroad bestowed medals and other awards on him for advancing science, aviation, peace, and good character. These prestigious recognitions included the Navy Cross and promotion to commander of the French Legion of Honor, the highest award France could give a foreigner. Several universities conferred honorary doctorates on him. The infatuated seniors of Wellesley, the women's college, adopted him as the honorary member of their graduating class. Aviation groups appointed him advisor, and the American Federation of Labor proposed that he arbitrate a strike in Virginia. Songs and poems were written about him; paintings and busts were created. It was suggested that the newly discovered planet be named "Byrd" (but astronomers settled on "Pluto").[2]

Byrd was also cited by the *New York Times* and several animal welfare organizations, including the ASPCA and the American Humane Association, for his devotion to his huskies. No one asked for comment from Gould, still smarting from memories of his beloved dogs butchered because the hard-nosed admiral would not fly food to them—a decision not well publicized.[3]

Other expedition members were similarly acclaimed by their towns and states and various organizations, and several were promoted by their employers. New Hampshire named a new highway the "Chinook Trail," after Walden's lost lead dog. One of the biggest celebrations was for Paul Siple. Erie declared a holiday and held a parade to welcome him home, and the Boy Scouts threw a four-state jamboree near the city for the memorable occasion.[4]

Byrd attended many events honoring the brave veterans of his expedition, including those with whom relations were strained. A master at keeping up appearances, he delivered the after-dinner address at a banquet thrown by the Masons in honor of brother Balchen, deeming the Norwegian "a perfect shipmate and companion." With an equally straight face, Balchen replied that he hoped to be kept in mind if the admiral mounted another expedition. (In truth, although Byrd and Balchen probably did not like each other, they maintained a business friendship during the expedition and for some time after.) Byrd also went to functions for Owen and Smith, heaping praise on both a great "enemy" and a rebel who thought the admiral a thief.[5]

Families of many of the members had kept scrapbooks containing messages from Railey, *New York Times* radiograms decorated with a sketch of Little America's transmission towers and the zig-zag symbol for radio waves, and countless newspaper clippings. The men saw for the first time the tremendous public impact of the south polar flight.

The *Times* had emblazoned a triple-deck banner headline over its first page and filled most of the first six pages with stories about the momentous accomplishment on both the day of the historic flight and the day after. On each of the next three days the newspaper ran Byrd's personal account in two columns under a triple-deck headline. Companies took out advertisements for products that had helped the flight; one example was a full-page ad touting Tydol engine oil. Stories told of ministers' basing their Sunday homilies on the flight and of a congregation's reverently burying newspapers reporting the dramatic event in the cornerstone of a new church.[6]

The President of the American Geographical Society, Isaiah Bowman, praised the *New York Times* for making the expensive expedition possible by keeping public interest alive. Besides printing stories almost daily, the paper had sent an antarctic exhibit on a tour of theater lobbies throughout the country. Bowman declared that the paper had gone beyond commercial objectives and had made a contribution to science as substantial as that of any scientific institution. Byrd echoed these sentiments and said of the remarkable radio operation that the *Times* "could not hope for a return commensurate with the expense of arranging and maintaining this unique communication." Not surprisingly, the *Times* agreed. The paper had run an editorial chastising the blasé audience at a Broadway movie theater for not applauding a newsreel showing the *Times*'s radio room receiving the thrilling first transmissions from Antarctica; a loyal reader had written later that the unjaded crowd at his east-side theater had clapped enthusiastically.[7]

In recognition of Owen's steady stream of stories filed from the ice, the Pulitzer Prize committee awarded the unhappiest explorer the 1930 prize for reporting.[8]

There was, however, a glaring flaw to the volumes of stories by Owen and other newsmen, and even to the biographies about Byrd. Incredibly, almost none of the hundreds of thousands of words told anything truly personal about Byrd or the people around him. The stories offered virtually nothing about likes and dislikes, attitudes and beliefs, mannerisms and idiosyncracies, interests and hobbies, habits, faults, temperaments, possessions, families—not even what the men looked and sounded like. Byrd was written about like a disembodied god—and his men like attending angels—all-good and perfect, all things to all people. Flipping through the scrapbooks, the expedition's members knew that not only Byrd's reserve and but also his influence and censoring pencil had more than a little to do with that unfocused, profitable image.

The wholesome front of the expedition appealed to educators. The American Geographical Society distributed booklets about the expedition to schools, which incorporated lessons about Byrd and his scientists into the curricula. A teacher published an instruction plan that used the heroic explorers as models of how children can become successful if they eat healthful food and brush their teeth. (The good teacher did not have a copy of the dental report that pointed out that some members had not taken care of their teeth.) The American Geographical Society, as well as the National Geographic Society and Byrd himself, received thousands of requests from curious children for information about the expedition. Byrd delivered a series of three lectures over NBC for the youngsters.[9]

Although the masses adulated Byrd, observers detected a slackening in fervor when compared with that of the roaring Twenties. Frederick Lewis Allen, who chronicled the jazz age, said that the ballyhoo of the decade had spent itself by the end, partly because Byrd's exploits and others like them "had been overpublicized, and heroism, however gallant, lost something of its spontaneous charm when it was subjected to scientific management and syndicated in daily dispatches. . . . Byrd's south polar flight made him a hero second only to Lindbergh in the eyes of the country at large, but in the larger centers of population there was manifest a slight tendency to yawn." The director of England's Scott Polar Research Institute quipped that the necessity to invent a daily gossip column must have been the most repugnant hardship Byrd faced.[10] Contrary to the opinion expressed by the American Geographical Society's president, the director submitted that the blaring publicity soon bored people and so had not been advantageous to science. The intellectuals did indeed yawn, unfortunately so turned off by the synthetic appearances that they failed to go beyond them and recognize the genuine accomplishments of Byrd and his men.

Byrd, of course, was suspicious of anyone who implied that Little America had been less than heavenly, and when some writers disparaged him and his men by calling them the "Rover Boys" and otherwise putting them down, the angered admiral snapped that his critics were nothing but "smart alecks" and "self-styled sophisticates." He blamed his own devil incarnate, Russ Owen, for much of the sniping. Byrd wrote to Arthur Sulzberger that Owen was feeding wrong information to "sophisticates around New York who write. . . . Owen is doing me a great deal of harm, and is going around giving an entirely wrong impression. No matter what he says to you—he is doing this." Byrd asked Sulzberger to rein Owen in.[11]

On 3 July, exhausted by all the functions he had had to attend, Byrd retreated with his family to a friend's three-hundred-acre farm in New Hampshire so they could spend the rest of the summer together on a long vacation. Guards kept the curious away. In a blue mood, Byrd had written his brother Harry the previous day: "I am tired and fed up with the whole business and am only going through with it as a duty. Thank heaven the receptions will soon be over." In other writings, the explorer had commented ruefully that he had not had much of a family life for the past ten years because of his activities. Even on this vacation, however, he had to collaborate with Murphy on his book and sally forth frequently to meet obligations.[12]

Putnam wanted to bring Byrd's book out in time for Christmas sales, so the writers had to rush. Their task would have been easier had Byrd worked on the manuscript during slow periods at Little America as planned. Byrd had thought sales of his first book were far short of their potential because of what he felt was lackluster promotion by Putnam, even though Railey had tried to persuade the admiral that sales had been as good as could be expected. Pouting, Byrd explained that apparently it was not worthwhile to spend much time writing and that he seemed to lack authorship ability anyway. So Byrd had no rough draft. Fortunately, Murphy was able to borrow liberally from the *New York Times*'s stories. George H. Putnam promised he would spend almost full time promoting the book.[13]

Byrd sent Gould a letter on 17 September, asking him to write material in a hurry for the book, a request that caused more friction between the two leaders. Gould, annoyed at the rush, replied that he wished Byrd had asked sooner and did not see how to get anything written on time. Byrd wrote back: "I am disappointed not to get anything from you in response to my strong appeal. . . . As leader of the expedition, it seems to me that I should have a report of the trip." Gould obeyed Byrd's imperious request, speedily composing an appendix on the sledge trip. Byrd, having finished his manuscript on 22 October, sent typeset galleys to Gould for checking.[14] On 19 November, the admiral wrote Gould another letter all but commanding obedience: "I have not a word from you in answer to my urgent plea that you check my book with me. That . . . is the most natural thing in the world for a leader to do, and I feel that I am within my rights in asking this of you." Gould, in the final existing letter of the episode, responded that only three chapters and his appendix had been sent him.

The detailed book, titled *Little America*, ran longer than four hundred pages, with sixty-nine photos and four maps. It was done in the same sanctimonious, superficially personal, often saccharine vein as all the preceding writings. Byrd emphasized his own role and placed most of his men in the background as shadows. He omitted almost all negative aspects, sometimes so as not to hurt people, other times to serve his own purposes. He never referred at all to the Harbor Board; to Owen's "disloyalty" or firing; to the drinking, fighting, personality clashes, or Mulroy's ostracism; to Walden's demotion; to the problems with his ships' captains; or to the theft of Smith's diary. Byrd criticized no one and lauded many. He mentioned Dick Brophy and his break-down only in passing, did not reveal that he had been second in command, and never even gave the one-time exec's first name. The serious dispute between Byrd and Gould over air support for geology and the sledge dogs came off as a minor disagreement. Byrd did not reveal that he pleaded with the whalers to evacuate his entire expedition in mid-January. He said that among his reasons for asking for some help and back-up support from the whalers was that Mason had appendicitis. The admiral made no mention of the black stowaway who was a member for a month, of the Loyal Legion, of the Wright mechanic who left the expedition, of the competition from Wilkins, or of the frantic attempt to reach the snowmobile in the Ford plane with two engines dead. The admiral did claim to have personally discovered Marie Byrd Land and its bordering mountains, to have switched the location of the polar flight cache on purpose, and to have navigated for all his flights. On the other hand, neither did he mention diving into the icy ocean to rescue Roth or kneeling in thanksgiving after finding the party at the Rockefeller Mountains.

Byrd announced in the book that he was naming the mountains he saw on his last major flight the Edsel Ford Range, after his "dear friend" (and major contributor).[15] It may be that Byrd withheld naming the mountains while he tried to talk Ford into contributing more than Rockefeller, since the mountains to be christened were bigger and more significant than the Rockefeller Mountains. The financial records of the expedition show that, besides the polar plane, Ford also contributed $50,000 while the expedition was in the field, but the records do not indicate whether the contribution was before or after the discovery of the Edsel Ford Mountains.

Paramount's movie, *With Byrd at the South Pole,* which the studio called a documentary, came out that summer. Only partially a "talkie," it opened with an introductory monologue by a uniformed Byrd standing at the *New York*'s helm, and announcer Floyd Gibbons breathlessly narrated the part about the polar flight; but most of the black-and-white film was a musically scored silent. Reviewers, including those in England, generally praised it, but the truest summations were given by the *Times* of London—"sentimental . . . slush"—and the Manchester *Guardian*—"vulgar." The film had all the flaws of Byrd's book and many more besides. Scenes were faked, happenings invented, and incidents distorted, at best to simplify things and at worst—and far more often—to wring tears and nervous sweat from audiences: a man floats away on an iceberg and is rescued, an old dog limps alone from the base to catch up to its former partners on the trail and has to be destroyed. The music was heavy with pieces like Sousa's "Stars & Stripes Forever," played when Byrd rescues Gould in the Rockefeller Mountains. Most of the scientific activities and exploratory flights—most activities of any significance—were omitted. The movie was a melodramatic fairy tale of a hero braving the antarctic cold, of his worshipful sidekicks and cute dogs, of the lovable penguins and seals he met, and of his earthshaking flight over the South Pole. The star was quite willing to give paying movie customers what they wanted, or what the studio thought they wanted; he commented, "I was afraid the picture would be overdramatized, but if anything it was underdone." The movie industry liked the picture and, recognizing the efforts and sacrifices of the two Paramount cameramen, awarded the documentary the 1930 Oscar for photography.[16]

The August issue of the *National Geographic* magazine featured the illustrated story of the expedition. Afterward, Byrd wrote what appeared to be personal letters to expedition members not mentioned in the article. The notes were identically worded, however. In a tone of pique, he wrote apologetically that he had intended to insert a statement in the final draft of the article about "you," but the magazine never gave him the chance.[17] Byrd's attention to this detail shows the importance he attached to maintaining good relations with his men and, perhaps, a readiness to employ white lies in his business.

Byrd sold the story of the expedition in several forms. He sent the *New York*—crewed by expedition members who acted as guides, and laden with antarctic equipment, a model of Little America that McKinley and others had made during the winter, and other exhibits—on a tour of coastal cities to bring in money through admission charges. (The *Bolling*—the Cinderella ship to the end—was not displayed. Byrd sold her to an arctic sealing outfit for $15,000.) Abraham & Strauss, the New York department store, held a week-long exhibition of expedition gear. Luna Park, a popular amusement center for New Yorkers, erected a 350-foot diameter, 50-foot tall cyclorama of Little America, painted by thirty artists. Two of the artists also rendered a series of oils of expedition scenes, which were exhibited first in the windows of the *New York Times*'s building and later in other cities.[18]

At the end of October, Byrd began his series of lectures in cities and towns throughout the land. At each appearance he was usually feted by whatever city he was in and escorted to the lecture hall, where he spoke and showed a movie different from the Paramount epic. His normal fee was sixty percent of the gross with a guaranteed minimum of $1,500.[19]

A *New York Times* reader, who identified himself as a European newly arrived in America, wrote a letter to the editor expressing his amazement that Byrd should be so revered and yet have to resort to crass commercialism to raise money. The government did want to do something tangible for Byrd, however. As the expedition had been on its way home a congressman had proposed striking and selling a commemorative fifty-cent piece, the proceeds to help pay the explorer's debts. Byrd requested that the bill not be introduced, asserting that there would be no deficit.[20] Perhaps he meant there would be no lack he could not overcome on his own. He may have wanted to avoid the potential strings attached to such a grant, the fund-raising problems that might arise if the public thought of his enterprises as government sponsored in any way, and embarrassment should his handsome personal profits come to light.

Congress then proposed striking a special gold medal to honor Byrd. As he told his men, he insisted that all of them be given gold medals, declaring to the government "that if this could not be done, the leader himself would not accept a gold medal." The government finally selected a design through a nationwide competition and struck sixty-six gold metals for the main expedition members and sixteen silver and bronze medals for the others. Curiously, no presentation ceremonies were held. The medals were simply shipped to Byrd, who forwarded them to the recipients. Evidently neither Byrd nor the government felt the travel costs of a reunion were affordable. Congress also passed a bill conferring citizenship on thirteen foreign expedition members, thus ending the threat to deport Balchen.[21]

The men's appreciation of the opposite sex had been heightened by living in a womanless world for so long. Sometimes long-standing marriage plans had been postponed because of the expedition. Most of the single men, including many of the older confirmed bachelors, rushed to the wedding altar within months after returning, several marrying girls met in New Zealand. In a surprising development, an enraged women named Bertha Dietrich saw the wedding picture of Claire D. Alexander in a newspaper and swore out an arrest warrant for him. She claimed he was really Claire Alexander Dietrich, her faithless husband who had walked out on her and their two babies in 1922, and charged him with nonsupport and bigamy.[22]

The happiness of most of the weddings was offset by the problems many men had in getting jobs as the awful depression deepened. Although almost all the ice party found employment, half the ships' crews were out of work, and they turned to the admiral for help. McKinley, Byrd's adjutant during demobilization, gave questionnaires to the jobless for distribution to potential employers, but got only two job offers. Byrd himself hired twelve men to work on the New York's tour, helped Demas get a scholarship and offered him and a sailor money to help pay for college, and dedicated proceeds from an expensive limited edition of his book to his expedition's unemployed. (Selling for $50 each, the one thousand autographed special copies were made of deluxe stock and had extra photos).[23] By the end of the year, thankfully, only two or three men had not found work.

In what seems another instance of mindless bureaucracy, Malcolm Hanson told Byrd that the Naval Research Laboratory, for whom the radio chief had run experiments in Antarctica, had made it clear to him that his antarctic service was outside the lab's mainstream work and that his career would suffer accordingly. Taking personal affront, Byrd wrote to Hanson, "I am prepared to ask that my promotion be cancelled if they do not recognize you. I would not hesitate a moment."[24]

Byrd helped even disaffected members. He wrote off $1,300 that Dean Smith owed the expedition and offered to pay the interest on a debt of $2,100 owed to others that Smith could not soon repay.[25]

Byrd's caring attitude toward his men was partly just good business. To demand loyalty, he had to give loyalty. To recruit good people for future enterprises, he had to treat his present corps well. To maintain his pristine image in the fishbowl in which he lived, he had to avoid even the appearance of unfairness. Byrd was outraged when any of his men questioned his fairness and was quick to respond with a dressing down and a demand for an apology, as when Parker and Tennant complained that the admiral had not done all he should to help them financially. Byrd went much further than he had to, however. When Claire Alexander Dietrich, his legal problems apparently resolved, spurned a job the admiral had arranged and demanded $1,000, Byrd dropped the ingrate. But Byrd want to do something for Dietrich's mother if she was really being evicted from her home as her son had claimed in his dunning letters. Byrd wrote to a contact where the mother lived to see if the story were true (it was not).[26] The contact was general manager of the Reading, Pennsylvania, *Times*, and a cynic could point to the opportunity for favorable press coverage. Later, however, with no possibility of publicity, the forgiving admiral gave Dietrich yet another chance by again arranging a job that he not only accepted but excelled in, to Byrd's astonishment and delight. Byrd seems to have acted not strictly out of self-interest, but at least partly from a genuine sense of higher obligation.

Byrd magnanimously gave permission in several cases for expedition members to publish books before the end of the two-year embargo they had all agreed to (although he admitted the legal standing of the embargo was weak). Books about the expedition were written during this period and within a short while afterward by Siple (arranged before the expedition by Putnam), O'Brien (another boys' book, about the geological sledge trip), Gould, Owen, and Harry Adams (of the ships' crews). Charles McGuinness, another sailor, wrote an autobiography with chapters covering the expedition. An independent author, Coram Foster, beat Byrd into print by five months with a sloppy potboiler about the expedition, apparently derived from news accounts. Other independents wrote the story of the Paramount twins (an inaccurate volume, as bad as the movie, that one suspects was really composed by the studio's publicity department), a juvenile biography of Balchen, and a polar history featuring Byrd's expedition. Charles Murphy's wife, Jane B. Walden—no relation to the dog driver—wrote a biography of Igloo. Later, Balchen, Smith, Bursey, and Railey wrote autobiographies, and biographers wrote additional juvenile and adult stories about Byrd and Balchen, which included experiences from the expedition. Byrd, Siple, and Owen wrote other books that touched on the first expedition.

Gould and Owen wrote the best books: honest as far as they went, mature, uncloying, and unpretentious. The men wrote discreetly; neither one directly contradicted Byrd, offered a negative view, or leveled any significant criticisms. Gould commended Byrd, noting that his outstanding characteristic was concern for the safety of his men, and the greatest compliment to his leadership was his running the largest expedition without death or great suffering or even a minor casualty. Gould expressed his regret that the public did not understand or really appreciate science, forcing explorers to trade on sensationalism to finance expeditions. His troubles with Byrd could be read only between the lines. Owen mentioned that there was drinking and revealed the existence of the Harbor Board, although he touched those topics lightly. He referred to personality conflicts without getting specific. His book was not published until 1934, although he had gotten Byrd's permission to write in 1930. Owen had formally thanked Byrd for the permission granted "in accordance with the conditions stipulated," which the reporter did not spell out. On the flyleaf of the copy he sent to Dean Smith, Owen scribbled: "What a shame it has to be so abridged." ("Sure enough, the contents gave little hint that anything had transpired that was not all sweetness and light. Discretion was either still imposed or had become a habit," Smith commented later.)[27]

Gould was angry with Byrd for giving O'Brien, the black sheep of the geological party, permission to write, especially since O'Brien's book would come out ahead of Gould's. The second in command had refused to give O'Brien photographs of the sledge trip for his book and, too late to block permission to publish, asked the admiral not to write the foreword. Although Byrd, too, had differences with O'Brien, he wrote a brief foreword anyway. Byrd, explaining that he made an effort "always to be just and fair," told Gould that O'Brien was destitute, the book would do no harm, and as a juvenile story it would not compete with the exec's account. But Gould—as protective of his own interests as Byrd was of his—remained furious. After the book came out, Gould wrote Goodale, "I think O'Brien's book is unfortunate. It gives a frightfully silly aspect to our journey from a mature point of view. I am sorry that he was permitted to write it."[28]

Byrd apparently censored—or tried to censor—McGuinness's autobiography. The publisher sent a draft for review to Adams, the other sailor-author, and Adams showed the chapters on the expedition to Byrd. Byrd told Adams the book would hurt the expedition and said he wanted to meet the publisher, but no further record of the incident exists.[29]

Readers eager for vicarious adventure flocked to buy the books. Byrd's sold one hundred thousand copies at $5.00 apiece. Owen's went into its third printing in less than ten weeks. O'Brien's had a second printing three months after issue. Siple's had eight printings and was translated into five languages. Gould's became a classic of polar literature and was reissued many years later.

Byrd also gave his men early permission to give lectures and reported he knew of at least thirty who did so, sometimes in competition with him. He allowed Gould, McKinley, and Lofgren to use the expedition's films in their appearances. Siple made a tour of fifty Boy Scout camps, presumably speaking gratis.[30]

The admiral viewed Melville's lectures and two further literary endeavors, from Owen and O'Brien, as attacks. Byrd heard that Melville was saying in his appearances that the commander showed little concern for his men after the expedition. Byrd wrote Melville to dissuade him from his course and got other members to do the same. The admiral also tried to get a maritime official and the Masons to put a stop to the captain's criticisms.[31]

Owen collaborated with a playwright, George Hummel, in writing a drama about an aviation expedition to Antarctica, headed by a leader inclined to mysticism. The expedition was threatened with mutiny when the relief ship could not at first get through. Beyond superficial resemblances, however, the fictional expedition had little in common with Byrd's enterprise: the leader was ineffectual, men died, and full-blown mutiny erupted. Gould learned about the drama and told Byrd it was really based on Greely's arctic expedition. The exec explained that Hummel had used the antarctic setting, and brought in Owen, to capitalize on the publicity surrounding Byrd. The admiral, nevertheless, fumed to Railey, "It is undoubtedly a very vicious thing. I think Sulzberger should be told about it." Byrd got a copy of the script, which showed Hummel and Owen as co-authors, but what, if anything, the admiral did about the play is unknown. The show, titled *The World Waits*, opened on Broadway on 25 October 1933—without any reference to Owen in the publicity or the playbill. The play got a good review from Brooks Atkinson, the *Times*'s theater critic, who identified it with the Byrd expedition and mentioned that Owen had worked on the script.[32] (A fictionalized Byrd expedition later served as the setting for the classic science fiction short story and movie "The Thing," by a writer unconnected with Byrd. Byrd's expeditions also inspired the juvenile bestseller *Mr. Popper's Penguins*.)

O'Brien wrote an article for an obscure magazine, *Real America*, that apparently mentioned the expedition's problems with drinking and that debunked Byrd's navigational claims. Byrd was away at the time, but an assistant, assuredly in touch with the admiral, rounded up letters from other members rebutting O'Brien's charges; the letters were to be used if the article ignited a scandal. An existing, unsigned copy of a rebuttal denied vigorously (and mendaciously) that alcohol was abused on the expedition, and stated irrelevantly that Byrd could navigate because he had learned to do so at Annapolis.[33] O'Brien's article attracted no attention, however.

As for the canine members of the expedition, Walden claimed his own dogs, several were taken as pets, and Goodale took the others to mind until Byrd's next expedition. Sadly, most of Byrd's dogs died of distemper within a year after their return.[34]

Two events centering on the expedition's dogs illustrated the importance attached to the expedition and the exalted status of pooches in the treacly popular culture then. Byrd was in Memphis to give a couple of lectures when he got word that Igloo was near death. He canceled the lectures—standing up a senator, the mayor, and other dignitaries who were scheduled to honor the leader—and rushed home to Boston. His sick pet died before he arrived. The grieving explorer laid Igloo in a white casket with silver handles. With Czegka as one of the pallbearers, Byrd buried his companion in a pet cemetery, then placed a spray of roses over the grave, marked with a white marble shaft inscribed with the words, "Igloo—More Than a Friend." *Literary Digest* ran a two-page obituary.[35]

The funeral rites for Igloo looked understated compared to those for Unalaska, a husky from the expedition who was run over by a car in Monroe, Louisiana. Some three thousand mourning school children took part in the ceremonies when he was buried in front of the American Legion Home, over the objections of people who complained the site was inappropriate since it was dedicated to war dead. Later, another throng of children surrounded the grave when two girls raised a large white veil to reveal a half-ton stone monument bearing a bronze plaque with the inscription, "Sacred to the Memory of Unalaska." The youngsters piled flowers on the grave. City officials announced that, when the new high school opened in two months, a portrait of the heroic husky would hang in the foyer.[36]

Byrd and his scientists still had a key project ahead of them: producing technical reports to fill what the admiral envisioned as "four fat volumes" that Gould would edit. On 30 August, Byrd wrote to Goodale, "The scientific staff will be kept intact until the work is completed. The expedition owes it to the country to do all possible to analyze and compile the scientific results." In another letter to Goodale, the admiral wrote that the volumes were significant because they "will last when everything else is forgotten." From England, Griffith Taylor said the whole scientific world eagerly awaited the results. In praising *Little America*, the *New York Times*'s book reviewer commented, "One hopes that the detailed scientific records will be published ere long. They are necessary to round out the story."[37]

But the project ran into difficulty, much like the dispute between Byrd and Gould over air support for the geological party, although this time the clash was more damaging. None of the expedition's members ever commented publicly on the fiery conflict, but the surviving correspondence tells an intriguing story.

.17.

The Vanishing Volumes

ON 2 September 1930, Gould, freshly married and back from his honeymoon, was in New York City on unpaid leave from the University of Michigan, and he was ready to tackle the scientific volumes. He wrote Byrd, "I think you know how very greatly I want the scientific research of the expedition the best that has yet come out of the antarctic." The geologist pointed out that ". . . It of course involves a vast amount of work for me. I therefore think it wise that we understand definitely at the outset that the work shall be carried on in the dignified manner we have planned so long." Gould highlighted the need for offices, equipment, expert assistance, and funds. He estimated a project cost of $50,000. The newlywed stressed the need of money for the project and for his salary: ". . . I dare not undertake this task without assurance that the wherewithal to complete it will be forthcoming, nor do I feel that I can assume the task as a labor of love."[1]

Byrd wrote back reassuringly: ". . . you mustn't worry about finances because I am responsible for getting you into your present situation and I am going to see you through it." Although he was so thorough when really dedicated, Byrd apparently made no formal arrangements to pay salaries or expenses to his scientists. Taking instead

269

an ad hoc approach, he wrote to Haines in mid-October, "The National Geographic Society will pay your salary for October–December. I don't feel you should use your own money as you started to do."[2]

The first sign of trouble with the chief scientist came in a 22 November letter from Gould to Byrd: ". . . There is one matter that I am genuinely sorry about and that is that as geographer of the expedition I have never been consulted about the maps, and there were some conspicuous errors in the one published in the *National Geographic* magazine. . . ." Byrd did not answer Gould, and his reticent attitude throughout their correspondence toward the maps and Gould's function as geographer is puzzling. Gould wrote later to Byrd: ". . . maps are a prime essential. All of the data must be at my disposal." He demanded "full access to map materials, photos, etc." Byrd replied, ". . . I have taken responsibility for the geography of our flights," and told Gould that a friend, navy cartographer Howard Saunders, had been retained to work on the aerial photos. The admiral explained that he considered Saunders one of the best in his field. Later, Byrd wrote to Gould, ". . . My contribution [to the volumes] will be small and perhaps just the geography of our flights and navigations. . . . It was never my intention for you to do the actual work on our maps. I mean the ones to be made as a result of our flights."[3]

The analysis of the aerial photos was a major project. McKinley said it was the biggest task of its nature ever undertaken. Since the analysts had little ground control—features mapped from the ground that also appeared in aerial photos—they had to extract information laboriously from shadows, figuring in the altitude, time, and camera angle when each picture was taken. They would scrutinize two thousand miles of horizon to search for anything that might have been missed in flight.[4]

Gould exclaimed that he could not understand why Byrd went to the expense of hiring Saunders, declaring to the admiral that McKinley, working in cooperation with the American Geographical Society, should have been the one to do the maps. McKinley felt the same way and angrily but unavailingly insisted he was fully qualified to do the work.[5]

Why did not Byrd tell Gould of the plans about the maps at the beginning? Why did the leader pay his own man to do them—was McKinley really not as competent? Why could not Saunders report through Gould, as the other scientists were supposed to, instead of reporting directly to the admiral? Byrd never gave Gould or anyone else the answers. So loathe to rely on others, Byrd may simply have wanted complete control of an endeavor so close to him. Otherwise, the unexplained matter may be another of the questionable circumstances surrounding Byrd's flights—or it might have reflected some unstated policy of Byrd's concerning the entire scientific volumes project.

Gould booked lectures almost solidly from November through March and could devote only part of his time to the scientific volumes. On 11 December, McKinley wrote dejectedly to Byrd that the scientific work had practically stopped,[6] moaning that people who had taken part in surveying work, and others who had the expedition's data or knew where they were located, had scattered. ". . . I was told that Larry Gould had charge of all these matters," McKinley remarked pointedly.

In fact, demobilization was the one phase of the expedition that had escaped Byrd's careful planning. Equipment and records, and the men who knew their whereabouts, were scattered in often unknown places, too. The meteorological record book Gould had assiduously kept for Haines on the trail, for example, had not been seen since they had left Antarctica.[7]

Byrd was moved by McKinley's letter to jostle Gould: "Will you please outline for me what each scientist is doing? . . . Give me the plan of operation. Do you know where you can get hold of the scientific data, and where is it being compiled? . . ." Byrd followed this letter with a stronger one on 10 January 1931:

> . . . from a number of sources I have heard some criticism of you to the effect that you are not and have not been giving the time you should . . . to the scientific work of the expedition. This must have started with several members of the expedition who have thought that you should have done more to bring order out of the chaos of demobilization.
>
> Don't let this worry you because . . . I am the one who should be the judge of these things, but I suggest that you stress the scientific end where possible and proceed vigorously. . . . I shall await . . . your reply on the plans, etc., of the scientific work. I will do everything in my power to aid all of you. . . . I am doing all I can possibly do. . . .[8]

Gould, enraged, wrote back on 17 January:

> I naturally resent your statement that I have been criticized. . . . I will not let that pass. I insist that you be specific both as to the nature and the source of criticisms. I note that "this must have started with several

members of the expedition, etc." This seems doubtful to me since there is but one member . . . Mike Thorne, who is conversant with what I have been doing. You owe me a prompt explanation, Dick.

You ask me for "plans, etc., of the scientific work" and add "I will do everything in my power to aid all of you." May I in this connection remind you of a letter which I wrote to you on Sept. 2 outlining the needs for the scientific work? . . . You have not yet given any answers to my proposals.

He reminded Byrd of the original plea for offices, expert assistance, and funds, and continued:

You expect results but you have placed no tools in my hands. . . .

I have been given to understand by Norm Vaughan that you have four men busy on the scientific work. It seems a bit irregular, to say the least, that I was not consulted about this. . . . To prepare any plan I must know what you have been doing. And the means . . . from the time you made the first commitment as to what was to be done with the scientific results. . . . Things have been too vague and now I must have specific information.[9]

After receiving Gould's letter, Byrd wrote testily to McKinley: "I am afraid that Larry thinks that I have not done enough for him and that I have not paid enough attention to him. . . . He is certainly on the wrong track now." Then the admiral responded in exasperation to Gould: ". . . there are many more than four men working on the scientific results. . . . I have taken it for granted all along that you knew all about the things these fellows are doing. . . ."[10]

Byrd's heavy financial burden must have played a large role in his tentative attitude toward the scientific project. The final accounting for the expedition showed a total cost of $1.1 million. The admiral wrote a letter in January 1931 to the expedition's members, candidly summarizing the expedition's monetary situation: "The expedition debt is up to $120,000, which I have assumed as a personal obligation, but the books and lectures have been successful, so that the debt can be paid, and we will be able to put $40,000 or so in the scientific work, which is our biggest obligation. The *City of New York* has been a failure, $17,000 is owed on it, but it at least has given employment to some of the men. We have gotten $22,000 from the motion pictures and we expect and hope they will do better." Byrd's figure about the total owed is confirmed by the 30 December 1930 report of his auditors, which showed a debt of $119,400.[11] By paying it with what he considered his own funds, Byrd thus became the largest single contributor to his own expedition.

As Americans grew too poor to spend much money at box offices, however, the highly profitable lectures soured a bit. Byrd wrote later to a friend, "In lectures, because of the depression, I'm talking in smaller places and charging less, but having full houses."[12]

Byrd had suffered two reverses late in 1930 that may also have been relevant. On 18 November, Byrd's good friend Charlie Bob, one of the biggest contributors, had been indicted (and later jailed for two years), charged with defrauding investors in his Metal & Mining Shares, Inc., of $6 million. The sharpie had paid the expedition's salaries and been an easy touch for emergency funds (although he had never produced the money for the promised "Byrd Beacon," announced before the expedition had left). In his distress, Bob sued to get back $150,000 he said he had donated to Byrd. Byrd said the contribution was far less, and in fact the expedition's records had Bob down for $83,000.[13] The fact that a significant portion of the expedition's expenditures had been financed by stolen funds was obviously embarrassing to Byrd. Mountains that had been named for Bob were suddenly found to be "nonexistent," and his name was dropped from the maps then in preparation.

Two weeks after Bob's indictment, Hilton Railey, Byrd's business manager, fund-raiser, and stateside alter ego throughout the expedition, resigned when accused of mismanagement. In a letter to Byrd, Railey refuted the admiral's charges: ". . . You will not discover 'heedless extravagance,' 'disregard of overhead,' or even 'carelessness' under pressure." Railey, whose annual salary was a princely $26,550, was also accused of overcharging for his services, reprimanded for "entirely negative" public relations, and blamed for the failure of the *New York*'s tour. Railey, in turn, posed accusatory questions to his boss: "Are you determined to be unjust to me? If not, will you take more pains to ascertain the facts before you make reckless statements?" (Byrd and Railey reconciled before the next expedition, which the business manager joined for a brief time.)[14]

On 6 February 1931, Byrd wrote a conciliatory letter to Gould:

> . . . I think we need to have a number of conferences. Also, regarding the matter you are holding against me, I think that we should get together and talk things over, that is if you care to. . . . Our respective duties and work have kept us from seeing enough of each other. I will

write no more along this line until I see how you feel about this thing.

In regard to . . . your letter, I was writing in a friendly spirit and did not expect to be jumped on. . . . Many is the time I have written to my brother in this same spirit. . . . I gather from your letter that the fault lies with me, if there is any. If you doubt that it does, I am willing to take the responsibility. . . . Until I hear from you, I will take the entire responsibility for any failures in the progress of the work.[15]

Byrd added that he thought it advisable to get a scientific body to help with expert assistance and office space.

Unmollified, Gould shot back: "None of your letters quite answers the specific things I asked you about in my letter to you of Jan. 17. . . . I find that you had made certain commitments as to the disposition of scientific data before we had even left the ice. You never told me about this. . . ."[16]

In a March 3 letter, Byrd snapped at Gould: "I cannot and will not stand for the tone of several of your communications to me lately. . . . I have tried time and again to impress on you that the burden on my shoulders is almost more than a man can bear."[17]

The day before, Byrd had written Haines as if the relationship with Gould was undisturbed, referring to an otherwise unrecorded conference with the exec: "Larry and I had a talk the other day and it was agreed that I should jump in and help as much as I can with the compilation of the scientific data, since I have certain facilities such as a secretary. . . . Because of the press of circumstances I have to some extent neglected my duty in this matter, but am now 'full speed ahead.' "[18]

A week later Byrd told a reporter he expected the scientific project to take eight to nine more months. Shortly after, Haines and the Carnegie Institution, for whom Davies had gone to Antarctica, both informed Byrd that the labor would last about a year.[19]

On 31 March, Byrd wrote Gould: "While in Washington I had a long conference with Haines, Hanson, Berkner, and Davies. . . . It looks as if it will take seven books of medium size." He stuck a needle in Gould, who was still making the lecture circuit: "We were all sorry you could not be there." Acting as if in direct charge of the project, Byrd suggested a format for the reports, noted that he had tried to arrange for Hanson and Haines to get time off from their regular jobs to work on the effort, and mentioned that he was "getting in outlines from the fellows in response to the letter I wrote."[20] The outlines, he revealed in other correspondence, were for presentation to Rockefeller, the expedition's largest contributor.

Two months later, Gould wrote apologetically to Byrd concerning the geological report: "I am sorry to be so slow about getting a properly detailed outline of my prospective report. . . . I naturally want to discuss the whole matter of publication with you—and there are a lot of things that I would like to talk with you about . . . [including] plans for your further exploration. Some interesting possibilities have arisen for me. . . ." The "interesting possibilities" referred to Gould's chance to run his own antarctic expedition. Byrd, who was then laying the groundwork for a second expedition, replied: "I have heard from other sources about your proposed expedition. Hope it goes through with you all right." Gould wrote back on 5 June that he had no definite plans for an expedition and would discuss the matter with Byrd before doing anything.[21]

Byrd apparently heard soon thereafter that Gould was seriously considering using Little America as his base. The commander sped a telegram to Gould on 29 June: "Hope you will make no further moves until you acquaint me with more details what you propose to do from Little America." The next day Byrd wrote to affirm that he would make every effort not to be selfish about his base. Gould responded to Byrd on July 2. The reply affronted Byrd, who repeated the offending passage in his response: "In your letter . . . there is the following paragraph—'When I discussed my prospective plans with you I thought you would be glad to have us who shared with you in the task of building Little America use it again. Naturally, if you do not want it we shall make other plans.' There is nothing in my letter that warrants that paragraph. I did not, as [it] indicates, say that I did not want you to go to Little America. . . . I don't think that paragraph is either fair or necessary."[22] Byrd said he could not permit use of Little America without discussing the matter with his biggest subscribers. Then, practically accusing his second in command of lying, he asserted that although Gould had said plans were nebulous, Byrd had heard that Gould was already raising money for an expedition.

The admiral also heard that Gould had been gossiping that Charlie Lofgren, who had departed, had quit as secretary because he was fed up with Byrd. Simmering, he wrote McKinley on 26 July: ". . . Gould is entirely disloyal to make the remark [about Lofgren]. He also said that I was accepting money to pay up the deficit of the expedition when I had no deficit." Byrd pointed out that his office staff automatically declined offers to help with the deficit because there was none. He seems to have referred to his taking the debt off the expedition's books and assuming it as a personal liability. He had told Gould only two months before, "I am still paying out on the expedition 'left-overs' etc. the interest on a million dollars. It has been a 'tough bag to hold.' "[23]

Despite his close relations with wealthy patrons—the Fords and Rockefellers visited his vacation home that summer—Byrd probably had decided not to press them for further contributions for the first expedition because he was already talking to these men about kicking in to a second expedition.[24]

As shown by Byrd's implacable hostility toward Owen, the admiral practically lost his reason when anybody talked about him behind his back. In his letter to McKinley, Byrd's further comments sounded as if he had reverted to the dark suspiciousness of the antarctic winter: "[Gould's] statement also is written in a malicious attempt to discredit me with the men of the expedition. The attempt is apparently being made to turn the members of the expedition against me. . . . Mike Thorne has made the statement that he and Gould are going back to Little America to finish the work that I should have done there." He requested McKinley to tell Gould that Byrd would not tolerate this disloyalty.

On 27 July, Eddie Goodale, exhibiting extraordinary gall, sent a letter calling Gould on the carpet. Goodale gave Byrd copies of the letter and of Gould's reply, indicating that a devious admiral had been behind the effort. Goodale wrote: ". . . in conversations with you in the antarctic and since we have returned you have given me the decided impression that your loyalty to Byrd may justly be broken due to unfair play on his part. Is this so? . . . Let's get things straight. When was the expedition debt cleared up? Did the bonuses of Paramount and *New York Times* cover the entire amount? If so, did Byrd accept money thereafter for his personal gain, under the guise of clearing the deficit? Did Charlie Lofgren leave Byrd because Charlie was 'fed up' with him? The answer to these questions will tell me your attitude towards the admiral." In response, Gould declared he did not have to answer to his sledging companion, directing Goodale to ask Byrd for the answers. Byrd, in a letter to Goodale, said, "I consider that the finances of the expedition are not Gould's affair. . . .

For three years I got nothing from the expedition, and as you know my expenses were simply enormous. It would be very difficult for me to tell you the amount that has gone out the past three years from my personal funds. . . . Paramount did not anywhere near come up to my expectations."[25]

In his 26 July letter to McKinley, Byrd had revealed that "there has been some pretty direct evidence that [arctic explorer and publishing heir George P.] Putnam is after my scalp. I thought that he and I were friends. . . ." Putnam was an old chum of Gould's, who dedicated his book both to his bride and to Putnam. In the subsequent letter to Goodale, Byrd, pleading incomprehension, went on, ". . . Gould is living in Putnam's apartment, and it has astonished me beyond measure to find these two fellows apparently doing these things against me. For the life of me, I cannot think of anything unfair that I did to Gould in the antarctic or since our return."

As in Antarctica during winter, when Byrd had been so anxious about the faithfulness of his men and they had presented him a declaration of their devotion, a group of expedition members again arranged a testimonial reaffirming their loyalty. They also wanted to thank the admiral for the help he had given many of them, for the complimentary copies of his book and of a private photo album McKinley had produced—a kind of yearbook of the expedition—and for Byrd's other thoughtful gestures toward the men in the difficult times since the gang had broken up. Beside the document, they also decided to give him an Annapolis ring (he had apparently lost his). They had taken up a collection among themselves by mail—a letter exists identifying Bubier, the author of the winter declaration, as a solicitor—to raise $5.00 apiece. The group held a dinner for Byrd in Boston in September to present their gifts. The citation they wrote read in part: ". . . The prolonged sojourn in southern latitudes was a significant experience, but it was chiefly so by reason of your sound direction and your unslacking personal sympathies. The influence of that leadership and those sympathies you did not withdraw with the formal demobilization of the expedition. . . . You have steadily maintained contact with all of us. For many, the period of readjustment to normal life, especially in these hard times, brought a measure of hardship and despair; but those qualities founded in friendship and loyalty that we who have been with you beyond latitudes 78° North and South know are fundamental in your character came swiftly into play; and all of us, if only because the unity of our association renders the lot of one the lot of all, were benefited." In his thank-you notes, Byrd wrote, "After all the knocks I've taken, it was pretty wonderful to have your sincere expression towards me." No involvement by Byrd in getting up the testimonial is recorded. It had not been signed by all expedition members, however, and it is recorded that after the presentation Byrd asked McKinley to get other signatures and instructed Demas in the touchy matter of getting O'Brien's signature.[26] The *New York Times* published the testimonial, probably on Byrd's initiative.

Gould wrote Byrd a scorching letter about the event: "I am sorry not to be seeing you now—but I was not invited to the party and only heard of it accidentally. For some reason, I have been completely ignored in the whole festivity except for my signature. I was not invited even to participate in the proposed gift, and when I discovered that things were misrepresented to me to get my signature then I became [illegible word] disturbed. I have the impression that the whole matter is designed to serve as personal aggrandizement for the person getting it up. When I discovered the 'lay of the land' . . . I protested to Bubier as he will no doubt tell you. I think the whole matter has been badly managed, and there is little spontaneity about it."[27]

On 12 October, apparently trying to repair the damage he felt Gould was causing, Byrd wrote Bernt Balchen, who was close to Gould, asking for a meeting to discuss how people had been lying to Balchen about Byrd.[28]

Byrd also disclosed to Balchen a tremendous hit from the depression. He had been devastated financially: "The aftermath of the expedition has been a terrible burden for one man to bear alone. . . . I have lost over $30,000 on the *City of New York* exhibit, and . . . have a personal loss close to $200,000. . . ." He also mentioned the $200,000 loss to Lofgren and attributed it mysteriously to "the mismanagement of a friend of ours." The loss Byrd cited was undoubtedly a combination of the expedition's debt, which Byrd had assumed personally, and his losses in the stock and bond markets. Consistent with his statements, his tax return for 1931 claimed a loss of $99,097 on the sale of securities. Even so, he reported a taxable income in 1931 of $93,981 including, before other deductions, $117,400 from lectures, $90,100 from books, and $4,000 in pay as a retired admiral. The year before had been his best financially, when he had had a net income of $171,000. Independently, Marie Byrd had an income in 1930 of $55,590 from the Ames trust, which dropped to $7,800 in 1931.[29] The investment losses were a calamity. Byrd earned peak income at the conclusion of his enterprises, which were years apart. He invested the money and, during the intervening years when he earned relatively little, he drew from his savings to live on and start up the next enterprise.

Byrd wrote a memorandum to Gould, undated but probably from the fall of 1931, wailing about his financial misfortunes and overburdening responsibilities, and indicating that the confidence in his investments that Marie had expressed in a radiogram just before the stock market's crash had been unwarranted: "The expedition itself is fun and healthy. It is the preparation and aftermath that take years off a man's life. . . . I myself had a tremendous loss . . . because I neglected my private affairs for expedition work, and the firm I was dealing with put much of my eggs in a basket that went busted [sic]. . . . When I returned I found many uncertainties, financially speaking, not the least of which was the uncertainty of whether I could carry the burden thrust upon my shoulders without breaking down physically. . . ." Then Byrd added an apparent dig at Gould: "While I was struggling, with no time for social amenities, some of those to whom I had given my friendship, and for whom I had done the most, saw fit to misunderstand me. . . ."[30]

Adding to the weight on Byrd's shoulders was Marie's health. She had become seriously ill in spring with an undisclosed condition, and her sickness had lingered through the summer. She seems to have recovered by winter.[31]

In early November, Byrd arranged for the National Geographic Society to take over the job of coordinating the scientific work, effectively relieving Gould of the responsibility. Byrd wrote a brusque note telling Gould of the arrangement and asking the chief scientist to inform him by return mail when the geological report would be completed.[32]

The cartographer Harold Saunders was named project supervisor. The society had agreed only to get the scientific reports ready for printing, so Byrd would still have to pay the publication costs himself. Convinced that he was giving as much to the project as necessary or possible, he informed Goodale, "My expense on this scientific work is going up so high that I am trying to keep it down as much as possible."[33] But he did not specify how much he was spending or what he was paying for. Given Gould's complaints and the almost total lack of progress on the project, it is hard to imagine that the admiral could have been giving out much.

The chill between Byrd and Gould was deep. Neither man would communicate cordially with the other for years. Since a public rupture would hurt both of them, they kept their differences pretty much to themselves. Characteristically, Byrd wrote to Dr. Coman, for example, on 13 November: ". . . In regard to Gould, our relationship down south, as you know, was very pleasant, and whenever I have seen him upon our return there has been no apparent change. No disagreeable word has passed between us. He was unduly impatient in one or two letters and I set him straight. That is all."[34]

Byrd himself had less time than ever for the scientific volumes. He began detailed planning for the next chapter in his career—his return to Little America. The professional explorer (displaying a certain lack of economic acumen) announced that he would sail the next September because "I am convinced that the depression is on the wane." At the same time, Byrd knew that his professional credibility was at stake. As he commented to Goodale, who was writing about trail equipment for a section on logistics: ". . . It is my desire to have the scientific work completed before we leave for the antarctic . . . We would be much criticized for starting on another expedition before the work of this one had been completed. . . . The expedition will live or die by the work that you fellows are doing."[35]

Early in March 1932, Ralph Shropshire mailed in his hydrographic paper from the Buffalo, New York, Museum of Natural Science, which had paid his salary while he worked on it. Shropshire's was the first and only report ready for publication. Siple had sent his biology report, but Gould and Saunders both thought it needed extensive rewriting, and Coman, nominally chief biologist, considered the young student's research so embarrassingly amateurish that he would not return the copy he had been sent.[36]

Hanson had made little progress on his report. On the ice, the admiral had bawled out Hanson for not completing projects on time, and Byrd called the other to task again, this time for not answering letters as well as for procrastinating: "I . . . am a bit shocked to hear that the scientific work is not to be turned out before September— that is over two years since our return." Later, displaying the little-seen hard side of his nature, Byrd wrote bitterly to Saunders that Hanson "did not answer my very strong letter. . . . I will not stand for such treatment any longer—I shall cut him off my list if he doesn't do something about it."[37]

Saunders wrote Gould on 4 March and pleaded with him to submit something on geology—anything he could—for the volumes. Ten days later, Gould replied astringently that laboratory work costing $500 was necessary, "and as yet Admiral Byrd has not provided the moneys to authorize me to have this done. . . . We are not in a position financially to undertake this work and we are waiting authorization from Byrd to go ahead with it at the expense of the expedition."[38]

Byrd wrote McKinley almost despondently on 16 March: "All the savings of my life up to 1931 plus a lot more has gone." The next day the admiral again wrote McKinley, sending the letter to his home instead of his office for stronger confidentiality and asking him to destroy the communication after reading. The tone was bitter and the message, conveying suspiciousness, was somewhat cryptic: ". . . won't you try to impress on Gould that I am not a multimillionaire. I have evidence from several sources that he thinks I am rolling in wealth. The good Lord only knows how I pulled through in the antarctic with the set of influences which I now know worked against me. If the real truth were known, I guess it is the best job I ever did. The handicaps were almost insuperable on account of the genius with which some supposed friends worked against me. . . ."[39]

Byrd wrote another bitter letter to Saunders on 20 April, groaning that the scientific volumes were failing because Byrd had had to delegate responsibilities to others. The next day he again wrote Saunders with an amazing assertion, given that Byrd had prevented Gould from acting as geographer: "It is true that I appointed [Gould] Geographer of the Expedition, but later found that this was a mistake, and he has not in my opinion acted as geographer." In another note ten days later the leader advised Saunders to press Gould to answer Saunders's letters, writing "I think he is peeved because I avoid seeing him. . . . All I ask of him is to do his work and to let me alone."[40]

In the summer, some odd, inexplicable byplay occurred in the estrangement between Byrd and Gould. Gould had named a peak in the great horst Admiral Mountain to honor Byrd. On 9 June, Byrd wrote Saunders, "I will write Gould about naming this mountain after him. He might have some strenuous objections to it." Nine days later he again wrote Saunders, "I have not heard from Gould in regard to naming the mountain after him, so we can go ahead and name it." Later, Gould wrote Byrd expressing surprise that Admiral Mountain had become Mount Gould.[41]

To McKinley, on 11 July, Byrd wrote another letter about his financial catastrophe: "I am having the most desperate possible time, and not only have lost nearly all the funds I have spent my lifetime to make, but am almost threatened with bankruptcy. I am far worse off than when I left for the antarctic." To Gould, Byrd said that he was netting so little that "I am not even paying an income tax this year." (He did pay next to nothing in federal tax for 1932—$11.)[42]

Ironically, and with his characteristic forgiveness and sense of obligation, he managed to scrape up $500 to donate to Charlie Bob, the big spender whose suit against Byrd had been unsuccessful and who was apparently in even worse shape than the man Bob had supported so heavily.[43]

The depression was to deal Byrd another major blow. He would not be able to get the money for a second expedition. On 26 July 1932, in a replay of his aborted initial attempt to launch the first expedition six years earlier, he announced that he was postponing the second "indefinitely," but he hoped for no more than a year.

Time flew but the scientific project dragged. Saunders told Gould on 17 March 1933 that Haines and the Carnegie Institution (working on the data from Davies, who had gone back to Canada) were completing their reports, but that the project was "pretty much at a standstill." On 15 April, in the depths of the depression, Byrd told Coman, "I . . . cannot personally spend any more on the scientific work than I already have. I simply have not got it to spend." The project nevertheless limped along. In September, Byrd told Gould, "I have got practically all the scientific work accounted for but yours." Gould replied that he could finish it by the holidays.[44]

Byrd accepted defeat, at least temporarily, on the project, having determined to leave for Antarctica in the fall of 1933. On 7 September, he announced reluctantly that he had decided to delay publication until his return.

Gould continued to belittle Byrd in private. In a letter to Balchen, referring to Byrd's isolation at a subbase during the second expedition, Gould wrote, "[Is] there anything more silly and cheap than his present attempt to be heroic? Even his blindest admirers are bound to see through this inanity." In the same letter, still hoping to mount his own expedition, the geologist mentioned the possibility of himself, Vaughan, and Crockett crossing Antarctica by sledge from a point below Argentina to Little America before Byrd left, and chortled, "Can you imagine how happy Byrd would be to bring us out?????" Writing much later to Balchen, Gould commented, "You ask . . . whether Byrd's motivation rises from a deep-seated motivation which requires him over and over to prove himself to himself. This probably is true. . . ."[45]

With only the remaining correspondence as a guide, deciphering the maneuvers and true intentions of Byrd and Gould throughout the attempted production of the scientific volumes has to depend on guess-work. At the start of the expedition, Byrd probably had intended to publish the scientific results as other expeditions had. Despite his numerous protestations to the contrary, however, he seems not to have given the commitment that the project required. He had left all post-expedition work out of his detailed planning. Incredibly, he made no overall provisions to pay the scientists afterward or to arrange any facilities or funding for their work, and he resisted Gould's prodding to do so, even describing the exec's efforts as "on the wrong track."

Raising cash for the project was obviously a problem. Byrd's expertise was making money through spectacular shows; it would be hard even for a draw like him to attract contributions, especially in a sick economy, so that someone in a laboratory could study something like the fluctuating diurnal patterns in horizontal and vertical geo-magnetic vectors. But he certainly could do better at procuring funds than the scientists themselves, and Gould clearly regarded that fund-raising as the admiral's job. Any shred of hope that Byrd would fully fund the project himself was dashed when he almost went broke, but his reluctant behavior before then is confounding. It could be explained by assuming that, at the end of the expedition when Byrd took a hard look at the financial implications of the project, he privately decided not to go through with it. An attempt at fund-raising to clean up the first expedition would have clashed with his campaign to finance the second expedition, difficult enough in the depression. He would not have wanted to add to the unexpected $120 thousand he already had to pay out of his own pocket. Byrd never said so, but he may have wanted the scientists to find their own backing—just as he wanted the sledge teams to do their jobs on their own without any help from him, even as he lauded their goals and professed full support. To say so outright might have led to image-damaging charges that he did not care about science and had abandoned his scientists. He may have hoped the scientists would take the hint from his uncharacteristic inaction and continual whining about his nearly unbearable burdens.

If this explanation is true, Byrd's curious attitude toward the mapping of his flights may have signaled his true intentions. He wanted this mapping completed because it fulfilled his own project, but it would have been awkward to give Gould and McKinley money for that effort alone when they were also concerned with mapping the sledge trip and the surveys of the barrier. If Byrd really did not want to underwrite the other work, he solved the problem by taking over flight mapping and paying his own cartographer.

Gould's behavior is puzzling. It is a wonder that he started on the scientific volumes at all since he and Byrd had barely been civil with each other at least since the expedition ended and probably since the sledge trip. No naif, he must have realized within a few weeks if not days of starting that the project was failing badly, for whatever reason. But instead of forcing an immediate showdown that would have led either to Gould's quietly resigning or Byrd's wholeheartedly supporting the effort, the project head contented himself with sending occasional huffy letters. He continued where he had left off after his sledge trip—hanging on, but not working hard for Byrd's enterprise. Instead, he devoted most of his time to working for himself, making money through lecturing and writing his book, and trying to form his own antarctic enterprise. He may not have wanted to abandon the project totally and lose credit for the volumes while there was any chance they could eventually succeed; furthermore, if he resigned, he might be blamed for the project's failure.

Byrd never did publish the scientific volumes. With the suspension of effort that became permanent, the work of Byrd's first Antarctic Expedition had ceased.

.18.

Byrd and the Byrd Expedition

JUDGMENTS of the expedition tend to be colored by judgments of Byrd himself, so the two views have to be clearly separated. Balchen could make that distinction, carefully referring to the greatness of Byrd's achievements and not the greatness of the man—whom Balchen had come to hate—during an interview with the *Saturday Evening Post*.[1]

Byrd was clearly not the superman he was made out to be. He was not even a good aviator. He was a poor pilot and a fumbling navigator, and he trembled when he flew. Nor was he the paragon he tried to appear. Egocentric and insecure, Byrd pursued his personal goals relentlessly. He occasionally drank when he should not have. At times he acted underhandedly or bent the truth—flagrantly lying at least once—and exaggerated his accomplishments. He distanced himself from the other leaders on the expedition and found sharing authority difficult. Davies commented, "I think Byrd was quite jealous of the degree of affection shown by nearly all of us to Larry and Bernt."[2] Byrd sought blind loyalty from the lower-ranking members and tried to unite them behind him and his personal aims. In a way calculated to achieve his ends, he practiced showmanship, sought personal glorification, and managed his heroic image to an extent that some others found offensive. In fairness to Byrd, he had to be conscious of publicity to pay his bills. He was, as he stated, in the "hero business."

Although Byrd might be criticized for not handling leadership challenges with finesse and for alienating many of his top people, he had reason to fear losing control of his expedition. The crew of Smith's flight that discovered Marie Byrd Land had disobeyed the leader's orders and nearly ruined his careful orchestration. One of his ship's captains flirted with mutiny, and the other may have contemptuously disregarded orders. In his relations with Gould, Byrd regretted the one time he had given in to the geologist, when the trip to the Rockefeller Mountains had resulted in the loss of the Fokker and a scare for the safety of several men.

Owen believed that Byrd was motivated by ambition and vanity.[3] His behavior, although sometimes inexcusable, was no worse and often better than that of many self-serving climbers. When measured against other leaders, Byrd comes out well. He falls way short mainly when measured against the image of perfection that he himself created. He certainly got the job done, however. Although Gould, perhaps justifiably, felt unfairly treated, the geologist would never have climbed the antarctic mountains without Byrd. Although Balchen did not like Byrd, the pilot would never have flown over the South Pole without the commander.

Byrd had many fine qualities. He was deeply concerned about the safety of all his men, and often he went out of his way to promote their welfare. Many of the lower-ranking men were devoted to him. At least two members of the Loyal Legion, Siple and Demas, remained unceasingly loyal. Siple accompanied Byrd on all his expeditions and worked closely with him for the rest of the admiral's life. Demas spent his retirement years defending the memory of Byrd against charges that the explorer had never reached the North Pole on the first of his famous flights.

The keys to Byrd's behavior during his first antarctic expedition are his unwavering ambition, his overarching image consciousness, his intense sense of loyalty, his almost pathological suspiciousness, and his uncompromising attitude. He set his primary personal and professional goals and put all his effort into them, never compromising for secondary goals or other peoples' goals such as the geological sledge mission or the scientific volumes. He regarded his heroic image as his most vital asset for attaining his goals, constantly chiseling it and protecting it from erosion, sometimes by dubious means, even in dealings with close associates. Absolute loyalty from others to him, and from himself to others when their goals did not conflict with his (unless their safety was at stake), meant more to him than any other virtue. If you were for Byrd, he was for you. If you were not, he was against you. Quick to suspect faithlessness, he regarded anything less than full acceptance from others as intolerable opposition. He could never have been close to Gould and Balchen, who had their own big ambitions and strong egos. It was a foregone conclusion that Byrd would loathe Russell Owen, who had virtually sole power to project Byrd's image to the world during the expedition but had different goals, a critical outlook, and a big mouth.

Byrd had suffered major disappointments in launching and conducting his expedition: the death of his first executive officer and the insanity of the replacement; the lack of enough shipping capability to get all equipment and supplies to the ice; the loss of the Fokker and the consequent curtailed flying and aerial-photography programs; and, of course, the failure to publish the technical volumes, which hurt the historical treatment of the expedition (although most of the scientific findings were eventually published separately in scholarly journals). In all probability, Byrd did not personally discover Marie Byrd Land or the Edsel Ford Mountains, and he was afraid that he might have missed the South Pole. The follow-up work ended in frustration, bitterness, and financial distress.

The admiral, however, could look back on his enterprise as a whole with abundant pride and satisfaction. A superb organizer and planner, he had overcome adversity and, through his expedition, accomplished almost all his goals: flew close enough to the pole to get credit; broadened the influence of aviation and radio and gained operating data and experience to improve their performance under polar conditions; discovered two mountain ranges; claimed a vast new territory for the United States; gathered geological information on the great horst and the Rockefeller Mountains; proved the existence of Scott Island and the nonexistence of Carmen Land; charted depths in the Southern

Ocean; collected a year's worth of data on weather, geomagnetism, the aurora, the behavior of radio waves, and other scientific phenomena in a scientifically virgin part of Antarctica; extended U.S. influence to Antarctica; and boosted America's international prestige. In the process, he had provided the world with two years of excitement and armchair adventure.

Most remarkable of all, Byrd formed and ran the expedition essentially by himself. He had help, of course, but as he often said the almost unbearable burdens really were on the shoulders of one man against the world. With the coming of big government, society may never see his like again.

An outstanding accomplishment of Byrd's mission, especially in contrast to preceding expeditions, was that he fulfilled his goal of no deaths, no major injuries, no wintertime mental breakdowns, and no nutritional illnesses. At the end of his *National Geographic* article, in a summary statement that rang true and recalled his similar words on departing almost two years previously, Byrd wrote that ". . . what matters more to me than anything else is that we left not a single man in Antarctica." Save for the evacuation episode, the well-being of the expedition was never subject to crisis. Byrd's care, caution, and thoroughness were largely responsible for that achievement. Partly because he had astutely selected Gould as second in command, Byrd also avoided discord among his men serious enough to thwart the expedition's success. Martin Ronne, the old veteran of Amundsen's expeditions, wrote Byrd that the Little America venture ". . . was for me the best expedition in every way. . . ."[4]

Byrd increased his own prestige, won promotion to Rear Admiral, and significantly furthered his career. He established the professional niche he had long sought for himself. He gained a wealth of experience and information about antarctic exploration and launched himself toward becoming America's "Mr. South Pole." Although he lost a fortune in the depression, he made a lot of money from the expedition. In addition, he helped others, including Balchen and Gould, to go on to distinguished careers (although Balchen, who became an air force colonel, later blamed Byrd for blocking a promotion to general).

Byrd's expedition made great contributions to science, technology, exploration, and American influence. Relying partly on dogs, skiers, and a wooden ship and partly on aircraft, an automobile, radio, and electricity, all efficiently organized in a businesslike way, he helped antarctic explorers out of the romantic era and into the age of advanced technology and bureaucratic expeditions. The techniques he pioneered form the basis of modern antarctic operations.

Byrd's machinations and pretensions helped to gain him space on the pages of newspapers, but his achievements earned him and his expedition a place in the pages of history.

Epilogue

BYRD's second private expedition to Little America in 1933–35 was famed for weekly voice radio broadcasts to the general public and for Byrd's stay in isolation at Advance Base, where he had to be rescued from what was said to be carbon-monoxide poisoning. The enterprise was one of Antarctica's greatest scientific expeditions and one of the most adventure-filled.

In 1939–41, Byrd led a combined private/government expedition as head of the U.S. Antarctic Service, which was to have run a continuing effort that would have been resupplied annually. He established two bases—at Little America and on the Antarctic Peninsula—but returned to the United States for the first winter. Before long, the navy eased him out of effective command and thwarted his plans to go back with the relief ships. The spread of World War II ended the enterprise prematurely.

During the war, Byrd returned to active duty in the navy's Bureau of Aeronautics, surveying islands in the Pacific and planning contingent air bases. The regular navy, put off his flamboyance and politically obtained promotions, shut him out of direct participation in the war.

The navy mounted an expedition based at Little America in 1946, Operation Highjump; but fearing that Byrd would exploit it for his personal aggrandizement, the navy installed him not as commanding officer but as officer-in-charge, an essentially powerless post, like the presidency of many countries.

In the mid-1950s, a dozen nations launched a series of coordinated antarctic expeditions in connection with the planned International Geophysical Year (IGY) of 1957–58, the event that was also to mark the launching of the first space satellites. Larry Gould was in charge of planning the U.S. antarctic program. Byrd again was appointed as officer-in-charge of the U.S. Navy's effort, Operation Deep Freeze, which supported a corps of civilian scientists. On the first trip south in 1955, the old admiral was ignored to the point of insult.

Between polar missions, Byrd served as head of various humanitarian, international, and political groups. After a long period of ill health, he died at home in Boston of what was described only as a heart ailment on 11 March 1957, at age sixty-eight.

After Byrd's first antarctic expedition, other Americans mounted antarctic ventures. At the beginning of 1934, only a short time before Byrd returned to Antarctica, Lincoln Ellsworth, in partnership with Wilkins, sailed to Little America to fly across the continent. Balchen, Braathen, and Coman were in the party. The project was aborted when the bay's ice split under their plane and wrecked it. The next year, Ellsworth tried to fly to Little America from the Antarctic Peninsula, but bad weather stopped him. In November 1935, he and pilot Herbert Hollick-Kenyon made the flight from the peninsula to Byrd's old base. Again with Wilkins, Ellsworth ran a summer-only expedition to the antarctic coast of the Indian Ocean in 1938.

In 1947–48, Martin Ronne's son Finn, an immigrant to America who had been with Byrd on his second and third antarctic expeditions, ran a scientific and exploratory venture to the Antarctic Peninsula, adding the Ronne Ice Shelf to the maps. (In his 1979 biography, Finn Ronne claimed that Byrd had confessed in 1930 to Isaiah Bowman, President of the American Geographical Society, that his famous flight to the North Pole had actually been off the mark by 150 miles. Ronne said that Bowman, in revealing this information, swore Ronne to secrecy until after Bowman's death, which came in 1950. When asked about Byrd's character in a private 1967 interview, however, Ronne disparaged Byrd but did not even hint that he had missed the North Pole.)

Byrd had predicted a continuing American expedition in an interview with the *New York Times* on his way home after his first expedition. Presciently, he pictured an aircraft squadron transported by an icebreaker through the pack even before it broke up, then the planes carrying scientists throughout Antarctica. Byrd guessed that a continuous expedition could map the continent in five or six years. He declared such an expedition would be so expensive it would need government backing (which he considered not likely). In another far-seeing statement, he envisioned permanent stations in Antarctica.[1]

His predictions essentially came to pass when the American IGY expedition was continued indefinitely, with the main base on Mc-Murdo Sound's side of Ross Island and with several other bases on the continent. The civilian scientific effort is called the U.S. Antarctic Research Program (USARP), and the navy's logistic support mission is still known as Operation Deep Freeze. The overall expedition is run by the National Science Foundation. Techniques and equipment—such as windproof fabrics—that were developed on or for the Byrd expeditions are still used.

The United States never officially ratified the territorial claims made by Byrd and America's other antarctic explorers. In 1959, America and eleven other nations having interests in Antarctica signed the Antarctic Treaty, agreeing to hold claims in abeyance and preserving the continent for science.

Through the decades of exploration by many countries since Byrd's first expedition, Antarctica has been entirely mapped, and even the nature of the land beneath the ice is generally known. The great horst, now known as the Transantarctic Mountains, ends not far from Gould's last camp in Marie Byrd Land. The ocean under the barrier, now known as the Ross Ice Shelf, does not continue across the continent but ends approximately at a line connecting the end of the horst with the Rockefeller Mountains. If all the ice melted and the ocean flooded low-lying areas, about half of Antarctica—roughly that part containing the pole and lying mostly in the eastern hemisphere—would be a plateau fringed partly by the horst. The rest, where Byrd's first expedition concentrated—Marie Byrd Land, the Rockefeller and Edsel Ford Mountains, the sea covered by the barrier—would be a vast archipelago. A huge island (Roosevelt Island) was discovered under the ice south of Little America where Gould predicted, confirming the belief that this island slowed the seaward movement of the barrier at Byrd's camp.

No new animals or enclaves of life have been discovered or are expected to be found on Antarctica or on the nearby islands as Byrd had hoped.

Byrd's first antarctic expedition heavily influenced the subsequent lives of most members, many of whom gave society the benefits of their unique experiences in Antarctica.

Many members of the winter party served with distinction in World War II. Eleven made post-war careers in the military or as civilians working for the military, nine of them as specialists in cold-weather operations. Ten followed careers in military or civilian aviation. Four were killed in air crashes.

Gould, Berkner, and Siple achieved worldwide eminence in science. They, with Goodale and Bursey, played key roles in both the American and international aspects of the IGY and in the establishment of the continuing USARP–Operation Deep Freeze expedition.

Of the foreign-born members, only Ronne, Braathen, and Davies returned permanently to their original homelands.

The following items summarize the available but often limited information about the subsequent lives of the members of the winter party of Byrd's first expedition:

Bernt Balchen returned to Antarctica as chief pilot for the Ellsworth-Wilkins expedition. He served as Amelia Earhart's technical advisor for the first solo transatlantic flight by a women. He helped to establish Norwegian Airlines but joined the U.S. Air Corps as a captain during the war, helping to establish an air base in Greenland and flying many daring missions to rescue downed aviators and to supply the Norwegian underground. After the war, Balchen assumed the presidency of Norwegian Airlines, which under him became the parent company of Scandinavian Airlines. Returning to active duty with the air force, he commanded the 10th Rescue Squadron in Alaska and won promotion to colonel.

Balchen was the subject of a 1950 biography. He wrote an autobiography, which was published in 1958. Byrd died during the writing. Balchen said the admiral's influential family and friends put legal pressure on himself and his publisher to kill the book, already printed, because of revelations and evaluations of the admiral not to the family's liking—including the statement that Floyd Bennett had hinted strongly that he and Byrd had never reached the North Pole. Balchen cut or toned down material they found objectionable and, at his own expense, arranged another printing.

Gould, who remained Balchen's lifelong friend, subsequently warned him in a letter about the other dangers of being too candid: "I am quite sure that the National Geographic Society with all the power it has—and I have discovered it is very great—would immediately rise to denounce you as a detractor of Byrd. I am not sure but that the Navy, much as they hated him, would likewise rise to his defense. . . . Byrd is an established myth, and I think we have to leave it to history to take care of that. I honestly believe that none of us who was intimately associated with him should be concerned directly with it."[2]

In 1971, nevertheless, in an interview published in an aviation history—and in a press conference shortly after—Balchen claimed that Bennett had actually confessed that he and Byrd had never reached the North Pole.[3]

Balchen died of bone cancer 17 October 1973, at age seventy-three.

Quin A. Blackburn   led the Queen Maud Range geological party on Byrd's second expedition. Blackburn worked for the U.S. Bureau of Land Management, and he died 8 February 1981, at age eighty-two.

George H. Black   won many decorations in the European theater of the war, and he remained in the army as a career sergeant. Black died 28 July 1965, at age sixty-eight.

Christoffer Braathen   served as a flight mechanic on the Ellsworth-Wilkins expedition and worked with Balchen at Norwegian Airlines. Braathen was killed as a passenger in the crash of a private plane on 1 August 1937, at age forty-two.

Kennard F. Bubier   advanced to lieutenant colonel in the marines then, with Demas, worked eleven years for Lockheed Corporation. Bubier reportedly died sometime after 1978.

Jacob Bursey worked on a ship on the Great Lakes after the expedition and later led a dog team exploration party on the U.S. Antarctic Service Expedition. Joining the U.S. Coast Guard, he participated in three arctic expeditions and rose to the rank of lieutenant commander. He also served as a technical advisor on Operation Deep Freeze. Bursey published an autobiography in 1957, and he died 23 March 1980, at age seventy-six.

Arnold H. Clarke attended MIT with Byrd's help after the expedition, joining the Woods Hole Oceanographic Institute. Clarke died 12 March 1976, at age seventy-two.

Francis D. Coman resumed duties at Johns Hopkins after the expedition but signed on as physician to the Ellsworth-Wilkins expedition. Coman earned his Ll.D. degree in 1940. During the war he served as a consultant to the War Production Board and to the Quartermaster General's Office. Ironically, during the last five years of his life, Coman worked closely with Siple, from whom he had been aloof on Byrd's expedition. Coman died in his sleep at age fifty-six on 21 January 1952, at the Canadian-U.S. Test and Development Center near Fort Churchill on Hudson Bay, reportedly after running nude in thirty-degree-below weather, repeating the stunt he had pulled at Little America.[4]

Frederick E. Crockett prospected for gold in the southwest. With his wife, an anthropologist, he organized an expedition to the islands in the southern and western Pacific in the mid-1930s. Crockett served in the OSS and was an instructor at an arctic training camp in Colorado during the war. He headed a real estate office for most of his career, dying at age seventy on 17 January, 1978, after heart surgery.

Victor H. Czegka joined Byrd's second expedition as general manager. Czegka died 18 February 1973, at age ninety-two.

Frank T. Davies did extensive work in the arctic. He also played a key role in Canada's space satellite program. Davies died 23 September 1981, at age seventy-seven.

Joe De Ganahl rose to lieutenant commander. He was killed 21 July

1943, at age thirty-nine, when the navy plane he was piloting crashed near Sitka, Alaska. Famed sprinter Charlie Paddock also died in the crash.

Epaminondas J. Demas   with help from Byrd, got a scholarship to New York University. After graduating, Demas joined Byrd's second expedition. Later, Demas worked with Bubier for Lockheed Corporation as an aeronautical engineer. Demas died 17 November 1979, at age seventy-two.

James A. Feury   owned and operated a tavern, although he reportedly quit drinking later in life. He died 30 December 1977, at age seventy-eight.

Edward E. Goodale   served as a consultant to the air corps, establishing bases in northern Canada and Greenland at the beginning of the war; some of this work was with Vaughan. Later commissioned, Goodale directed search-and-rescue missions in the North Atlantic, rising to lieutenant colonel. He joined the U.S. Weather Bureau, becoming deputy chief of polar operations and supervising the establishment of arctic weather stations. He helped to plan and run antarctic operations for IGY and directed New Zealand's operations for USARP. Reportedly having suffered from Alzheimer's disease, Goodale died sometime after 1986.

Charles F. Gould   went back to working as a merchant seaman. He reportedly died sometime before 1978.

Laurence M. Gould   never launched his own antarctic expedition. Gould joined the faculty of Carleton College and founded the Department of Geology and Geography. During the war he served as chief of the arctic branch of the Arctic, Desert, and Tropic Information Center of the air corps. He was elected president of Carleton. Gould became a member of the National Science Foundation's board, chairman of the U.S. IGY antarctic committee, chairman of the Committee on Polar Research of the National Academy of Sciences, president of the International Scientific Committee on Antarctic Research, and president of the American Association for the Advancement of Science.

Gould corresponded once in a while with Byrd. Over the years, although they sometimes worked at cross purposes, their letters became friendlier. In letters for Harrison's newsletter, circulated among expedition members, Gould has mentioned Byrd with nothing but high regard. Gould is living in Arizona at this writing.

William C. Haines returned to Little America with Byrd's second expedition as third in command. Haines became assistant meteorologist at the St. Louis Weather Bureau. He died 7 April 1956, at age sixty-nine.

Malcolm P. Hanson rose to commander. He worked in England on the development of radar and was reportedly one of the top three engineers on that project.[5] Hanson died in August 1942, at age forty-seven, when his navy plane crashed on a secret mission in the Aleutians, presumably in a radar experiment.

Henry T. Harrison returned to the Weather Bureau, then became flight dispatcher for United Air Lines at Cleveland. He served as a meteorologist in the air corps during the war. Harrison became director of meteorology for United Air Lines. He is living in North Carolina at this writing.

Harold I. June rose to chief aviation pilot, the highest enlisted rank in the navy. He joined Byrd's second expedition as chief pilot. June represented United Aircraft Corporation overseas, returning to active duty in the navy during the war. He joined Kaman Corporation, the helicopter manufacturer, then went back to United Aircraft. June died 22 November 1962, at age sixty-seven.

Charles E. Lofgren accompanied Byrd on a cross-country lecture tour after the expedition. Lofgren served as a personnel officer in the navy during the war and rose to commander. Resuming his position as head of the Fleet Reserve Association, he became a registered lobbyist representing navy and marine enlisted men. Lofgren died of cancer at age seventy-seven on 26 November 1971.

Howard F. Mason served in the navy during the war and then became a civilian electronics engineer with the navy. Mason is living in Washington state at this writing.

Ashley C. McKinley received the U.S. Air Corps's Legion of Merit award for exceptional service in testing and developing cold-weather equipment during the war. He advanced to colonel, and he died on 11 February 1970, at age seventy-three.

Thomas B. Mulroy worked for the U.S. Maritime Administration. He died in June 1962, at age sixty-five.

John S. O'Brien wrote several books for boys about arctic adventure. He died of cancer on 6 December 1938, at age forty-one.

Russell Owen returned to the *New York Times*. He wrote two books about polar regions besides his book on Byrd's expedition. Owen died of a heart attack at age sixty-three on 3 April 1952.

Alton N. Parker became a pilot for TWA. He died of a heart attack at age forty-seven on 30 November 1942.

Carl O. Petersen converted to Paramount cameraman for Byrd's second expedition. Petersen joined the navy and became a lieutenant on the aircraft carrier *Ranger*. He died 10 November 1941, at age forty-three.

Martin Ronne returned to Norway and died in the spring of 1932 at age seventy-two.

Benjamin Roth reportedly died sometime before 1978.

Joseph T. Rucker returned to Paramount, and died on 21 October 1957, at age seventy.

Paul A. Siple graduated from college and went on to earn his Ph.D. in geography. Siple worked with Byrd in running all the succeeding private and government expeditions with which the admiral was associated, returning to Antarctica six times and spending more time there than any other person in history. During the war, Siple served the army as an expert on cold-weather operations, rising to the rank of lieutenant colonel. He spent most of his post-war career as a science advisor to the army's Research and Development Department, where he worked with Coman. Siple developed the concept of the windchill factor, working out the equation on which the table is based. He was named president of the Association of American Geographers, and he was posted in Australia as the science advisor to the U.S. embassies in Australia and New Zealand. Siple died of a heart attack on 25 November 1968, at age fifty-nine.

Dean C. Smith worked for American Air Lines, Leaming Curtiss Company, Fairchild Aviation, Hughes Tool Company, and Douglas Aircraft Company. In 1934 he received the Harmon trophy as America's most outstanding aviator. He became president of the National Air Pilots Association. In 1954 Byrd, in a mellow mood and estranged from Balchen, wrote Smith about the flights to rescue Gould's party in the Rockefeller Mountains and to lay the polar flight's supply cache: "I still find myself . . . regretting that I did not recognize those two magnificent exploits of yours by making you the pilot of the plane that flew to the south pole. It is sometimes difficult for a leader to see things clearly. I now think that you showed bigness not to get sore as hell at me."[6] (One wonders if Byrd's flattery and exceptional generosity toward Smith were designed to make Smith feel better about Byrd and forget about writing an exposé.) In 1961 Smith wrote a revealing book about his flying career before and during the Byrd expedition. Smith died of a heart attack on 4 March 1987, at age eighty-six.

Sverre A. Strom became master of a yacht in Boston. He served as a coast guard port captain in the arctic during the war. He became police chief of Worcester, Massachusetts, but he was an arctic specialist with the rank of captain in the air force's Strategic Air Command at the time of his death on 15 June 1950, at age fifty-six.

George W. Tennant continued as an itinerant cook. He died of a heart attack on 15 February 1953, at age seventy.

George A. Thorne reportedly died in the crash of his private plane in the late 1930s.

Willard Van der Veer returned to Paramount. No information is available after the mid-1970s.

Norman D. Vaughan represented the United States in the dog sled races in the 1932 winter Olympics at Lake Placid. He performed search-and-rescue work for the air corps in Europe and northern Canada during the war. In the Battle of the Bulge, he used dog teams to make spectacular rescues of the crews of disabled tanks, and he made a postwar career in the air force's search-and-rescue division. He owned a sporting goods store but became superintendant of maintenance at the University of Alaska. Late in life, while in his seventies, he was in the news again for competing in the Iditarod dog sledge race from Anchorage to Nome. Vaughan is living in Alaska at this writing.

Arthur T. Walden died of a heart attack at age seventy-six after helping his eighty-six-year-old wife out of a burning house, on 26 March 1947.

The following information concerns a few other key people who were involved with the expedition:

Lloyd V. Berkner returned to the National Bureau of Standards after the expedition, then joined the Carnegie Institution. He served as a navy captain during the war. He administered the first military assistance program under the North Atlantic Treaty. Berkner became president of several scientific organizations: the university group that runs Brookhaven National Laboratory, the International Council of Scientific Unions, the space science board of the National Academy of Sciences, and the Graduate Research Center of the Southwest. He is called the Father of the IGY for proposing it in 1950. Berkner died of a heart attack at age sixty-two on 4 June 1967.

Gustav L. Brown became captain of a mail liner. He died 3 December 1950, at age fifty-eight.

Richard G. Brophy was wounded by police while fleeing after attempting to steal a taxi in 1935, and he was committed to a mental hospital. In 1937, he announced plans for an autogyro expedition to the arctic. He was found dead of natural causes in a hotel room on 28 May 1938, at age forty-seven.

Charles J. V. Murphy wintered over at Little America on Byrd's second expedition. Murphy spent the rest of his career as a writer for *Fortune* magazine, serving as the Washington Bureau's chief for fourteen years. He continued to ghostwrite for Byrd. Murphy ghosted books for the Duke and Duchess of Windsor and wrote books under his own name about the Windsors and others. He wrote the classic children's story "Little Toot." Murphy died 29 December 1987, at age eighty-three.

Hilton H. Railey became, in 1931, the business manager of an unsuccessful Wilkins-Ellsworth project to sail a submarine to the North Pole. He undertook a series of other interesting jobs and wrote a book about his career in 1938. No information is available after that date.

On his second antarctic expedition, Byrd recovered the Ford plane he had flown over the South Pole, which is now on display at the Ford Museum in Dearborn, Michigan, and the Fairchild, which also flew on the second expedition. The Fairchild flew for twenty-five more years for various owners. Overhauled and cannibalized, but still largely the plane Byrd's pilots flew, it is now owned by the Smithsonian Institution but on indefinite loan to the Virginia Aviation Museum in Richmond.

The expedition's flagship, the *City of New York*, reportedly caught fire and was destroyed in Nova Scotia some time before 1982. No information is available on the fate of the *Eleanor Bolling*.

In December 1955, during the initial Operation Deep Freeze, Byrd and Siple returned to the site at Little America where the buildings of Byrd's first expedition had been erected. The camp was deeply buried—all they could see were the tips of the sixty-five-foot-tall radio towers barely poking out of the snow. The sides of what had been the Bay of Whales had come together, obliterating the once-huge indentation. Late in 1987, the entire Bay of Whales section broke away from the barrier and floated off. All of Little America now lies somewhere at the bottom of the great Southern Ocean.

Notes

PREFACE

1. Montague, *Oceans, Poles and Airmen*, 289–300.
2. Correspondence and records, Byrd papers, box 86.1 files 3, 6–11, 13, 15–19, 22–23; box 93 files 20–22, 30–31; box 1024 files 2–7.

CHAPTER 1

1. Byrd, *Skyward*, 204.
2. Ibid.
3. *Literary Digest*, 27 July 1927, 34–35.
4. Byrd, *Skyward*, 29.
5. Ibid., 30.
6. Ibid., 79, 122; Hoyt, *Last Explorer*, 43, 50.
7. Hoyt, *Last Explorer*, 7.
8. Byrd, *Skyward*, 140.
9. Ibid., 343.
10. Ibid., 142; Grosvenor, NEA address; Hoyt, *Last Explorer*, 76.
11. Byrd to Amundsen, 23 Feb. 1926, Wilson files.
12. Hoyt, *Last Explorer*, 100.
13. Balchen, *Come North With Me*, 54.
14. Byrd, *Discovery*, xiii; Murphy, *Struggle*, 221.

15. Byrd, *Little America*, 7.
16. Morris and Smith, *Ceiling Unlimited*, 255.
17. Byrd, *Skyward*, 236.
18. Balchen, unidentified manuscript, Balchen papers, National Archives.
19. Montague, *Oceans, Poles and Airmen*, 69.
20. Ibid., 35.
21. Green, *Dick Byrd*, 209.
22. Joe and Olga Hill, *In Little America with Byrd*, 6.
23. *N.Y. Times*, 7 July 1927.

CHAPTER 2

1. *N.Y. Times*, 7 July 1927.
2. Ibid., 3 July 1927.
3. Balchen, *Come North*, 125.
4. *N.Y. Times*, 14 July and 7 Sept. 1927; Balchen, *Come North*, 149.
5. *N.Y. Times*, 5 Aug. 1927.
6. Ibid., 8 Aug. 1927.
7. Balchen, *Come North*, 129; *N.Y. Times*, 5 Aug. 1927.
8. Joyce to Wilkins, 15 Aug. 1927, Byrd papers, box 12 file 8; Byrd, "Crusaders," *Saturday Evening Post*, 22 Sept. 1928, 174.
9. Howe, *Popular Mechanics*, 196; Murphy, *Struggle*, xii; *N.Y. Times*, 7 July and 12 Mar. 1928.
10. Hoyt, *Last Explorer*, 71; Byrd, *National Geographic*, 128; *N.Y. Times*, 1 July 1928.
11. Mason, speech, 13, 14–15; Railey, *Touch'd With Madness*, 116–117.
12. Byrd, *Little America*, 36, 259; Hoyt, *Last Explorer*, 167; *N.Y. Times*, 7 July 1927 and 1 July 1928.
13. *N.Y. Times*, 7 July, 1 Dec., 4 Dec., and 26 Dec. 1927, and 29 July 1928; *Literary Digest*, 7 Apr. 1928, 36–38; Byrd to Amundsen, 26 Mar. 1928, Wilson files; Byrd, *Saturday Evening Post*, 21 Apr. 1928, 54.
14. *N.Y. Times*, 26 Nov. 1927, and 1 July and 15 Aug. 1928; Byrd, *Saturday Evening Post*, 21 Apr. 1928, 54; Green, *Dick Byrd*, 265; Byrd, *Little America*, 22, 25; master of Kane Lodge to Byrd, 28 Feb. 1930, Byrd papers, box 13; Strom to Melville, undated, Byrd papers, box 154 file 39. Quotation is from Byrd, *Skyward*, 307.
15. Byrd, *Saturday Evening Post*, 21 Apr. 1928, 12.
16. Ibid., 13.
17. Siple, personal interview; Byrd, *National Geographic*, 128; *N.Y. Times*, 1 July 1928. Quotation is from *N.Y. Times*, 18 Mar. 1928.
18. Carter, *Little America*, 40; Hoyt, *Last Explorer*, 71.
19. Carter, *Little America*, 39; Bernays, *Biography of an Idea*, 346; Hoyt, *Last Explorer*, 261.
20. Contracts, Byrd papers, box 1008 file 14; Railey to Byrd, radiogram, 17 Jan. 1930, Byrd papers, box 10.1 file 13; Byrd to ship's crew, memo, 24 Dec. 1928, Byrd papers, box 13; Byrd, *Skyward*, 325.
21. Byrd, *Skyward*, 324; Hoyt, *Last Explorer*, 71.
22. Andrews, *This Business of Exploring*, 14.

23. Byrd, *Skyward*, 234; Bruno, *Wings Over America*, 170. Quotation is from Demas, diaries, 30 June 1929.
24. Demas, diaries, 11 July 1929.
25. Byrd, *Skyward*, 221; Murphy, *Struggle*, 321.
26. Murphy, *Struggle*, 51; Hoyt, *Last Explorer*, 157.
27. Murphy, *Struggle*, 359; Smith, *By the Seat*, 178.
28. *N.Y. Times*, 25 Dec. 1927, and 31 Mar. 1928; Konow to Byrd, correspondence, 14 July 1927, Byrd papers, box 108 file 11; Owen, *South of the Sun*, 103; Balchen, *Come North*, 133; Byrd to Amundsen, 13 February 1927, Wilson files; Byrd, *National Geographic*, 129.
29. *N.Y. Times*, 15 Mar. and 2 June 1928; Byrd to Liberty National Bank, Byrd papers, box 107 file 8.
30. Knight and Durham, *Hitch Your Wagon*, 137; *N.Y. Times*, 23 Aug. and 14 and 23 Sept. 1927, and 6 May 1928.
31. Balchen, *Come North*, 134; *N.Y. Times*, 12 Oct. 1927, and 9 Apr. and 28 May 1928.
32. *N.Y. Times*, 10 Apr. 1928; Balchen, *Come North*, 134.
33. Byrd, *Little America*, 37.
34. *N.Y. Times*, 13 Mar. and 27 Apr. 1930.
35. Ibid., 11 Mar. 1928; Siple, *A Boy Scout With Byrd*, 153, and *Ninety Degrees South*, 75; Simmons, *Target Arctic*, 60. Quotation is from Byrd, *Skyward*, 280–281.
36. Balchen, *Come North*, 139; *N.Y. Times*, 20 and 26 Apr. 1928.
37. *N.Y. Times*, 19 June, 5 Aug., and 5 Dec. 1927, and 29 Apr. and 9 May 1928; Murphy, *Struggle*, 329.
38. Montague, *Oceans, Poles and Airmen*, 221.

CHAPTER 3

1. *N.Y. Times*, 19 May 1928.
2. Ibid., 18 and 30 May 1928; *Nation*, 30 May 1928, 603.
3. *N.Y. Times*, 5 and 7 June and 22 Aug. 1928.
4. Byrd to Railey, radiogram, 5 Aug. 1929, Byrd papers, box 12 file 2; Murphy, *Struggle*, 366. Quotation is from Earl Hanson, *The Nation*, 418–420.
5. *N.Y. Times*, 29 Sept. 1928.
6. Byrd, *Little America*, 29; Hoyt, *Last Explorer*, 164.
7. *N.Y. Times*, 20 and 22 June, 1 and 19 July, and 3 Aug. 1928; Byrd, *National Geographic*, 128.
8. Carter, *Little America*, 36.
9. *N.Y. Times*, 2, 4, 19, and 20 June 1928; Railey, *Touch'd With Madness*, 100.
10. Quotation is from Railey, *Touch'd With Madness*, 112. Byrd to Railey, radiogram, 10 Apr. 1929, in Byrd's diary.
11. Byrd, *Little America*, 10–11; Railey, *Touch'd With Madness*, 109.
12. Byrd, *Little America*, 245; Byrd to Amundsen, 13 Dec. 1927 and 26 Mar. 1928, Wilson files.
13. *N.Y. Times*, 1 July, 17 Aug., and 2 Oct. 1928; Carter, *Little America*, 44.
14. Byrd, *Little America*, 35.
15. Hoyt, *Last Explorer*, 61; McGuinness, *Sailor of Fortune*, 242; *N.Y. Times*, 19 July, 2 and 3 Aug., and 20 Sept. 1928; Byrd, *National Geographic*, 156; Byrd, *Little America*, 15.

16. *N.Y. Times*, 1 July, 2 and 17 Aug. 1928; Hoyt, *Last Explorer*, 165.

17. *N.Y. Times*, 15 Aug. 1928.

18. *Literary Digest*, 15 Sept. 1928, 41; *N.Y. Times*, 3, 9 and 16 Aug. and 17 Sept. 1928.

19. *N.Y. Times*, 4, 24, and 29 Aug. 1928, and 10 Aug. 1930.

20. Ibid., 22 June, and 4, 8, 9, 11, 20, and 26 Aug. 1928. Quotation is from 9 Aug. 1928.

21. Ibid., 18 and 19 Aug. 1928; Byrd, *Little America*, 22, 194; Byrd, *National Geographic*, 233; Hoyt, *Last Explorer*, 51. Quotation is from *N.Y. Times*, 7 July 1927.

22. *N.Y. Times*, 18 Mar. and 29 July 1928.

23. Ibid., 3 and 7 July and 7 Sept. 1927, and 11 Mar., 1 Apr., 1 July, and 3 Aug. 1928; salary records, Byrd papers, box 120 file 2; Byrd, *Saturday Evening Post*, 21 Apr. 1928, 58.

24. Personnel contracts, Byrd papers, box 12 file 5.

25. *N.Y. Times*, 20 and 23 Aug. 1928.

26. Harrison, diary, 22 Aug. 1928.

27. Ibid., 31 Aug. 1929; *N.Y. Times*, 13 July 1928.

28. Carter, *Little America*, 39; *N.Y. Times*, 26 Aug. 1928.

29. Siple, *Boy Scout*, 5; Siple, diaries, 25 Aug. and 7 Sept. 1928; *N.Y. Times*, 27 and 31 Aug. and 18 Sept. 1928.

30. Siple, diaries, 25 Aug. 1928; Byrd, memo to expedition, 10 Jan. 1929, Byrd papers, box 13; *N.Y. Times*, 28 Aug. and 1 Oct. 1928.

31. Carter, *Little America*, 47, 50; *N.Y. Times*, 26 Aug. 1928.

32. *N.Y. Times*, 31 Aug. 1928.

33. Carter, *Little America*, 48; Adams, *Beyond the Barrier With Byrd*, 54.

34. Adams, *Beyond the Barrier With Byrd*, 57; *N.Y. Times*, 20 Sept. 1928.

35. *N.Y. Times*, 21 Sept. 1928.

36. Ibid., 19 and 21 Sept. 1928.

37. Ibid., 1 Oct. 1928; Byrd, *Little America*, 11; Murphy, *Struggle*, 364.

38. Murphy, *Struggle*, 366.

39. Murphy, *Struggle*, 366; Railey to Byrd, radiogram, 13 Jan. 1931, Byrd papers, box 132 file 75; *N.Y. Times*, 29 and 30 Sept. 1928.

40. *N.Y. Times*, 11 Mar., 9 Aug., 30 Sept., and 1 and 4 Oct. 1928.

41. *N.Y. Times*, 6 Oct. 1928; Smith, *By the Seat*, 182.

42. *N.Y. Times*, 11 and 12 Oct. 1928; Byrd, *Skyward*, 300. Quotation is from *N.Y. Times*, 11 Oct. 1928.

43. Gould, diaries, 26 Jan. 1929; Hatch, *The Byrds*, 311; Murphy, *Life*, 30 Oct. 1939, 29; Steinberg, *Admiral Byrd*, 37; Hoyt, *Last Explorer*, 34.

44. *N.Y. Times*, 6 Oct. 1928.

45. Paper headed "Dec. 2, 1928, enroute San Pedro, Cal.," Byrd papers, box 10.1 file 8.

46. *N.Y. Times*, 20 May 1929.

47. Ibid., 11 Oct. 1928.

48. Ibid.; Murphy, *Struggle*, 335. Quotation is from Byrd, *Skyward*, 281.

49. *N.Y. Times*, 11 Oct. 1928.

CHAPTER 4

1. *N.Y. Times*, 26 Aug. 1928 and 16 Apr. 1929; Smith, manuscript, 149, 652–653; Smith, *By the Seat*, 653; Demas, diaries, Sept. 1928.

2. Owen, *South of the Sun*, 39; Balchen, *Come North*, 159; Demas, diaries, 25 Oct. 1928; R. E. Byrd to M. A. Byrd, 12 and 16 Nov. 1928, Byrd papers, box 13 file 18; R. E. Byrd to M. A. Byrd, undated, Byrd papers, box 1007 file 6.

3. Demas, diaries, 31 Oct.–3 Nov. and 4 Nov. 1928.

4. *N.Y. Times*, 16 Aug. 1928; Byrd, *National Geographic*, 128; Carter, *Little America*, 35.

5. Siple, diaries, 3 Sept., 12 Oct., and 9 Dec. 1928; Siple, personal interview; Harrison, diary, 12 Oct. 1928; Davies, oral history tape.

6. Demas, diaries, Sept. 1928; Harrison, diary, 31 Aug. and 18 and 24 Sept. 1928; Siple, diaries, 30 Aug. and 22 and 27 Sept. 1928; Balchen, *Come North*, 161.

7. Harrison, diary, 17 Sept. 1928; *N.Y. Times*, 17 and 18 Sept. 1928; Siple, diaries, 16, 17, and 18 Sept. 1928; Siple, personal interview.

8. Adams, *Beyond the Barrier With Byrd*, 248; *N.Y. Times*, 21 Apr. 1928; Siple, diaries, 15 Sept. 1928; Siple, personal interview; list of contributors, Byrd papers, box 13 file 5.

9. Harrison, diary, 16 and 19 Sept. and 26–27 Oct. 1928; Demas, diaries, 26–27 Oct. 1928.

10. Harrison, diary, 24 Oct. 1928; Siple, personal interview.

11. Adams, *Beyond the Barrier With Byrd*, 86, 98; Gould, diaries, 3 Nov. 1928; Harrison, diary, 1 and 4 Nov. 1928; Siple, diaries, 1 and 3 Nov. 1928.

12. Byrd, *Little America*, 15; Carter, *Little America*, 36, 53; Adams, *Beyond the Barrier With Byrd*, 59; *N.Y. Times*, 16 Aug. 1928 and 5 Dec. 1950, Brown obituary; Demas, diaries, Nov. 1928; Gould, typed diary, VI–14.

13. Siple, *Boy Scout*, 17.

14. Adams, *Beyond the Barrier With Byrd*, 85.

15. Bursey, *Antarctic Night*, 1; Byrd to Gould, 30 May 1931, Byrd papers, box 153 file 35; Gould to Byrd, 8 July 1931, Byrd papers, box 153 file 35.

16. *N.Y. Times*, 3 Aug. 1928.

17. Byrd, *Little America*, 34; *Literary Digest*, 6 Apr. 1929, 71; Murphy, *Struggle*, 1; *N.Y. Times*, 1 July and 4 Sept. 1928, and 13 July 1930.

18. Hoyt, *Last Explorer*, 174.

19. Ibid.

20. *N.Y. Times*, 22 Nov. 1928.

21. Byrd, *Little America*, 50; Byrd, *National Geographic*, 137; Demas, diaries, 5 Nov. 1928; *N.Y. Times*, 9 Nov. 1928, and 5 Jan. 1929.

22. Byrd, *Little America*, 13, 43; Hunt, *My Second Home*, 9–15.

23. Carter, *Little America*, 136; *Current History*, 30 Jan. 1930, 747; *Literary Digest*, 14 Dec. 1929, 8; *N.Y. Times*, 6 Apr. and 29 Nov. 1929.

24. *N.Y. Times*, 18 Nov. 1928; Siple, *Boy Scout*, 21; Gould, typed diary, VI–16; *World Almanac*, 1929, summary for 14 Nov.

25. Siple, personal interview.

26. *N.Y. Times*, 20 Nov. 1928.

27. Owen, *The Antarctic Ocean*, 227.

28. Harrison, diary, 29 Nov. 1928.

29. Adams, *Beyond the Barrier With Byrd*, 107; Gould, typed diary, VI–16.

30. Owen, *South of the Sun*, 41.

31. Gould, diaries, 26 Jan. 1929.
32. Byrd, *Little America*, 54; Byrd, *National Geographic*, 138; Owen, *The Conquest of the North and South Poles*, 103; Owen, *South of the Sun*, 12.
33. Demas, diaries, 29 Nov. 1928; Byrd, *Little America*, 55; *N.Y. Times*, 2 Dec. 1928 and 11 Jan. 1929.
34. Owen, *Conquest*, 106.
35. Siple, *Ninety Degrees*, 39; Owen, *Conquest*, 104.
36. *N.Y. Times*, 11 Apr. and 3 Aug. 1928; Harrison, diary, 4 Dec. 1928; Siple, *Boy Scout*, 23.
37. Demas, diaries, Dec. 1928; Harrison, diary, 7 Dec. 1928; Siple, diaries, 5 Dec. 1928.
38. *N.Y. Times*, 19 July and 13 Dec. 1928; Byrd, *Little America*, 61; Demas, diaries, Oct. 1928; Harrison, diary, 6 Oct. 1928; Siple, diaries, 6 Oct. 1928.
39. *N.Y. Times*, 5 Dec. 1928.
40. Byrd, *Little America*, 16, 50; Gould, typed diary, VI–19; Hatch, *Byrds*, 312.
41. Smith, *By the Seat*, 188; *N.Y. Times*, 26 Dec. 1928; Siple, diaries, 14 Dec. 1928.
42. Gould, typed diary, VI–19; *N.Y. Times*, 1 Apr. 1928; Adams, *Beyond the Barrier With Byrd*, 227; Byrd, *Little America*, 221; Carter, *Little America*, 60; Gould, *Cold*, 3.
43. Byrd, *National Geographic*, 141; *N.Y. Times*, 21 Dec. 1928.
44. Harrison, diary, 22 Dec. 1928.
45. Siple, diaries, 24 Dec. 1928.
46. Adams, *Beyond the Barrier With Byrd*, 132, 133; Blackburn, diary, 25 Dec. 1928; *N.Y. Times*, 23 Dec. 1928 and 27 Dec. 1971; Lofgren personnel form, Byrd papers, box 12 file 1; Demas, diaries, Dec. 1928.
47. Christmas script, 1928, Byrd papers, box 10.1 file 15.
48. Blackburn, diary, 25 Dec. 1928.
49. Byrd, *National Geographic*, 143
50. *N.Y. Times*, 28 July 1927; Byrd, *Little America*, 79; Carter, *Little America*, 63.
51. Byrd, *Little America*, 79.
52. Balchen, unidentified manuscript, 181, Balchen papers, National Archives; Blackburn, diary, 26 Dec. 1928.
53. Bursey, *Antarctic Night*, 54; Blackburn, diary, 26 Dec. 1928.
54. *N.Y. Times*, 29 July, 3 Oct., and 28 Dec. 1928; Hayes, *Antarctica*, 342; Siple, diary, 22 Dec. 1928.
55. Bursey, *Antarctic Night*, 54.
56. Expedition order, 28 Dec. 1928, Byrd papers, box 13; *N.Y. Times*, 29 Dec. 1928.
57. Gould, diaries, 28 Dec. 1928.
58. Blackburn, diary, 30 Dec. 1928; Demas, diaries, 30 Dec. 1928.
59. Byrd, *Little America*, 92.
60. Byrd, *National Geographic*, 144.

CHAPTER 5

1. Byrd, *National Geographic*, 150; Siple, *Scout to Explorer*, 13.
2. Byrd, *Little America*, 94; Byrd, *National Geographic*, 149.

3. Bursey, *Antarctic Night*, 50; Siple, diaries, 18 Dec. 1928; Gould, diaries, 6 Jan. 1929.

4. Brophy to Byrd, radiogram, 4 Jan. 1929, Byrd papers, box 13; Byrd to *N.Y. Times*, radiogram, 5 Jan. 1929, Byrd papers, box 13.

5. Hoyt, *Last Explorer*, 196; Carter, *Little America*, 69.

6. Demas, diaries, 4, 28, and 30 Jan. 1929; Harrison, diary, 7 Jan. 1929; Byrd, *Little America*, 171; Siple, *Boy Scout*, 46.

7. Byrd, *Little America*, 96; Siple, diaries, 21 Jan. 1929.

8. Byrd, *Little America*, 108; Demas, oral history tape; *N.Y. Times*, 6 Jan. 1929.

9. Blackburn, diary, 6 and 8 Jan. 1929; Harrison, diary, 8 Jan. 1929; Siple, diaries, 8 Jan. 1929; Coman to Birchall, radiogram, 14 Jan. 1929, Byrd papers, box 13 file 20; Byrd, memorandum, 20 July 1929, Byrd papers, box 1019 file 12.

10. Montague, *Oceans, Poles and Airmen*, 259; Smith, *By the Seat*, 192.

11. Byrd, memorandum, 20 July 1929, Byrd papers, box 1019 file 12; Coman to Birchall, radiograms, 11 Jan. 1929, Byrd papers, box 28.1.

12. Byrd to Birchall, radiogram, 14 Jan. 1929, Byrd papers, box 49 file 13; Owen to Birchall, radiogram, 20 Jan. 1929, Byrd papers, box 49 file 13.

13. R. E. Byrd to M. A. Byrd, 31 Jan. 1929, Byrd papers, box 1007 file 6.

14. Byrd, *Little America*, 52; *N.Y. Times*, 27 July 1927 and 11 Mar. 1928; Brody, *Popular Mechanics*, 380

15. *N.Y. Times*, 11 Mar. and 25 Dec. 1928, and 13 Sept. 1929.

16. Siple, diaries, 19 Jan. 1929.

17. Blackburn, diary, 30 Dec. 1928.

18. Siple, diaries, 20 Jan. 1929.

19. Ibid., 24 Jan. 1929; Harrison, diary, 24 Jan. 1929; Gould to Byrd, radiogram, 25 Jan. 1929, Byrd papers, box 13 file 20; Blackburn, diary, 25 Jan. 1929; Bursey, *Antarctic Night*, 62; Byrd, *Little America*, 115.

20. Blackburn, diary, 25 Jan. 1929.

21. *N.Y. Times*, 16 Aug. 1928.

22. Gould, diaries, 26 Jan. 1929; Demas, diaries, 4, 7, and 30 Jan. 1929.

23. Demas, diaries, 28 Jan. 1929; Clarke, diary, 28 Jan. 1929; Byrd, *National Geographic*, 158.

24. Demas, diaries, 29 Jan. 1929.

25. Ibid., 31 Jan. 1929; Byrd, *National Geographic*, 158; Balchen, *Come North*, 171; Blackburn, diary, 30 Jan. 1929; Owen, *South of the Sun*, 66; Siple, personal interview.

26. Demas, diaries, 31 Jan. 1929; Hatch, *Byrds*, 316; Siple, personal interview.

27. Harrison, diary, 31 Jan. 1929.

28. *N.Y. Times*, 14 Sept. 1928; Balchen, unidentified manuscript, 246, Balchen papers, National Archives; Byrd, *Little America*, 37.

29. Owen, *Conquest*, 115.

30. Hatch, *Byrds*, 252; Demas, diaries, 29 Jan. 1929.

31. Harrison, diary, 2 Feb. 1929.

32. Byrd to McKinley and Mrs. Brophy, radiogram, 3 Oct. 1929, Byrd papers, box 13; Harrison, first Byrd expedition alumni newsletter, 29 Nov. 1974, Harrison papers.

33. Bursey, *Antarctic Night*, 85.

34. Gould, diaries, 23 Feb. 1929.

35. Smith, *By the Seat*, 193.

36. Balchen, unidentified manuscript, 190–202, Balchen papers, National Ar-

chives; *N.Y. Times*, 1 July 1928; Hoyt, *Little America*, 210; Clarke, diary, 10 Feb. 1929; Demas, diaries, 6 Feb. 1929; O'Brien report, undated but with May 1929 papers, Byrd papers, box 10.1.

37. Byrd, *National Geographic*, 150; Carter, *Little America*, 71; Clarke, diary, 28 Feb. and 1 Mar. 1929.

38. Hoyt, *Last Explorer*, 233; Demas, diaries, 10 Feb. 1929; Blackburn, diary, 21 Jan. 1929.

39. Adams, Beyond the Barrier With Byrd, 143; Byrd, *Little America*, 147; Clarke, diary, 20 Feb. 1929.

40. Blackburn, diary, 23 Feb. 1929; Byrd, diary, 19 June 1929, Byrd papers, box 12 file 2; Byrd to director of Buffalo's Museum of Science, Byrd papers, box 154 file 35; Gould, diary, VI–2; Harrison, diary, 9 Jan. 1929.

41. Carter, *Little America*, 77; Siple, personal interview; Byrd, diary, 25 Apr. 1929, Byrd papers, box 12 file 2; Greason to Balchen, 13 and 19 Apr. 1932, Balchen papers, accession no. 1007578, Air Force History Center.

42. Byrd, *Little America*, 147; Demas, diaries, 22 Feb. 1929; Gould, diary, V2–14.

43. Quotation is from *Literary Digest*, 15 Sept. 1928, 41. *N.Y. Times*, 21 Aug. 1928.

44. *N.Y. Times*, 5, 10, 21, and 23 Aug. 1928; Siple, *Boy Scout*, 153; Siple, personal interview.

45. Siple, diaries, 30 Dec. 1928 and 22 Feb. 1929; *N.Y. Times*, 5 Aug. 1928; Carter, *Little America*, 67; Siple, *Boy Scout*, 58, and *Ninety Degrees*, 41.

46. *N.Y. Times*, 16 Feb. 1929.

47. Demas, diaries, 24 Feb. 1929; McGuinness, *Sailor*, 263; Siple, diaries, 24 Feb. 1929.

48. Byrd, *Little America*, 153.

49. Blackburn, diary, 27 Feb. 1929; Byrd, *National Geographic*, 169.

50. Siple, *Boy Scout*, 68.

51. Gould, diaries, 8 Apr. 1929 and V2–37; Clarke, diary, 3 Apr. 1929; Blackburn, diary, 28 Apr. 1929.

52. Gould diaries, 3 Feb. and 4 Mar. 1929; *N.Y. Times*, 8 Mar. 1929; Owen, *Conquest*, 138; Siple, diaries, 5 Mar. 1929.

53. Balchen, *Come North*, 165; *N.Y. Times*, 11 Mar. 1928.

54. Byrd, *Little America*, 1; list of contributors, Byrd papers, box 13 file 5; Adams, *Beyond the Barrier With Byrd*, 39, 54; Byrd, *Little America*, 363.

55. R. E. Byrd to M. A. Byrd, 28 Nov. 1928, Byrd papers, box 13 file 18; Brophy to Byrd, radiogram, 20 Dec. 1928, Byrd papers, box 13 file 6; Byrd to Brophy, radiogram, 2 Jan. 1929, Byrd papers, box 13.

56. *Yankee* magazine interview manuscript, Wilson files.

57. Quotation is from Bursey, *Antarctic Night*, 72. Byrd, *Little America*, 170.

58. Siple, diaries, 14 Mar. 1929; Demas, diaries, 19 Oct. 1929.

CHAPTER 6

1. Adams, *Beyond the Barrier With Byrd*, 203; Byrd, *National Geographic*, 152; Clarke, diary, 6 Oct. 1929.

2. Demas, diaries, Jan. 1929. Quotation is from Byrd, *National Geographic*, 153.

3. Knight and Durham, *Hitch Your Wagon*, 147; Smith, *By the Seat*, 178. Quotation is from Byrd, *Little America*, 14.

4. Demas, diaries, Feb. 1929. Byrd, *Saturday Evening Post*, 22 Sept. 1928; *Little America Times*, 30 Sept. 1934, 363; *N.Y. Times*, 28 May 1928 and 23 Nov. 1962; Adams, *Beyond the Barrier With Byrd*, 228.

5. Smith, *By the Seat*, 194.

6. Byrd, *National Geographic*, 155; Harrison, diary, 24 Jan. 1929.

7. Demas, diaries, 11 Jan. 1929.

8. Balchen, unidentified manuscript, 1–36, Balchen papers, National Archives.

9. Smith, *By the Seat*, 182.

10. Owen, *South of the Sun*, 152; Adams, *Beyond the Barrier With Byrd*, 227; Byrd, *Little America*, 14; Balchen, *Come North*, 18; Murphy, *Struggle*, 263; *N.Y. Times*, 20 Jul. 1927 and 21 Mar. 1928; Smith, *By the Seat*, 183.

11. Demas, diaries, 26 and 27 Jan. 1929.

12. Gould, diaries, 27 Jan. 1929; Siple, *Boy Scout*, 46.

13. Byrd, *Little America*, 120.

14. Ibid., 124.

15. Ibid., 125; Carter, *Little America*, 76.

16. Demas, diaries, 5 and 13 Feb. 1929; Gould, typed diary, V2–8; Harrison, diary, 14 Feb. 1929; Siple, *Boy Scout*, 49, and diaries, 28 Jan. 1929.

17. Harrison, first Byrd Expedition alumni newsletter, 2 Nov. 1982, Harrison papers.

18. *N.Y. Times*, 11 May and 5 Aug. 1928; Adams, *Beyond the Barrier With Byrd*, 233.

19. Byrd, *National Geographic*, 208; Demas, diaries, Oct. 1928.

20. Gould, diaries, 17 Feb. 1929; Demas, diaries, 19 Feb. 1929.

21. Quotation is from Smith, manuscript, 683. Byrd, *Little America*, 10, 243; *N.Y. Times*, 11 Aug. 1929.

22. Smith, manuscript, 685.

23. Smith, *By the Seat*, 197.

24. Smith, manuscript, 691.

25. Blackburn, diary, 18 Feb. 1929. Quotation is from Smith, manuscript, 691–694.

26. Smith, *By the Seat*, 195.

27. *N.Y. Times*, 21 Feb. 1929.

28. Byrd, *Little America*, 143.

29. R. E. Byrd to M. A. Byrd, radiogram, 18 Feb. 1929, Byrd papers, box 13 file 18; Harrison, diary, 18 Feb. 1929; Clarke, diary, 18 Feb. 1929; Gould, typed diary, V2–13; Gould, diaries, 2 Mar. 1929; Blackburn, diary, 19 Feb. 1929.

30. R. E. Byrd to M. A. Byrd, radiogram, 21 Feb. 1929, Byrd papers, box 13 file 18; R. E. Byrd to M. A. Byrd, radiogram, 22 Feb. 1929, Byrd papers, box 1007 file 6.

31. Montague, *Oceans, Poles and Airmen*, 259.

32. Harrison, personal communication; Smith, *By the Seat*, 191.

33. Gould, *Cold*, 8, and diaries, 2 Mar. 1929; Clarke, diary, 20 Feb. 1929; Demas, diaries, 20 Feb. 1929.

34. Smith, personal communication; *N.Y. Times*, 19 Aug. 1928 and 10 Mar. 1929; Byrd, *Alone*, 158.

35. Demas, diaries, 21 and 26 Feb. 1929.

36. Byrd, *Little America*, 69, 171.

37. Gould, typed diary, V2–15 and V2–33; Clarke, diary, 11 Apr. 1929.
38. Demas, diaries, 17 Mar. 1929.
39. Ibid., 16 Mar. 1929; Siple, diaries, 16 Mar. 1929; Gould, personal notes from Antarctican Society lecture, 1968.
40. Adams, *Beyond the Barrier With Byrd*, 234; Demas, diaries, 19 Mar. 1929; Siple, diaries, 16 Mar. 1929.
41. Smith, manuscript, 689–699; Demas, diaries, 17 Mar. 1929.
42. Owen, *South of the Sun*, 87.
43. Demas, diaries, 17 Mar. 1929.
44. Smith, manuscript, 701–702.
45. Balchen, *Come North*, 94–95.
46. Quotation is from Owen, *South of the Sun*, 87. Byrd, *Skyward*, 59.
47. Smith, manuscript, 702–703; *N.Y. Times*, 24 Mar. 1929.
48. Smith, *By the Seat*, 204.
49. Ibid.
50. Quotation is from Smith, manuscript, 707. Balchen, *Come North*, 177.
51. Byrd, *Little America*, 178.
52. Harrison, personal communication.
53. Smith, manuscript, 711–712.
54. Harrison, diary, 18 Mar. 1929; Siple, diaries, 18 Mar. 1929.
55. *N.Y. Times*, 21 Mar. 1929.
56. Owen, *Conquest*, 134.
57. Gould, *Cold*, 27, 126.
58. Taylor, *Antarctic Adventure and Research*, 77; *N.Y. Times*, 27 Sept. 1928.
59. Gould, typed diary, V2–26.
60. Gould, *Cold*, 33; *N.Y. Times*, 24 Mar. 1929.
61. Byrd, *Little America*, 186; Gould, *Cold*, 36.
62. Byrd to Balchen and June, memo, 4 May 1929, Byrd papers, box 10.1 file 8.
63. Brown to Byrd, radiogram, 25 Sept. 1929, in Byrd's diary; Byrd to members, bulletin board notice, 20 Apr. 1929, Clarke papers; Byrd, diary, 15 and 24 May 1929; Demas, diaries, 21 May 1929.
64. Byrd, diary, 14 Apr. 1929.
65. *N.Y. Times*, 14 Sept. 1929 and 26 June 1930; Byrd, *Little America*, 270; Byrd, bulletin board notice, 20 Apr. 1929, Clarke papers.
66. Byrd, bulletin board notice, 6 May 1929, Clarke papers; Demas, diaries, 1 May 1929; Gould, typed diary, V2–7; Byrd, bulletin board notice, 20 Apr. 1929, Clarke papers; *N.Y. Times*, 26 Mar. 1929. Quotation is from Railey to Byrd, radiogram, 27 Apr. 1929, in Byrd's diary.
67. Byrd, *Little America*, 196.
68. Harrison, diary, 18 Apr. 1929; Demas, diaries, Mar. 1929; Owen, *South of the Sun*, 83.

CHAPTER 7

1. Gould, diaries, 20 Jan. 1929; Siple, *Boy Scout*, 56.
2. Byrd, *Little America*, 233.
3. Smith, manuscript, 735.

4. Byrd, *Little America*, 225.

5. Davies, oral history tape; Demas, diaries, 27 May 1929.

6. Gould, *Cold*, 55; Siple, *Boy Scout*, 55.

7. Demas, diaries, 23 Feb. 1929.

8. Siple, diaries, 25 Apr. 1929; Gould, *Cold*, 60; Siple, *Boy Scout*, 89.

9. Demas, diaries, 8 Apr. 1929; Siple, *Boy Scout*, 80. Quotation is from Gould, *Cold*, 66.

10. Owen, *Conquest*, 169, and *South of the Sun*, 106.

11. Owen, *South of the Sun*, 29.

12. Byrd, *Little America*, 157; Gould, *Cold*, 2; personnel forms, Byrd papers, box 12 file 1.

13. Harrison, diary, 29 Apr. and 29 July 1929.

14. Byrd, *Little America*, 200; Davies, oral history tape; Owen, *South of the Sun*, 235.

15. Byrd, *Little America*, 193; Carter, *Little America*, 93; *N.Y. Times*, 29 June 1930.

16. Owen, *Conquest*, 122.

17. *N.Y. Times*, 26 Dec. 1928; Byrd, *National Geographic*, 142; Carter, *Little America*, 94, 150; Owen, *Conquest*, 123; Siple, *Boy Scout*, 91; Owen, *South of the Sun*, 188, 192; Byrd, *Little America*, 101; Davies, oral history tape; Siple, *Ninety Degrees*, 41–42.

18. *N.Y. Times*, 11 Apr. 1928; Owen, *South of the Sun*, 64.

19. Carter, *Little America*, 94; Demas, diaries, 25 and 29 Apr. 1929; Gould, *Cold*, 48, and diaries, 29 Apr. 1929; *N.Y. Times*, 16 June 1929.

20. Siple, *Ninety Degrees*, 42.

21. Byrd, *Little America*, 168; Carter, *Little America*, 99; Gould, *Cold*, 64; Siple, diaries, 30 June 1929.

22. Byrd, *Discovery*, 73, and *Little America*, 221; Harrison, first Byrd expedition alumni newsletter, 29 Nov. 1979; Gould, *Cold*, 48, 53; Owen, *South of the Sun*, 96; Gould, typed diary, V2–37; Bursey, *Antarctic Night*, 80; Carter, *Little America*, 94; Harrison, diary, 3 May 1929.

23. Owen, *South of the Sun*, 40–41; *N.Y. Times*, 13 Sept. 1929; Siple, diaries, 5 Aug. 1929.

24. Gould, *Cold*, 58.

25. Carter, *Little America*, 99; Clarke, diary, 14 Apr. and 24 May 1929; Siple, diaries, 6 June 1929.

26. Byrd, *Little America*, 224; *N.Y. Times*, 1 July 1929, IX, 3; Siple, *Boy Scout*, 90; Owen, *South of the Sun*, 121; Carter, *Little America*, 95–96; Gould, *Cold*, 59.

27. Byrd, *Little America*, 207; Siple, *Boy Scout*, 90; Harrison, diary, 29 Apr. 1929.

28. Byrd, *National Geographic*, 143; Davies, oral history tape; Siple, *Boy Scout*, 91.

29. *N.Y. Times*, 19 May 1929; Slate and Cook, *It Sounds Impossible*, 114; Clarke, diary, 13 Apr. 1929; Harrison, diary, 13 Apr. 1929; Carter, *Little America*, 101; Gould, *Cold*, 49.

30. Owen, *South of the Sun*, 160; Clarke, diary, 13, 19, and 20 Apr. 1929; Byrd, *Little America*, 220; Gould, *Cold*, 49; Demas, diaries, 19 Apr. 1929; Harrison, diary, 20 Apr. 1929; Siple, diaries, 20 Apr. 1929.

31. Byrd, *National Geographic*, 172; Clarke, diary, 2 Aug. 1929; Byrd, diary,

27 Apr. 1929; Byrd to Meinholtz, radiogram, 1 June 1929, in Byrd's diary; Gould, typed diary, V2–42; Harrison, diary, 17 Apr. and 25 May 1929; Siple, diaries, 8 June 1929.

32. Byrd to Broadcasting Co. of New Zealand, radiogram, 28 May 1929, Byrd papers, box 10.1 file 7.

33. Gould, *Cold*, 44.

34. *N.Y. Times*, 1 Sept. 1928 and 3 Mar. 1931; Gould, *Cold*, 50; Davies, oral history tape; Owen, *Conquest*, 148; Gould, typed diary, V2–40; Demas, diaries, 5 May 1929.

35. Clarke, diary, 31 Mar. 1929; Bursey, *Antarctic Night*, 77; Smith, *By the Seat*, 215.

36. Siple, *Ninety Degrees*, 44; Byrd, *Alone*, 74; Demas, diaries, 5 Mar. 1929; *N.Y. Times*, 1 Apr. 1929; Siple, diaries, 17 Aug. and 24 Sept. 1929.

37. Demas, diaries, Feb. and 29 Sept. 1929; Siple, *Ninety Degrees*, 308; Owen, *South of the Sun*, 161; Smith, *By the Seat*, 214.

38. Hatch, *The Byrds*, 319; Siple, *Ninety Degrees*, 306; Steinberg, *Admiral Byrd*, 85; Owen, *South of the Sun*, 94; Carter, *Little America*, 70, 85.

39. Hatch, *The Byrds*, 318; Blackburn, diary, 5 Aug. 1929.

40. Byrd, *Little America*, 20, 57, and 209; Byrd, *Alone*, 30.

41. Owen, *The Antarctic Ocean*, 226; Siple, diaries, 28 and 29 May 1929; Hoyt, *Last Explorer*, 6, 231; Siple, *Ninety Degrees*, 123. Quotations are from Clarke, diary, 1 Dec. 1928 and 12 July 1929.

42. Carter, *Little America*, 98; Gould, *Cold*, 64; Byrd, diary, 7 Sept. 1929.

43. Carter, *Little America*, 94; Harrison, diary, 28 Apr., 23 May, 9, 22, and 27 June, 17 July, and 6 Aug. 1929.

44. Siple, diaries, 25 Apr. and 24 June 1929; Balchen, *Come North*, 179, 180; Demas, diaries, 24 May 1929; Owen, *South of the Sun*, 89; Siple, personal interview; Hoyt, *Last Explorer*, 230.

45. Byrd, *Little America*, 81; Harrison, first Byrd expedition alumni newsletter, 29 Nov. 1974; Balchen, *Come North*, 167.

46. *N.Y. Times*, 25 Aug. 1929; Owen, *Conquest*, 118; Gould, *Cold*, 35.

47. Gould, *Cold*, 46; Byrd, *Little America*, 362; *N.Y. Times*, 17 Oct. 1929.

48. Byrd, *Little America*, 241, 249; Gould, *Cold*, 47, 74.

49. Owen, *South of the Sun*, 41, 84; Harrison, first Byrd expedition alumni newsletter, 29 Nov. 1974; personnel forms, Byrd papers, box 12 file 1; Byrd, *Discovery*, 102; Carter, *Little America*, 98.

50. Byrd to dog team drivers, memo, 3 June 1929, Byrd papers, box 10.1 file 5.

51. Byrd, *Little America*, 241, 242, 255; Demas, diaries, 6 and 18 Aug. 1929.

52. Smith, manuscript, 640; Smith, *By the Seat*, 180.

CHAPTER 8

1. Byrd, diary, 17 Apr. 1929; Demas, diaries, 14 Apr., 22 and 29 May, July, and 15 Oct. 1929; Siple, diaries, 4 Jan., 16 and 18 Apr., and 11 June 1929.

2. Byrd to Railey, radiogram, 30 May 1929, in Byrd's diary; Byrd to Railey, 25 June 1929, in Byrd's diary; Railey to Byrd, 25 June 1929, in Byrd's diary; Railey to Byrd, 31 July 1929, in Byrd's diary.

3. Demas, diaries, 4 Apr., 9 May, and 29 June 1929; Byrd, diary, 10 May

1929; Gould, diaries, 12 May 1929; Harrison, diary, 8 Apr. and 10 May 1929; Blackburn, diary, 9 May 1929; Gould, typed diary, V2–46; Siple, diaries, 9 May 1929.

4. Harrison, first Byrd expedition alumni newsletter, 29 Nov. 1977; Blackburn, diary, 10 May 1929; Clarke, diary, 10 May 1929; Bursey, *Antarctic Night*, 79; Owen, *South of the Sun*, 102; Siple, diaries, 10 May and 8 Sept. 1929.

5. Demas, diaries, 10 May 1929; Siple, diaries, 10 May 1929.

6. Siple, diaries, 13 May 1929; Demas, diaries, 17 and 23 May 1929.

7. Gould, diaries, 27 May 1929; Harrison, diary, 25 and 26 May 1929; Demas, diaries, 26 May 1929; Siple, diaries, 26 and 27 May 1929.

8. Gould, diaries, 29 and 31 May 1929.

9. Demas, diaries, 20 June 1929; Harrison, diary, 20 June 1929.

10. Demas, diaries, 15 May and 11 and 20 June 1929; Owen, *South of the Sun*, 118, 119; Demas, oral history tape; Bursey, *Antarctic Night*, 82.

11. Demas, diaries, 28 Apr. and 14 July 1929; Siple, diaries, 27 Apr., 6 May, and 14 July 1929, and *Ninety Degrees*, 320; bulletin board notice, undated, Byrd papers, box 10.1 file 8; Davies, oral history tape; Harrison, diary, 14 July 1929.

12. *N.Y. Times*, 19 May 1929; Siple, diaries, 21 Apr. 1929; Clarke, diary, 28 July 1929; Lida Hanson, *The Story of Malcolm Hanson*, 134; Davies oral history tape; Owen, *South of the Sun*, 107.

13. Adams, *Beyond the Barrier With Byrd*, 229; *N.Y. Times*, 9 Apr. 1928 and 14 Mar. 1929; Demas, diaries, 6 Feb. 1929 and 21 Jan. 1930.

14. Siple, diaries, 25 June 1929; Byrd to Railey, radiogram, 8 Aug. 1929, Byrd papers, box 10.1 file 3; Clarke, diary, 9 Aug. 1929; Demas, diaries, 29 Sept. 1929; Owen, *South of the Sun*, 56, 100, 105, 136; Siple, *Ninety Degrees*, 138.

15. Demas, diaries, 17 Sept. 1929; Byrd to Railey, radiogram, 29 Jan. 1929, Byrd papers, box 48 file 6; Byrd, *Alone*, 19.

16. Harrison, diary, 4 Aug. 1929; Carter, *Little America*, 98; Murphy, *Struggle*, 13; Byrd, unidentified papers, Byrd papers, box 10.1 file 8; Siple, diaries, 24 May 1929; Demas, diaries, 2 Mar. 1929; Byrd, diary, 3 Oct. 1929.

17. Siple, diaries, 31 Aug. 1929; Harrison, diary, 4 Aug. 1929.

18. Demas, diaries, 4 July 1929; Davies, oral history tape; Owen, *South of the Sun*, 128.

19. Gould, diaries, 6 July 1929; Harrison, diary, 4 July 1929; Demas, diaries, 4 July 1929; Gould, typed diary, V2–65.

20. Demas, diaries, 19 May 1929; Harrison, diary, 19 May and 4 July 1929; Siple, diaries, 1 Apr. and 5 July 1929; Owen, *South of the Sun*, 91; Smith, *By the Seat*, 95; Steinberg, *Admiral Byrd*, 85; Smith, manuscript, 749.

21. Carter, *Little America*, 60; Demas, diaries, 4 and 5 July 1929; Harrison, diary, 4 July 1929; Smith, manuscript, 743–744.

22. Clarke, first Byrd expedition alumni newsletter, Harrison papers, 29 Nov. 1974; Harrison, diary, 3 Sept. 1929.

23. Demas, diaries, 5 July 1929.

24. Ibid., 1 June and 6 July 1929; Harrison, diary, 6 July 1929.

25. Demas, diaries, 12 July 1929. Quotation is from Byrd, diary, 13 July 1929.

26. Demas, diaries, 12 and 14 July 1929.

27. Siple, *Boy Scout*, iii.

28. Demas, diaries, 14 and 15 July 1929.

29. Byrd, memo, 20 July 1929, Byrd papers, box 1019 file 12.

30. Byrd to Railey, radiogram, 8 Aug. 1929, in Byrd's diary; Byrd to Owen,

2 Sept. 1930, Byrd papers, box 154 file 22; bulletin board memo, 13 Oct. 1929, Byrd papers, box 13.

31. Smith, *By the Seat*, 192; Montague, *Oceans, Poles and Airmen*, 259.

32. Byrd to Railey, radiogram, 21 Aug. 1929, in Byrd's diary, is one example; Byrd to Lyman, radiogram, 14 Aug. 1929, Byrd papers, box 10.1 file 3.

33. Demas, diaries, 2 Aug. 1929

34. Byrd to Railey, radiogram, 4 May 1929, in Byrd's diary; Railey to Byrd, radiogram, 29 May 1929, in Byrd's diary; Byrd to Railey, radiogram, 29 May 1929, in Byrd's diary.

35. Siple, diaries, 7 Jan. 1930.

36. Montague, *Ocean, Poles and Airmen*, 259; Smith, *By the Seat*, 192.

37. Demas, diaries, 2 Aug. 1929; Owen, *Conquest*, 137, 144; Owen, *South of the Sun*, 79, 80, 120; Siple, personal interview; Coman, prescription for Owen, 18 Apr. 1929, Coman papers; Harrison, diary, 12 Dec. 1929.

38. *N.Y. Times*, 7 June 1929; Siple, *Ninety Degrees*, 317.

39. *N.Y. Times*, 29 June 1930; Harrison, diary, 7 Sept. 1929; Demas, diaries, 7 Sept. 1929.

40. Owen, *Antarctic Ocean*, 226.

41. Siple, diaries, 21 July 1929.

42. Script, unidentified, Byrd papers, box 1002 file 4.

43. Byrd to De Ganahl, 11 Sept. 1930, Byrd papers, box 153 file 25.

44. Siple, diaries, 21 July 1929.

45. Demas, diaries, 28 July 1929.

46. Byrd to Crockett, 3 Aug. 1930, Byrd papers, box 153 file 21; Byrd to De Ganahl, 11 Sept. 1930, Byrd papers, box 153 file 25; Charles Gould to Byrd, 27 July 1933, Byrd papers, box 153 file 37; Clarke, diary, 26 Aug. 1929.

47. Gould to Balchen, 12 Apr. 1958, Gould papers; *Yankee* magazine interview draft, Wilson files. Mitchell quoted in Balchen, *Come North*, 60.

48. Byrd to Brown, radiogram, 8 Apr. 1929, in Byrd's diary.

49. R. E. Byrd to M. A. Byrd, radiogram, 17 Sept. 1929, Byrd papers, box 1007 file 1.

50. Balchen, unidentified manuscript, Balchen papers, National Archives; Siple, diaries, 24 June 1929; Demas, diaries, 29 May 1929.

51. Demas, diaries, 30 May 1929; Harrison and Davies correspondence, first Byrd expedition alumni newsletter, 29 Nov. 1975.

52. Harrison, personal communication; Siple, diaries, 1 Aug. 1929; Clarke, diary, 1 Aug. 1929; Blackburn, diary, 1 Aug. 1929; Demas, diaries, 31 July 1929; *N.Y. Times*, 11 Aug. 1929.

53. Byrd to Railey, radiogram, 5 Aug. 1929, in Byrd's diary; Railey to Byrd, radiograms, 16 and 17 Aug. 1929, in Byrd's diary; Lofgren to Bayer, radiogram, 5 Aug. 1929, Byrd papers, box 10.1 file 3.

54. *N.Y. Times*, 24 Apr. 1928; Siple, *Ninety Degrees*, 182; Balchen, *Come North*, 178; Owen, *South of the Sun*, 187; Harrison, diary, 18–19 Nov. 1929; Montague, *Oceans, Poles and Airmen*, 256, 264; Smith, manuscript, 645.

55. Balchen, manuscript, "The Strange Enigma of Admiral Byrd," Gould papers; Balchen, unidentified manuscript, 225i, Balchen papers, National Archives; Byrd to Tapley, radiogram, 6 Apr. 1929, in Byrd's diary; Bayer to Byrd, radiogram, 8 Apr. 1929, in Byrd's diary; Byrd to Brown, radiogram, 8 Apr. 1929, in Byrd's diary; Carter, *Little America*, 93; Montague, *Oceans, Poles and Airmen*, 259.

56. Owen, *Conquest*, 142; Owen, *South of the Sun*, 149; Balchen, unidentified manuscript, 223, Balchen papers, National Archives.

57. Siple, diaries, 30 Aug., 14 Sept., 15 and 16 Oct., and 23 Dec. 1928, and 6, 8, and 24 Sept. 1929; Demas, diaries, May 1929; Gould, diaries, 3 Nov. 1928, and typed diary, V1–12.

58. Carter, *Little America*, 106; Gould, *Cold*, 65, 101; Owen, *Conquest*, 146; Siple, *Ninety Degrees*, 322; Demas, diaries, 14 June 1929.

59. *N.Y. Times*, 13 Sept. 1929; Byrd, *Little America*, 231, 232; Siple, diaries, 3 July 1929; Owen, *South of the Sun*, 151; Byrd, *National Geographic*, 175; Gould, diaries, 3 June 1929; Demas, oral history tape.

60. Harrison, diary, 1 Aug. 1929.

61. Mason, speech, 9 Oct. 1982, Wilson files.

62. Byrd, *Little America*, 221; Smith, bulletin board notice, 9 July 1929, in Clarke papers; *N.Y. Times*, 23 June 1929; Owen, *South of the Sun*, 122; Demas, diaries, 23 May and 10 Aug. 1929; Mason, speech, 9 Oct. 1982, Wilson files; Byrd to Railey, radiogram, 30 Aug. 1929, Byrd papers, box 10.1 file 2.

63. *N.Y. Times*, 22 Dec. 1929; R. E. Byrd to M. A. Byrd, radiogram, 11 Sept. 1929, in Byrd's diary; Railey to Byrd, radiogram, 22 Aug. 1929, in Byrd's diary.

64. Gould, diaries, 9 Aug. 1929.

65. Harrison, diary, 20 Aug. and 3 Sept. 1929; Gould, *Cold*, 104.

66. Byrd, *Little America*, 272; *National History*, Sept. 1930, 538; *N.Y. Times*, 23 Feb. 1930.

67. Demas, diaries, 20, 21, and 22 Aug. 1929; Harrison, diary, 6 Aug. 1929; Blackburn, diary, 22 Aug. 1929; Clarke, diary, 22 Aug. 1929; Owen, *South of the Sun*, 105, 281.

68. Gould cited in Carter, *Little America*, 108; Demas, diaries, 22 Aug. 1929; Harrison, diary, 22 and 23 Aug. 1929; Owen, *South of the Sun*, 167; Siple, diaries, 22 Aug. 1929.

69. Demas, diaries, 31 Aug. 1929.

70. Clarke, diary, 2 Sept. 1929; Demas, diaries, 2, 3, and 4 Sept. 1929.

71. Gould, *Cold*, 100.

72. Harrison, diary, 2 and 26 Oct. 1929; Owen, *Conquest*, 119.

73. *N.Y. Times*, 16 Sept. 1929; Harrison, diary, 18 Sept. 1929; Demas, diaries, 2 and 6 Oct. and 13 Dec. 1929; Siple, diaries, 2 Oct. 1929; Owen, *South of the Sun*, 260; Blackburn, diary, 15 Sept. 1929.

74. Byrd, *Little America*, 224–225, 279.

75. Ibid., 280; Owen, *Conquest*, 118; Harrison, diary, 30 Sept. and 12 Oct. 1929.

76. Harrison, diary, 15 Sept. and 19 Oct. 1929. Carter, *Little America*, 99; Siple, diaries, 11 Sept. 1929.

77. Sullivan, *Quest for a Continent*, 118; *N.Y. Times*, 1 Mar. 1929.

78. Harrison, diary, 23 May and 25 Sept. 1929; Siple, diaries, 23 May 1929; *N.Y. Times*, 14 Mar. and 15 and 30 Sept. 1929; Demas, diaries, 19 July and 25 Sept. 1929.

79. *N.Y. Times*, 19 Mar. 1929; Byrd to Railey, radiogram, 30 July 1929, in Byrd's diary; Meinholtz to Byrd, radiogram, 17 Sept. 1929, Byrd papers, box 10.1 file 1; Railey to Byrd, radiogram, 26 July 1929, in Byrd's diary; Clarke, diary, 15 July and 27 Sept. 1929; Demas, diaries, 15 July 1929.

80. Demas, diaries, 1 June and 19 July 1929; Harrison, diary, 19 June and 17 Sept. 1929.

81. Byrd to Railey, radiogram, 5 Aug. 1929, in Byrd's diary.
82. Ibid., 21 Sept. 1929; Birchall to Owen, radiogram, 26 Sept. 1929, in Byrd's diary; Byrd to Railey for Bowman, radiogram, 25 Sept. 1929, in Byrd's diary; Byrd, diary, 25 Sept. 1929.

CHAPTER 9

1. Demas, diaries, 27 Mar. and 19 and 28 Sept. 1929; Bursey, *Antarctic Night*, 77; Byrd, *Little America*, 69, 275–277; Harrison, diary, 14 Sept. 1929; Owen, *South of the Sun*, 185; Hoyt, *Last Explorer*, 237.
2. Clarke, diary, 1 Oct. 1929; Siple, diaries, 26 Sept. and 10 Oct. 1929.
3. Report of geological party, Byrd papers, box 12 file 16; Byrd, memo to geological party, 19 Sept. 1929, in Byrd's diary.
4. Byrd, memo to members, 8 Aug. 1929, Byrd papers, box 10.1 file 3; Byrd to Walden, memo, 27 Sept. 1929, Byrd papers, box 13.
5. Owen, *South of the Sun*, 58; Siple, *Ninety Degrees*, 4, 42; Siple, *Boy Scout*, 42; Siple, diaries, 24 May 1929; Siple, *Scout to Explorer*, 111. Quotation is from Siple, diaries, 3 May 1929.
6. Gould, diaries, 4, 6, and 9 Oct. 1929.
7. Byrd, diary, 7 Oct. 1929; Blackburn, diary, 4 Oct. 1929; Gould, *Cold*, 105, and diaries, 7 Oct. 1929; Harrison, diary, 11 Oct. 1929.
8. Gould, diaries, 12 and 13 Oct. 1929; Siple, diaries, 11 Oct. 1929.
9. Gould, *Cold*, 108.
10. Gould, diaries, 13 Oct. 1929; Harrison, diary, 13 Oct. 1929; Demas, diaries, 1 Mar. and 13 Oct. 1929.
11. Owen, *South of the Sun*, 200, 201; Gould, *Cold*, 113; Harrison, diary, 13 Oct. 1929; Siple, diaries, 14 Oct. 1929.
12. Clarke, diary, 13 Oct. 1929; Harrison, diary, 13 and 14 Oct. 1929.
13. Davies, oral history tape.
14. Gould, diaries, 9 Oct. 1929; Siple, diaries, 26 Sept. 1929.
15. *N.Y. Times*, 16 Oct. 1929; Siple, diaries, 15 Oct. 1929.
16. Harrison, diary, 17 Oct. 1929; Siple, diaries, 16, 17, and 18 Oct. 1929; Byrd, *Little America*, 397; Gould, *Cold*, 117–118, and diaries, 17 Oct. 1929.
17. Byrd, *Little America*, 288; Demas, diaries, 15 Oct. 1929; Gould, *Cold*, 117; Harrison, diary, 15 Oct. 1929; *N.Y. Times*, 18 Oct. 1929.
18. Gould, *Cold*, 118; Byrd, *Little America*, 362; Harrison, diary, 19 July and 18 Oct. 1929.
19. Gould, *Cold*, 73, 139; Byrd, *Little America*, 290.
20. Gould, *Cold*, 119; Demas, diaries, 18 Oct. 1929.
21. Byrd, *Little America*, 290.
22. Siple, diaries, 12 Jan. 1929; Harrison, diary, 14 June 1929; Murphy, *Life*, 30 Oct. 1939, 29.
23. Hoyt, *Last Explorer*, 91.
24. Byrd to geological party, radiogram, 21 Oct. 1929, in Byrd's diary.
25. Byrd to Strom, 20 Oct. 1929, in Byrd's diary; Strom to Byrd, undated, in Byrd's diary.
26. Owen, *Conquest*, 148; Byrd, diary, 25 Oct. 1929; Owen, *South of the Sun*, 203.
27. Demas, diaries, 29 Oct. 1929; Owen, *South of the Sun*, 221.

28. Byrd, *Little America*, 299; Siple, diaries, 17 Oct. 1929.
29. Byrd, diary, 1 Nov. 1929; Demas, diaries, 1 Nov. 1929; Siple, diaries, 1 Nov. 1929.
30. Demas, diaries, 28 Oct. 1929; Siple, *Boy Scout*, 102; O'Brien, *By Dog Sled*, 176.
31. Gould, diaries, 11 June 1929, and typed diary, V2–57; O'Brien, *By Dog Sled*, 17.
32. O'Brien, *By Dog Sled*, 20.
33. Coman to Gould, 25 Nov. 1929, Gould papers.
34. Demas, diaries, 5 Nov. 1929; Harrison, diary, 5 Nov. 1929; Siple, *Boy Scout*, 101.
35. Carter, *Little America*, 113; Owen, *Conquest*, 148; Byrd, *Little America*, 134, 304.
36. Bursey, *Antarctic Night*, 87; Gould, *Cold*, 128.
37. Byrd, diary, 25 Oct. 1929; Siple, diaries, 25 Oct. 1929.
38. Harrison, diary, 29 Oct. 1929; *N.Y. Times*, 1 Mar. 1930; Smith, manuscript, 776; Byrd to Railey, radiogram, 12 Nov. 1929, in Byrd's diary.
39. M. A. Byrd to R. E. Byrd, radiogram, 7 Oct. 1929, Byrd papers, box 1007 file 1.
40. Harrison, diary, 10 Nov. 1929; Coman to Gould, 25 Nov. 1929, Gould papers; Owen, *South of the Sun*, 220.
41. Owen, *South of the Sun*, 220.
42. Lofgren to Byrd, memo, undated, Byrd papers, box 154 file 7.
43. Byrd to Owen, 20 Nov. 1929, Byrd papers, box 13.
44. Carter, *Little America*, 121; Owen, *South of the Sun*, 220.

CHAPTER 10

1. Demas, diaries, 20 Nov. 1929.
2. Ibid., 9 Nov. 1929; Byrd, *Little America*, 306.
3. *N.Y. Times*, 21 Mar. 1928; Smith, *By the Seat*, 185.
4. Siple, *Boy Scout*, 99.
5. Harrison, diary, 15 Nov. 1929.
6. R. E. Byrd to M. A. Byrd, radiogram, 15 Nov. 1929, Byrd papers, box 1007 file 1.
7. Smith, manuscript, 762.
8. *N.Y. Times*, 16 Apr. 1929.
9. Carter, *Little America*, 118; Harrison, diary, 18 Nov. 1929.
10. *N.Y. Times*, 20 Nov. 1929.
11. Ibid., 21 Nov. 1929.
12. Smith, *By the Seat*, 222.
13. Byrd, *Little America*, 320; Hoyt, *Last Explorer*, 249; *N.Y. Times*, 21 Nov. 1929.
14. Smith, *By the Seat*, 223.
15. Siple, diaries, 3 Oct. 1929; Balchen, *Come North*, 181; *N.Y. Times*, 8 Oct. 1930.
16. Smith, *By the Seat*, 224.
17. Blackburn, diary, 19 Nov. 1929; Clarke, diary, 19 Nov. 1929.
18. *N.Y. Times*, 22 Nov. 1929; Demas, diaries, 18 Nov. 1929.

19. Owen, *South of the Sun*, 237; Demas, diaries, 19 Nov. 1929; Smith, manuscript, 760; Balchen, *Come North*, 184.
20. Balchen, *Come North*, 186; Montague, *Oceans, Poles and Airmen*, 295–296.
21. Balchen, *Come North*, 55; Smith, personal communication; Montague, *Oceans, Poles and Airmen*, 48.
22. Demas, diaries, 14 Aug. and 6 Nov. 1929; Harrison, diary, 18 and 19 Nov. 1929; Siple, diaries, 20 Nov. 1929.
23. Siple, diaries, 23 Nov. 1929; Demas, diaries, 24 Nov. 1929.
24. *World Almanac*, 1930, news of 1929, 1 July 1929.
25. Demas, diaries, 25 Nov. 1929; Harrison, diary, 27 Nov. 1929.
26. Clarke, diary, 26 Nov. 1929.
27. Knight and Durham, *Hitch Your Wagon*, 185; Harrison, diary, 30 Nov. and 13 Dec. 1929.
28. Balchen, unidentified manuscript, Balchen papers, National Archives, 235; Fokker, *Flying Dutchman*, 265.
29. Byrd to Gould and McKinley, memos, 28 Sept. 1929, in Byrd's diary; Owen, *South of the Sun*, 213.
30. Byrd, *National Geographic*, 207.
31. Harrison, diary, 23 Nov. 1929.
32. Owen, *Conquest*, 150; Byrd, *Little America*, 326; Byrd to Berkner, radiogram, 21 Nov. 1929, Byrd papers, box 13 file 1.
33. Byrd, *National Geographic*, 207.
34. Ibid., 208; Montague, *Oceans, Poles and Airmen*, 261.
35. Knight and Durham, *Hitch Your Wagon*, 188.
36. Byrd, *Little America*, 235; Balchen, *Come North*, 189.
37. Balchen, *Come North*, 190.
38. Ibid.
39. *N.Y. Times*, 18 June 1930.
40. Smith, *By the Seat*, 221.
41. Ibid., 220
42. Montague, *Oceans, Poles and Airmen*, 262; Harrison, diary, 8 Feb. 1930.
43. Owen, *South of the Sun*, 250; Byrd, *Little America*, 313.
44. Ibid., 329; Byrd, *National Geographic*, 195; *N.Y. Times*, 21 Nov. 1929.
45. Gould, *Cold*, 150, 151; Byrd to Gould, radiogram, 28 Nov. 1929, Byrd papers, box 13; Byrd to Gould, radiogram, 2 Dec. 1929, Byrd papers, box 13.
46. *N.Y. Times*, 20 and 22 Nov. 1929.
47. Byrd, *Little America*, 344.
48. Roberts, *Great Exploration Hoaxes*, 133; Montague, *Oceans, Poles and Airmen*, 261.
49. Byrd to Railey, radiogram, 16 Dec. 1929, Byrd papers, box 48 file 7; committee report, National Geographic Society, 9 Jan. 1931, Byrd papers, box 1002 file 2; *N.Y. Times*, 1 Apr. 1931.
50. McKinley to Byrd, undated letter, Byrd papers, box 154 file 10.
51. Byrd, *Little America*, 329.
52. Smith, manuscript, 771; Owen, *South of the Sun*, 220.
53. Siple, diaries, 30 Nov. 1929; Owen, *South of the Sun*, 256; Demas, diaries, 30 Nov. 1929; Carter, *Little America*, 129; Blackburn, diary, 30 Nov. 1929; Demas, oral history tape; Harrison, diary, 30 Nov. 1929; Clarke, diary, 30 Nov. 1929.
54. Mason, speech, Wilson files; Byrd, *National Geographic*, 219; *N.Y. Times*, 3, 13, and 20 Dec. 1929.

55. *N.Y. Times*, 8 Dec. 1929; Harrison, diary, 3 Dec. 1929; Swanson to Byrd, radiogram, 2 Dec. 1929, Byrd papers, box 48 file 7; Byrd to Railey, radiogram, 12 Dec. 1929, Byrd papers, box 10.1; Byrd to expedition's New York office, radiogram, undated (but identified in other references as 21 Dec. 1929), Byrd papers, box 48 file 7.

56. Blackburn, diary, 2 Dec. 1929; *N.Y. Times*, 8 Dec. and 20 Dec. 1929; R. E. Byrd to M. A. Byrd, radiogram, 4 Dec. 1929, Byrd papers, box 13.

CHAPTER 11

1. Clarke, diary, 5 Dec. 1929; Demas, diaries, 5 Dec. 1929; Harrison, diary, 5 Dec. 1929.

2. Clarke, diary, 3 Dec. 1929; Harrison, diary, 3 Dec. 1929; *N.Y. Times*, 4 Dec. 1929.

3. Byrd, *Little America*, 350, 351; Byrd, *National Geographic*, 219.

4. Byrd, *Little America*, 352–353, 355; Byrd, *National Geographic*, 219.

5. Byrd, *The Geographical Review*, April 1933.

6. Ibid., 184; Byrd, *Little America*, 142; *N.Y. Times*, 21 Feb. 1929.

7. McKinley, Smith, and Berkner to Byrd, radiogram, 19 Feb. 1929, Byrd papers, box 13 file 8.

8. When Gould camped at the Rockefeller Mountains, he saw a distant peak he took to be the Matterhorn. Two different bearings were given from his campsite. In a 20 May 1929 report radioed to the secretary of the navy, which located Gould's camp at 78-90-05S, 154-7W (Byrd papers, box 10.1 file 7), Byrd stated, "From this point the peak bore 58 degrees from true north, and a triangulation indicated it to be about 70 miles distant. . . . [It] is probably over 5,000 in height." On 2 Sept. 1930, Gould wrote Byrd (Byrd papers, box 153 file 37), "The true bearing of the Matterhorn from the Rockefeller Mountains is N 65 deg. E." For Byrd's paper in *The Geographical Review*, his postexpedition cartographer, Harold Saunders, drew La Gorce as a ridge whose ends intersect both bearings. Saunders placed La Gorce peak 50 miles from Gould's camp, using a longitude of 154-27W for the camp, but the shift makes little difference. On a modern map, La Gorce peak is well to the west of both bearings and McKinley peak is to the east. If either bearing was correct, or nearly so, Gould was looking toward the farther mountains of the Edsel Ford Range, but no peak appears to be within sight on or close to either bearing.

9. Owen, *Antarctic Ocean*, 231; Gould, *Cold*, 181.

10. Byrd, *Little America*, 351; Siple, diaries, 5 Dec. 1929; Harrison, diary, 5 Dec. 1929; Smith, manuscript, 773; Montague, *Oceans, Poles and Airmen*, 263.

11. Byrd, *Discovery*, 7; Byrd, *Little America*, 356; Smith, *By the Seat*, 216.

12. *N.Y. Times*, 1 Jan. 1930.

13. Demas, diaries, 29 Mar., 18 Aug., 8 Nov., and 8 Dec. 1929; *N.Y. Times*, 13 Dec. 1929; Byrd to Gould, radiogram, 11 Dec. 1929, Byrd papers, box 13.

14. M. A. Byrd to R. E. Byrd, radiogram, 30 Nov. 1929, Byrd papers, 1007 file 1; Smith, manuscript, 773.

15. Byrd, *Little America*, 359.

16. Clarke, diary, 14 Dec. 1929; Harrison, diary, 14 Dec. 1929; Owen, *South of the Sun*, 260; Byrd to Gould, radiogram, 14 Dec. 1929, Byrd papers, box 13.

CHAPTER 12

Note Most of the information in this chapter comes from Gould, *Cold*; Byrd, *Little America*, pp. 393–412 (the appendix, written by Gould, on the geological sledge trip); and O'Brien, *By Dog Sled for Byrd*.

1. O'Brien, *By Dog Sled*, 61; Gould, *Cold*, 128–129.
2. Gould, *Cold*, 131, 134.
3. Gould, diaries, 18 Nov. 1929.
4. Gould, *Cold*, 139–140; Byrd to Gould, radiogram, 20 Nov. 1929, Byrd papers, box 13 file 1.
5. Harrison and Smith, personal communications; Clarke, diary, 18 Oct. 1929.
6. Gould, diaries, 11 Dec. 1929.
7. Gould, typed diary, V3–12, 24 Nov.
8. Gould, diaries, 23 and 25 Nov. 1929.
9. O'Brien, *By Dog Sled*, 117.
10. Byrd, *Little America*, 399.
11. Gould, *Cold*, 157; Byrd to Berkner, radiogram, 21 Nov. 1929, Byrd papers, box 13 file 1.
12. Gould, *Cold*, 163–169.
13. Ibid., 170.
14. Gould, typed diary, V3–18.
15. Gould, *The Geographical Review*, 194; Owen, *Antarctic Ocean*, 242.
16. Gould to Byrd, radiogram, 28 Dec. 1929, Byrd papers, box 10.1 file 9.
17. Gould, *Cold*, 192.
18. Byrd, *Little America*, 408.
19. Gould, *Geological Society of America Bulletin*, 1392, and *Cold*, 42; Byrd, *Little America*, 408.
20. *N.Y. Times*, 29 Nov. 1930.
21. Gould, diaries, 7 Jan. 1930.
22. Byrd, *Little America*, 362, 374; Brody, *Popular Mechanics*.
23. Harrison, diary, 19 Jan. 1930; Harrison, personal communication.

CHAPTER 13

1. *N.Y. Times*, 18 Jan. 1930; Hayes, *The Conquest of the South Pole*, 263; Taylor, *Current History*, 970.
2. Gould, *The Geographical Review*, 180, and *Cold*, 211–212, 332.
3. Taylor, *Current History*, 969.
4. Byrd, *Little America*, 225, 262; Grimminger and Haines, *Monthly Weather Review Supplement No. 41*, 1; Harrison, diary, 1 Jan., 24 Apr., and 2 July 1929; Siple, *Boy Scout*, 57; Demas, diaries, Feb. 1929; Owen, *Conquest*, 144.
5. Harrison, personal communication, and diary, 13 Apr., 23 July, 23 Sept., 18 Oct., and 20 Dec. 1929; Haines to Byrd, 21 Mar. 1931, Haines papers; Grimminger and Haines, *Monthly Weather Review Supplement No. 41*, 3.
6. Harrison, diary, 28 Dec. 1929.
7. Haines, *Monthly Weather Review*, 117; Owen, *Conquest*, 140.
8. Byrd, *Little America*, 233; *N.Y. Times*, 24 Nov. 1929 and 23 Feb. 1930; *The Philadelphia Inquirer*, 7 Jan. 1988.
9. Rudmose Brown, *Polar Regions*, 52.

10. Gould, *Cold*, 261; Byrd, *Little America*, 266.

11. Demas, diaries, 27 Feb. 1929; Gould, *Cold*, 38; Davies, oral history tape; Siple, diaries, 1 Aug. 1929.

12. *N.Y. Times*, 12 May 1929.

13. Byrd, *Little America*, 266; Davies, oral history tape; Gould, *Cold*, 161; *N.Y. Times*, 24 Nov. 1929.

14. Mason, speech, Wilson files; "At the Bottom of the World With Byrd," *Popular Mechanics*, 236.

15. Byrd, *National Geographic*, 174; *N.Y. Times*, 27 Apr. 1930; Berkner, *Bureau of Standards Journal of Research*, abstract.

16. Byrd, *Little America*, 269; *N.Y. Times*, 25 July and 17 and 29 Aug. 1929; Gillmor, *Early History of Upper Atmospheric Physics Research in Antarctica*, 241; Owen, *Conquest*, 173; Byrd, *National Geographic*, 177.

17. Davies, oral history tape; Owen, *South of the Sun*, 30.

18. Taylor, *Current History*, 970.

19. *N.Y. Times*, 4 Sept. and 31 Dec. 1929.

20. Ibid., 28 Sept. and 8 Dec. 1929; Railey, *Touch'd With Madness*, 118; Owen, *Conquest*, 171–172.

21. *N.Y. Times*, 23 Apr. 1930.

22. Byrd, *Little America*, 297; Gould, *Cold*, 11.

23. Byrd, *Little America*, 226, 266; Davies, oral history tape; Gould, *Cold*, 109.

24. Byrd, *Little America*, 226.

25. Owen, *South of the Sun*, 264–265.

26. Siple, *Boy Scout*, 123; Byrd, *National Geographic*, 161.

27. Harrison, diary, 20 and 21 Jan. 1930; *N.Y. Times*, 23 Jan. 1930.

28. *N.Y. Times*, 20 Dec. 1929; Taylor, *Current History*, 968.

29. Byrd, *Little America*, 358; Siple, *Boy Scout*, 127, 129; Owen, *South of the Sun*, 272.

30. *N.Y. Times*, 28 Sept. 1930; Siple, diaries, 23 May and 13 Nov. 1929 and 18 Jan. 1930; Siple, *Boy Scout*, 117; Siple, *Ninety Degrees*, 46; Gould, *Cold*, 57.

31. Harrison, diary, 25 Jan. 1930; Owen, *South of the Sun*, 277–278; Siple, diaries, 25 Jan. 1930.

32. *N.Y. Times*, 22 Sept. 1929.

CHAPTER 14

1. *N.Y. Times*, 2 Dec. 1929.

2. Ibid., 19, 21, and 22 Dec. 1929; Siple, diaries, 22 Dec. 1929.

3. Owen, *South of the Sun*, 256, 263; Harrison, diary, 4 Dec. 1929.

4. Harrison, diary, 24 Dec. 1929; Owen, *South of the Sun*, 268.

5. Blackburn, diary, 25 Dec. 1929; Demas, diaries, 25 and 26 Dec. 1929

6. *N.Y. Times*, 20 Dec. 1929.

7. Clarke, diary, 30 Dec. 1929; Harrison, first Byrd expedition alumni newsletter, 29 Nov. 1975.

8. Harrison, diary, 17 Dec. 1929 and 1 Jan. 1930; Clarke, diary, 31 Dec. 1929; Demas, diaries, Mar. and 31 Dec. 1929, and 1 Jan. 1930.

9. Harrison, diary, 12 Oct. and 17 Dec. 1929.

10. Byrd to Railey, radiogram, 17 Jan. 1930, Byrd papers, box 48 file 6; Byrd, *Little America*, 363; *N.Y. Times*, 26 Dec. 1929 and 20 Apr. 1930.

11. Demas, diaries, 15 Dec. 1929.

12. Harrison, diary, 17 Dec. 1930.

13. Ibid., 12 Jan. 1930; *N.Y. Times*, 12 Jan. 1930.

14. Harrison, diary, 14 Jan. 1930.

15. Ibid.

16. Demas, diaries, 14 Jan. 1930; Harrison, diary, 14 and 15 Jan. 1930; Owen, *South of the Sun*, 274; Siple, diaries, 15 Jan. 1930.

17. Harrison, diary, 15 Jan. 1930; Byrd, *Little America*, 16, 372; Byrd to Railey, radiogram, 30 July 1929, in Byrd diary; Owen, *South of the Sun*, 273.

18. Harrison, diary, 15 Jan. 1930; Siple, diaries, 16 Jan. 1930; Clarke, diary, 16 Jan. 1930; Byrd, *Little America*, 366; Byrd to Railey, radiograms, 29 Jan. 1930, Byrd papers, box 10 file 14 and box 48 file 6.

19. Harrison, diary, 15 Jan. 1930.

20. Ibid.; Demas, diaries, 16 Jan. 1930.

21. Demas, diaries, 15 Jan. 1930; Gould, *Cold*, 254.

22. Clarke, diary, 24 Jan. 1930; bulletin board notice on whaler messages, Siple papers.

23. Harrison, diary, 16 Jan. 1930; Gould, *Cold*, 254.

24. Byrd, *Little America*, 141; Harrison, diary, 16 Jan. 1930; Siple, diaries, 5 Jan. 1930.

25. Harrison, diary, 18 Jan. 1930; Siple, diaries, 18 Jan. 1930; Byrd, *Little America*, 365, 373.

26. Owen, *South of the Sun*, 274; Hoyt, *Last Explorer*, 252.

27. Harrison, diary, 18 Jan. 1930; *N.Y. Times*, 18 June 1950, Strom obituary; Byrd to Railey, radiogram, 20 Jan. 1930, Byrd papers, box 48 file 6.

28. Smith, *By the Seat*, 230; Owen, *South of the Sun*, 278; Byrd, *Little America*, 375.

29. Clarke, diary, 1 Jan. 1930; Harrison, diary, 18 Jan. 1930; Siple, diaries, 18 Jan. 1930; Smith, personal communication.

30. Harrison, diary, 21 Jan. 1930; Byrd, *Little America*, 365.

31. Railey, *Touch'd With Madness*, 114, 130; Byrd, *National Geographic*, 226.

32. *N.Y. Times*, 26 Jan. 1930.

33. Railey, *Touch'd With Madness*, 125–126, 130; Byrd to Railey, radiogram, 22 Jan. 1930, Byrd papers, box 48 file 6; *N.Y. Times*, 25 Jan. 1930.

34. Railey, *Touch'd With Madness*, 126–127, 130; Byrd, *Little America*, 250, 378; Byrd, *National Geographic*, 223; Demas, diaries, 22 Jan. 1930; Harrison, diary, 22 Jan. 1930; Byrd to Railey, radiogram, 22 Jan. 1930, Byrd papers, box 48 file 6.

35. McGuinness, *Sailor of Fortune*, 267; Melville to Byrd, radiogram, 24 Jan. 1930, Byrd papers, box 117 file 2; Byrd to Railey, radiogram, 24 Jan. 1930, in Byrd's diary; Berkner to Owen, radiogram, 22 Jan. 1930, Byrd papers, box 13; Byrd to Melville, radiogram, 23 Jan. 1930, Byrd papers, box 117 file 2; Demas, diaries, 23 Jan. 1930; Berkner to Owen, radiogram, 23 Jan. 1930, Byrd papers, box 117 file 2; Harrison, diary, 22 Jan. 1930.

36. Byrd, bulletin board notice, 24 Jan. 1930, Byrd papers, box 13.

37. Demas, diaries, 27 Jan. 1930; Owen, *South of the Sun*, 276; Smith, manuscript, 779.

38. Byrd to Railey, radiogram, 24 Jan. 1930, Byrd papers, box 48 file 6.

39. Hoyt, *Last Explorer*, 253; Railey, *Touch'd With Madness*, 130.

40. Byrd, *Little America*, 319; Railey, *Touch'd With Madness*, 122, 130.

41. Byrd to Railey, radiogram, 28 Jan. 1930, Byrd papers, box 48 file 6; Railey to Byrd, radiogram, 29 Jan. 1930, Byrd papers, box 48 file 6.

42. Byrd, *Little America*, 379; Railey to families of expedition members, 28 Jan. 1930, Clarke papers.

43. Byrd, *Little America*, 376, 380.

44. Gould, *Cold*, 256; Byrd, *Little America*, 362; Harrison, diary, 19 Jan. 1930.

45. Siple, *Boy Scout*, 138.

46. Demas, diaries, 21 Feb. 1930; Gould to Byrd, telegram, 26 Jan. 1931, Byrd papers, box 1002 file 13; Gould, typed diary, V3–41.

47. Harrison, diary, 31 Jan. 1930; Gould, *The Geographical Review*, 195.

48. Siple, *Boy Scout*, 141.

49. Demas, diaries, 29 and 30 Jan. 1930; Harrison, diary, 29 and 30 Jan. 1930; Clarke, diary, 30 Jan. 1930.

50. Clarke, diary, 26 Jan. 1930; Demas, diaries, 24 and 30 Jan. and 1 and 2 Feb. 1930.

51. Gould, diaries, 19–24 Jan. 1930; Harrison, diary, Jan. and 28 Jan. 1930; Davies, oral history tape; Smith, *By the Seat*, 230; Freeman, draft of article for *True* magazine, 4 June 1962; Balchen papers, accession no. 1007462, Air Force History Center; Carter, *Little America*, 144; Hatch, *The Byrds*, 319.

52. Demas, diaries, 30 and 31 Jan. 1930; Goodale to Gould, 27 July 1931, Byrd papers, box 153 file 37; Gould to Balchen, 12 Sept. 1933, Balchen papers, accession no. 1007579, Air Force History Center.

53. Demas, diaries, 19, 24, and 25 Jan. 1930.

54. Owen, *South of the Sun*, 281; Harrison, first Byrd expedition alumni newsletter, 29 Nov. 1975; Harrison, personal communication.

55. Demas, diaries, 7 Jan. 1930; Harrison, first Byrd expedition alumni newsletter, 29 Nov. 1975; Harrison, personal communication, 1985.

56. Owen, *South of the Sun*, 278.

57. Byrd to Brown, radiogram, 28 Jan. 1930, Byrd papers, box 1002 file 22.

58. Byrd, *Little America*, 373, 380.

59. Ibid., 380.

60. Byrd to Brown, radiograms, 29 Jan. 1930, Byrd papers, box 13.

61. Adams and McGuinness to Byrd, radiogram, 30 Jan. 1930, Byrd papers, box 13.

62. Brown to Byrd, radiogram, 30 Jan. 1930, Byrd papers, box 13; Gould and McKinley to Brown, radiograms, 31 Jan. 1930, Byrd papers, box 13.

63. Brown to Byrd, radiogram, 1 Feb. 1930, Byrd papers, box 13. Brown to Larry, Mac, and "the rest of the bunch," radiogram, 1 Feb. 1930, Byrd papers, box 117 file 5.

64. Byrd, *Little America*, 381.

65. Byrd to Mrs. Mason, radiogram, 7 Mar. 1930, Byrd papers, box 13; Demas, diaries, 7 Feb. 1930; Siple, diaries, 5 Feb. 1930.

66. Byrd, *Little America*, 365.

67. Siple, diaries, 6 Feb. 1930; Demas, diaries, 7 Feb. 1930; Harrison, diary, 7 Feb. 1930.

68. Harrison, diary, 7 Feb. 1930; Siple, diaries, 7 Feb. 1930; Byrd to Railey, radiogram, 7 Feb. 1930, Byrd papers, box 13.

69. Byrd, *Little America*, 387.

70. Demas, diaries, 13 Feb. 1930; Clarke, diary, 15 Feb. 1930.

71. Harrison, diary, 9 Feb. 1930.

72. Bulletin board notice, 24 Dec. 1929, Clarke papers; Harrison, diary, 11 Feb. 1930; Byrd to Walden, Vaughan, and Goodale, radiogram, 9 Apr. 1930, Byrd papers, box 19.

73. Demas, diaries, 11 Feb. 1930; Siple, diaries, 14 Feb. 1930; Smith, manuscript, 780.

74. Harrison, diary, 17 Feb. 1930; Clarke, diary, 28 Feb. 1930.

75. Bulletin board notice, 5 Feb. 1930, Clarke papers; Cohen to Byrd, radiogram, undated, Clarke papers.

76. Byrd, *Little America*, 383–386.

77. Shropshire to Saunders, 6 Apr. 1933, Saunders papers; Byrd to Saunders, 30 Apr. 1932, Saunders papers; Byrd to Melville, radiogram, 20 Jan. 1930, Byrd papers, box 117 file 2; Melville to Byrd, radiograms, 20, 23, and 24 Jan. 1930, Byrd papers, box 117 file 2.

78. Siple, diaries, 17 Feb. 1930.

79. Byrd, *Little America*, 265; Hoyt, *Last Explorer*, 255.

80. Byrd, *Little America*, 389; Owen, *Conquest*, 164.

81. Siple, *Boy Scout*, 143; Demas, diaries, 18 and 19 Feb. 1930; Demas oral history tape; Harrison, diary, 19 Feb. 1930.

CHAPTER 15

1. *N.Y. Times*, 28 Feb. and 2 Mar. 1930; Harrison, diary, 3 Mar. 1930.

2. Byrd, *National Geographic*, 227; *N.Y. Times*, 27 Feb. 1930.

3. Harrison, diary, 28 Feb. 1930; Demas, diaries, 26 Feb. 1930; *N.Y. Times*, 28 Feb. 1930; Owen, *South of the Sun*, 288.

4. Memos and signature sheets for expedition members, 9 Mar. 1930, Byrd papers, box 13.

5. Harrison, diary, 11 Mar. 1930.

6. Siple, *Boy Scout*, 214; *N.Y. Times*, 15 Mar. 1930.

7. Harrison, diary, 10 and 12 Mar. 1930; Siple, *Ninety Degrees*, 49; Smith, *By the Seat*, 214; *N.Y. Times*, 30 Apr. 1930; Smith, manuscript, 723.

8. Smith, *By the Seat*, 232.

9. *N.Y. Times*, 12 and 13 Mar. 1930.

10. Byrd to Meinholtz, radiogram, 9 Mar. 1930, Byrd papers, box 118; Byrd to Railey, radiogram, 9 Mar. 1930, Byrd papers, box 13.

11. Harrison, diary, 18 and 22 Mar. 1930; *N.Y. Times*, 16 and 21 Mar. 1930.

12. *N.Y. Times*, 19 Mar. 1930; Siple, *Boy Scout*, 147.

13. Harrison, diary, 25 Apr. 1930; *N.Y. Times*, 29 Aug. 1928.

14. R. E. Byrd to M. A. Byrd, undated, Byrd papers, box 1007 file 6.

15. Byrd to Railey, radiogram, undated but filed with 29 Apr. 1930 material, Byrd papers, box 13.

16. Fosdick to Byrd, 16 Nov. 1927, Byrd papers, box 107 file 20; Byrd to Railey, radiogram, 27 Aug. 1929, in Byrd's diary.

17. Byrd to Berkner, radiogram, 24 Aug. 1929, Byrd papers, box 10.1 file 2.

18. *N.Y. Times*, 18 and 24 Mar. 1930; Siple, diaries, 26 May 1929; R. E. Byrd to M. A. Byrd, undated, Byrd papers, box 1007 file 6.

19. Clarke, diary, 1 Apr. 1930; *N.Y. Times*, 27 Apr. 1930.

20. Harrison, diary, 2 and 3 Apr. and 12 May 1930; Clarke, diary, 2 Apr. 1930.

21. Clarke, diary, 18 Apr. 1930; *N.Y. Times*, 20 Apr. 1930; Siple, *Boy Scout*, 149

22. *N.Y. Times*, 6 Sept. 1928, 7 and 19 Apr. 1930, 15 May 1930, and 10 June 1930; Harrison, diary, 8 Apr. 1930; Hoyt, *Last Explorer*, 256.

23. *N.Y. Times*, 27 Feb. 1930; West, *With Admiral Byrd in Little America*, 86.

24. *N.Y. Times*, 25 and 27 May 1930.

25. Ibid., 19 Apr. and 11 June 1930.

26. Railey to Byrd, 13 Jan. 1931, Byrd papers, box 132 file 75.

27. Harrison, diary, 7 June 1930.

28. Ibid., 16 June 1930; Smith, *By the Seat*, 232; Smith, personal communication; Owen to Jones, radiogram, 11 June 1930, Byrd papers, box 13.1; Byrd to Smith, 6 Sept. 1954, Byrd papers, box 95 file 34; Roberts, *Great Exploration Hoaxes*, 134.

29. Slate and Cook, *It Sounds Impossible*, 114.

30. M. A. Byrd to R. E. Byrd, undated, Byrd papers, box 1004 file 5; Dickie Byrd to R. E. Byrd, undated, Byrd papers, box 1002 file 4.

31. R. E. Byrd to M. A. Byrd, radiogram, 27 Jan. 1930, Byrd papers, box 1007 file 1; R. E. Byrd to M. A. Byrd, undated, Byrd papers, box 1007 file 6; R. E. Byrd to M. A. Byrd, undated, Byrd papers, box 1007 file 6; M. A. Byrd to R. E. Byrd, radiogram, 9 June 1930, Byrd papers, box 1007 file 1.

32. "Wanted: New Poles for Byrd to Conquer," *Literary Digest*, 5 July 1930, 40.

33. Ibid., 41; Clarke, diary, 19 June 1930. Quotation is from *N.Y. Times*, 20 June 1930.

34. *Collier's* magazine, 78.

35. *N.Y. Times*, 15 and 21 June 1930. Quotation is from *National Geographic*, Aug. 1930, 228.

36. Balchen, *Come North*, 194–195; Balchen, unidentified manuscript, 252, Balchen papers, National Archives; Byrd to Balchen, 6 Sept. 1930, Balchen papers, accession no. 1007578, Air Force History Center; Byrd to commissioner of naturalization, 26 Aug. 1930, Byrd papers, box 153 file 3.

CHAPTER 16

1. *N.Y. Times*, 5 Mar. and 25, 27, and 28 June 1930; Steinberg, *Admiral Byrd*, 32.

2. *N.Y. Times*, 28 Oct. 1929, 22 Feb. 1930, 15 and 26 Mar. 1930, 19 and 29 June 1930, 9 July 1930, 26 and 31 Oct. 1930, 11 Dec. 1930, and 21 Jan. 1931.

3. Ibid., 3 and 29 Mar., 10 Apr., 21 May, and 18 July 1930.

4. Ibid., 9 and 29 June 1930.

5. Ibid., 24 and 29 June and 16 Sept. 1930.

6. Ibid., 2 Dec. 1929.

7. Ibid., 23 and 26 Jan. and 9 June 1929; Bowman, *Scientific Monthly*, Apr. 1930, 341; Byrd, *Natural History*, Sept. 1930, 532.

8. *N.Y. Times*, 13 May 1930.

9. Ibid., 20 and 23 Apr. 1930; Dickson, *Hygeia*, 270; Grosvenor, NEA address.

10. Quotation is from Allen, *Only Yesterday*, 293–294. Scott, *The Geographical Journal*, 252.

11. Byrd, *Rotarian*, 57; Byrd to Sulzberger, Byrd papers, box 1002 file 10.

12. *N.Y. Times*, 10 June and 15 July 1930; R. E. Byrd to H. F. Byrd, 2 July 1930, Byrd papers, box 12 file 12; Byrd, *Little America*, 5.

13. Byrd to Putnam, radiogram, 18 Apr. 1929, Byrd papers, box 10.1 file 8; Byrd to Railey, radiogram, 27 July 1929, Byrd papers, box 10.1 file 14; Byrd to Railey, radiogram, 25 Jan. 1930, Byrd papers, box 10.1 file 14; Byrd to Railey, radiogram, 17 Jan. 1930, Byrd papers, box 10.1 file 14.

14. Byrd to Gould, 17 Sept. 1930, Byrd papers, box 153 file 35; Gould to Byrd, undated, Byrd papers, box 153 file 35; Byrd to Gould, 22 Sept. 1930, Byrd papers, box 153 file 35; *N.Y. Times*, 23 Oct. 1930.

15. Byrd, *Little America*, 256.

16. *N.Y. Times*, 29 June and 27 July 1930; Cohen to Byrd, telegram, 6 Nov. 1930, Byrd papers, box 154 file 33.

17. One example: Byrd to Clarke, 16 Aug. 1930, Byrd papers box 153 file 17.

18. Siple, diaries, 15 June 1929; Byrd to Goodale, 22 Aug. 1930, Goodale papers; *N.Y. Times*, 18 July 1930; *N.Y. Times*, 23 Apr., 23 June, and 5 Oct. 1930.

19. *N.Y. Times*, 23 June and 28 Sept. 1930; Murphy, *Life*, 30 Oct. 1930; Steinberg, *Admiral Byrd*, 91.

20. *N.Y. Times*, 26 Mar. and 21 Aug. 1930.

21. Byrd to Goodale, 5 Sept. 1930, Goodale papers; *N.Y. Times*, 28 Jan., 2, 13, 20, and 30 May, 21 June, 3 and 20 Aug., 11 Oct., and 18 and 19 Dec. 1930; Clarke, diary, Sept. 1931.

22. Byrd, *Alone*, 97; *N.Y. Times*, 22 July 1930.

23. *N.Y. Times*, 24 June, 20 Oct., and 27 Nov. 1930 and 3 Jan. 1931; Byrd to Barter, 26 May 1931, Barter papers; Demas, diaries, 31 Jan. 1930; Demas, oral history tape.

24. Byrd to Hanson, 11 Mar. 1932, Saunders papers.

25. Byrd to Smith, 17 Oct. 1931, Byrd papers, box 154 file 38.

26. Byrd to general manager of Reading *Times*, 22 May 1931, Byrd papers box 153 file 2.

27. Owen to Byrd, 10 July 1930, Byrd papers, box 154 file 22; Smith, manuscript, 680.

28. Gould to Byrd, 9 Sept. 1930, Byrd papers, box 153 file 35; Gould to Byrd, 21 Aug. 1930, Byrd papers, box 153 file 35; Gould to Byrd, 12 Jan. 1931, Byrd papers, box 153 file 35; Byrd to Gould, 29 Jan. 1931, Byrd papers, box 153 file 35; Gould to Byrd, telegram, 26 Feb. 1931, Byrd papers, box 1002 file 13; Gould to Goodale, 14 June 1931, Goodale papers.

29. Byrd to Adams, Byrd papers, box 153 file 1.

30. *N.Y. Times*, 13 Apr. 1932.

31. Correspondence in Byrd papers, box 15 file 16; Strom to Melville, undated, Byrd papers, box 154 file 39.

32. Owen script, Byrd papers, box 9 file 10; Gould to Byrd, 9 Feb. 1932, Byrd papers, box 153 file 37; Byrd to Railey, 22 Aug. 1933, Byrd papers, box 142 file 14; *N.Y. Times*, 26 Oct. 1933.

33. Byrd to Gould, 18 Oct. 1934, and MacDonald to Bursey, 3 Oct. 1934, Byrd papers, box 154 file 20; unidentified letter, Byrd papers, box 154 file 20.

34. Byrd to O'Brien, 22 Apr. 1931, Byrd papers, box 154 file 20.

35. *N.Y. Times*, 21 and 22 Apr., 30 May, and 1 June 1931; *Literary Digest*, 9 May 1931, 30.

36. *N.Y. Times*, 10 July 1931.

37. Byrd, *Little America*, ix; Gould, diaries, 2 Feb. 1930. Byrd to Goodale, 22

Aug. 1930, and 31 July 1931, Goodale papers; Taylor, *Current History*, 970; *N.Y. Times*, 30 Nov. 1930.

CHAPTER 17

1. Gould to Byrd, 2 Sept. 1930, Byrd papers, box 153 file 35.
2. Byrd to Gould, 5 Sept. 1930, Byrd papers, box 153 file 35; Byrd to Haines, 11 Oct. 1930, Haines papers.
3. Gould to Byrd, 22 Nov. 1930, Byrd papers, box 153 file 35; Gould to Byrd, 17 Jan. 1931, Byrd papers, box 1002 file 13; Byrd to Gould, 6 Feb. 1931, Byrd papers, box 153 file 35.
4. *N.Y. Times*, 22 Apr. 1930; McKinley, *National Geographic*, 484.
5. Gould to Byrd, 12 Feb. 1931, Byrd papers, box 1002 file 13; McKinley to Byrd, undated, Byrd papers, box 154 file 10.
6. Gould itineraries, Byrd papers, box 153 file 35; McKinley to Byrd, 11 Dec. 1930, Byrd papers, box 15 file 16.
7. Gould to Saunders, 3 May 1932, Saunders papers.
8. Byrd to Gould, 20 Dec. 1930 and 10 Jan. 1931, Byrd papers, box 153 file 35.
9. Gould to Byrd, 17 Jan. 1931, Byrd papers, box 1002 file 13.
10. Byrd to McKinley, 2 Feb. 1931, Byrd papers, box 154 file 10; Byrd to Gould, 3 Feb. 1931, Byrd papers, box 1002 file 13.
11. Railey to M. A. Byrd, 21 Jan. 1931, Byrd papers, box 1005 file 7; Byrd to expedition members, 15 Jan. 1931, Haines papers.
12. Byrd to Saunders, 9 Mar. 1932, Saunders papers.
13. *N.Y. Times*, 1 Dec. 1930; Byrd to Mrs. Bob, 31 Jan. 1932, Byrd papers, box 133 file 24; memo on contributions, undated but in 1930–31 file, Byrd papers, box 111 file 26.
14. Railey to Byrd, 13 Jan. 1931, Byrd papers, box 132 file 75; letter from a supplier to Czegka, 5 June 1933, Byrd papers, box 55 file 10.
15. Byrd to Gould, 6 Feb. 1931, Byrd papers, box 1002 file 13.
16. Gould to Byrd, 12 Feb. 1931, Byrd papers, box 1002 file 13.
17. Byrd to Gould, 3 Mar. 1931, Byrd papers, box 1002 file 13.
18. Byrd to Haines, 2 Mar. 1931, Haines papers.
19. Haines to Byrd, 21 Mar. 1931, Haines papers.
20. Byrd to Gould, 31 Mar. 1931, Byrd papers, box 153 file 35.
21. Gould to Byrd, 27 May 1931, Byrd papers, box 153 file 35; Byrd to Gould, 30 May 1931, Byrd papers, box 153 file 35; Gould to Byrd, 5 June 1931, Byrd papers, box 153 file 35.
22. Byrd to Gould, telegram, 29 June 1931, Byrd papers, box 153 file 35; Byrd to Gould, 28 July 1931, Byrd papers, box 153 file 35.
23. Byrd to McKinley, 26 July 1931, Byrd papers, box 154 file 12; Byrd to Gould, 30 May 1931, Byrd papers, box 153 file 35.
24. Byrd to Balchen, 20 June 1931, Balchen papers, accession no. 1007578, Air Force History Center.
25. Goodale to Gould, 27 July 1931, Byrd papers, box 153 file 37; Byrd to Goodale, 28 July 1931, Byrd papers, box 153 file 37.
26. *N.Y. Times*, 13 Sept. 1931; Bubier to Clarke, 12 Aug. 1931, Clarke papers; Byrd to Haines, 15 Sept. 1931, Haines papers; Byrd to Demas, 1 Oct. 1931,

Demas papers; McKinley to Byrd, 4 Jan. 1932, Byrd papers, box 154 file 11.

27. Gould to Byrd, dated only "Friday afternoon," Byrd papers, box 153 file 35.

28. Byrd to Balchen, 12 Oct. 1931, Byrd papers, box 1011 file 67.

29. Byrd to Lofgren, 25 Sept. 1931, Byrd papers, box 154 file 7; tax returns, Byrd papers, box 1004 file 15, box 1016 file 24.

30. Byrd to Gould, memorandum, undated, Byrd papers, box 153 file 35.

31. Byrd to Clarke, 27 June 1931, Byrd papers, box 153 file 17; Byrd to Gould, 30 May 1931, Byrd papers, box 153 file 35; Byrd to Parker, 30 Sept. 1931, Byrd papers, box 154 file 24.

32. Byrd to Goodale, 12 Nov. 1931, Goodale papers; Byrd to Gould, 12 Nov. 1931, Byrd papers, box 153 file 35.

33. Byrd to Goodale, 18 Nov. 1931.

34. Byrd to Coman, 13 Nov. 1931, Byrd papers, box 153 file 19.

35. *N.Y. Times*, 13 Sept. 1931; Byrd to Goodale, 31 July 1931.

36. Saunders to Shropshire, 5 Mar. 1932, Shropshire to Saunders, 18 Mar. 1939, and Coman to Saunders, 28 Mar. 1933, Saunders papers.

37. Byrd to Hanson, 11 Mar. 1932, and Byrd to Saunders, 30 Apr. 1932, Saunders papers.

38. Saunders to Gould, 4 Mar. 1932, and Gould to Saunders, 14 Mar. 1932, Saunders papers.

39. Byrd to McKinley, 16 Mar. 1931 and 17 Mar. 1932, Byrd papers, box 154 file 10.

40. Byrd to Saunders, 20, 21, and 30 Apr. 1932, Saunders papers.

41. Byrd to Saunders, 9 and 18 June 1932, and McKercher to Saunders, 2 Nov. 1932, Saunders papers.

42. Byrd to McKinley, 11 July 1932, Byrd papers, box 154 file 10; Byrd to Saunders, 18 June 1933, Saunders papers; tax returns, Byrd papers, box 1016 file 24.

43. Note, Byrd papers, box 133 file 24.

44. Saunders to Gould, 17 Mar. 1933, Saunders papers; Byrd to Coman, 15 Apr. 1933, Byrd papers, box 153 file 19; Byrd to Gould, 21 Sept. 1933, and Gould to Byrd, 25 Sept. 1933, Byrd papers, box 153 file 35.

45. Gould to Balchen, 27 Apr. 1934, Balchen papers, Air Force History Center; Gould to Balchen, 12 Apr. 1958, Gould papers.

CHAPTER 18

1. Balchen to Gould, 24 Mar. 1958, Gould papers.
2. Davies, first Byrd expedition alumni newsletter, 29 Nov. 1975.
3. Owen, *Antarctic Ocean*, 226.
4. Ronne to Byrd, 4 Dec. 1930, Byrd papers, box 154 file 29.

EPILOGUE

Note The epilogue is largely based on Harrison, "Some Facts About Members of Winter Party, Byrd Antarctic Expedition I," 15 Apr. 1978, Harrison papers: Hoyt, *The Last Explorer*; Sullivan, *Quest for a Continent*; and *New York Times* obituaries.

1. *N.Y. Times*, 18 May and 21 June 1930.
2. Gould to Balchen, 12 Apr. 1958, Gould papers.
3. Montague, *Oceans, Poles and Airmen*, 289–300.
4. Davies, oral history tape.
5. Lida Hanson, *Malcolm Hanson*, 157.
6. Byrd to Smith, 17 July 1954, Byrd papers, box 95 file 34.

Select Bibliography

ARCHIVED PAPERS

Air Force History Center, Bolling Air Force Base, Washington, D.C.
Bernt Balchen. Microfilm of the papers that Balchen gave the air force. Accession numbers 1007461, 1007462, and 1007578 contain much of the material related to Byrd.

National Archives, Washington, D.C.
Virtually all the material related to Byrd's first expedition, except the Hanson papers, is in the Center for Polar and Scientific Archives, Record Group 401.
Bernt Balchen
Leland Barter
Quin A. Blackburn
Arnold H. Clarke
F. Dana Coman
Victor H. Czegka
Frank T. Davies
Epaminondas J. Demas
Edward E. Goodale
Laurence M. Gould
William C. Haines
Malcolm P. Hanson (Record Group RG 72, S/67/43, box 83. Naval Research Laboratory correspondence concerning Hanson's work during Byrd's expedition)
Harry T. Harrison

333

Harold E. Saunders
Paul A. Siple

Ohio State University Libraries, Columbus, OH.
  Richard E. Byrd. Contents of thirty-five file cabinets of Byrd's personal and business records. Also contains many papers of Marie A. Byrd and Richard E. Byrd, Jr. Location of documents by box and file numbers refers to the temporary arrangement existing in July 1988 and described by the "preliminary inventory" of the papers.

University of Wyoming Library, Laramie, WY.
  Dean C. Smith. Contains the unedited version of the manuscript for Dean Smith's autobiography, *By the Seat of My Pants*. The draft of the section on Byrd's expedition is much longer and differs in small ways from the published book's version. In personal correspondence, Smith stated that the draft accurately reflects his thoughts and memories, including the portions cut or changed for publication by the editor.

OTHER PAPERS

Alison Wilson. Files of correspondence, literature, and photocopied papers concerning Byrd and the first expedition in the office of Ms. Wilson of the National Archives staff. Included are the text of a 9 Oct. 1982 speech by Howard F. Mason, "Radio Communications on the First Byrd Antarctic Expedition," delivered before the Society of Wireless Pioneers; a draft of a 1986 interview with Norman D. Vaughan for *Yankee* magazine; and photocopies of correspondence between Byrd and Amundsen.

DIARIES

All but Vaughan's diary are in the writers' archived papers.

  Quin A. Blackburn. One volume from Dec. 1928 to Dec. 1929.
  Richard E. Byrd. Typed sheets covering Apr. 1929 to early Jan. 1930. Mostly copies of radiograms interspersed with a few personal notes mainly, it seems, to provide information for Byrd's book.
  Arnold H. Clarke. One volume from Sept. 1928 to June 1930.
  Epaminondas J. Demas. Copybook, small notebook, small leatherbound, and typescript diaries from Oct. 1928 to Feb. 1930.
  Laurance M. Gould. Manuscript and typescript diaries, in three volumes, and manuscript trail journal with diary notes from Oct. 1928 to Jan. 1930.
  Henry T. Harrison. One volume from Aug. 1928 to June 1930.
  Paul A. Siple. Manuscript and typescript diaries from Aug. 1928 to Mar. 1930.
  Norman D. Vaughan. A few pages of a loose-leaf diary, from Dec. 1928, in Siple's papers.

OTHER ARCHIVAL RECORDS

All in the National Archives, Center for Polar and Scientific Archives, Record Group 401.

Oral history tapes

Reminiscenses of Epaminondas J. Demas, recorded 4 May 1972, and Frank T. Davies, recorded 13 Mar. 1972, in the Demas and Davies papers.

Movie

With Byrd at the South Pole, a 1930 Paramount documentary, in James E. Mooney's papers.

Newsletter

First Byrd Expedition alumni newsletter, published annually by Henry Harrison since 1974 and deposited with his papers.

PERSONAL SOURCES

Letters to Eugene Rodgers

Edward E. Goodale, one letter, 1966; Henry T. Harrison, six letters from Dec. 1985 to May 1986; Dean C. Smith, two letters, May 1986.

Interviews

Paul A. Siple, 22 Mar. 1967; Finn Ronne, 16 Mar. 1967.

Lecture Notes

Laurance M. Gould, talk to Antarctican Society about Byrd's first expedition, 18 Oct. 1968.

BOOKS BY PERSONNEL OF BYRD'S FIRST EXPEDITION

Adams, Harry. *Beyond the Barrier With Byrd*. New York: M. A. Donohue & Co., 1932.
Balchen, Bernt. *Come North With Me*. New York: E. P. Dutton & Co., 1958.
Bursey, Jack. *Antarctic Night*. New York: Rand McNally & Co., 1957.
Byrd, Richard E. *Alone*. New York: G. P. Putnam's Sons, 1938; Ace Books, undated. (Citations are to Ace paperback edition.)
———. *Discovery*. New York: G. P. Putnam's Sons, 1935.
———. *Little America*. New York: G. P. Putnam's Sons, 1930.
———. *Skyward*. New York: G. P. Putnam's Sons, 1928.
Gould, Laurence M. *Cold*. New York: Brewer, Warren & Putnam, 1931.
McGuinness, Charles J. *Sailor of Fortune*. Philadelphia: MacRae-Smith Co., 1935.
O'Brien, Jack S. *By Dog Sled for Byrd*. Chicago: Thomas S. Rockwell Co., 1931.
Owen, Russell E. *The Antarctic Ocean*. New York: Whittlesey House, 1941.
———. *The Conquest of the North and South Poles*. New York: Random House, 1952.
———. *South of the Sun*. New York: The John Day Co., 1934.
Railey, Hilton H. *Touch'd With Madness*. New York: Carrier & Evans, 1938.
Siple, Paul A. *A Boy Scout With Byrd*. New York: G. P. Putnam's Sons, 1931.

——. *Ninety Degrees South*. New York: G. P. Putnam's Sons, 1959.
——. *Scout to Explorer*. New York: G. P. Putnam's Sons, 1936.
Smith, Dean C. *By the Seat of My Pants*. Boston: Little, Brown, & Co., 1961.

JOURNAL AND MAGAZINE ARTICLES BY PERSONNEL OF THE FIRST EXPEDITION

Berkner, Lloyd V. "Some Studies of Radio Transmission Over Long Paths Made on the Byrd Antarctic Expedition." *Bureau of Standards Journal of Research* (Feb. 1932).
Byrd, Richard E. "The Conquest of Antarctica By Air." *The National Geographic Magazine* (Aug. 1930).
——. "Crusaders." *Saturday Evening Post* (22 Sept. 1928).
——. "The Flight to Marie Byrd Land." *Geographical Review* (Apr. 1933).
——. "How I Select My Men." *Saturday Evening Post* (21 Apr. 1928).
—— (with Albert D. Barker). "Over the South Pole by Air." *Natural History* (Sept. 1930).
Gould, Laurence M. "The Ross Ice Shelf." *Bulletin of the Geological Society of America* (30 Sept. 1935).
——. "Some Geographical Results of the Byrd Antarctic Expedition." *Geographical Review* (Apr. 1931).
Haines, William. "The Green Flash Observed October 16, 1929, at Little America by Members of the Byrd Antarctic Expedition." *Monthly Weather Review* (Mar. 1931).
—— and George Grimminger. "Meteorological Results of the Byrd Antarctic Expeditions, 1928–30 and 1930–35." *Monthly Weather Review Supplement No. 41* (Oct. 1939).
McKinley, Ashley. "Mapping Antarctica from the Air." *National Geographic Magazine* (Oct. 1932).

OTHER BOOKS

Allen, Frederick Lewis. *Only Yesterday*. New York: Harper & Bros., 1931.
Andrews, Roy Chapman. *This Business of Exploring*. New York: G. P. Putnam's Sons, 1935.
Bernays, E. L. *Biography of an Idea*. New York: Simon & Schuster, 1965.
Bertrand, Kenneth J. *Americans in Antarctica 1775–1948*. New York: American Geographical Society, 1971. (Bibliography cites many of the scientific papers resulting from Byrd's first expedition.)
Bruno, Harry. *Wings Over America*. New York: McBride & Co., 1942.
Carter, Paul A. *Little America*. New York: Columbia University Press, 1979.
Fokker, Anthony. *Flying Dutchman*. New York: Arno Press, 1931.
Foster, Coram. *Rear Admiral Byrd and the Polar Expeditions*. New York: A. L. Burt & Co., 1930.
Gillmor, C. Stewart. "Early History of Upper Atmospheric Physics Research in Antarctica," *Upper Atmosphere Research in Antarctica* (vol. 29 of *Antarctic Research Series*). Washington, D.C.: American Geophysical Union, 1978.
Green, Fitzhugh. *Dick Byrd*. New York: G. P. Putnam's Sons, 1926

Hanson, Lida. *The Story of Malcolm Hanson.* Privately published, 1946. (Copy in Library of Congress.)

Hatch, Alden. *The Byrds of Virginia.* New York: Holt, Rinehart & Winston, 1969.

Hayes, J. Gordon. *Antarctica.* London: The Richards Press, 1928.

———. *Conquest of the South Pole.* London: Thornton Butterworth, 1932.

Hill, Joe Jr. and Ola D. Hill. *In Little America With Byrd.* New York: Ginn & Co., 1937.

Hoyt, Edwin J. *The Last Explorer.* New York: John Day Co., 1968.

Hunt, A. Leigh. *My Second Home: Admiral Byrd in New Zealand.* Wellington, New Zealand: self published. (Copy in New York City public library.)

Joerg, W. L., ed. *Problems of Polar Research.* New York: American Geographical Society, 1928.

Joerg, W. L., ed. *The Geography of the Polar Regions.* New York: American Geographical Society, 1928.

Knight, Clayton and Robt. Durham. *Hitch Your Wagon.* Drexel Hill, Pennsylvania: Bell Publishing Co., 1950.

Miller, Francis Trevelyan. *The World's Great Adventure.* Self published.

Montague, Richard. *Oceans, Poles and Airmen.* New York: Random House, 1971.

Morris, Lloyd and Kendall Smith. *Ceiling Unlimited.* New York: Macmillan Co., 1953.

Murphy, Charles J. V. M. *Struggle.* New York: Frederick A. Stokes Co., 1928.

Roberts, David. *Great Exploration Hoaxes.* San Francisco: Sierra Club Books, 1982.

Ronne, Finn. *Antarctica, My Destiny.* New York: Hastings House, 1979.

Rose, Lisle A. *Assault on Eternity.* Annapolis: Naval Institute Press, 1980.

Rudmose-Brown, R. N. *The Polar Regions.* London: Methuer & Co., 1927.

Simmons, George. *Target Arctic.* Philadelphia: Chilton, 1965.

Slate, Sam J. and Joe Cook. *It Sounds Impossible.* New York: Macmillan Co., 1963.

Steinberg, Alfred. *Admiral Richard E. Byrd.* New York: G. P. Putnam's Sons, 1960.

Sullivan, Walter S. *Quest for a Continent.* New York: McGraw-Hill, 1957.

Taylor, Thomas G. *Antarctic Adventure & Research.* New York: D. Appleton & Co., 1930.

Thomas, Lowell. *Sir Hubert Wilkins.* New York: McGraw-Hill, 1961.

Walsh, George. *Gentleman Jimmy Walker.* New York: Praeger, 1974.

West, Wallace. *With Admiral Byrd in Little America.* Racine, Wisconsin: Whitman Publishing Co., 1934.

Whalen, Grover A. *Mr. New York.* New York: G. P. Putnam's Sons, 1955.

OTHER MAGAZINE AND JOURNAL ARTICLES

Anonymous

"Admiral Byrd Receives New Honor From the Society." *National Geographic Magazine* (Aug. 1930).

"Antarctic Flights 1928–1929." *Geographical Review* (Apr. 1929).

"At the Bottom of the World With Byrd." *Popular Mechanics* (Aug. 1930).

"Byrd Bags His Second Pole." *Literary Digest* (14 Dec. 1929).

"Byrd Circles South Pole by Airplane." *Current History* (Jan. 1930).

"Byrd's Iggie has Yapped at His Last Huskie." *Literary Digest* (9 May 1931).

"Byrd to Receive Unique Tribute From School Children." *Journal of the National Education Assoc.* (Mar. 1931).

Editorial. *Collier's* (14 June 1930).
"Franklin and Byrd." *The Nation* (30 May 1928).
"How Female Huskies Lead Byrd's Mushers." *Literary Digest* (6 Apr. 1929).
"A Million-Dollar Attack on the South Pole." *Literary Digest* (15 Sept. 1928).
"Now the Birdmen will Invade The Antarctic." *Literary Digest* (23 June 1928).
"Putting Byrd's Eskimos on Ice to Get Them to the South Pole." *Literary Digest* (7 Apr. 1927).
"Wanted: New Poles for Byrd to Conquer." *Literary Digest* (5 July 1930).
"What Byrd Found." *Literary Digest* (12 July 1930).

Authored

Anthony, Malcolm. "Silent Lady." *American Magazine* (July 1930).
Booth, James W. "Who Owns the South Pole?" *Popular Mechanics* (Apr. 1930).
Bowman, Isaiah. "Antarctica." *Science Monthly* (Apr. 1930).
Brody, John T. "Dog Heroes of the White Hell." *Popular Mechanics* (Sept. 1930).
Dickam, Belle L. "An Account of Teaching Health by Reference to the Byrd Expeditions." *Hygeia* (Mar. 1937).
Emmons, Gardner. "Meteorological Results of the Byrd Antarctic Expeditions, 1928–30 and 1933–35." *The Geographical Review* (Jan. 1940).
Hanson, Earle. "The Race to the South Pole." *The Nation* (24 Oct. 1928).
Hanson, Earle. "What Is the Use of Antarctic Exploration?" *World's Work* (Apr. 1930).
Horowitz, August, ed. *Little America Times*. New York. (Newsletter about antarctic affairs begun during Byrd's second antarctic expedition. Copies in Library of Congress.)
Howe, J. Olin. "At the Bottom of the World." *Popular Mechanics* (Aug. 1930).
Murphy, C. J. V. M. "Admiral Byrd." *Life* (30 Oct. 1939).
Rogers, Kendall. "Furniture Designed for Byrd Expedition." *House Beautiful* (Feb. 1929).
Rudmose-Brown, R. N. "Some Problems of Polar Geography." *Smithsonian Institution Annual Report* (1929).
Saunders, Harold E. "The Flight of Admiral Byrd to the South Pole." *Proceedings of the American Philosophical Society* (29 June 1940).
Scott, J. M. "Admiral Byrd's Expedition." *Geographical Journal* (Mar. 1930).
Taylor, Griffith. "Byrd's Scientific Achievement in the Antarctic." *Current History* (Aug. 1930).

MISCELLANEOUS

Grosvenor, Gilbert. Introduction of Byrd for an address to the National Education Association. (In Library of Congress.)
The *New York Times* extensively covered Byrd and the planning, field work, and aftermath of the expedition.

Index

ABOUT THE AUTHOR

Eugene Rodgers was graduated from Villanova University in 1961 with a B.S. in chemistry. He studied the history of science for two years at the University of Wisconsin graduate school while working as a research assistant in the school's science writing apprenticeship program.

In 1963 Rodgers became public information officer for the U.S. Antarctic Research Program, the nation's continuing scientific expedition. He served with the program for two years, splitting his time evenly between Washington, D.C., and U.S. bases in Antarctica and New Zealand.

Rodgers worked as a freelance writer before becoming director of science public relations for Westinghouse Electric Corporation in 1967. He became a speech writer for the nuclear industry's trade association in 1975 and for the head of the government's nuclear program in 1976. Subsequently, Rodgers served as a speech writer for the senior executives of Virginia Power, United Technologies Corporation, and IBM. In 1987 he founded a national newsletter on research activities in the electric power industry. As a freelance writer, he contributes frequently to Time-Life Books.

Rodgers married Carol D. Huber in 1977. They have a son, Eric, and a daughter, Catherine. Now a resident of suburban Richmond, Virginia, Rodgers is studying toward a graduate degree in finance at Virginia Commonwealth University.

The Naval Institute Press is the book-publishing arm of the U.S. Naval Institute, a private, nonprofit professional society for members of the sea services and civilians who share an interest in naval and maritime affairs. Established in 1873 at the U.S. Naval Academy in Annapolis, Maryland, where its offices remain today, the Naval Institute has more than 100,000 members worldwide.

Members of the Naval Institute receive the influential monthly naval magazine *Proceedings* and substantial discounts on fine nautical prints, ship and aircraft photos, and subscriptions to the Institute's recently inaugurated quarterly, *Naval History*. They also have access to the transcripts of the Institute's Oral History Program and may attend any of the Institute-sponsored seminars regularly offered around the country.

The book-publishing program, begun in 1898 with basic guides to naval practices, has broadened it scope in recent years to include books of more general interest. Now the Naval Institute Press publishes more than forty new titles each year, ranging from how-to books on boating and navigation to battle histories, biographies, ship guides, and novels. Institute members receive discounts on the Press's more than 300 books.

For a free catalog describing books currently available and for further information about U.S. Naval Institute membership, please write to:

Membership Department
U.S. Naval Institute
Annapolis, Maryland 21402
or call, toll-free, 800-233-USNI.

THE NAVAL INSTITUTE PRESS

BEYOND THE BARRIER

The Story of Byrd's First Expedition to Antarctica

Designed by Alan Carter

Set in Caslon 540 (text) and Caslon Open (display)
by NK Graphics, Inc., Baltimore, Maryland

Printed on 60-lb. Glatfelter B-16, smooth antique
finish (text), and 70-lb. Glatco Gloss (photo section),
and bound in Holliston Crown Linen by
Maple-Vail, Inc., York, Pennsylvania

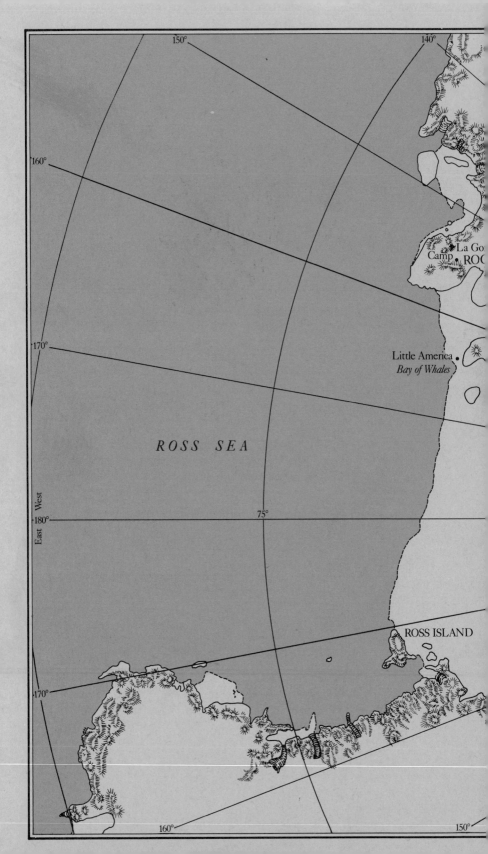